# Cookery
## for the Catering Industry

For Peter Carden

With many Thanks
for your Help and Support

Stuart Phelps

June 92

# Cookery
## for the Catering Industry

**Douglas Sutherland BA (Hons) MHCIMA**

*Formerly Head of*
*The Department of Food & Fashion,*
*North Devon College of Further Education*


**Stuart Rhodes MCFA (CG)**

*Lecturer in Food Studies*
*Harrogate College of Arts & Technology*

**Northcote House**

© Douglas Sutherland & Stuart Rhodes 1992
First published in 1992 by Northcote House Publishers Ltd, Plymbridge
House, Estover Road, Plymouth PL6 7PZ, United Kingdom.
Tel: Plymouth (0752) 735251. Fax: (0752) 695699. Telex: 45635.

ISBN 0-7463-0573-7

**British Library Cataloguing-in-Publication Data**
A catalogue record for this book is available from the British Library

Typeset by PDQ Typesetting, Stoke-on-Trent
Printed by The Cromwell Press, Melksham, Wiltshire

# Contents

## 1 Industrial Studies                                                 15

The hotel and catering industry, 15. Professional bodies and trade associations, 18. Management's and employee's social responsibilities, 19. Trade unions within the industry, 20. Healthy eating guidelines, 21. Commodity estimating guide, 24. Simple percentage food costs, 26. Self-assessment questions for industrial studies, 28.

## 2 Cold Preparation                                                   29

The competency defined, 29. Purpose of cold preparation, 29. Organisation and preparation, 29. Safety and hygiene — general rules, 30. General rules for efficient production and presentation, 31. Techniques associated with cold preparation, 31. Equipment used in cold preparation, 32. Self-assessment questions for cold preparation, 32. Cold sauces and basic preparations, 33. Basic cuts of vegetables, 35. Batters, 36. Binding agents, 38. Cold butter sauces, 39. Salads, 40. Hors-d'oeuvre, 43. Fish preparation, 51. Cuts of meat, 55. Sandwiches, 67. Pâtisserie and confectionery, 68. Cold sweets, 80. Cheese, 82.

## 3 Boiling          *Bouillir*                                        84

The competency defined, 84. The purpose of boiling, 84. Methods of boiling foods, 85. Advantages of boiling, 85. Effects of boiling on foods, 86. General rules for efficient boiling, 86. Organisation and preparation for boiling, 87. General safety rules for boiling, 88. Degrees of cooking for boiling, 88, Equipment used for boiling, 89. Techniques associated with boiling, 89. Self-assessment questions for boiling, 89. Stocks, 90. Glazes, 93. Cooking liquors, 94. Blanc, 94. Soups, 95. Sauces, 109. Boiling shellfish, 124. Boiling eggs, 125. Farinaceous dishes, 126. Boiling of meats, 132. Boiled vegetables, 133. Boiled pâtisserie dishes, 143. Rice puddings, 153. Savouries, 155.

## 4 Poaching          *Pocher*                                        157

The competency defined, 157. Reasons for poaching, 157. Methods of poaching, 157. Organisation and preparation for poaching, 158. Advantages of poaching, 159. Effects of poaching on foods, 159. General rules for efficient poaching, 159. General safety rules, 160. Techniques associated with poaching, 160. Equipment used in poaching, 161. Self-assessment questions for poaching, 161. Poached egg dishes, 162. Poached fish dishes, 165. Poached mousses, 172. Poached pâtisserie, 175. Poached savouries, 177.

# Acknowledgements

We would like to thank the following staff of Harrogate College of Arts and Technology for their support and assistance in the compiling of this book.

The Principal: P A Clarke BSc MIBiol FBIM ACP

Head of Division of Catering and Hairdressing: B K Sharples

For secretarial work: Monika Harrison, Grace MacHutchinson and Shirley Haste

We would also like to thank the full-time students of Catering, Harrogate College of Arts and Technology for their involvement and co-operation.

*Douglas Sutherland*
*Stuart Rhodes*


To my dear wife, Helen, in deep appreciation of her constant encouragement and patience.

*Douglas Sutherland*

# Preface

The various elements (of a practical nature) which are the core of the competency based approach to **food preparation** are essentially processes which demonstrate independent skills in specific areas of cookery. They are:

| *English* | | *French* |
|---|---|---|
| Cold Preparation | | |
| Boiling | – | *Bouillir* |
| Poaching | – | *Pocher* |
| Stewing | – | *Etuver* |
| Braising | – | *Braiser* |
| Steaming | – | *Vapeuriser* |
| Baking | – | *Cuire* |
| Roasting (Pot Roasting) | – | *Rôtir (Poêler)* |
| Grilling | – | *Griller* |
| Shallow Frying | – | *Sauter* |
| Deep Fat Frying | – | *Frire* |
| Microwave Cookery | – | *Micro Onde* |

It is the skill process which is important rather than concern over individual recipes. In other words, it is the **process** which is the key factor irrespective of the item being processed, be it fish, poultry, meat or whatever. To acquire proficiency (**competency**) in each specialist component, the student must learn to think about and plan each task in a logical sequence. This is the approach adopted throughout this book.

# Introduction

The specific aim of this book is to meet the needs of the Competency approach to food preparation which is now the main thrust of the revised City and Guilds of London Institute examinations 706 series — *Cookery for the Catering Industry*.

Each chapter is headed by a comprehensive review of the competency based skills, and the reader is given a wide-ranging insight into each of the Principles of Cookery together with supporting material, in order to meet the contemporary and future requirements of the major examining body — the City and Guilds of London Institute.

The contents also relate directly to the **Caterbase Project** of the Hotel and Catering Training Company. Additionally, those students who are studying under the aegis of other national bodies, such as BTEC (Business and Technician Education Council) and similar schemes, will also find much of interest within the book's pages.

We have adopted an integrated approach as far as ancillary subject matter is concerned, on the basis that we believe the reader will recognise that each practical task must, of necessity, require that the operator obtains an understanding of certain elements over and above mere recipe interpretation. Such elements will include **communication, planning, doing and checking**.

For the above reasons, we have chosen to head each practical component with a review of the various items of equipment appropriate to the competency under discussion, together with correct methods of work with proper emphasis on hygiene and safety factors. The bulk of the formulae will be capable of easy conversion to larger scale production needs if required.

Of course, working conditions are not, unfortunately, always ideal, but the well-tutored craftsperson who is familiar with the best techniques will be able to adapt much more readily as a result of his or her breadth of professional knowledge and expertise. In that sense the learning process is a continuing activity which should endure throughout the individual's working life. Our sincere wish is that this work will assist the reader to achieve the best possible standards as part of a professional approach to cookery.

# How to use this book

*Structure*

The structure of the book follows the methods of cookery approach: from boiling through to microwave cookery as detailed in the current syllabus of the City and Guilds.

*Portions*

Where possible we have introduced multiple portion quantities for each recipe. On the left-hand side of the page are the quantities for *four portions* while on the right-hand side the recipe has been increased to *ten or more portions* or the equivalent in the case of liquids, thus allowing students to use the book both in college classroom situations and in the workplace environment.

*Measures*

Looking to the future of the catering industry in an international context we have included only metric measures, so allowing you the purchaser to use this book in any country in which you choose to work.

# Weights and measures

*Abbreviations*

| | |
|---|---|
| Kilogram | kg |
| Gram | g |
| Decilitre | dl (one-tenth of a litre) |
| Millilitre | ml |

Set out below is a list of conversions from imperial to metric detailing the precise weights and measures of grams, decilitres and millilitres.

*Imperial/metric conversion*

**Approximate weights**

| *ounces* | *grams* |
|---|---|
| 1 | 28 |
| 1½ | 42 |
| 2 | 56 |
| 2½ | 70 |

| | |
|---|---|
| 3 | 84 |
| 3½ | 98 |
| 4 | 115 |
| 4½ | 130 |
| 5 | 142 |
| 5½ | 156 |
| 6 | 170 |
| 6½ | 185 |
| 7 | 200 |
| 7½ | 215 |
| 8 | 230 |
| 8½ | 245 |
| 9 | 256 |
| 9½ | 270 |
| 10 | 285 |
| 10½ | 300 |
| 11 | 315 |
| 11½ | 330 |
| 12 | 342 |
| 12½ | 356 |
| 13 | 370 |
| 13½ | 385 |
| 14 | 400 |
| 14½ | 414 |
| 15 | 427 |
| 15½ | 442 |
| 16 | 456 |

## Liquid measure

| | | | | |
|---|---|---|---|---|
| ¼ dl | = | 1 fl oz | = | 28.5 ml |
| ¾ dl | = | 2½ fl oz | = | 70 ml |
| 1 dl | = | 3½ fl oz | = | 100 ml |
| | | 5 fl oz | = | 140 ml |
| ¼ litre | = | 9 fl oz | = | 250 ml |
| | | 10 fl oz | = | 285 ml |
| | | 15 floz | = | 425 ml |
| ½ litre | = | 18 fl oz | = | 500 ml |
| | | 20 fl oz | = | 570 ml |
| ¾ litre | = | 27 fl oz | = | 750 ml |
| 1 litre | = | 35 fl oz | = | 1000 ml |
| | | 40 fl oz | = | 1 litre 140 ml |

## Length

| | | |
|---|---|---|
| ¼ in | = | 7 mm |
| ½ in | = | 12 mm |
| 1 in | = | 25 mm |
| 2 in | = | 5 cm |
| 4 in | = | 10 cm |
| 6 in | = | 15 cm |
| 12 in | = | 30 cm |

## Temperature conversion

$$°F - 32 \div 9 \times 5 = °C$$
$$°C \div 5 \times 9 + 32 = °F$$

| Fahrenheit °F | Centigrade °C |
|---|---|
| 98 | 37 |
| 212 | 100 |
| 220 | 104 |
| 250 | 121 |
| 260 | 127 |
| 275 | 135 |
| 290 | 143 |
| 300 | 149 |
| 310 | 154 |
| 320 | 160 |
| 330 | 165 |
| 340 | 171 |
| 350 | 177 |
| 375 | 182 |
| 380 | 191 |
| 400 | 204 |
| 410 | 210 |
| 420 | 215 |
| 430 | 221 |
| 440 | 227 |
| 450 | 232 |
| 460 | 238 |
| 475 | 246 |
| 480 | 249 |
| 500 | 260 |

# Chapter 1
# Industrial Studies

## The hotel and catering industry

### The size of the industry

The Hotel and Catering Industry ranks as the third largest in the United Kingdom's league of major industries. It employs a labour force of well in excess of two million people and, over the next decade, is expected to grow even bigger. Indeed, it could become the number one industry by the end of the century. It is an industry which is composed largely of small units, many of which employ ten or less individuals. Conversely, it also has some fifty hotel chains including one, Forte Hotels, which is the world's biggest hotel group, with more than 20,000 rooms at its disposal and a great many more subsidiary catering operations as well. The company operates more than 300 hotels throughout the world (many of them of international repute and renown), and is a front runner in terms of training and staff development.

### Economic aspects of the industry

The importance of the industry as a major contributor to the economic prosperity of the nation is profound. It is the biggest single dollar earner, and through the medium of tourism earns some £6,000 million per annum. A great number of people are undoubtedly attracted into the industry because of its cosmopolitan nature and the degree of mobility which is obtainable through the wide range of jobs on offer. Indeed, there are more jobs available than there are trained people to fill them; a point which is not surprising when one considers the scope of job opportunities.

### The structural organisation of the industry

Altogether, there are some fourteen sectors which go to make up the range of specialist services provided. They are:

hotels, restaurants, industrial catering, hospital and welfare catering, transport catering (air, sea, railways), public houses, wine and cocktail bars, clubs, contract catering, fast food outlets, Armed Forces, educational establishments, residential and non-residential establishments.

Each of the above sectors will provide one or more of the following services: food, drink and accommodation.

Within the framework of each specialist service, a vast number of skilled personnel are required to meet the needs of the customers. For example, if we look more closely at the main food preparation occupations (within a commercial/welfare context), the actual preparation of meals can involve: chefs or cooks and ancillary staff such as kitchen assistants, kitchen porters, storekeeper and cleaning staff. In terms of a full kitchen brigade such as one would find in a premier hotel, the staffing structure can be set out as follows.

### Chef de partie responsibilities

| | | |
|---|---|---|
| Sauce chef | — Chef saucier: | All sauces except fish sauces; all entrées of meat, poultry and game, except roasts. |
| Roast chef | — Chef rôtisseur: | All items for roasting and deep frying. |
| Grill chef | — Chef grillardin: | All items from the grill including grilled fish. |
| Larder chef | — Chef garde-manger: | All cold fare including aspics, salads, and sandwiches. Also supplies the main kitchen with prepared raw meats, fish, poultry and game, and makes all hors-d'oeuvre, pâtés, terrines and pâté en croûte. |
| Fish chef | — Chef poissonnier: | All hot fish dishes, fish stocks and fish sauces. |
| Vegetable chef | — Chef entremettier: | All vegetables, potato dishes, savouries including savoury soufflés and farinaceous items. |
| Pastry chef | — Chef pâtissier: | Prepares all sweets and pastries, as well as iced confections, petits fours and fruit baskets. |
| Relief chef | — Chef tournant: | The relief chef, who works in any department as required. |
| Soup chef | — Chef potager: | Makes all the soups and usually the egg dishes. |
| Breakfast chef: | | Usually combines the duty with that of kitchen staff cook. |

Each partie will have an appropriate number of commis and apprentices or trainees. In addition, in very large brigades other specialists could include:

chef de nuit, chef tourier, chef froitier, confiseur, glacier, boucher, hors-d'oeuvrier, kitchen clerk and aboyeur. There would also be one or more general staff cooks working independently of the main kitchen brigade.

Obviously, not all work situations would merit such a comprehensive number of high-grade specialist staff. At the other end of the spectrum, the food production element may only involve a single cook and a general assistant and as previously mentioned the industry norm is made up of small units employing ten or less individuals.

Contemporary trends now play a major role as far as basic food preparation methods are concerned. There is a tremendous take-up of ready prepared meat and poultry (much of it portion packed) as well as the vast range of frozen vegetables and fruits, which means that semi-skilled and unskilled kitchen helpers are no longer necessary. However, the demand for fully trained chefs has never been greater, both at home and abroad. After the completion and formal training (usually by attendance at a technical college) and the acquisition of recognised qualifications, mainly through the medium of the City and Guilds of London Institute's examination system, young trainee chefs can opt to specialise in whichever branch of the kitchen appeals most. Such highly skilled specialists as the chef pâtissier, chef garde-manger or chef saucier, are greatly sought after and the demand for such skills invariably exceeds supply. The career prospects are excellent, and the monetary rewards are commensurate with the skills of the respective specialism.

## Front of house occupations

The same applies to 'front of house' occupations involving food and beverage service, reception and accommodation services which, between them, employ trained specialists adept at meeting the most demanding requirements of the customer. A brief synopsis of the career opportunities will illustrate aptly the many and varied tasks undertaken:

| *Food and Beverage Services* | *Accommodation Services* | *Reception Services* |
| --- | --- | --- |
| Trainee waiter/waitress | Housekeeping trainee | Trainee receptionist |
| Commis waiter/waitress | Room maid | Receptionist |
| Station waiter/waitress | Floor housekeeper | Shift leader |
| Head waiter/waitress | Hotel housekeeper | Head receptionist |
| Restaurant manager/ | | Front office manager/ |
| manageress | | manageress |

The hotel and catering industry is big business. There are some 200,000 full-time opportunities created each year, all of which benefit from a sophisticated Careers Advisory Service run by local education authorities, and by the Department of Employment through a nationwide network of Job Centres. The industry also has its own specialist London-based Department of

Employment run **Hotel and Catering Trades Centre** (see page 405).

# Professional bodies and trade associations

*Professional bodies*

**The Hotel and Catering and Institutional Management Association** is the professional body for managers in the food and accommodation services industry. It sets and maintains standards of managerial education, experience and practice for the benefit of its members, the industry and the general public.

Membership is open only to those who meet the strict education and industrial standards required and who accept the Code of Conduct and the disciplinary procedures of the Institute.

The various grades of HCIMA membership fall into two broad categories. There are corporate members (fellows, honorary fellows, life members and members) and non-corporate members (associates, licentiates, intermediates and students). Fellows are the most senior grade of corporate membership and are entitled to use the designatory letters FHCIMA.

Naturally, each grade of membership has its own strict criteria for the award of a specific degree of status.

*Trade associations*

Some associations exist primarily for the advancement of cookery, one of the most prominent being the **Cookery and Food Association** (see page 405) which in turn incorporates the **Craft Guild of Chefs**. There is also the **Chefs and Cooks Circle** (see page 405). The latter is a member of the World Association of Cooks' Societies (WACS), and as such is the only British organisation eligible to select and send British National Teams to compete in international Culinary Olympics. The teams sent achieve outstanding successes world wide. Most professional chefs belong to one or the other association and derive much benefit from the wide range of services which they provide, e.g. a monthly or quarterly journal, an exchange of professional knowledge and up-to-date information about new techniques and equipment, as well as a close involvement in gastronomic festivals both at home and abroad.

The **British Hotels, Restaurants and Caterers Association** serves the needs of its members who are involved in running a business pertaining to the catering industry. Members receive the Association's journal, and can also avail themselves of professional advice covering such topics as recent legislation affecting their business interests; advice on technical issues and the purchasing of equipment; and many other important commercial matters.

### Other development agencies

A significant part of the training offered is through *youth training*, which is available through a large number of different organisations. There are training agents, large companies, colleges and other agents who get together a number of companies to organise training programmes. In some areas there are now TECs (Training Enterprise Councils) which organise all kinds of training including YT in their area. Details of the latter are obtainable at all Careers Centres and Department of Employment Job Centres.

Courses are available for all age ranges and include retraining for new occupations. **The Hotel and Catering Training Company,** which also has several regional offices, offers a nationwide coverage through locally based training programmes delivered through purpose-designed training centres. Details of the schemes can be obtained from any of the Regional Offices (Scottish, Central, Western or Southern) or by writing to the Head Office (see page 405). Local information can be supplied by any of the Training Centres of which there are more than sixty throughout England and Scotland.

Because schemes are constantly being revised and updated, it is advisable to keep in contact with your local Careers Officer or similar agent, e.g. HCTC representative, when seeking out course information.

# Management's and employees' social responsibilities

Management's responsibility to employees may be seen in the provision of steady employment at reasonable wages under satisfactory working conditions. There must be opportunity for individual development and progress with facilities for further training and instruction which will enable an employee to gain satisfaction and fulfilment from their daily work. Satisfactory working conditions are to be interpreted in a wider sense than just adequate physical facilities, and should include supervision which, whilst firm, is sympathetic and encouraging, and far removed from the principle of enforcing discipline by the 'fear of the sack'.

The employee also has a number of moral obligations. These can best be summed up under the headings of personal attitudes and general behaviourial patterns towards others. It is essential to develop and maintain a good standard of courtesy towards one's colleagues (including the management). A constant striving to do one's best at all times by exercising courtesy, tact and good humour, even when working conditions are not ideal, will go a long way to encouraging a reciprocal set of values in the rest of the team.

Punctuality is the keynote when arriving at the workplace, and a fair day's work for a fair day's pay is a sound work ethic. Personal health care should be underlined by a good standard of personal cleanliness and adequate rest. Both aspects are the responsibility of the individual.

# Trade unions within the industry

It has to be stated that despite the size of the industry's total labour force, only a very small percentage of its workers belong to any sort of trade union, and what membership there is is concentrated mainly within the industrial catering sphere. As far as hotels and restaurants are concerned, the impact of unionisation is extremely low. Quite concerted efforts have been made by various unions in recent years to recruit catering workers into one union or another. There are several big trade unions which are available to the catering employee. They are:

**General and Municipal Workers Union (GMWU)**
**Union of Shop, Distributive and Allied Workers (USDAW)**
**Transport and General Workers (TGW)**

Dependent upon which sector of the industry a person is working in, whether local government, transportation or health, it is possible to belong to a more specific union body, e.g. **National Union of Public Employees (NUPE)**, **National Union of Railwaymen (NUR)** or even one associated with the airlines.

What are the reasons for the low rate of unionisation?

1. As already stated, the industry is made up largely of small units (ten or less workers) and the rapport which frequently exists between employer and employee is often 'family' orientated. In other words, perhaps the individual employee does not really feel the need to belong to a union as far as personal interest/welfare is concerned.

2. A high proportion of workers change their jobs fairly frequently. Because of the ease with which workers can move about from one job situation to another, union officers experience difficulty in recruiting new members.

3. A significant number of staff recruited into the catering industry come from countries outside the United Kingdom. As a result, there may be a basic ignorance on the part of many as to the functions of a trade union, as well as a fear that if they do join it will have adverse repercussions as far as the employer is concerned.

4. It must also be recognised that not everyone is keen on becoming a trade union member. After all, it is still a matter of choice in most situations.

5. Finally, there are some organisations whose attitude towards trade union membership is unsympathetic. There may be a bar to workers belonging to any sort of trade union.

### Trade union aims and objectives

The first aim of a trade union is to look after the best interests of its members and advance their cause. They will negotiate with the employers in such areas as rates of pay and hours of work, paid leave (holidays) and general conditions of work. The union negotiators are extremely skilled in their work, and their primary aim is always to advance the well-being of their members and defend their rights.

Broadly speaking, the main responsibility of management is to advance the interests of the business, that is, the shareholders or, in the case of a privately owned company, the proprietor. Understandably, there are occasions when there is a conflict of interest between the two sides (unions and management) and this is where the skill of the negotiator comes into play. However, there are times when each side fails to reach a mutually compatible agreement. At this stage of the proceedings, there may be cause to call in an independent body, such as ACAS.

### Advisory, Conciliation and Arbitration Service (ACAS)

**The Advisory, Conciliation and Arbitration Service** is a respected, totally independent review body whose officers will act to effect conciliation between both parties, and hopefully arrive at a satisfactory settlement without the matter reaching the stage of a tribunal hearing. Industrial tribunals are more concerned that disputes are settled by the process of conciliation, rather than having to resort to judicial procedures imposed by a tribunal judiciary hearing.

# Healthy eating guidelines

### Nutritional requirements

For proper health and efficiency an individual must eat sufficient of all the principal nutrients which constitute the optimum diet. Such nutrients are present in varying amounts in a wide range of foods and it is therefore possible to manage an adequate food intake in a number of ways to suit local tastes and varying food supplies.

The optimum requirements will differ between sexes and occupations. Thus a male's dietary needs in terms of *calories* can be in the following range:

2,500 (sedentary occupation/lifestyle)

3,000 (moderately active occupation/lifestyle)
4,500 (very active physically demanding occupation/lifestyle)

whilst a woman's calorific needs can be in the following range:

2,100 (sedentary occupation/lifestyle)
2,500 (moderately active occupation/lifestyle)
3,000 (very active occupation/lifestyle)

The above figures are meant as a general guide. If less than the optimum requirements of nutrients are supplied by a diet, then a decline in efficiency and well-being may well show itself by signs of lassitude and tiredness, with more serious health risks resulting over the longer term.

A large number of the recipes found in this book may be altered to reflect the eating trends of today's consumers. By and large, modern consumers are much better informed, with demands for increased fibre content together with reduced cholesterol levels in the food that they eat, whether within the home or when eating-out. Such demands are based, rightly, on the belief that all will benefit from the new healthier diets. This healthy eating can be further improved by an increased intake of fresh produce, especially fresh fruit and vegetables.

Throughout the text, you will be given various alternatives whereby recipes can be modified in line with healthy eating or weight reducing diets such as: wholemeal flour in place of white flour; plain yoghurt in place of fresh cream, and so on. However, it is as well to remember as professional caterers that we should not alter a dish beyond general recognition, and that we should always inform the customer of any major adjustment to the ingredients of a recipe/dish. For example, the caterer should not serve a cream soup on the menu and finish the item with plain yoghurt (in place of fresh cream) without making this fact quite clear to the customer beforehand. Such knowledge can be conveyed as part of the menu information, or passed on verbally at the point of taking the customer's order.

A balanced diet will contain adequate amounts of fruit, vegetables, meat, fish and poultry, together with nuts, rice and dried pulses such as lentils and chickpeas.

Alternatively, many people have chosen to follow a vegetarian diet, with a good balance of fresh fruit and vegetables, dried pulses and nut products on a regular basis. It is all a matter of personal choice.

No single food contains all the nutrients that we need to keep healthy, which is why we require a good balance of all the nutrients to maintain our bodies (and minds) in a healthy condition.

The body is a machine, and it needs fuel, obtained from carbohydrates, proteins and fat. These are converted into energy which is measured in *calories* — the more calories, the more power for the machine.

If your body takes in too much power, i.e. too many calories, it simply stores it up — as fat. If you eat less food that you need your body consumes the power it has stored — and you lose weight. However, nobody should even contemplate going on a diet without first obtaining medical advice and dietary guidance. Single-minded attempts at slimming can be dangerous to one's health! An individual's correct weight (in a health sense) depends on height and body build and that is why expert medical advice is essential before starting any weight-reducing regime.

We also need minerals and vitamins for bodily growth and a well-balanced metabolism. A serious shortage of any of these essential elements can cause diseases of the bones, skin and bodily functions. To help to avoid illnesses such as heart strain, tooth decay, excess weight, anaemia, high blood pressure, etc. it is important to maintain a well-balanced diet on a daily basis.

## Reduction of cholesterol in the diet

The main sources of cholesterol in the diet are margarine, butter and cream. Fortunately, there are now readily available both margarines and butters which are low in cholesterol and some of these are suitable for use in catering. Low-fat cream is also available containing up to half the fat of standard cream. Fresh double cream contains a high fat level of approximately 48 per cent, whipping cream 35 per cent and single cream the lowest fat level of 18 per cent. By simply selecting a cream with a lower fat content, the level of fat intake in the diet can be reduced. The fat level can be reduced even further by finishing soups and sauces with plain yoghurt where appropriate. However, this will drastically alter the finished flavour of the dish and, as already mentioned, the customer should be informed of any such substitution.

When cream is the thickening agent in a dish, care must be taken as to the fat content of the cream used — single cream will not thicken sauces, because of its low fat content. Neither will yoghurt for similar reasons.

The use of polyunsaturated fats and oils will also aid the reduction of cholesterol in the diet. However, remember that low-fat spreads are not suitable for cooking purposes because of their high water content.

## Increasing fibre in the diet

An increased fibre content in the diet can be realised in several ways:

1.  By introducing more fresh fruit and vegetables.

2.  By using brown rice in place of white, and wholewheat pasta in place of the standard variety.

3.  By substituting wholemeal for white flour in pastry.

All are measures which will add quite substantially to our fibre intake. In addition a large number of sauces, especially the brown and miscellaneous sauces, may be made using brown flour in the roux in place of white flour.

Fibre is made up from a complex variety of substances and is found only in plant cell walls. There are two types of fibre, soluble and insoluble.

*Soluble fibre* is found in fruits and vegetables. The best sources, however, are pulses such as kidney beans and lentils, and such items as pearl barley, porridge oats and rye bread.

Soluble fibre forms a sticky substance in the stomach and is believed to restrict the amount of fat the body absorbs. It is also thought that soluble fibre affects the production of insulin in the body. Insulin controls the blood sugar levels which determine how hungry we feel—so an increase in the intake of soluble fibre may reduce those hunger attacks during the day!

*Insoluble fibre* is found mainly in wheat-based items such as breakfast cereals, bread, flour, bran and the more fibrous vegetables. It acts like a sponge in the stomach soaking up moisture from the foods we eat, and then swelling in the stomach so making us feel full up.

# Commodity estimating guide

*Fresh vegetables*

The average weight of trimming varies with each type of vegetable. A reasonable cooked portion of vegetables to be served would be 85 g. Therefore the amount puchased should be in relation to the waste in preparation:

| | |
|---|---|
| Broad beans | 450 g will produce 140 g prepared, or 2 portions |
| French beans | 450 g will produce 280–340 g prepared, or 4–5 portions |
| Broccoli and cauliflower | 450 g will produce 230 g prepared, or 2–3 portions |
| Cabbage | 450 g will produce 340 g prepared, or 3–4 portions |
| Marrow | 450 g will produce 340 g prepared, or 3–4 portions |
| Brussel sprouts | 450 g will produce 280–340 g prepared, or 3–4 portions |
| New potatoes | 450 g will produce 340 g prepared, or 3–4 portions |
| Main crop potatoes | 450 g will produce 225 g prepared, or 2–3 portions of most potato dishes |
| Spinach—leaf | 450 g will produce 225–340 g prepared, or 2–3 portions |
| Garden peas | 450 g will produce 225 g prepared, or 2–3 portions |

*Fresh meat*

**Weight loss in cooking**
Generally, one can asume a weight loss of about 30 per cent in the roasting and grilling of meats, and consideration of any bone content could increase the percentage loss to about 50 per cent. This means that to obtain a yield of 225 g of cooked meat from a joint on the bone, it would be necessary to purchase 450 g. Therefore assuming that the policy is to serve 112 g of cooked meat to each

customer, one needs to double this amount in purchasing; so that a 6 kg rib of beef will serve 24 people with 112 g each; alternatively, a 6 kg rib of beef will serve 32 people with 84 g portions.

### Portion control

The nature of the establishment and the charges made will largely determine the size of the portions served. The following is a guide to what is acceptable:

| *Meat* | *per person* |
|---|---|
| Steak sirloin | 168–225 g |
| Steak rump | 168–225 g |
| Steak fillet | 112–170 g |
| Minute steak | 84–142 g |
| Steak T-bone | 340 g |
| Lamb chop | 112–170 g |
| Best-end cutlets (2 each) | 112–170 g |
| Pork chops | 112–170 g |
| Veal escalopes | 142 g |
| Gammon | 112–170 g |

| *Fish* | *per person* |
|---|---|
| One portion Dover sole (whole) | 340 g |
| Two portions Dover sole (whole) | 562–780 g |
| Dover sole fillet | 112–142 g |
| Plaice fillet | 112–142 g |
| Salmon steaks | 168–225 g |

| *Poultry* | *Weight (undrawn)* | |
|---|---|---|
| Poussin (single) | 570 g | 1 bird per person |
| Poussin (double) | 800 g | 1 bird per 2 persons |
| Spring chicken | 1 kg 340 g | 3 portions per bird |
| Autumn chicken | 2 kg | 4 portions per bird |
| Capons | 3 kg | 8 portions per bird |

| *Boiling fowl* | | |
|---|---|---|
| Small birds | 2 kg | 7 portions per bird |
| Large birds | 3 kg | 9 portions per bird |

All poultry will lose about 25 per cent on drawing, and about 50 per cent on roasting and bone loss. Thus, a 3 kg capon will lose 728 g in drawing = 2 kg 272 g; after roasting and bone loss (the carcass) 50 per cent of the 2 kg 272 g will then leave about 1 kg 126 g of actual meat.

Therefore, allow 112 g of chicken if served off the bone (breast meat), and 170 g if served on the bone (wing or leg).

| | |
|---|---|
| Ducklings | Allow 3 portions per 1 kg 340 g bird |
| Ducks | Allow 4 portions per 1 kg 812 g bird |
| Geese | Allow 6 portions per 2 kg 720 g bird |
| Turkeys | Turkeys will lose 25 per cent of their weight in drawing, and 40 per cent in roasting and bone loss (the carcass). Thus a 9 kg turkey will lose 2¼ kg in drawing = 7¾ kg, and 40 per cent of the original weight in roasting and carcass weight, with the actual meat production being 3 kg 171 g. It is usual to serve 50/50 dark and white meat, with an average portion being 84–112 g. The total number of portions is therefore 28 per 9 kg turkey. |

# Simple percentage food costs

The aim of the percentage system of kitchen control is to produce a predetermined percentage of profit upon the selling price of food served. The percentage of profit required is decided upon by the management, the most usual percentage being a 60 per cent profit, which means the average cost of the food should be 40 per cent.

Having determined the required percentage of profit, an appropriate amount will be added to the cost price of all the kitchen dishes, or to the cost price of set meals if these are served. The system is applied by the percentage being worked out upon the entire food side of the business, usually upon a daily basis.

First of all, the cost of the day's food is totalled up. This figure is ascertained by reference to the quantities used and to the prices paid. Secondly, the total takings (food sales) for the day are confirmed. And to these two figures the following formula is applied:

$$\text{Takings} - \text{cost of purchase} = \text{gross profit}$$

$$\frac{\text{Gross profit} \times 100}{\text{Takings (sales)}} = \text{gross percentage}$$

Here is an example:

| | £ |
|---|---|
| Takings | 300 |
| Purchases | 120 |
| Gross profit | 180 |

$$\text{Kitchen percentage} = \frac{180 \times 100}{300} = 60\%$$

In practice the percentage is usually taken to two decimal points.

If we use one of our poultry items (turkey) as an example of how to determine the selling price per portion in order to achieve a 60 per cent gross profit margin (that is, 40 per cent food cost), the calculations would be as follows:

Assume that the purchase price of the turkey is £1.90 per kg. The bird weighs 9 kg, therefore the purchase price is £17.10. The number of portions produced is 28, so the cost per portion is 61.1p. To find out the selling price, the formula is as follows:

$$\text{Selling price} = \frac{\text{Food cost}}{\text{Kitchen percentage}} \times 100$$

$$\text{Selling price} = \frac{61.1 \times 100}{40} = 152.7p$$

Single dishes or complete menus can be accurately costed and priced according to the desired margin of profit using the above formula. A quick 'at a glance' chart is as follows:

| *Food cost* | *Multiply* | | | *Approximate selling price* | *Gross profit* |
|---|---|---|---|---|---|
| 50% | × 2 | (2) | @ 61.1p = | 122p | 50% |
| 45% | × 2⅔ | (2.22) | @ 61.1p = | 137p | 55% |
| 40% | × 2½ | (2.5) | @ 61.1p = | 153p | 60% |
| 33⅓% | × 3 | (3) | @ 61.1p = | 183p | 66⅔% |
| 55% | × 1¾ | (1.75) | @ 61.1p = | 107p | 45% |
| 60% | × 1⅔ | (1.66) | @ 61.1p = | 101p | 40% |

In the above calculations, we have used the arbitrary figure of 61.1p, which is the cost of our turkey portion. Naturally, any other figure can be substituted according to the required food cost percentage calculation.

Once the management has decided upon the kitchen percentage required, and the food cost has been worked out, we can then find out the selling price of any article, either single dishes or complete menus. As already stated, the more usual kitchen percentage is 40 per cent food cost, giving a gross profit margin of 60 per cent. However, that is only part of the story, because the business will incur costs other than the cost of food. Such costs or expenses are referred to as *overheads*, and must be deducted from the gross profit.

### Overheads

Overheads will include rent, rates, heating and lighting, maintenance/repairs, wages and depreciation. The last of these is monies set aside to cover the cost of replacing worn out equipment and fittings.

Other overheads of a more variable nature will include laundry, stationery and advertising. When all these costs have been accounted for, usually on an annual basis, we can establish precisely what amount of net profit the business is producing. Unfortunately, it is sometimes the case that a net loss is the outcome of the year's trading. For that reason, the shrewd business person will monitor his or her income and expenditure on a more frequent basis, monthly at least. In that way, should the trading pattern prove unsatisfactory, steps can be taken to correct deficiencies, perhaps by increasing menu prices or stricter portion control. Either way, no business is going to function indefinitely unless the net profit margin is satisfactory.

The above is a very condensed summary of the financial aspects of restaurant management. It does, however, serve to emphasise the necessity of strict budgetary control if one is to remain successful (and solvent) in a catering business enterprise. It simply is not enough being a super cook or chef. The prosperous chefs are those who are also keen businessmen.

# Self-assessment questions for industrial studies

1. There are fourteen major sectors within the hotel and catering industry; can you name seven?
2. Which body represents the industry in a professional (managerial) sense?
3. Can you name at least three trade associations?
4. What do the letters 'HCTC' stand for?
5. Can you briefly describe management's social responsibilities to the employee?
6. The employee has a set of moral obligations towards fellow workers (including management); briefly describe what those obligations are.
7. To keep fit and healthy, a sensible diet should be supported by other measures; what are they?
8. Trade union membership in the catering industry is very small. Can you name at least two possible reasons for the low level of recruitment?
9. What is the primary aim of a trade union as far as its members are concerned?
10. What is the main function of the Advisory, Conciliation and Arbitration Service (ACAS)?

When you have completed these questions check your answers with fellow students and your chef or lecturer.

# Chapter 2
# Cold Preparation

## The competency defined

This section refers to the basic preparation and production of raw foods and cooked foods for presentation as cold dishes. The range of dishes covered includes savoury and sweet items, wholemeal recipes and notes on cuts of fish, meat and poultry.

## Purpose of cold preparation

There are many reasons for serving dishes cold; they include the following:
1. To provide foods suitable for travel, such as picnic hampers and working lunches.
2. For presentation on cold buffets or salad bars, with or without the modern take-away facilities.
3. To provide colour, texture, fibre and a fresh vitamin content for the diet, as in salads.

Cold preparation is necessary and is used for many types of food, including cold sauces, salad dressings, salads and hors-d'oeuvre, as well as the preparation of cold dishes for buffets and counter service, and basic preparations such as forcemeats, marinades, mousses and dressed shellfish, such as crab, lobster and prawns.

## Organisation and preparation

The larder chef (*chef garde-manger*) would be the person who is responsible for overseeing the production of all cold preparations (except for sweet items). His section will prepare all the meat, poultry, fish and game for cooking by other specialist sections in the main kitchen. Such preparation would include all types of offal as well. The larder section is also responsible for all cold buffet work including hors-d'oeuvre, salads, dressings and sandwiches, etc.

In very large traditional partie systems, there would be a number of chef specialists who are responsible to the *chef garde-manger* for specific tasks, including:

| | |
|---|---|
| *Chef froitier:* | Cold buffet work. |
| *Chef hors-d'oeuvrier:* | Production of hors-d'oeuvre. |
| *Boucher (butcher):* | All butchery work. |

First-class organisation in the preparatory stages is essential for the efficient functioning of this very important section. It is the 'power house' which is responsible for supplying the main kitchen with all their raw materials.

Plenty of space is needed, not only in the form of tabling, but also in terms of refrigeration facilities. Meat, poultry, fish and game should be kept under refrigeration as much as possible—not left out in the open. It is a complex department to organise given the large amount of *mise en place* (preparation in advance) with which this part of the organisation is concerned. Some idea of the nature of the work-load can be gleaned from the following production schedule.

| | |
|---|---|
| *Hors-d'oeuvre and salads*: | To include composite and single varieties; all cold sauces to include mayonnaise and its derivatives; fish and shellfish cold sauces (for fish cocktails); compound butters; and simple and compound salads. |
| *Fish and shellfish preparation*: | For the main kitchen (to be cooked); and also the elaborate cold and decorated fish items for the buffet. |
| *Poultry and game*: | The preparation and dressing, including cuts, of poultry and game for the main kitchen. Also, all cold items for the buffet. |
| *Butchery*: | The dissection/jointing of carcass meat including beef, lamb, mutton, pork, veal and bacon sides (including ham and gammons). |
| *Miscellaneous items*: | To include forcemeats, stuffings, marinades and brines, and a range of classical garnishes, such as quenelles and salpiçon, sandwiches and canapés, and also reception savouries. |

The above range is not exhaustive, but will certainly act as a guide.

# Safety and hygiene—general rules

When working in the larder it is important that you observe a high standard of hygiene, both personal and otherwise, when dealing with food and equipment. On a personal level you must wear clean chef's whites daily and never use your apron for wiping your hands. Always ensure that your hands are clean, and that you scrub them thoroughly after visiting the lavatory. Avoid contact with your hair, nose and mouth (all sources of infection).

Regarding food, fish should be kept in a separate refrigerator and away from other foods. Never store cooked and raw meats in the same refrigerator, the reason being the ever-present danger of cross-contamination by harmful bacteria. In other words, the bacteria present in uncooked foods such as raw chicken or meat may pass from raw foods to cooked foods which may then be eaten by an unsuspecting customer resulting in food poisoning which can be very serious indeed.

With regards to equipment, never cut raw foods and cooked foods (especially meats) on the same cutting board or with the same knife—unless they have been thoroughly cleansed in the mean time. This sort of practice can cause food poisoning for the same reasons as above.

# General rules for efficient production and preparation

High standards of work are always essential in this section of the kitchen brigade, as the quality of the finished dish is affected by the quality of the basic *mise en place*. You should always take special note of which foods will go together, with regards to texture, flavour and colour ( a good example of this is when making an *hors-d'oeuvre varié*). Also, note which cooked and non-cooked foods will go together to produce an exciting dish, such as cooked meat or fish with a specific salad.

An artistic flair is essential in producing decorative work, such as decorated hams or whole salmon, especially for cold buffets. The ability to produce quick and simple designs for decoration is a skill to be developed. Points to be remembered when serving cold foods include the following:

1. The appearance must be crisp and appealing to the customer.
2. Never over-decorate foods or use too much colour as this may detract from the overall eye appeal of the finished product. Incidentally, some colours should never be used—blue is one example, at least as far as fresh foods are concerned. Royal icing is a different matter.

# Techniques associated with cold preparation

*Carving*: The slicing of meats and poultry for service.
*Chopping*: The cutting of foods, such as onion, parsley and other herbs and vegetables into very small pieces. Parsley should be quite finely chopped and then dried in the corner of a clean kitchen cloth to expel excess moisture.

*Dressing*: Refers to two different processes, firstly coating a food, such as a salad, with a dressing such as sauce vinaigrette or oil; and secondly, the portioning of foods on dishes for service in the restaurant.

*Garnishing*: This is a final touch added to dishes of food, and is placed around or by the side of the main item; watercress, tomato, lemon or parsley are typical examples.

# Equipment used in cold preparation

The equipment used in this section is quite varied and includes: assorted bowls and basins, whisks, blenders, sieves, trays, ricers and spoons. All equipment should be washed in hot, soapy water and rinsed in clean hot water, then thoroughly dried before being stored for future use.

Of course, the items listed form only a small part of the equipment required in a busy larder section and do not take into account such items as mincing machines, bowl choppers, gravity feed slicers, small and large size scales, pie moulds and terrines for making raised pies (*pâté en croûte*). There are also, of course, the numerous special tools for butchering the various meats. Some examples are: boning knives, butcher's saws (tenon and bow types), choppers, cleavers, and a range of slicing knives.

# Self-assessment questions for cold preparation

1. Can you describe in general terms the work of the larder section?
2. Apart from the *chef garde-manger*, name three other specialists who may be employed in this section in a large kitchen brigade.
3. Name some of the miscellaneous items which are produced in the larder section.
4. What do you understand by the term '*mis en place*'?
5. How can cross-contamination be caused?
6. Detail four techniques associated with cold preparation.
7. Name ten small and medium-sized pieces of equipment found in the larder section.
8. Explain why strict standards of hygiene are essential in the catering industry.
9. What is a cartouche?
10. What is a tomato concassé?

When you have completed all these questions check your answers with your fellow students and chef or lecturer.

# Cold sauces and basic preparations

## Introduction to cold sauces and basic preparations

It is essential in all aspects of cookery that the basic preparations and sauces are of the highest possible standard and quality. Only then can you ensure that the finished dishes will be of the highest standard. This is especially the case with cold work, so make sure that you work cleanly and use the best materials.

### White chaud-froid sauce — Sauce chaud-froid blanc

| | | |
|---|---|---|
| 1 litre | Chicken velouté | 4 litres |
| ½ litre | Aspic jelly (ordinary) | 2 litres |
| ¼ litre | Double cream | 1 litre |

1. Bring the chicken velouté to the boil in a shallow pan (sauteuse) and begin a steady process of reduction, stirring constantly to avoid burning on the bottom.
2. Add the aspic jelly and the cream by degrees until the velouté has reduced by about one-third in volume.
3. Check the seasoning and setting consistency, and pass through a tammy cloth into a clean container. The sauce should be of a masking consistency, but not too thick.
4. Allow to cool and use just before setting-point is reached.
5. If not for immediate use, cover the bowl with foil and keep in the refrigerator.
6. Re-heat in a shallow pan stood in a tray of hot water (bain-marie style).

### Pink chaud-froid sauce — Sauce chaud-froid aurore

| | | |
|---|---|---|
| ½ kg | Fresh tomatoes | 1½ kg |
| 1 litre | Chicken velouté | 4 litres |

1. Cook the tomato flesh *(concassé)* in 50g of butter to a pureé.
2. Add the chicken velouté and bring to the boil.
3. Check the seasoning and pass through a tammy cloth into a clean bowl.
4. The sauce should be an attractive rose pink in colour and have a delicate flavour of tomato.

### Brown chaud-froid sauce — Sauce chaud-froid brun

| | | |
|---|---|---|
| 1 litre | Demi-glace or good jus lié | 4 litres |
| ¾ litre | Aspic jelly (ordinary) | 3 litres |
| ½ glass | Dry sherry or Madeira wine | 1 dl |

1. Bring the demi-glace or *jus lié* to the boil in a sauteuse and, stirring

constantly, reduce the volume by about one-third adding the aspic jelly by degrees during the process of reduction.
2. Add the sherry or Madeira, and check the seasoning and setting consistency.
3. Pass through a tammy cloth into a clean container, and allow to cool.
4. Use just on setting-point for masking or coating small and large items.

Note: Using *jus lié* will give a much lighter sauce.

## Salad dressings and sauces

There is nothing to equal the flavour of home-made salad dressing and mayonnaise. Both items will keep for several weeks. French dressing can be bottled and retained under normal larder/cupboard conditions, whilst mayonnaise will keep perfectly well in a foil covered basin or similar utensil in the refrigerator.

### French dressing

*Vinaigrette*

| | | |
|---|---|---|
| 6 tablespoons | Olive oil | 1 litre |
| 2 tablespoons | French wine vinegar | 50 ml |
| 1 teaspoon | French mustard | 20 g |
| | Salt, milled pepper | |
| | Small pinch of castor sugar | 25 g |

1. Blend all the ingredients together and bottle up for future use.
2. This dressing may be varied by the addition of some finely chopped parsley, chives, tarragon and chopped chervil.
3. Always shake well before using.

### Mayonnaise

| | | |
|---|---|---|
| 125 ml | Olive oil | 1 litre |
| 2 | Egg yolks | 16 |
| | Salt, ground white pepper | |
| 1 dessertspoon | Vinegar | 100 ml |
| 1 coffeespoon | English mustard (optional) | 15 g |

1. Whisk the yolks and salt together in a suitable basin, then add the vinegar.
2. If using mustard, blend in at this stage.
3. Add the oil carefully at first to form a fairly thick consistency, after which the oil can be added until all is absorbed.
4. The resulting mayonnaise should be of a stiff consistency. The latter can now be corrected by the addition of one or two teaspoons of boiling water whisked in at the end.

Note: In cold weather, it is essential to warm the oil slightly to prevent the mayonnaise from 'turning'. If this should occur, the sauce may be brought back by placing a dessertspoon of very hot water into a clean basin, then dribbling in the curdled sauce whilst still whisking.

# Basic cuts of vegetables

Depending on the ultimate use of vegetables, they may be required to be cut into a variety of shapes and sizes. Below is a list of the basic vegetable cuts you will be using.

*Brunoise — Very small dice*
Cut the vegetables into manageable lengths.
Cut the lengths into slices no thicker than 2 mm.
Cut the slices into strips no thicker than 2 mm.
Cut the strips into squares no thicker than 2 mm.
Used mainly in garnishing soups.

*Julienne — Very thin strips*
Cut the vegetables into lengths of no more than 4 cm.
Cut the lengths into the thinnest possible slices.
Cut the slices into the thinnest possible strips.
Used as garnish for soups, entreés and salads.

*Jardinière — Thick cut bâtons (also known as bâtons)*
Cut the vegetables into 1½ cm lengths.
Cut the lengths into 3 mm slices.
Cut the slices into bâtons 3 × 3 × 18 mm.
Commonly used as a cut for vegetable service, e.g. carrots.

*Macédoine — Large dice*
Cut the vegetables into manageable lengths.
Cut the lengths into ½ cm slices.
Cut the slices into ½ cm strips.
Cut the strips into ½ cm dice.
Commonly used as a cut for hot vegetables, soups and salads.

*Paysanne — Thin sliced shapes*
There are four main acceptable methods of presenting paysanne; all are sliced thinly:
    1 cm slices of triangular shape
    1 cm slices of square shape
    1 cm slices of rough sided rounds
    1 cm slices of round shape

Commonly used in soups such as minestrone or vegetable broths.

**Tomato concassé**

1. Remove the eye of the tomato (stalk end) with the point of a small vegetable knife.
2. Plunge each tomato into near boiling water for a few seconds, then place into a basin of cold water.
3. When all the tomatoes have been treated in this way, begin at the stalk end and peel away the skin. They should remove quite easily.
4. Cut each tomato across laterally, and remove the seeds with a teaspoon leaving the shell of the tomato half intact.
5. Cut the flesh into neat dice and use as required.

Tomato prepared in this way has many uses both as a garnish and in savoury items and sauces.

# Batters

There are a number of batters used for deep frying foods. The recipe denotes which batter to select. Batters are used as protective covers for foods being cooked or for a parcel to hold foods if using stuffed pancakes.

**Frying batter**                                            *Pâté à frire*

| | | |
|---|---|---|
| 230 g | Strong flour | 460 g |
| 15 g | Yeast | 30 g |
| 10 ml | Oil | 20 ml |
| 100 ml | Milk (tepid heat) | 200 ml |
| 140 ml | Cold water | 280 ml |
| | Pinch salt and sugar | |

1. Cream the yeast with the sugar, and dilute the yeast mixture with the tepid milk. Add the water.
2. Beat into the sieved flour and salt, and blend to a smooth mixture. Finally, add the oil.
3. Cover with a cloth and allow to ferment for about 1 hour.

The batter will keep for 2–3 days if necessary in a cool place. It can be used for both savoury and sweet items.

**Egg batter 1**

| | | |
|---|---|---|
| 200 g | Plain flour | 500 g |
| 1 | Egg | 3 |
| 2½ dl | Milk/water | 6 dl |
| | Salt | |
| 2 tablespoons | Oil | 4 tablespoons |

1. Shake the flour and salt through a fine sieve into a bowl of suitable size for

the volume of batter being made.
2. Make a well in the centre of the flour, adding the egg and milk.
3. Beat to a smooth batter.
4. Beat in the oil and allow to stand covered for 30 minutes before using.

## Egg batter 2

| | | |
|---|---|---|
| 200 g | Plain flour | 500 g |
| 2 tablesepoons | Oil | 5 tablespoons |
| 2½ dl | Milk/water | 6 dl |
| 2 | Egg whites | 5 |
| | Salt | |

1. Shake the flour and salt through a fine sieve into a bowl of suitable size for the volume of batter being made.
2. Add the milk and beat to a smooth batter.
3. Beat in the oil and leave to stand for 30 minutes before using.
4. Beat the egg whites until stiff and fold into the batter when ready to be used.

## Baking powder batter

| | | |
|---|---|---|
| 200 g | Plain flour | 500g |
| 1 teaspoon | Baking powder | 2½ teaspoons |
| 2½ dl | Milk/water | 6 dl |
| | Salt | |

1. Shake the flour, salt and baking powder through a fine sieve into a bowl of suitable size for the volume of batter being made.
2. Create a well in the centre of the flour and add the milk.
3. Beat until a smooth batter is made.

## Pancake batter

| | | |
|---|---|---|
| 112 g | Medium flour | 225 g |
| | Pinch salt | 7 g |
| 1 | Egg | 2 |
| 1 | Egg yolk | 2 |
| 140 ml | Water | 280 ml |
| 140 ml | Milk | 280 ml |
| 20 ml | Salad oil | 40 ml |
| 15 g | Castor sugar (for sweet pancakes) | 30 g |

1. Sieve the flour, and blend in the egg, yolk, oil, salt, milk and water to form a smooth batter.
2. Strain into a clean basin, and rest in a cool place before using. The batter will keep for 2–3 days in a cool place.

# Binding agents

Panadas are used in the basic preparation of forecemeats, fish and meat farces. They help to bind ingredients together and extend the volume of the basic dish so allowing for an increased number of portions for service. There are three panadas: bread, flour and frangipane.

### Bread panada                                    *Panade au pain*

| | | |
|---|---|---|
| 1 litre | Milk | 5 litres |
| 1 kg | Fresh white breadcrumbs | 5 kg |
| | Salt and pepper | |

1. Boil the milk and add the breadcrumbs, mix in well using a wooden spoon.
2. Add the salt and pepper to taste.
3. Keep mixing on the stove top until the panada is thick and smooth in texture.
4. Pour on to a lightly buttered tray and spread out evenly.
5. Leave to go cold before use.

### Flour panada                                    *Panade à la farine*

| | | |
|---|---|---|
| 1 litre | Water | 5 litres |
| 225 g | Butter or margarine | 1 kg 125 g |
| 700 g | Plain flour | 3½ kg |
| | Salt and pepper | |

1. Boil the water and butter or margarine in a pan with salt and pepper.
2. Add the flour and mix in well until smooth with a wooden spoon, off the heat.
3. Place back on to the stove until completely cooked, 5–15 minutes.
4. Spread on a buttered tray, butter the surface and allow to go cold.

### Frangipane panada                               *Panade à la frangipane*

| | | |
|---|---|---|
| 1 litre | Boiling milk | 5 litres |
| 16 | Egg yolks | 80 |
| 350 g | Clarified butter or margarine | 1¾ kg |
| | Salt and pepper | |
| | Grated nutmeg | |

1. In a suitably sized pan place the egg yolks, clarified butter and flour, season and add a small amount of grated nutmeg.
2. Mix well with a wooden spoon until smooth.
3. Add the boiling milk, a little at a time, over a gentle heat.
4. When all the milk is added continue to mix over heat until smooth and cooked, 5–10 minutes.

5. Pour on to a buttered tray, spread out evenly and allow to go cold before use.

# Cold butter sauces

Cold butter sauces are usually served with grilled or deep-fried foods such as fish or meat. They are sliced and laid on top of the fish or meat to moisten and flavour them.

### Anchovy butter                                   *Beurre d'anchois*

| 50 g | Butter | ½ kg |
| | Anchovy essence to taste | |

1. Blend the butter and anchovy essence together; use enough essence to lightly colour the butter and give a gentle flavour of anchovy.
2. Roll into a cylindrical shape in greaseproof paper and chill until required.
3,. Cut into ½ cm thick slices with a warm knife. Serve on crushed ice or on the food being served.

Serve with grilled and fried fish dishes.

### Butter for snails                          *Beurre à la bourguignonne*

| 100 g | Butter | ½ kg |
| 25 g | Brunoise of shallots | 75 g |
| 15 g | Garlic paste | 25 g |
| 25 g | Finely chopped parsley | 50 g |
| | Pepper to taste | |

Mix all ingredients together in a suitable sized mixing bowl. Roll in greaseproof paper to a cylindrical shape. Chill until required.

### Shrimp butter                                 *Beurre de crevettes*

| 100 g | Butter | 1 kg |
| 100 g | Peeled shrimps | 1 kg |
| | Seasoning as required | |

Mix well together and pass through a sieve. Roll in greaseproof paper to a cylindrical shape and chill until required.

### Parsley butter                              *Beurre maitre d'hôtel*

1. Blend the juice of two fresh lemons with each kg of butter, 50 g of finely chopped parsley and two good pinches of cayenne pepper.
2. Roll in greaseproof paper to a cylindrical shape and chill until required.

Served with grilled and shallow-fried meats, fish and poultry.

# Salads

### Introduction to salads

These are commonly found on buffet tables or as side salads to accompany a main course. More substantial salads may often be found as starters on menus in restaurants and popular eating houses. The dishes listed here are popular examples in common use.

**Potato salad**                          *Salade de pomme de terre*

| | | |
|---|---|---|
| 400 g | Potatoes | 1 kg |
| 1–2 tablespoons | French dressing | 70 ml |
| | Chopped chives or finely | |
| | chopped onions | 75 g |
| 65 ml | Mayonnaise | 125 ml |
| | Freshly chopped parsley | |

1. Choose medium-sized potatoes which, after washing, should be steamed in their jackets until just cooked through.
2. Peel and cut into dice, then marinade by sprinkling with the French dressing. Lightly blend in the chopped chives or onions before binding with the mayonnaise.
3. When serving, dust the top with the freshly chopped parsley.

**New potato salad**

| | | |
|---|---|---|
| 200 g | New potatoes | 1 kg |
| 2 tablespoons | Mayonnaise | 125 ml |
| 2 tablespoons | Fresh cream | 75 ml |
| | Chopped chives | 50 g |
| 1 dessertspoon | French dressing | 25 ml |

1. Wash and steam the new potatoes in their skins. Allow to cool slightly before peeling and cutting across into slices (not too thick).
2. Semi-whip the cream and blend with the mayonnaise.
3. Sprinkle the potatoes with the French dressing and chopped chives and fold in the cream/mayonnaise sauce.

**Russian salad**                          *Salade russe*

| | | |
|---|---|---|
| 100 g | Diced cooked carrots | 1 kg |
| 100 g | Cooked garden peas | 1 kg |
| 100 g | Cooked diced white turnip | 1 kg |
| 100 g | Cooked diced French beans | 1 kg |
| 5 ml | Mayonnaise | 750 ml (¾ litre) |
| 1–2 tablespoons | Vinaigrette | 125 ml |

1. Cook the prepared vegetables in lightly salted water until just tender.
2. Rinse off under running water (to refresh) and drain in a colander.
3. Blend the mixture together and sprinkle with the vinaigrette.
4. Finally, bind gently with the mayonnaise.

## Rice salad                                                  *Salade de riz*

Prepare a rice pilaff in the following manner:

1. Finely chop one medium-size onion, and one clove of garlic.
2. Place approximately 30 g butter into a suitable oven-proof pan, and add the onion and garlic.
3. Allow to cook gently for 2–3 minutes without allowing to take on any colour. Stir continuously during this process.
4. Add 180 g of long grain rice and stir over the heat until it becomes transparent and the rice absorbs the butter.
5. Season with salt and milled pepper, and cover the rice with boiling chicken stock—about 350 ml.
6. Cover the pan with a well-buttered circle of greaseproof paper and a tight-fitting lid.
7. Place in a hot oven, 230–250°C, and cook for about 15 minutes, until the rice is cooked and all the stock is absorbed.
8. Remove from the oven and turn out immediately into a cool pan.
9. Stir in a large knob of butter, using a fork to separate the rice grains and use as required.

*For the rice salad* blend into the rice the following ingredients:

| | |
|---|---|
| 50 g | **Small diced red pimentoes** |
| 50 g | **Diced tomato concassé** |
| 50 g | **Cooked garden peas** |
| 25 ml | **French dressing** |

1. Use two forks to blend in the garnish to avoid mashing the rice grains.
2. Check the seasoning.
3. Dress slightly dome-shaped in shallow earthenware dishes.

## Beetroot salad                                        *Salade de betterave*

| | | |
|---|---|---|
| 250 g | **Cold boiled beetroot** | 600 g |
| 10 g | **Brunoise of onion** | 25 g |
| ½ dl | **Vinaigrette** | 1 dl |

1. Cut the beetroot into bâtons or macédoine.
2. Bind with the vinaigrette and arrange in an earthenware ravier.
3. Sprinkle with the brunoise of onion and finely chopped parsley and serve.

## Cucumber salad                           *Salade de concombres*

| | | |
|---|---|---|
| ½ | Cucumber | 1¼ |
| | Finely chopped parsley | |
| ½ dl | Vinaigrette | 1 dl |

1. Peel the cucumber and cut into thin round slices or alternatively cut into bâtons.
2. Bind the cucumber with the vinaigrette and arrange neatly in an eathenware ravier dish.
3. Sprinkle liberally with finely chopped parsley and serve.

## Tomato salad                              *Salade de tomate*

| | | |
|---|---|---|
| 250 g | Tomatoes | 600 g |
| 10 g | Brunoise of onion | 25 g |
| ½ | Chiffonade of lettuce | 1 |
| ½ dl | Vinaigrette | 1 dl |
| | Finely chopped parsley | |

1. Blanch the tomato and remove skins.
2. Slice and arrange neatly in earthenware service dishes on a bed of chiffonade of lettuce.
3. Sprinkle with brunoise of onion.
4. Nap with vinaigrette, sprinkle liberally with finely chopped parsley and serve.

## Japanese salad                            *Salade japonaise*

| | | |
|---|---|---|
| 100 g | Large concassé of tomato | 250 g |
| 50 g | Fresh pineapple pieces | 125 g |
| 2 | Oranges cut into segments | 5 |
| 2 | Red apples | 5 |
| 4 | Lettuce quarters | 10 |
| | *or* | |
| | Lettuce hearts | |
| | Finely chopped parsley | |
| 1 dl | Acidulated cream | 2 dl |

1. Mix the tomato concassé, pineapple and oranges together gently.
2. Core and dice the apple and mix with the above ingredients.
3. Bind the ingredients with acidulated cream and arrange on the lettuce quarters or hearts.
4. Sprinkle liberally with finely chopped parsley and serve.

## Mimosa

*Salade mimosa*

| | | |
|---|---|---|
| 2 | Bananas | 5 |
| 4 | Oranges | 10 |
| 50 g | Green grapes | 125 g |
| 4 | Lettuce hearts | 10 |
| 1 dl | Acidulated cream | 2 dl |
| | Finely chopped parsley | |

1. Peel and slice the bananas.
2. Segment the oranges.
3. Bind with acidulated cream and grapes.
4. Arrange neatly in the lettuce heart.
5. Sprinkle liberally with finely chopped parsley.

## Niçoise salad

*Salade niçoise*

| | | |
|---|---|---|
| 200 g | Cooked whole French beans | 500 g |
| 10 g | Anchovy fillets | 25 g |
| 5 g | Capers | 15 g |
| ½ dl | Vinaigrette | 1 dl |
| 100 g | Blanched tomatoes | 250 g |
| 10 g | Stoned black olives | 25 g |
| 100 g | Macédoine of cooked potato | 250 g |
| | Salt and pepper | |
| | Finely chopped parsley | |
| 1 | Chiffonade of lettuce | 2 |

1. Cut the whole French beans into large diamonds.
2. Quarter the blanched tomatoes and remove pips.
3. Gently mix together the macédoine of potato, French beans, tomatoes and olives.
4. Add the vinaigrette and seasoning.
5. Arrange in an earthenware ravier on a bed of chiffonade of lettuce.
6. Garnish with the capers and the anchovy fillets, which should be cut in half lengthways.
7. Sprinkle liberally with finely chopped parsley and serve.

# Hors-d'oeuvre

*Introduction to hors-d'oeuvre*

These dishes may be served either as starters in their own right or as part of a selection of starters on an hors-d'oeuvre trolley. They are also commonly served as a salad or evening main course. They are very varied in style and the common ones have been included here.

## À la grecque style hors-d'oeuvre

The first part of the preparation is the special *à la grecque* marinade or cooking liquor made from the following:

| | | |
|---|---|---|
| 1 | Lemon (juice only) | 4 |
| 25 ml | Olive oil | 100 ml |
| 250 ml | Water | 1 litre |
| 6 | Peppercorns | 24 |
| 6 | Coriander seeds | 24 |
| 15 g | Salt | 60 g |
| ½ | Bay-leaf | 2 |
| 1 sprig | Thyme | 2 |

1. Bring all the ingredients to the boil and simmer gently for 10 minutes.
2. Do not strain the resulting marinade. Use as required.

### Celery à la grecque      Céleri à la grecque

1. Choose the heart of a small head of celery and cut into 40 cm lengths.
2. Cover with cold water and some lemon juice, and bring to the boil.
3. Immediately, run under cold water to refresh.
4. Drain and arrange in a shallow pan.
5. Cover with *à la grecque* (barely) and simmer until tender.
6. Arrange neatly in a suitable dish with some of the cooking liquor and garnish.
7. Serve well chiled.

### Cauliflower à la grecque      *Chou-fleur à la grecque*

1. Choose a small cauliflower and divide into florets or small sprigs.
2. Blanch for 10 minutes as above, and then refresh and drain.
3. Arrange in a shallow pan, cover with the marinade and cook covered until the sprigs are just cooked but still slightly crisp.
4. Arrange in a shallow dish with some of the liquor, and serve well chilled.

### Portugaise style hors-d'oeuvre

| | | |
|---|---|---|
| 250 ml | Tomato juice | 1 litre |
| 100 g | Tomato concassé | 400 g |
| 25 g | Tomato purée | 100 g |
| 1 small | Garlic clove | 2 |
| 25 g | Onion (finely diced) | 100 g |
| 50 g | Sultanas (optional) | 200 g |
| point | Bay-leaf | 1 |
| | Salt and milled pepper | |
| 50 ml | White wine vinegar | 200 ml |
| 50 ml | Olive or vegetable oil | 200 ml |
| 25 g | Soft brown sugar | 100 g |

1. Cook the chopped onion in the oil together with the chopped garlic in a covered pan so that the contents do not take on any colour, but are soft and transparent.
2. Meanwhile, prepare the tomato flesh by removing the eyes (stalk end) from the tomatoes before plunging them for a few seconds into very hot water. Remove immediately, and skin with the point of a small knife.
3. Cut across laterally and remove the seeds with a teaspoon leaving the tomato halves. Cut the latter into neat 1 cm dice.
4. Add half the tomato concassé to the cooked onion along with the remainder of the ingredients.
5. Allow to simmer gently for approximately 10 minutes. Check the seasoning and use as required.

**Note:** Whichever item is being prepared portugaise style, such as cauliflower sprigs, leeks, or button onions, should be cooked by first blanching (as with *à la grecque* style) then simmered in the sauce until just tender.

When dishing up, present with the sauce in a shallow dish and sprinkle the top with the remaining tomato concassé and a dusting of chopped parsley. Do not strain the cooking liquor.

Fish too can also be prepared in the same manner, such as fresh herrings, mackerel and soft roes.

## Herrings portugaise                    *Harengs portugaise*

1. Use fresh herrings prepared into fillets.
2. Cut the fillets across in a slantwise manner into neat pieces.
3. Place a little oil in a shallow pan and allow to heat up.
4. Turn the pieces of fish over in the oil just long enough to set the flesh firmly.
5. Transfer into a clean pan and cover barely with the portugaise preparation and a buttered cartouche of greaseproof paper and foil.
6. Allow to cook in a moderate oven for about 15 minutes. Remove and cool.
7. Arrange the herring portions in a shallow dish and mask with the sauce.
8. Finally, sprinkle lightly with chopped parsley. Serve very cold.
9. Other fish is prepared in the same way.

## Soused herrings

| | | |
|---|---|---|
| 4 | Herrings | 10 |
| 50 g | Carrots | 125 g |
| 1 | Bay-leaves | 3 |
| 10 | White peppercorns | 25 |
| 50 g | Shallots | 125 g |
| ½ dl | Vinegar | 1¼ dl |
| | Fresh thyme | |
| | Salt and pepper | |
| | Picked parsley | |

1. Gut, scale and fillet the herrings.
2. Wash in cold running water.
3. Dry and season with the salt and pepper.
4. Roll, with the skin on the outside surface.
5. Sit the rolled fish fillets in an earthenware dish or other container suitable for the oven.
6. Wash, peel and re-wash the carrots and peel the shallots.
7. Slice the shallots and carrots into thin rings, as for paysanne.
8. Blanch the rings in boiling water for 3–5 minutes.
9. Add to the rolled fish fillets and add the remaining ingredients.
10. Cover with a cartouche and cook in a moderate oven for about 20 minutes.
11. Allow the soused herrings to go cold, leaving covered with the cartouche to prevent excess evaporation of moisture.
12. Transfer to a clean service dish with the shallot and carrot rings.
13. Serve garnished with picked parsley and covered with a little of the cold cooking liquor.

## Egg mayonnaise                                      *Oeuf mayonnaise*

| | | |
|---|---|---|
| 4 | **Cold hard-boiled eggs** | 10 |
| 4 | **Slices of cucumber** | 10 |
| 4 | **Slices of tomato** | 10 |
| | **Chiffonade of lettuce** | |
| 2 dl | **Mayonnaise** | 5 dl |
| | **Paprika** | |
| | **Picked parsley** | |
| 4 | **Slices of lemon** | |

Egg mayonnaise may be served in any of three styles:

1. As part of an hors-d'oeuvre trolley—slice the eggs and arrange in raviers, dilute the mayonnaise to coating consistency and nap over the eggs, sprinkle with a little paprika, and serve.
2. As an individual hors-d'oeuvre—arrange by cutting the egg in half lengthways and sitting yolk side down on a bed of lettuce, nap with diluted mayonnaise and garnish with cucumber, tomato, parsley and lemon, sprinkle with paprika and serve on a side plate.
3. As a main course—allow two eggs for a main course and serve as above on a main course plate, with an additional garnish of potato salad, russian salad and mácedoine of cooked beetroot; extra cucumber and tomato may also be served.

## Stuffed eggs

| | | |
|---|---|---|
| 4 | **Cold hard-boiled eggs** | 10 |
| | **Thick mayonnaise to bind** | |
| 20 g | **Butter** | 50 g |
| | **Salt and white ground pepper** | |

1. Cut the eggs in half, lengthways.
2. Remove the yolks, without damaging the egg-white halves.
3. Push the yolks through a fine wire sieve.
4. Using a wooden spoon mix the egg yolk, butter and mayonnaise in a bowl and season.
5. Arrange and garnish the egg-white halves as for any of the three methods given for egg mayonnaise.
6. Sit the cases hollow part uppermost and using a piping bag with a large star nozzle, pipe a rosette of egg yolk mixture back into each case, and serve.

**Assorted fillings for stuffed eggs**

1. Add a little tomato ketchup to the basic mixture—*oeuf farcie au tomate*.
2. Add a little pureé of spinach to the basic mixture— *oeuf farcie aux épinards*.
3. Add anchovy essence to the basic mixture—*oeuf farcie aux anchoise*.
4. Add duxelle to the sieved egg yolk and bind with mayonnaise—*oeuf farcie duxelle*.
5. Add a little pureé of prawns to the basic mixture—*oeuf farcie aux crevettes roses*.

**Quails eggs**                                    *Oeufs de caille*

Allow 6 eggs per portion. Served hard-boiled, cold on a bed of washed mustard cress, on a polished silver flat or white porcelain plate. Serve accompanied with brown bread and butter.

**Liver Pâté**

| 25 g | Butter | 60 g |
|---|---|---|
| 50 g | Belly pork | 125 g |
| 50 g | Leg of pork | 125 g |
| 100 g | Chicken livers | 250 g |
| 15 g | Finely cut onions | 35 g |
| 1 | Crushed clove of garlic | 2 |
| | Finely chopped fresh thyme | |
| | Finely chopped fresh parsley | |
| | Finely chopped chervil | |
| 50 g | Sliced streaky bacon | 125 g |
| | Milled sea salt | |
| | Fresh milled pepper | |
| 1 dl | Single cream | 2 dl |
| 1 | Measure of brandy | 2 |

1. Dice the liver into 2 cm pieces.
2. Melt the butter in a frying-pan and add the herbs, garlic and onions and liver.
3. Sweat without colour.
4. Dice the pork as finely as possible.

5. Season with salt and pepper.
6. Add the pork to the pan and sweat until cooked.
7. Line earthenware terrines with rindless rashers of streaky bacon.
8. Pass the pâté mixture through a fine mincer twice and then through a drum sieve or alternatively put through a food blender and then sieve.
9. Mix in the cream and brandy.
10. Adjust the seasoning.
11. Pour into the lined terrines and cover with more streaky bacon.
12. Cover with a buttered cartouche and lid.
13. Stand in a tray of water, coming half-way up the side of the terrine, and cook in a moderate oven for 1–1½ hours.

**Note:** The action of the water helps to prevent the outer surfaces of the pâté burning in the oven.

Stages 11 to 13 may be omitted and the pâté poured into individual dishes or pots, capped with clarified butter and chilled for service, omitting also the streaky bacon. Serve accompanied with hot fingers of toast and usually garnished with lettuce and wedges of lemon.

**Smoked salmon** *Saumon fumé*

Smoked salmon is produced from prepared sides of fresh salmon, which have been placed in brine solutions and then smoked.

1. Trim the salmon edges and make sure that all the bones have been removed.
2. Carve the salmon as thinly as possible on a slight slant.
3. Dress on suitable serving plates, overlapping, allowing 25–30 g per person.
4. Decorate with sprigs of parsley.
5. Accompany with lemon wedges and brown bread and butter.

**Smoked trout** *Truite fumé*

Allow one per portion.

1. Remove the outer skin and also lift off the bone; the flesh comes away quite easily with the aid of a small sharp knife.
2. Serve the fillets garnished with prepared lemon slices, and a sprig of picked, washed parsley.
3. Smoked trout is also accompanied by horseradish cream made as follows: whisk a small quantity of fresh cream until semi-stiff; stir in a spoonful of grated horseradish, and finish the sauce with a pinch of cayenne pepper and salt to taste.

**Smoked eel** *Anguille fumé*

1. Skin the smoked eel and detach the fillets.

2. Cut across into fine strips.
3. Serve on a bed of lettuce leaves together with lemon wedges and/or horseradish cream, and with brown bread and butter.

## Fish and shellfish cocktails

Use any flaked, cooked white fish or shellfish, such as prawns, shrimps, crabmeat, lobster or a mixture as desired. In the case of shellfish, whichever sort is used it must, of course, first be removed from the shell. For this reason, and to save time, it is an advantage to use the frozen variety if appropriate.

With regard to white fish: cooked flaked cod, fresh haddock, whiting and the more expensive ones such as turbot and brill are all very suitable for the making of fish cocktails.

1. Wash and well drain some lettuce leaves before shredding into strips.
2. Set a generous spoonful in the base of glass goblet(s) or other individual choice of container.
3. Add one dessertspoonful of tomato concassé.
4. Add the selected fish items, and spoon over sufficient cocktail sauce to mask.
5. Decorate the top with one or two shelled prawns, and garnish the edge of the glass with a lemon slice, cut halfway through so that it will sit neatly on the rim of the glass.
6. Serve well chilled with brown bread and butter.

## Cocktail sauce                                          *Sauce Marie Rose*

| | | |
|---|---|---|
| 65 ml | Mayonnaise | 1 litre |
| 15 ml | Lemon juice | 40 ml |
| 4 spots | Tabasco sauce (optional) | 16 spots |
| 30 ml | Tomato juice | ¼ litre |
| 1 teaspoon | Worcester sauce | ⅛ dl |

Combine all the ingredients to a smooth consistency and check the seasoning for taste.

## Oysters                                                              *Huîtres*

As with all shellfish, the shell must be tightly closed to indicate that the oyster is quite fresh. Prepare as follows:

1. Open very carefully using an oyster knife.
2. Scoop out the oyster by separating it from the membrane and then replace into the deep half of the shell. Be careful to retain any of the juice with the oyster.

3. Serve on a bed of crushed ice with wedges of lemon and brown bread and butter.
4. Allow 6 oysters to a portion.

## Meat salad                                    *Salade de viande*

Almost any left-over cooked meat (roast or boiled) can be used.

| | | |
|---|---|---|
| 200 g | Cooked meat | 1 kg |
| 30 g | Tomato concassé | 200 g |
| 25 g | Finely chopped onion (or chopped chives) | 200 g |
| 15 g | Chopped parsley | 100 g |
| 4 | Pickled gherkins | 10–15 |
| 200 g | Cold boiled potato | 1 kg |
| 30 ml | French dressing | 200 ml |
| | Salt and milled pepper | |

1. Cut the meat into slices, then into strips.
2. Place into a china bowl and sprinkle with some of the dressing.
3. Allow to marinade for 20 minutes.
4. Meanwhile, slice the potatoes across into roundels and dice the gherkins into ½ cm pieces.
5. Blend the meat strips, tomato concassé, gherkins, chopped onions/chives and parsley together and lightly season with salt and pepper.
6. Arrange slightly mounded in a suitable dish or dishes and place a neat border of overlapping slices of potato round the edge,
7. Spoon the remaining dressing over the potato slices.
8. Dust the top with chopped parsely and serve well chilled.

## Chilled melon                                    *Melon frappé*

Six to eight portions may be obtained from one canteloup or honeydew melon.

1. Slice the melon in half, lengthways.
2. Remove all the seeds.
3. Divide into the required number of portions.
4. Cut through the melon, dividing into pieces; do not cut through the skin.
5. Cut the melon free of the skin, but leave standing on the shell portion.
6. Serve on a bed of crushed ice.
7. Accompany with castor sugar and ground ginger.

**Note:** Melon is also often served garnished with a slice of orange and stem ginger.

**Charantais melon**                      *Melon de charente*
**Ogen melon**                            *Melon de ogen*

Allow one melon per portion.

1.  Cut the top off the melon, to make a lid.
2.  Scoop out the seeds.
3.  Replace the lid and serve on a plate, chilled.

**Fresh grapefruit**                      *Pamplemousse*

| 2 | **Fresh grapefruit** | 5 |
| 4 | **Maraschino cherries** | 10 |
|   | **Picked parsley** |   |

1.  Cut the grapefruits in half.
2.  Remove the core and loosen the segments.
3.  Sit in individual dishes or plates.
4.  Garnish with a maraschino cherry in the centre of the grapefruit, and a small piece of picked parsley.

**Grapefruit cocktail**                   *Cocktail de pamplemousse*

| 4 | **Grapefruit** | 8 |
| 4 | **Maraschino cherries** | 10 |
|   | **Picked parsley** |   |

1.  Using a sharp paring knife, cut away the peel and pith.
2.  Divide into segments, removing all traces of skin and pips.
3.  Dress in coupes or cocktail glasses.
4.  Garnish with a maraschino cherry and picked parsley.

**Grapefruit and orange cocktail**        **Florida cocktail**

| 3 | **Grapefruit** | 8 |
| 2 | **Oranges** | 4 |
| 4 | **Maraschino cherries** | 10 |
|   | **Picked parsley** |   |

1.  Proceed as for grapefruit cocktail, mixing with the orange.
2.  Garnish and serve as for the grapefruit cocktail.

# Fish preparation

*Introduction to fish preparation*

Fish must be prepared in a hygienic manner; always wash the fish in cold running water and make sure that the inside cavity is thoroughly cleaned before proceeding to cut the flesh into the required format. This is to avoid the risk of contamination and eventual food poisoning.

### Cuts of fish

*Darne*: Cut from the middle of a large round fish such as salmon, cod or hake. The thickness is usually about 20–25 mm.

*Tronçon*: A cutlet from a large flat fish, such as turbot, brill or halibut. First cut the fish in half down the backbone and, from each half, cut clices, as shown below.

**Note**: When dividing large flat fish in half start at the tail end using a sharp, heavy knife.

*Suprême*: A slice cut from large fillets, the cuts being made obliquely through the thickness.

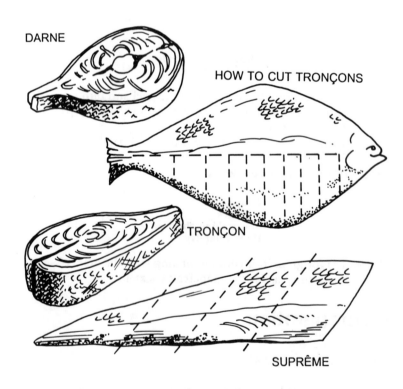

DARNE

HOW TO CUT TRONÇONS

TRONÇON

SUPRÊME

*Paupiettes*: Rolled fillets of small, flat fish, such as plaice or sole. They are often spread with a fish mousseline before rolling.

*Pliers*: Folded fillets of fish such as sole or plaice, sometimes spread with a fish farce, folded and poached.

*Goujons*: Cut from flat fillets of fish, such as sole or plaice. They are cut across the fillet in an oblique manner, and are then rolled cigar shape before cooking *à la meunière* or deep fried (*pané á l'anglaise*).

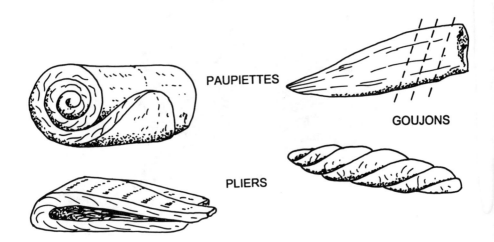

PAUPIETTES

GOUJONS

PLIERS

## Cold poached salmon

*Saumon froid*

| | | |
|---|---|---|
| 4 | Darnes of salmon | 10 |
| ½ | Large crisp lettuce | 1 |
| ¼ | Cucumber | ¾ |
| 100 g | Tomatoes | 250 g |
| 2 dl | Mayonnaise | 5 dl |

1. Poach the darnes of salmon and leave to go cold in the court bouillon.
2. Drain well and remove the centre bone and skin.
3. Garnish with the lettuce, slices of cucumber and tomato.
4. Serve the sauce in a sauce-boat or piped with a star nozzle on to the plate and finish with a piece of picked parsley.

## Crab preparation

Fresh crab is usually purchased ready boiled. If not, the crab should be cooked in a court bouillon for about 35 minutes according to the size.

The hen crab is considered to be the better. It should be undamaged when purchased with both claws intact.

After dressing, the crab is presented on a suitable dish, and served with a sauce vinaigrette and also sauce mayonnaise.

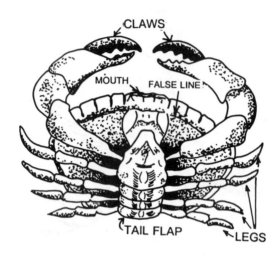

1. Twist off the legs and claws, and separate the body from the shell.
2. Crack the claws and remove the flesh with a small knife.
3. Remove the mouth and stomach bag by gentle pulling; they should come away in one piece.
4. Remove the meat, easing round the inside of the shell with the back of a fork. Turn all the meat into a basin, and reserve any coral for decoration. Then tap with a knife handle around the false line to trim back to the shell's hard casing.
5. Scrub and dry the shell and lightly oil the casing.
6. Taking the body of the crab discard the 'dead man's fingers'.
7. Remove any brown meat and add it to that in the basin.
8. Flake the white meat and season with vinaigrette dressing to taste.
9. Pass the soft brown meat through a sieve, and add about one-quarter of its weight in white, fresh breadcrumbs. Add a few spots of Worcester sauce and season with salt and milled pepper.
10. Arrange the white meat in the centre of the shell, and slightly mound. Dress the soft neatly on either side, and mark it criss-cross fashion with the blade of a small knife.
11. Decorate the centre white meat with very thin strips of anchovy fillet and

several capers.

12. Place lines of sieved, hard-boiled yolk of egg, chopped parsley, and sieved hard-boiled egg white down each side of the brown mixture.

13. Arrange the thin legs in a necklace on the flat dish to form a 'stand' on which to place the dressed crab. Garnish with a few crisp leaves of lettuce heart, and skinned, quartered tomato if desired.

Crab meat is also used for cocktails (as an alternative to prawns), and in crab patties and savoury crab pancakes.

## Cold chicken or ham mousse

*Mousse de volaille*

| 480 g | Chicken (cooked)<br>*or*<br>Ham (cooked) | 1200 g |
|---|---|---|
| 1½ dl | Cold chicken or ham velouté | 4 dl |
| 1¼ dl | Aspic jelly | 3 dl |
| 3 dl | Half-beaten whipping cream | 7½ dl |

1. Mince the cooked flesh twice and sieve.
2. Bind with the velouté.
3. Place in a bowl over ice and water.
4. Beat in the cream and taste for seasoning; do not add salt for ham mousse.
5. Beat in the aspic jelly.
6. Pour mixture into an aspic-lined mould and leave to set.
7. When set, turn out and use as required.

## Fish mousse (cold)

*Mousse de poisson*

Proceed exactly as for cold ham or chicken mousse using fish velouté.

**Note**: Dissolved gelatine may be used in place of aspic jelly if required. (see also pages 172–173.)

# Cuts of meat

*Introduction to cuts of meat*

Before you start dissecting (cutting up) joints of meat, you must know what all the joints are and where to find them on the carcass. Without this knowledge it will be impossible for you to dissect a carcass with any accuracy.

A correctly butchered carcass will give more portions of meat when cooked and so increase profitability.

Great care should be taken when butchering, as careless working may result in an accident. Never apply too much pressure or try to cut joints larger than you can safely handle.

The following pages list in detail the joints of meat on various animals used in Britain. The joints cut for use in the catering industry are different from those cut by butchers in high street shops for the retail trade, and you should therefore be careful not to confuse the two.

**Side of veal**

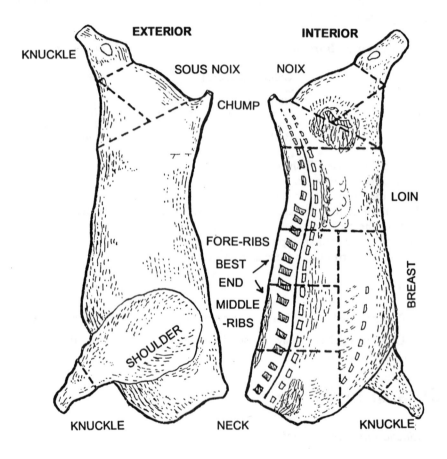

| Knuckle | *Jarret* |
| Leg (cushion, under-cushion and thick flank) | *(Noix, soux noix, gite à la noix)* |
| Loin | *Longe* |
| Breast | *Poitrine* |
| Shoulder | *Epaule* |
| Best end | *Carré* |
| Neck end and scrag | *Cou* |

## Cuts of veal

| Name of cut | Approx weight | Uses |
| --- | --- | --- |
| Knuckle | 2½ kg | Osso bucco, sauté, stewing. |
| Cushion | 3 kg | Roasting, braising, escalopes and sauté. |
| Under-cushion | 3 kg | Roasting, braising, sauté and escalopes. |
| Thick flank | 2½ kg | Roasting, braising, sauté and escalopes. |
| Loin | 4 kg | Roasting, grilling, frying (chops). |
| Best end | 3 kg | Roasting, grilling or frying (cutlets). |
| Shoulder | 6 kg | Roasting and braising, also stews. |
| Neck end | 3 kg | Stewing and sauté. |
| Neck (scrag) | 1½ kg | Stewing and stock. |
| Breast | 2 kg | Stewing or roasted (boned, rolled and stuffed). |

The two loins joined together constitute a *saddle*. This is usually cooked *poêlé* (dry braised).

A single *loin* which is boned and rolled with the kidney left in is called a 'Rognonade'. It is usually cooked as for the saddle.

## Offal from a carcass of veal

| Type | Uses |
| --- | --- |
| Liver | Shallow frying. |
| Kidneys | Sauté, pies and puddings. |
| Sweetbreads | Braising or shallow frying. |
| Head | Soup (e.g. mock turtle) or boiling. |
| Brains | Poached or shallow fried. |

Dutch and English milk-fed veal weighs much heavier because of production by intense farming methods. The average weight per side of Dutch veal is approximately 40–50 kg.

**Side of pork**

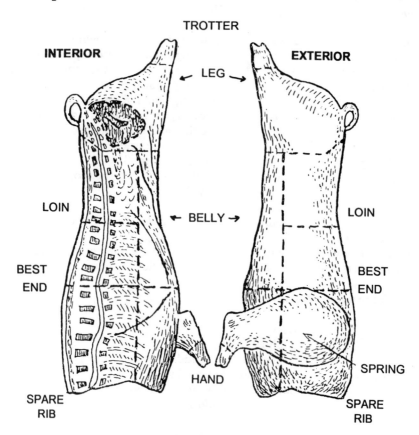

**Cuts of pork**

| Name of cut | Weight | Uses |
|---|---|---|
| Leg | 5½ kg | Roasting and boiling. |
| Loin and best end | 4½ kg | Roasting, grilling and frying. |
| Belly | 2 kg | Pickling, boiling and pies. |
| Spare rib | 2 kg | Roasting and pies. |
| Shoulder* | 3½ kg | Roasting, boiling and pies. |
| Head | 4 kg | Brawn. |

*The shoulder is divided into two:
(a) Hand and spring: shank end of the shoulder.
(b) Blade-bone: top part of the shoulder.

**Pork offal**

| Type | Uses |
|------|------|
| Liver | Frying and pâté. |
| Kidneys | Grilling or sauté. |
| Trotters | Grilling or boiling. |

The *head* is mostly used for manufacturing purposes.
*Bath chaps*: These are prepared pig's cheeks which are cooked and breadcrumbed; sold ready prepared as a regional speciality.
*Brawn*: The tongue and brain are usually removed, then the remainder of the head is made into brawn.

**Carcass of lamb**

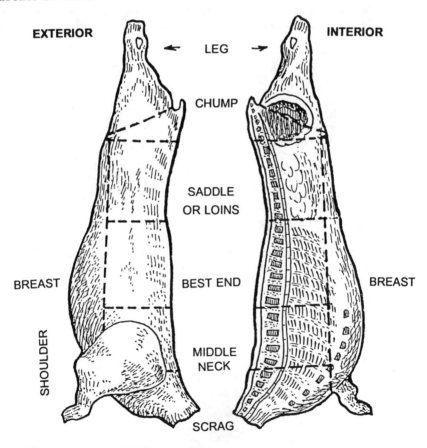

| Cuts of lamb | Weight | Uses |
|------|------|------|
| Shoulders (2) | 3 kg | Roasting, braising, stewing. |
| Legs (2) | 3½ kg | Roasting (mutton boiled), braised. |
| Breasts (2) | 2½ kg | Roasting, stewing, epigrammes. |

| Middle neck and scrag | 2 kg | Stewing or broth |
|---|---|---|
| Best ends (2) | 2½ kg | Roasting or cutlets fried or grilled. |
| Loins (2) | 3½ kg | Roasting whole as a saddle or *poêlé* (dry braised), chops or noisettes. |

*Chump chops* are cut from the top end of the leg about 20 mm thick. They can be grilled, fried or braised.

### Saddle and loin of lamb

A *baron* of lamb consists of the pair of hind legs and saddle presented as one piece. Half this joint dissected along the backbone is called a *quarter*.

The *saddle* refers to the two whole loins joined together. It can be roasted or cooked *poêlé* (dry braised). For banqueting purposes, it is usual to present the saddle 'short cut', i.e. minus the chump end. This enables the saddle to be carved lengthways and re-set upon the carcass for presentation in the room.

 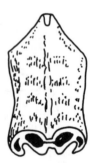

BARON OF LAMB OR MUTTON    SADDLE OF LAMB OR MUTTON

The two loins are produced by splitting the saddle lengthways with a lamb chopper. The loin(s) can then be cut up into chops; boned, stuffed and rolled for *poêlé*; or boned, tied with string, and cut between the string ties to make noisettes or rosettes.

NOISETTES OF LAMB

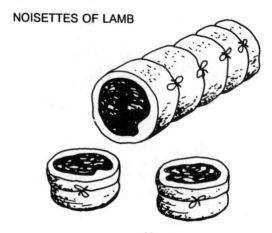

The *best end* of lamb consists of the first seven ribs of lamb. After trimming as in the diagram, they can be roasted whole or cut into cutlets for grilling or sauté.

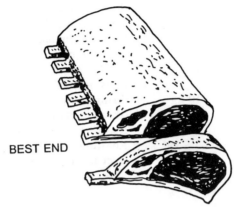

BEST END

## Side of beef

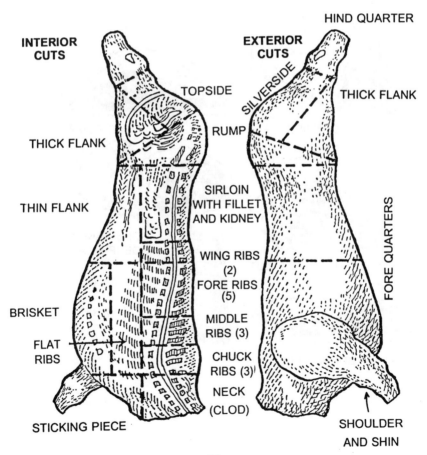

HIND QUARTER

INTERIOR CUTS

EXTERIOR CUTS

TOPSIDE

SILVERSIDE

THICK FLANK

THICK FLANK

RUMP

THIN FLANK

SIRLOIN WITH FILLET AND KIDNEY

FORE QUARTERS

WING RIBS (2)

FORE RIBS (5)

BRISKET

MIDDLE RIBS (3)

FLAT RIBS

CHUCK RIBS (3)

NECK (CLOD)

STICKING PIECE

SHOULDER AND SHIN

## Hindquarter cuts/uses

| Name of cut | Weight | Uses |
| --- | --- | --- |
| Thin flank | 10 kg | Stewing, boiling, pies, sausages. |
| Thick flank | 8 kg | Braising, stewing, pies, sausages. |
| Topside | 9 kg | Braising, braising steaks, second-class roasting joint. |
| Silverside | 11 kg | Pickled (then boiled), braising and braising steak. |
| Rump (and thick fillet) | 10 kg | Grilling, first-class braising joint; (thick fillet) roast and steaks. |
| Sirloin and fillet | 10 kg | Roasting, grilling, and frying steaks. |
| Wing rib | 5½ kg | Roasting. |
| Suet and kidney | 8 kg | Suet paste, pies and puddings. |

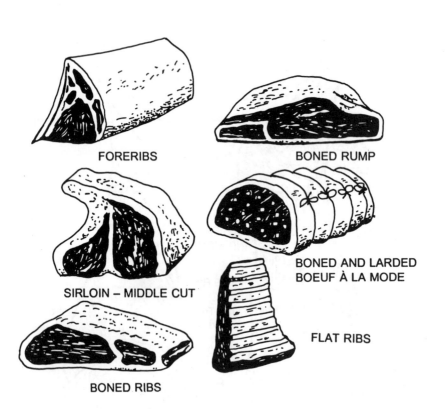

FORERIBS

BONED RUMP

SIRLOIN – MIDDLE CUT

BONED AND LARDED
BOEUF À LA MODE

FLAT RIBS

BONED RIBS

## Forequarter cuts/uses

| Name of cut | Weight | Uses |
| --- | --- | --- |
| Fore rib | 8 kg | Roasting. |
| Middle rib | 10 kg | Roasting and braising. |
| Flat rib | 3 kg | Braising, boiling stews. |
| Chuck rib | 12 kg | Braising and stews. |
| Brisket | 14 kg | Pickling, stews, pies and sausages |
| Sticking piece | 5 kg | Stewing and sausages. |
| Clod | 5 kg | Stews, pies and sausages. |
| Shin (shoulder) | 6 kg | Stews, consommé and beef tea. |

### Beef offal

| | |
| --- | --- |
| Heart | Stuffed and braised. |
| Kidney | Soup, pies and puddings. |
| Liver | Braising and frying. |
| Oxtail | Braising and soup. |
| Ox tongue | Pickled and pressed; also braised. |
| Tripe | Tripe and onions. |

## Cuts of beef for grilling

*Entrecôte*: Cut across the prepared *contrefilet* (boned-out loin). A standard *entrecôte* steak is about 10 mm thick to give a weight of about 200 g.

*Entrecôte double*: Cut similarly, but 25 mm thick, then lighly flattened with a wet cutlet bat to a thickness of 20 mm.

*Porterhouse steak*: Sometimes referred to as a 'T-bone' steak, it is a cut from the sirloin which joins the last rib bone of the wing rib. It is cut 40 mm thick, and will serve 2–3 persons usually. However, whereas the porterhouse will serve 2–3, the 'T-bone' steak is really for one person only. Its weight is about 650 g and is cut to a thickness of 10 mm.

*Entrecôte Minute*: This is similar to an *entrecôte* steak but is cut much thinner and batted out with a cutlet bat so that each side can be cooked in one minute or so.

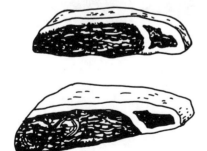

ENTRECÔTE AND ENTRECÔTE
DOUBLE

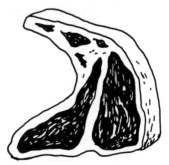

ɫ PORTERHOUSE, SIRLOIN OR
'T'-BONE STEAK

*Rump steak*: The rump is usually cut into long 20 mm thick slices across the grain. The outer edge of fat is trimmed to a depth of 10 mm, then the slice is cut across into individual portion rump steak of about 200 g in weight. The point steak from the rump is considered to be the choice cut.

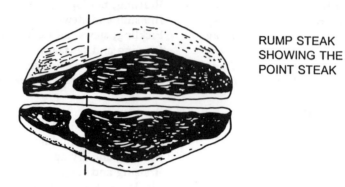

RUMP STEAK
SHOWING THE
POINT STEAK

Rump steak showing the 'point steak'. This has more flavour than other steaks but needs correct hanging to prevent it being tough to eat.

**Steaks from the fillet of beef**

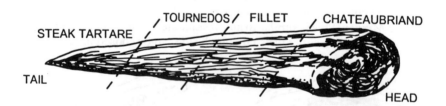

STEAK TARTARE   TOURNEDOS   FILLET   CHATEAUBRIAND

TAIL

HEAD

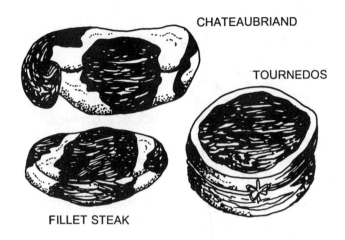

CHATEAUBRIAND

TOURNEDOS

FILLET STEAK

*Chateaubriand*: This is cut from the thick end of the fillet. It is a thick cut steak for two or more persons and can vary in weight from 350 g to 900 g. The usual practice is to flatten the meat across the grain with a cutlet bat to a depth of 50 mm for ease of grilling. It is generally tied with thin string to hold it in shape whilst grilling takes place.

*Fillet*: This is also cut from the head of the whole fillet into steaks of 20–25 mm thickness.

*Tournedos*: The meat for tournedos. They are usually 30–40 mm thick. They are often barded around with fat bacon and tied with string. Tournedos are grilled or sautéd according to requirements.

*Mignon*: Refers to the tail end of the fillet, which can be cut into 25 mm cubes for sauté or strips 40 × 50 mm for *sauté de boeuf stroganoff*, or steak tartare.

**Side of bacon**

The diagram shows the typical 'Wiltshire' cut including the breakdown of the whole gammon into cuts for grilling.

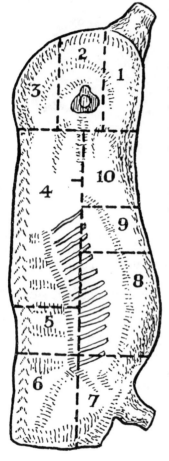

1. HOCK OF GAMMON
2. MIDDLE OF GAMMON
3. CORNER OF GAMMON
4. BACK OF BACON
5. THICK END OF BACK
6. COLLAR
7. FOREHOCK
8. BEST STREAKY
9. THIN STREAKY
10. FLANK

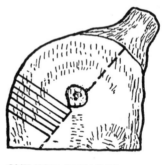

CUT FOR GRILLING

SIDE OF BACON

| Name of cut | Approx. weight | Uses |
|---|---|---|
| Gammon | 7 kg | Boiled, braised, grilled, fried. |
| Back | 9 kg | Grilled, fried. |
| Streaky | 4½ kg | Grilled, fried and lardons. |
| Collar | 4½ kg | Boiled, grilled and fried. |
| Forehock | 4½ kg | Boiled, grilled, pies. |
| Flank | 4 kg | Grilled, fried and lardons. |

# Sandwiches

## Introduction to sandwiches

Sandwiches are an important aspect of catering. The consumption of sandwiches by the public accounts for a major part of the financial turnover of the catering industry. A good sandwich can mean good business and high profits. A poor sandwich can mean no business and no profits.

Always use fresh bread and the freshest of ingredients. Never skimp on the quantity of fillings and always butter the bread to the edges of the crust.

Sandwiches may be made using any type of bread, white, granary, rye, wholemeal, all of which have their own distinctive flavours and textures to give a finished sandwich. Here are a few examples of classic sandwiches.

### Double decker and triple decker

Suitable for either toasted or untoasted bread, using any type of bread. For a double decker you need three slices of bread with the centre slice buttered on both sides and two complementing fillings, e.g. chicken mayonnaise in one layer and ham and tomato in the other layer.

For a triple decker use four slices of bread, the middle two slices buttered on both sides. Use three complementary fillings, such as ham and tomato, chicken mayonnaise, and egg salad.

### Toasted sandwiches

These consist of a hot filling inside two slices of hot toast, such as scrambled egg, fried egg, grilled bacon, tomato. More common now is the sandwich toaster, a machine which allows you to place a cold filling between two slices of bread buttered on the outside and placed between two hot plates and toasted. This has increased the variety of foods which may be placed into a toasted sandwich, to include items such as corned beef and onion, and cheese. In addition, any of the vol-au-vent or bouchée fillings are suitable for inclusion in toasted sandwiches.

### Club sandwich

This is probably one of the most popular of sandwiches served today. Three slices of toast are used, the centre slice buttered on both sides. In the first layer is lettuce, hot grilled bacon and mayonnaise, in the second layer is lettuce, slices of hard-boiled egg, slices of cold cooked chicken and mayonnaise.

### Bookmaker sandwich

Another popular sandwich—two slices of hot buttered toast with a filling of minute steak, served with salad garnish and mustard.

**Danish open sandwiches**                    **Scandinavian Smørrebrød**

These are prepared on buttered rye or pumpernickel bread with a wide variety of toppings, such as fish, smoked fish, boiled egg, vegetables and assorted salad items, continental sausages, and shellfish. A few examples would be as follows:

1. Hard-boiled egg, capers, gherkins, picked herring.
2. Chiffonade of lettuce, sliced hard-boiled egg, mayonnaise, salami.
3. Cold roast beef, gherkins, tomato slices.
4. Smoked salmon, shrimps, lettuce and lemon segments.
5. Chiffonade of lettuce, cold flaked smoked haddock, sieved with egg.

Presentation standards must be high, great care being given to how you arrange the food on the slices of bread. Garnish with picked parsley, watercress and radishes. Danish open sandwiches are often eaten with a knife and fork.

# Pâtisserie and confectionery

*Introduction to pâtisserie and confectionery*

This section covers a wide range of preparations for use in the making of desserts and confectionery. We cover crèmes, pastries, flans, pies, savarin doughs and other base preparations all of which go towards the completion of dishes in other parts of the book.

Great care should be taken when weighing out ingredients for *pâtisserie* and confectionery as a slight miscalculation can ruin a recipe.

It is essential when working on *pâtisserie* and confectionery that the highest levels of hygiene be maintained for the prevention of food contamination and eventual food poisoning. Always wear clean chef's clothing, make sure that all utensils are thoroughly cleaned before and after use, and regularly clean your hands between tasks.

*Fillings for Danish pastries*

**Cinnamon sugar cream**

| 112 g | Butter | 225 g |
| 170 g | Castor sugar | 340 g |
| 3 spots | Vanilla essence | 6 spots |
| ¼ coffeespoon | Powdered cinnamon | ½ coffeespoon |

1. Cream the butter and sugar together to a light consistency.

2. Beat in the vanilla essence and powdered cinnamon.
3. Keep in a covered basin in the refrigerator.
4. Use as required.

## Almond filling                                   *Farce amandine*

| | | |
|---|---|---|
| 112 g | Ground almonds | 225 g |
| 140 g | Butter | 280 g |
| 3 spots | Vanilla essence | 6 spots |
| 3 spots | Almond essence | 6 spots |

1. Cream the butter with the sugar, add the vanilla and almond essence.
2. Finally, blend in the ground almonds.
3. Keep in a covered basin in the refrigerator.
4. Use as required.

### Flavoured creams

These are made from whipping or double cream which is half whipped and sweetened with castor sugar, with the addition of a spirit, usually rum or brandy, to suit your taste.

## Chantilly cream

This is double or whipping cream, whipped and flavoured with castor sugar and vanilla essence. Often used for topping on meringues or trifles.

## Lindens cream

Half-whipped double cream, flavoured with castor sugar, port or marsala to taste, with 5 leaves of dissolved gelatine added during the whipping stage to each ½ litre of cream.
   Served with fresh fruit or used as a topping for trifle.
   A variation of this can be made by using another liqueur or wine, e.g. beaumes de venise, to flavour the cream and serving a glass of the same liqueur or wine with the cream and fresh fruit.

## Butter cream

| | | |
|---|---|---|
| 200 g | Soft butter | 400 g |
| 150 g | Icing sugar | 300 g |

1. Pass the icing sugar through a fine sieve into a suitably sized stainless steel or ceramic bowl.
2. Add the butter in small pieces.
3. Mix in until creamy and light.
4. Flavour and colour as for your requirements.

Used for making gâteaux and other small cakes and fancies.

## Royal icing

This is used for the icing of cakes such as wedding cake, christening cake and Christmas cake.

| 3 | Egg whites | 500 ml approx. |
| 450 g | Icing sugar | 3½ kg |
| 2 teaspoons | Lemon juice | ½ dl |
| | Trace of blue | |

1. Sieve the icing sugar into a suitable mixing bowl (or machine bowl).
2. Add two-thirds of the egg white and beat to a firm consistency.
3. Add the remaining egg white, lemon juice and blue trace.
4. Continue to beat to the required consistency.
5. For larger amounts which are blended in the machine, use a flat beater, and mix on slow speed.
6. Adjust the consistency of the icing with a little more egg white if necessary according to whether the icing is to be used for coating or piping.
7. Once made, keep covered with a damp cloth to prevent skinning over—or preferably, retain in a lidded polythene container.

It is good practice to sieve both the lemon juice and the egg whites, especially if the medium is required for piping purposes. A piece of fine muslin is ideal for the job. A small amount of glycerine (1–2 teaspoons for the smaller mix) will create a more mellow textured icing. The blue will counteract the yellowish tinge imparted by the egg white. In order to avoid too much aeration when blending, beat three-quarters of the icing sugar into the whites initially, then fold in the remainder to amalgamate. If the royal icing is allowed to stand overnight and re-beaten the following day, it will pipe much more easily—especially for fine line work, etc. Omit any glycerine content in icing made for piping purposes; the glycerine tends to make the texture too short especially for fine work.

If coloured icing is needed, omit the blue colour unless, of course, it is for a blue cake—such as Wedgwood. Naturally, sugar for coating purposes will be slightly softer than that needed for piping. If several coats are to be applied, the final coat will be thinned down with more egg white. In this way, a smooth, even coat will be obtained free from unsightly blemishes. If the icing is to be used over a period of several days, it will keep perfectly well in tightly lidded polythene/plastic food containers. There is no need to keep it under refrigeration.

If using dried egg white (albumen), the usual rate of make-up is:
45 g powdered albumen
300 ml cold water

1. Reconstitute by adding the cold water to the dried albumen.
2. After stirring well, it should be left in a covered container and allowed to stand in the refrigerator overnight. Before use, strain through muslin into a clean mixing bowl.
3. This amount of albumen will take approximately 1½ kg of sieved icing sugar.

Finally, always scald all utensils before making the icing. Everything must be free from grease; any trace of the latter will be detrimental to successful royal icing.

## Pastes

The production of a good quality paste is essential for the successful completion of main dishes, such as plain pies and pastries. Always follow the instructions carefully.

### Apple dumpling paste

| | | |
|---|---|---|
| 225 g | **Medium flour** | 900 g |
| Pinch | **Baking powder** | 30 g |
| 90 g | **White vegetable shortening** | 400 g |
| 25 g | **Castor sugar** | 100 g |
| 50 ml | **Cold water (approx.)** | 200 ml |

1. Sieve the flour and baking powder together.
2. Rub in the fat to fine crumbs, and make a bay.
3. Add the castor sugar and cold water to dissolve.
4. Finally, draw in the flour/fat and mix to a smooth paste.
5. Allow to rest before using. Keep in a cool place.

### Flan paste

| | | |
|---|---|---|
| 450 g | **Medium flour** | 1 kg 800 g |
| 285 g | **Butter or margarine** | 1 kg 140 g |
| 2 | **Eggs** | 8 |
| 28 g | **Castor sugar** | 115 g |
| Pinch | **Salt** | 15 g |

1. Sieve the flour and rub in the fat to fine crumbs.
2. Make a bay in the centre, and add the egg, sugar and salt.
3. Allow to dissolve then carefully draw in the flour and blend to smooth paste.
4. Wrap in greaseproof and refrigerate for approximately 30 minutes.

The larger amount of paste can be made on the machine using the dough hook, and blending in on *slow* speed.

## Savoury flan paste

| | | |
|---|---|---|
| 170 g | Medium flour | 680 g |
| 1 | Egg yolk | 4 |
| ½ dl | Cold water | 240 ml |
| Pinch | Salt | 15 g |
| 45 g | Grated parmesan cheese | 170 g |
| 112 g | Margarine or butter | 450 g |

1. Sieve the flour and rub in the fat to fine crumbs. Make a bay.
2. Add the grated cheese sprinkled over the flour mixture.
3. Add the yolks, water and salt and draw in flour, etc. to a smooth dough.
4. Wrap in greaseproof and rest before using.

**Note:** Use grated cheddar cheese in place of parmesan if desired.

## Cheese straws                                    *Paillettes au parmesan*

| | | |
|---|---|---|
| 225 g | Medium flour | 900 g |
| 140 g | Butter or margarine | 560 g |
| 170 g | Grated parmesan cheese | 670 g |
| ½ teaspoon | Salt | 30 g |
| | Point of cayenne pepper | |
| 2 | Eggs, beaten | 8 |
| ½ dl | Cold water | 240 ml |

1. Rub the fat into the sieved flour and make a bay.
2. Sprinkle on the grated parmesan cheese, and blend all to a smooth paste, using sufficient cold water to bind.
3. Allow the paste to rest in a cool place before using.
4. Roll the paste out to 7 mm thickness, and cut into 10 cm wide bands.
5. Then cut bands across into 7 mm wide strips. Twist or leave plain.
6. Tray up on greased baking trays.
7. Bake to golden brown at 210°C for several minutes. Cool on cake wires.

## Cornish pasty paste

| | | |
|---|---|---|
| 230 g | Medium flour | 900 g |
| 100 g | White vegetable shortening | 400 g |
| 70 ml | Cold water | 285 ml |
| pinch | Salt | 15 g |

1. Sieve the flour and rub in the fat to fine crumbs.
2. Make a bay and add the salt and cold water.
3. Blend to a smooth dough. Rest before using.

## Pizza dough

| 230 g | Strong flour | 900 g |
|---|---|---|
| 5 g | Yeast | 25 g |
| 140 ml | Milk at blood heat | 570 ml |
| 1 | Egg | 4 |
| 7 g | Butter | 28 g |
| ½ teaspoon | Salt | 15 g |
| ½ g | Castor sugar | 15 g |

1. Sieve the flour; dilute the yeast with the tepid milk.
2. Melt the butter and blend into the flour mixture together with beaten eggs and sugar.
3. Make up into a dough, cover and prove to double its size in a warm place.
4. Knock back and use as required.

## Danish paste

| 140 g | Strong flour | 565 g |
|---|---|---|
| 70 ml | Cold milk | 285 ml |
| | Pinch of mixed spice | 15 g |
| 15 g | Castor sugar | 60 g |
| 15 g | Yeast | 30 g |
| 1 | Small egg (size 3) | 3 |
| 1 teaspoon | Lemon juice | Juice of 1 lemon |
| 100 g | Firm unsalted butter | 400 g |

1. Dissolve the yeast and sugar in the cold milk.
2. Beat the egg and stir in milk; mix well.
3. Sieve the flour and spice, make a bay and add the milk mixture.
4. Blend all to a smooth dough. Rest covered in the refrigerator for 30 minutes.
5. Roll the dough out to a rectangle, and spread the butter in small pieces over two-thirds of the dough.
6. Fold into three.
7. Give one three-fold turn, then repeat.
8. Rest for a further hour in the refrigerator, covered with a damp cloth to prevent skinning over.
9. Give a further two complete turns making 4 turns in all.
10. Allow to rest before using.

## Sweet paste                    *Pâté à sucre*

| 230 g | Medium flour | 450 g |
|---|---|---|
| 112 g | Butter or margarine | 230 g |
| 56 g | Castor sugar | 112 g |
| 1 | Egg | 2 |

1. Sieve the flour and make a bay in the centre.
2. Add the sugar and egg and mix to a creamy consistency (this will help to dissolve the sugar crystals).

3. Add the butter (softened) and blend into the sugar and egg mixture.
4. Finally, draw in the flour and mix lightly to a smooth paste.
5. Wrap in greaseproof paper and refrigerate for at least 30 minutes before using.
6. Use a light dusting of flour when rolling out, and handle very lightly. This is rich paste with tender eating qualities. It is best made in advance of requirements.

## Viennese paste for torten bases

| | | |
|---|---|---|
| 260 g | Medium flour | 520 g |
| 112 g | Ground almonds | 225 g |
| 140 g | Butter | 280 g |
| 140 g | Icing sugar | 280 g |
| 1 | Egg plus 1 yolk | 2 plus 2 yolks |

1. Lightly blend together the butter and icing sugar, then add the egg and yolk to form a creamy consistency.
2. Meanwhile, sieve the flour and ground almonds together, and add to the butter, sugar and egg mixture.
3. Blend to a smooth paste and rub down lightly. Wrap in greaseproof paper and keep in the refrigerator for one hour before using.

**Note:** The paste is best made the day before it is required.

For torten bases, roll out a portion of paste to about 10 mm thick. Place on to a greased baking sheet and docker well before baking at 204°C for about 15 minutes to a nice golden brown. This pastry base is also suitable for a cheesecake foundation. Use a torten ring or flan ring as a guide to forming a circle according to the size of torten or cheesecake required.

If possible, it is advantageous to line the baking sheet with silicone paper. The latter can be used several times over.

## Fruit pie paste

| | | |
|---|---|---|
| 230 g | Medium flour | 900 g |
| Pinch | Salt | 10 g |
| 56 g | Butter or margarine | 230 g |
| 56 g | White vegetable shortening | 230 g |
| 30 g | Castor sugar | 122 g |
| ½ dl | Cold water (approx.) | 250 ml |

1. Sieve the flour and rub in the two fats to form fine crumbs.
2. Make a bay and add the sugar and salt dissolved in the water.
3. Draw in the flour mixture and blend lightly to a smooth paste.
4. Rest for 15 minutes in a cool place before using.
5. Use a light dusting of flour when rolling out, and blend any scraps into the main bulk.
6. Suitable for both plated fruit pies and also as a covering paste for the deep dish variety.

7. Before baking, brush the tops with weak eggwash and dust with granulated sugar for a crispy topping.

## Savoury pie paste

Use the above recipe but omit the sugar.

## Machine made short paste

*Stage 1. Cream up on 2nd speed:*
900 g Medium flour
400 g Cake margarine (or butter)
400 g White vegetable shortening
to a light consistency.

*Stage 2. Sieve together:*
900 g Medium flour
15 g Baking powder
Blend into the above mixture slowly to a crumbly consistency.

*Stage 3. Dissolve together:*
315 ml Cold water (approx.)
340 g Castor sugar
15 g Salt

1. Add to the main mixture on slow speed.
2. When the paste is sufficiently drawn together, stop the machine, taking care not to over-mix.
3. Use the flat cake beater at the creaming stage, and then change beater for the dough hook for stages 2 and 3.
4. The paste can be made in advance, then wrapped and refrigerated.

## Noodle paste                                    *Pâté à nouilles*

| 230 g | Strong flour | 900 g |
| 4 | Egg yolks | 16 |
| 1 | Egg | 4 |
| ¼ dl | Cold milk (approx.) | 125 ml |
| | Pinch of salt | |

1. Sieve the flour and make a bay. Add the remainder of the ingredients, and blend to a smooth dough.
2. Roll out a portion of the dough wafer thin. Meanwhile keep the remainder of the paste covered with a clean kitchen cloth to prevent skinning over and drying out.
3. Divide the rolled out paste into bands approximately 10 cm wide, then cut across into 7 mm wide strips.
4. Spread the strips out on a tray and dust with semolina. This will allow the *nouilles* to dry off before cooking in plenty of boiling, salted waer.

**Note:** This paste is also suitable for making ravioli, cannelloni and lasagne.

## Savarin paste

*Pâté à savarin*

| | | |
|---|---|---|
| 230 g | Strong flour | 900 g |
| 15 g | Yeast | 60 g |
| | Pinch of salt | |
| 1 dl | Fresh milk (tepid) | 425 ml |
| 3 | Eggs | 12 |
| 15 g | Castor sugar | 60 g |
| 112 g | Melted butter | 450 g |

1. Sieve the flour and make a bay. Dissolve the yeast in the tepid milk, and add to the bay along with the beaten eggs (slightly warmed).
2. Add the salt and blend all to a smooth paste. Cover with a clean cloth and allow to rest for about 30 minutes.
3. Beat in the melted butter, and then the sugar.
4. Pipe the mixture into greased savarin moulds (small or large) using a wide, plain nozzle (12 mm size).
5. Prove carefully until the mixture just reaches the top rim of the mould.
6. Bake at 215°C for about 20 minutes to a nice golden brown.

## Puff paste

*Feuilletage*

| | |
|---|---|
| 450 g | Strong flour |
| 450 g | Butter |
| 250 ml | Ice-cold water (approx.) |
| 10 g | Small pinch of salt |
| | Juice of ½ lemon *or* |
| | Pinch of cream of tartar |

1. Sieve the flour and rub in 56 g butter.
2. Form a block of the remainder of the butter, dust with flour and place aside.
3. Make a bay with the flour mixture, add the salt and lemon juice or cream of tartar.
4. Blend with water to a smooth, clear dough—ball-shaped.
5. Cut the dough crossways with a sharp knife, and cover with a cloth. Rest for 15 minutes in a cool place.
6. Roll out the dough to a star shape, leaving the centre part thick (like a cushion).
7. Place the block of butter on the centre and fold over the flaps to enclose the butter completely.
8. Dust with flour and roll out the dough keeping edges as straight as possible to about 45 cm long and 15 cm wide (18 × 6 in.). Fold into three; half turn to the left or the right before re-rolling—this is very important.
9. This constitutes one turn.
10. Place in a cool larder or refrigerator covered with a damp cloth (or cling film) and allow to rest for 15 minutes.
11. Repeat rolling and turning five times more, and rest in between each turn.

12. Finally, allow to rest before using.

If necessary, it is permissible to give double turns for the first four turns, then a single turn, and a further and final single turn to complete. However, it is essential to rest the paste in between each of the double turns, and also between each of the single and final turns. It is all a matter of circumstances and availability of time, etc.

Care when rolling out the dough to keep the sides straight and the corners square is very important if the correct quality of lamination is to be achieved. Failure to do so will result in disappointment with misshapen goods.

### Rough puff paste

| | |
|---|---|
| 450 g | **Strong flour** |
| 340 g | **Butter or margarine** |
| 250 ml | **Ice-cold water** |
| | **Pinch of cream of tartar** |
| 10g | **Salt** |

1. Cut the chosen fat into 2 cm dice. Sieve the flour with the salt.
2. Dissolve the cream of tartar in the water.
3. Lightly mix the cubes of fat with the flour, add the water and mix to a fairly firm dough.
4. Roll out the dough to a rectangle 30 cm × 15 cm and fold in three as for ordinary puff paste. This constitutes one single turn. Give six turns in all and take care to rest the paste in between turns.
5. Keep covered with a damp cloth in a cool place.

*Uses*: For puff meat pasties, sausage rolls and topping steak pies, etc. With care, quite a good quality article can be achieved with the usual flaky characteristics of puff paste.

### Wholewheat flour recipes

Today 100 per cent wholewheat flour is widely used both for flavour and to increase fibre intake. Best quality wholewheat flour contains no additives, and all the wheat's natural elements are retained throughout the stone grinding process including the bran which provides natural fibre. The latter is an essential element to maintain a healthy digestive system.

Wholewheat flour is best used freshly milled; the normal recommended 'use-by date' is 4–6 weeks. Like all flours, it should be stored in a cool, dry place.

High quality stoneground flour, such as Allinsons, is suitable for any recipe which requires a high protein content, such as bread and other yeast goods. Such a flour is a blend of Canadian and English wheats. Stoneground flour milled from high protein English wheat is suitable for making wholewheat pastry, biscuits, sponges and batters.

## Wholewheat bread

| | |
|---|---|
| **600 g** | **Wholewheat flour** |
| **15 g** | **Salt** |
| **15 g** | **Sugar** |
| **15 g** | **Vegetable fat** |
| **30 g** | **Yeast** |
| **425 ml (approx.)** | **Water at 43°C** |

1.  Rub the fat into the flour.
2.  Dissolve the yeast in the tepid water.
3.  Add the salt and sugar to the fat/flour mixture.
4.  Blend in the yeast/water to form a loose dough.
5.  Knead well and put to prove until double the size, taking all the usual precautions.
6.  When the dough is ready, knock back and divide off into suitable amounts, e.g. 450 or 900 g pieces.
7.  Place into greased bread tins, cover and prove until the dough reaches the top rim of the tin. Dust the top with flour (optional) and bake at 238° for 35–40 minutes.
8.  When baked, turn out and allow to cool on a wire rack.

**Note:** Wholewheat flours will always take up more liquid than ordinary white flour; with wholewheat flour, a slack dough is essential to achieve a nice, tender eating loaf with a good crumb structure and volume.

## Wholewheat pastry

| | | |
|---|---|---|
| **230 g** | **Wholewheat flour** | **900 g** |
| **115 g** | **Vegetable fat** | **450 g** |
| **10 g** | **Salt** | **30 g** |
| **130 ml** | **Water (approx.)** | **500 ml** |

1.  Rub the fat into the flour and make a bay. Add the salt and part of the water, and draw in the flour/fat mixture to form a soft dough.
2.  Allow to rest for several minutes after making up, and handle lightly when rolling out.

Suitable for all savoury dishes.

For a sweet pastry for fruit pies, etc., add 25 g soft brown sugar to the smaller mix (and 100 g to the larger quantity) before blending in the water.

## Choux paste                                        *Pâté à choux*

| | | |
|---|---|---|
| **70 g** | **Wholewheat flour** | **280 g** |
| **55 g** | **Butter** | **220 g** |
| **115 ml** | **Water** | **460 ml** |
| **2** | **Eggs** | **8** |
| | **Pinch salt/sugar** | |

1. Heat the water and butter to boiling-point, then remove from the heat.
2. Add the salt and sugar, and stir in the flour. Cook out for a minute or two over moderate heat until the mixture leaves the sides of the pan. Remove and cool slightly.
3. Beat in the eggs in several lots to form a firm piping consistency.
4. Use as required. Bake at 200°C for éclairs and cream buns, etc.

## Wholewheat suet paste

| | | |
|---|---|---|
| 230 g | Wholewheat flour | 920 g |
| 115 g | Shredded suet | 460 g |
| 15 g | Salt | 60 g |
| 140 ml | Water (approx.) | 570 ml |
| 20 g | Baking powder | 80 g |

1. Blend the suet with the flour and make a bay. Add the salt, baking powder and water. Draw in to a smooth dough.
2. Use as required for savoury puddings and dumplings.

**Note:**
1. For sweet suet paste, add 25 g soft brown sugar to the small mix (and 100 g to the large quantity), before blending in the water.
2. The salt can be dissolved in the water beforehand.
3. The baking powder can be lightly blended with the flour before adding the suet. Unlike plain white flour, it is not advisable to sieve wholewheat flour/baking powder to achieve distribution, otherwise, the coarser particles of bran are retained in the flour sieve.
4. As with other wholewheat flour pastes, the finished dough should be on the soft side to effect a tender eating suet crust or pudding

## Wholewheat scones

| | | |
|---|---|---|
| 230 g | Wholewheat flour | 920 g |
| 60 g | Butter | 230 g |
| | Pinch of salt | |
| 20 g | Baking powder | 60 g |
| 70 ml | Water | 285 ml |
| 70 ml | Milk at 45°C | 285 ml |
| 15 g | Sugar | 60 g |
| 15 g | Yeast | 60 g |

1. Dissolve the yeast in the warm milk and add a quarter of the sugar. Leave to ferment for 10–15 minutes.
2. Meanwhile, blend the butter with the flour and make a bay.
3. Add the salt, baking powder and remainder of the sugar.
4. Add the yeast liquid and form the whole into a soft textured dough.
5. Dust with flour, and roll out to a depth of 25 mm. Cut out with a round cutter approximately 6 cm in diameter.
6. Tray up on a greased baking tray, and bake at 190°C for approximately 15–20 minutes.
7. Cool on a wire rack.

Such scones are best handled lightly during the making-up process; do not use an excess of flour when rolling and cutting out. They need to be baked off smartly when ready.

# Cold sweets

The following is a small selection of cold sweets which are served in their own right and are commonly seen on menus of eating houses.

### Fresh fruit salad                                    *Salade des fruits*

| | | |
|---|---|---|
| 2 | Oranges | 12 |
| 2 | Dessert apples | 12 |
| 2 | Dessert pears | 12 |
| 60 g | Black grapes | 340 g |
| 60 g | Green grapes | 340 g |
| 2 | Bananas | 12 |
| 60 g | Red cherries   (if in season) | 340 g |
| 60 g | Black cherries (" "     "   ) | 340 g |
| 400 ml | Stock syrup | 2 litres |

1. Peel and prepare the oranges into segments free from pips and any pith.
2. Peel, quarter and core the apples and pears and cut into slices.
3. Skin, halve and remove the pips from the grapes.
4. Stone the cherries, and peel and slice the bananas just before service. Sprinkle the latter with lemon juice to avoid any discoloration.
5. Blend all the fruit together with the syrup and serve in suitable dishes well chilled.

Other fruits in season such as strawberries, raspberries and peaches, etc. may also be included.

### Chocolate mousse                                    *Mousse au chocolat*

| | | |
|---|---|---|
| 6 | Egg yolks | 18 |
| 112 g | Castor sugar | 36 g |
| 225 g | Plain chocolate | 675 g |
| 30 g | Softened butter | 90 g |
| 1 measure | Rum (optional) | 3 measures |
| 6 | Egg whites | 18 |
| 140 ml | Double cream (semi-whipped) | 420 ml |

1. Whisk the egg yolks and sugar in a suitable basin over a pan of hot water to the ribbon stage. Add the butter and take off heat.
2. Meanwhile, melt the chocolate in a separate basin over a pan of warm water. Remove when melted.
3. Blend the chocolate into the yolk/sugar mixture and add the rum.
4. Whisk the mixture until cool.
5. Fold the whipped cream into the chocolate mixture. Beat the egg whites until stiff and carefully fold in.

6.  Pour into suitable individual glasses and allow to set off in the refrigerator.
7.  Finally, decorate the top with a rosette of whipped cream and garnish with a sprinkling of coarsely grated chocolate or chocolate rolls.
8.  Serve with sponge fingers apart.

**Lemon mousse**                                                          *Mousse au citron*

| 400 g | Castor sugar | 800 g |
|---|---|---|
| 6 | Lemons (grated zest/juice) | 12 |
| 30 g | Leaf gelatine | 60 g |
| 6 | Egg yolks | 12 |
| 6 | Egg whites | 12 |
| 850 ml | Double cream | 1¾ litres |

1.  Whisk the egg yolks and sugar in a suitable basin over warm water to a thick consistency.
2.  Soak the leaf gelatine in cold water until soft, then remove and squeeze out the surplus water.
3.  Stir in the gelatine until melted, then add the zest and juice of the lemons.
4.  Cool the mixture and stir to the point of setting.
5.  Semi-whip the cream and fold into the mixture followed by the stiffly whipped egg whites.
6.  Pour into individual glasses or soufflé dishes (lined with paper collars to retain the height).
7.  Allow to set off in the refrigerator, then decorate the top with rosettes of whipped cream and a pinch of pistachio, or roasted flaked almonds.

**Lemon syllabub**

| 1 | Lemon |
|---|---|
| 10 g | Castor sugar |
| 140 ml | Sweet white wine |
| 285 ml | Double cream |

1.  Grate the zest of the lemon and strain the juice.
2.  Place into a mixing bowl together with castor sugar, wine and double cream.
3.  Whisk all together until the mixture becomes quite thick.
4.  Spoon or pour into goblets and place in the refrigerator.
5.  The syllabub is best made the previous day.
6.  For service, decorate the top with whipped cream and escort with sponge fingers.

# Cheese

*Cheese production*

Cheese is one of the major by-products of milk. All cheese is made from a base of curdled milk, and may be grouped in 4 classes:

1. Cheese made from fresh curds;
2. Cheese made from fermented curds at low temperature (soft textured);
3. Cheese made from curds fermented at a higher temperature, and having a hard, compressed texture;
4. Cheeses which have a mould element such as Stilton, Gorgonzola, Roquefort, Danish Blue.

There is also available a vegetarian cheese made with non-animal rennet.

Today, the bulk of cheese made in England is creamery manufactured, although more than 10 per cent is still made on the farm as against only 2 per cent French cheese being farm made.

The three main Farmhouse varieties are Cheddar, Cheshire and Lancashire. However, there are a great many English cheeses from which to choose, each dependent upon the type of milk used in the manufacture, e.g. pasteurised skimmed milk (Cottage Cheese); the hard cheeses such as English Cheddar made from warm pasteurised milk; and the cream cheeses, some of which are made either from whole cream, or from cream and milk mixed.

Not all cheeses are made from cow's milk. Other types of animal milk are used for speciality cheeses:

| | |
|---|---|
| *Roquefort* | Sheep's milk |
| *Liptauer* | Sheep's and cow's milk |
| *Greek feta* | Goat's and sheep's milk |

The above are but three examples of a great many more varieties, including buffalo milk cheese.

Most English cheeses are graded by experts. The two examining bodies who are involved in the grading system are:

1. The Milk Marketing Board, Thames Ditton, Surrey KT7 0EL who grade farmhouse produced cheese;
2. The National Association of Creamery Proprietors and Wholesale Dairymen Incorporate, 19 Cornwall Terrace, London NW1 4QP who grade creamery-produced cheese.

Each cheese is marked according to the following scale:

1. Extra Selected
2. Selected
3. Graded
4. Non-graded

Dependent upon whether the cheese is of the farmhouse variety, or produced at a creamery, so the cheese is graded at the place at which it was made. In any case, no cheese is graded which is less than ten days old, and the date of making must be stamped on every cheese.

The English Cheese Mark is awarded to cheese from England and Wales produced by a registered cheese-maker and which has been regularly checked for flavour, body and texture by the English Country Cheese Council Inspector. Only cheese made to this superior quality is entitled to a quality selected grade.

## Cheese storage

Whole cheeses will keep for a considerable time in a cool, airy store-room; they should be used in strict rotation. Alternatively, the bottom shelf of a cold room or larder is ideal. Any cut cheese should be closely wrapped in polythene, foil or cling film to prevent drying out. Store in a cool environment. Blue cheeses such as Dorset Blue Vinny, Blue Wensleydale or Stilton are best kept at a slightly lower temperature of 4°C (38°F).

## Cutting cheese

The style of cut is dependent upon the particular cheese. The round, flat cheeses such as Camembert and the square, flat sort such as Carré de L'Est should be portioned like a cake, that is cut into triangular wedges. The practice of scooping out half Stiltons with a cheese scoop is not to be recommended as it is very wasteful. Instead, the knife should be drawn flat across the surface on the basis of 'cut high', 'cut low', 'cut level'. In this way, each guest receives a decent portion of Stilton, and the establishment is not left with a thick shell of unusable cheese.

## Serving cheese

Cheese is a living organism, and must not be subjected to extremes of heat or cold, which will destroy its character and flavour. Before service, the cheeses should be brought to room temperature to bring out their full flavour. Do not remove too much cheese from storage at any one time. Use two or three good size wedges rather than several small pieces when setting out the cheese board. Keep the latter in a cool part of the restaurant to prevent the display from drying out. If possible, use a cheese board with a see-through cover for added protection.

# Chapter 3
# Boiling *Bouillir*

## The competency defined

Boiling is one of the 'wet methods' of cookery. Food is placed into a liquid (stock, water or milk) and by immersion cooked at a temperature of 100°C (212°F.). The term 'boiling' refers to the rapid bubbling movement of the liquid. A slower bubbling movement whereby the bubbles merely break the surface is known as simmering. The latter process is one more commonly used for two main reasons:

1. When foods are boiled, there is usually an undue amount of evaporation of the liquid, and consequently an abnormal amount of shrinkage.
2. The colour and the texture of certain foods can be adversely affected by too rapid boiling.

To the possible liquids which are generally used as the moistening agent, i.e. stock, water and milk, we can also add court-bouillon (see page 94), a prepared cooking liquid used for fish, etc. None of the liquids are usually thickened during the boiling process, with one exception, namely a *blanc*. This is a cooking liquor made up of water, lemon juice, flour and salt, which is used in the preparation of certain types of vegetables in order to help them to retain their 'whiteness' whilst cooking, and to avoid undue discoloration.

## The purpose of boiling

There are several reasons for utilising the boiling method of food preparation:

1. To render the item fit for consumption.
2. To make the item easy to digest.
3. To make the food both pleasant and agreeable to the palate.
4. To give the food a suitable texture and, dependent upon the item being processed, to make it tender or slightly firm according to the nature of the product.

# Methods of boiling foods

1. By plunging foods into cold liquids which are then brought up to boiling-point (100°C; 212°F). There are three main reasons for using this method:

(a) To ensure that the maximum flavour is extracted from the item, such as when making stock from bones.
(b) Gradually to soften the tougher and more fibrous foods such as root vegetables. Maincrop vegetables such as turnips, swedes and carrots are high in coarse cellulose content and will therefore take longer to cook than the early baby turnips and carrots.
(c) Whole fish such as fresh salmon are started off in cold liquid in order to help prevent damage to the final presentation caused by loss of shape, or the possibility of 'splitting' if boiled too rapidly. Furthermore, after cooking is completed, such fish are allowed to remain in the liquor (*court-bouillon*) until cold and set. Some items are brought to the boil fairly rapidly, whilst others are treated with much care and brought more slowly to the boil; whole salmon is a very good example.

2. By plunging foods into near boiling liquids which are then brought to boiling temperature, and the cooking process carried out. This alternative method is used mainly for the following reasons:

(a) To seal in the flavour of small cuts of fish such as salmon, cod, halibut or turbot steaks. The same principle will apply to some meat items, such as French-style boiled beef (*boeuf bouilli à la française*).
(b) To set the protein. The preliminary heat sets and hardens the protein which then forms a casing round the meat. Thus, the flavour and a certain amount of the natural juices are prevented from escaping into the liquid. For green vegetables such as cauliflower and garden peas, the action of boiling should be gentle. Whilst we are concerned to retain the bright green colour, care must be taken that the cellulose content of such vegetables does not becomes 'mashed' through excessive boiling.
(c) To reduce the total cooking time, as in the case of new potatoes and eggs.

Generally speaking, when foods are placed into boiling liquid, the latter is brought back to the boil fairly quickly before being allowed to *simmer* until cooking is completed.

# Advantages of boiling

There are several advantages in the adoption of the boiling method:

1. It can be labour saving in the sense that, once the process is under way, the minimum attention is required.
2. It is a fast, simple and safe procedure to add the required amount of (or extra) liquid to the pan during cooking.
3. It is very suitable for both large and small-scale cooking, and can be fairly economical on fuel.
4. It is a method which is most adaptable when preparing the cheaper, tougher cuts of meat, and the same will apply to poultry such as boiling fowl. It therefore makes it a very cost-effective method of cookery.
5. It maximises the starch and flavour extraction from foodstuffs as in the making of soups and stocks.
6. As far as green vegetables are concerned, boiling is the method adopted by the majority of cooks as a means of retaining the maximum colour. In addition, provided the cooking time is kept to the minimum, and the quantity of water used is not excessive, many of the nutrients can be conserved. In any case, it is always sound policy (nutritionally speaking) to serve a fruit juice and possibly a green salad as part of the menu, to counteract any loss of nutrients in the cooking process.

# Effects of boiling on foods

Boiling is used for a wide variety of foods, especially those of a tough, fibrous nature. It is a method which helps to break down such fibres and thus render the food more digestible. Many vegetables can be prepared in this way, and it is particularly suitable for the tuber and root class. It is also used for the reduction of various syrups, and the cooking of numerous farinaceous products (pasta) and eggs.

# General rules for efficient boiling

1. During boiling, all foods must be completely immersed throughout the cooking period.
2. Green vegetables should not be covered with a lid during the boiling process, as this can result in loss of colour and flavour because of adverse chemical reaction.
3. Any liquid loss due to excess evaporation must be replaced in order to maintain total submersion.
4. Any meats which have been salted (pickled in brine), such as silverside of beef, ox tongue, beef brisket, or legs of pork, should be soaked overnight, and then placed into fresh cold water for boiling. This will help to reduce excess salt.
5. To preserve natural flavour, fresh meat and poultry should be placed into boiling liquid; this has the effect of sealing in most of the natural

juices.

6. Any residue (scum) which is brought to the surface by the action of boiling, e.g. in the case of meat, must be carefully removed by skimming, and not allowed to boil back into the liquid.

7. All root vegetables (with the exception of new potatoes — a tuber) should be started in cold water; this has the effect of softening the large amount of cellulose which most mature root vegetables contain. It will also help to leach out any acrid taste (some root vegetables have more than others), which will enhance the flavour.

8. New potatoes retain a higher level of vitamin C when started in boiling water. After washing, they are usually cooked in their skins.

9. Stocks, sauces, soups and gravies should always be simmered gently (never boiled). Any surface residue should be removed by skimming. Stocks which are allowed to boil rather than simmer will turn cloudy. The general principle when making a stock (brown or white) is to extract the flavour from the bones and vegetables by prolonged simmering. The usual time for a basic white stock is 6–8 hours. Apart from frequent skimming during this time, the inside rim of the pot should also be wiped with a clean damp kitchen cloth. The eventual outcome is a clear, flavoursome article which is the foundation of all good cooking.

10. To be precise, although we refer to 'boiling' as one of the general methods of cookery, when applied to fish dishes, it is something of a misnomer. There are good reasons for this. The texture of fish is delicate; the fibres are loosely held together by connective tissue. They contain a large quantity of water, and during cooking, this tissue turns into gelatine. Because of the high percentage of water, the gelatine so formed is diluted and the fibres fall apart. Such fish is therefore much more successfully poached. Boiling is not a suitable method of cookery — especially when applied to white fish. In addition, as we have already observed, salmon is only brought to boiling-point before being drawn to the side of the main heat, and then allowed to cook very gently — well below boiling temperature.

# Organisation and preparation for boiling

In a traditional kitchen brigade system, operating as 'parties', the following specialist chefs de partie would be involved in some aspect of 'boiled food' preparation.

*Chef saucier:* — Butcher's meats, such as boiled beef, ox tongue, ham, gammon, leg of mutton, calf's head and poultry.

*Chef poissonnier:* — Fish dishes including shellfish.

*Chef garde-manger:* — The initial preparation of all fish, poultry, meats and offal, before cooking commences.

*Chef entremettier:*     Vegetables and farinaceous items.

As part of the traditional mise-en-place system, some food items, particularly vegetables, are prepared (cooked) in advance of the service and then *refreshed*; the latter refers to the practice of placing the items under running cold water until they are quite cold. Foods which are refreshed in this way will continue to cook in their own heat until they have cooled naturally. Boiled foods (vegetables) which have been refreshed are then re-heated in a 'chauffant' at the point of service. The 'chauffant' is merely a container of boiling salted water into which the vegetables are dipped to re-heat and then drained.

# General safety rules for boiling

1. Great care must be exercised when placing foods into or taking them out of boiling liquids. Splashing can harm not only the operator but also nearby colleagues.
2. Saucepan handles should always be turned away from the direct heat; they must not protrude over the edge of the stove or they may be accidentally dislodged or pulled over.
3. Always make sure that pans of the correct size for the job are used. If the pan is too small, boiling liquids will spill over the edge and may cause scalding.
4. Be most careful when moving pans containing boiling liquids from one area of the stove to another. Extreme care should also be taken if it is found necessary to remove boiling liquids from one part of the kitchen to another.

# Degrees of cooking for boiling

As a general rule, foods which are cooked by the boiling method are subject to thorough cooking, such as the tougher cuts of meat and some poultry. Most vegetables, however, are cooked to the stage referred to as 'al dente'. The latter is best defined as being just cooked but retaining a certain element of bite or crispness.

Temperatures should be controlled so that liquids are brought to the boil (or re-boil) as quickly as possible, after which the temperature is lowered so that the liquid simmers.

Pasta such as spaghetti and macaroni are further items which are cooked 'al dente'. Conversely, meat and poultry are cooked until tender.

The size, age and quality of raw foods used will determine the cooking times for various recipes. The better the quality of the raw product, the shorter the cooking time.

# Equipment used for boiling

Equipment used includes stock-pots, bratt pans, saucepans (of various sizes) and boiling kettles. They should be washed with hot water and detergent, then rinsed with fresh hot water and dried thoroughly after use. Saucepans should be stored upside down on pan racks. Always check that pans are properly clean before using, and that the pan handles are not loose.

It is very important when using copperware to make sure that each pan is adequately lined with tin. Indeed, any item which shows a defect in this respect should be put to one side and not used. Any 'green' discoloration on the outer surface of the copperware can be removed with a paste made up of vinegar and salt (after which, thoroughly rinse in hot water). Alternatively, a modern abrasive cleaning paste may be used. Faults should be reported, and the equipment placed aside for maintenance.

# Techniques associated with boiling

*Blanching and refreshing:*
1. In cold water: place foods, e.g. bones, into cold water and bring quickly to the boil. Wash immediately under running cold water until the item is quite cold.
2. In hot water: plunge the foods into boiling water, then immediately refresh under running water. This method is commonly used when skinning tomatoes.

*Soaking:* Prior to boiling, certain food items require soaking for a period of time to allow for softening, e.g. dried vegetables, pulses and dried fruits. Meats which have been pickled or dry cured also require soaking to remove excess salt.

*Skimming:* This is the removal of residue (scum) and other impurities from the surface of liquids during the cooking process.

# Self-assessment questions for boiling

1. What is the difference between boiling and simmering?
2. Why are root vegetables such as turnips, swedes and carrots started in cold water?
3. Why are new potatoes started in boiling water?
4. Can you name two items for menu inclusion used to counteract loss of nutrients when preparing green vegetables by the boiling method?
5. Why should stocks be simmered gently and not boiled during the cooking process?
6. Describe briefly the process of refreshing when applied to cooked

vegetables such as cauliflower, garden peas and French beans.
7. What is a 'chauffant'?
8. How would you describe the term 'al dente' when referring to cooked pasta?
9. Can you describe two methods of 'blanching'?
10. Describe two general safety rules applicable to the boiling method of cookery.

When you have completed these questions check your answers with your fellow students and chef or lecturer.

# Stocks

### Introduction to stocks

Stocks are used as the foundation of gravies, soups and sauces, and it is thus essential that the stock is of the highest possible standard if the end product is also to be of a high standard.

Stocks are liquids which contain soluble nutrients and flavours obtained from solid foods by a process of long and gentle boiling (simmering). This process takes between 6–8 hours, with the exception of fish stock which takes only 20 minutes and vegetable stocks which take 1 hour.

To achieve the highest possible standards when creating your basic stocks the following guidelines should be followed.

1. Never use unsound meat or bones in your stock, and never use rotting vegetables, as any food used which is of a poor quality will only taint the stock giving it a poor flavour and causing it to 'turn' (go rancid) quickly.
2. During cooking a scum will appear on the surface of the stock. This should be removed and not allowed to boil back into the stock. If the scum boils back into the stock it will cause the stock to go cloudy and bitter in taste.
3. During cooking, fat which is released from the food will float to the surface. This should be removed, to prevent both clouding and the finished stock tasting greasy.
4. Never allow the stock to boil too rapidly. Once brought to the boil it should simmer gently. If allowed to boil too rapidly it may go cloudy and there will be excess evaporation.
5. Never allow the stock to stop simmering, especially in hot weather. Changes in temperature may cause the stock to 'turn' (go rancid).
6. If stock is not to be used straight away, it should be strained, re-boiled, poured into clean containers of stainless steel or pot and placed somewhere to cool as quickly as possible before being stored in the refrigerator.
7. Never season stocks, as this will hinder the seasoning of the fare, soup or gravy to be made from the stock.

**Proportions of ingredients for all except fish stock and vegetable stocks**

| | |
|---|---|
| 2 kg | Bones, raw |
| 4 litres | Water |
| ½ kg | Assorted root vegetables: carrot, leek, onion, celery |
| | Bouquet garni |
| 15 | Peppercorns |

**Method for white stock**                                       *Fond blanc*

1. Break up the bones into small chunks.
2. Remove all fat and marrow.
3. Place into stock-pot of appropriate size, add cold water and bring rapidly to the boil.
4. Remove any scum from surface and sides of pan.
5. Wash, peel and re-wash vegetables.
6. Add prepared whole vegetables, bouquet garni and peppercorns to stock-pot.
7. Re-boil and then leave to simmer for 6–8 hours, remembering to skim the stock at regular intervals.
8. When ready, strain and cool before refrigerating or strain and re-boil for use straight away.

**Method for brown stock**                                       *Fond brun*

1. Break up the bones and brown either on the stove in a frying-pan with a small amount of fat or in a roasting pan in a very hot oven.
2. When brown, remove any fat and place the bones into stock-pot of appropriate size.
3. Allow any sediment in the pan to brown, swill out (déglace) with ½ litre of boiling water, scraping the bottom and sides of the tray with a wooden spoon, then add to the stock-pot.
4. Next pour in the cold water, bring it rapidly to the boil and remove any scum.
5. Turn down the heat and allow the water to simmer.
6. While the water is simmering wash, peel and re-wash the vegetables. Roughly chop them (mirepoix), fry in a small amount of fat until a deep brown colour, strain off any fat and then add the vegetables to the water and bones, along with the bouquet garni and peppercorns.
7. Allow to re-boil then simmer for 6–8 hours, skimming at regular intervals.
8. When the stock is ready, strain into a clean pan and either re-boil it for immediate use, or re-boil and place into storage containers, allowing it to cool before placing in the refrigerator.

When making brown stock it is permissible to add clean mushroom trimmings, tomato trimmings, etc. to aid with the flavour.

Due to the length of cooking time a high level of evaporation will occur. To counteract this add ½ litre of cold water just before stage 7. This will also encourage any scum to rise to the surface of the stock.

## Stocks used for white stews, soups and sauces

| | |
|---|---|
| White chicken stock | *Fond blanc de volaille* |
| White veal stock | *Fond blanc de veau* |
| White beef stock | *Fond blanc ou fond de marmite* |
| White mutton stock | *Fond blanc de mouton* |

## Stocks used for brown stews, gravies, soups and sauces

| | |
|---|---|
| Brown game stock | *Fond de gibier* |
| Brown chicken stock | *Fond brun de volaille* |
| Brown veal stock | *Fond brun de veau* |
| Brown beef stock | *Fond brun ou estouffade* |
| Brown mutton stock | *Fond brun de mouton* |

## White vegetable stock                    *Fond blanc de légumes*

| | |
|---|---|
| **500 g** | **Onion** |
| **500 g** | **Carrot** |
| **500 g** | **Leek** |
| **500 g** | **Celery** |
| **5 litres** | **Water** |

1. Wash, peel and re-wash the vegetables, then cut into rough dice (mirepoix).
2. Place into appropriate sized stock-pot.
3. Add the cold water.
4. Bring rapidly to the boil and then allow to simmer for 1 hour.
5. Skim at regular intervals if required.
6. When the stock is ready, strain into a clean pan and re-boil if required straight away, or re-boil and place into clean storage containers, allowing to cool before refrigerating.

Suitable for use in white vegetable soups, sauces, stews.

## Brown vegetable stock                    *Fond brun de légumes*

| | |
|---|---|
| **500 g** | **Onion** |
| **500 g** | **Carrot** |
| **500 g** | **Leek** |
| **500 g** | **Celery** |
| **50 ml** | **Vegetable oil** |
| **300 g** | **Tomato trimmings** |
| **300 g** | **Mushroom trimmings** |
| **10** | **Peppercorns** |
| **5 litres** | **Water** |

1. Wash, peel and re-wash the vegetables.
2. Cut the vegetables into rough dice (mirepoix).
3. Shallow fry the vegetables in the vegetable oil until a deep golden brown.
4. Drain off the vegetable oil and place the vegetables into a stock-pot of appropriate size.
5. Add the cold water and bring to boil as quickly as possible.
6. Add the tomato and mushroom trimmings and leave to simmer for at least 1 hour, skimming to remove any impurities at regular intervals.
7. When the stock is ready, drain into a clean stock-pot and re-boil if required for immediate use. If to be stored for future use, re-boil and pour into suitable storage containers, e.g. stainless steel or earthenware pots, and allow to cool before placing in refrigerator.

Suitable for use in brown vegetable soups, sauces and stews.

**Proportions of ingredients for fish stock**          *Fond de poisson*

| | |
|---|---|
| 100 g | Butter or margarine |
| 200 g | Onions, sliced |
| 2 kg | White fish bones: sole, plaice, turbot |
| ½ | Lemon, juice only |
| 5 | Peppercorns |
| 1 | Bay leaf |
| | Parsley stalks |
| 5 litres | Cold water |

1. Melt the fat in an appropriate sized pan with a thick base.
2. Add the onions, washed fish bones and other ingredients reserving the water until later.
3. Cover the pan with a lid and allow the ingredient to cook without colouring (sweat) for 5 to 10 minutes.
4. Add the cold water, bring to the boil, skim and simmer for 20 minutes.
5. Strain the stock into a clean container or pan dependent upon immediate requirements for stock.

Used as a base for fish soups, stews and sauces.

# Glazes

Glazes are made from white or brown beef stocks and from fish stock. The stocks are allowed to simmer and evaporate until they have reduced in volume to a thick sticky substance or gelatinous stage. This substance is known as a glaze and is stored in glass jars and kept well refrigerated. However, you must use the glaze within a period of 7 days to ensure freshness.

Glazes may be frozen, if stored in sterilised containers, for 2 to 3 months. Glazes are used to enhance the flavour of sauces, and it is also possible to use them as bases for sauces.

Glazes may also be turned into sauces by adding cream or whisking in a quantity of butter. However, these are very unstable sauces; they are difficult to make and have to be used immediately.

# Cooking liquors

### Court-bouillons

These are stocks created for foods (such as fish) with delicate flavours which would otherwise lose flavour in the cooking. By adding flavourings such as vegetables, herbs and peppercorns the foods being cooked are given extra flavour and seasoning by the court-bouillon.

### Court-bouillon for oily fish and shellfish

Suitable for trout, salmon, salmon-trout and assorted molluscs and crustacea shellfish.

| *1 litre* | | *5 litres* |
|---|---|---|
| 1 litre | Cold water | 5 litres |
| 5 g | Salt | 30 g |
| 50 g | Paysanne of carrots | 200 g |
| 50 g | Paysanne of onion | 200 g |
| | Parsley stalks | |
| 5 | Peppercorns | 15 |
| 1 | Bay-leaf | 3 |
| | Vinegar | |

1. Select a pan of appropriate size to cook the fish required.
2. Place all of the ingredients into the pan and bring quickly to the boil.
3. Leave the court-bouillon to simmer for 20 minutes to allow the ingredients to infuse with the water (to give flavour).
4. The court-bouillon is now ready to use. Whole fish should be placed gently into a cold court-bouillon, whilst cuts of fish and shellfish are placed gently into a simmering court-bouillon.

### White fish court-bouillon

When poaching white fish use water with the juice of 1 lemon and 5 g of salt to 1 litre of water.

# Blanc

This is a liquor used to cook foods which need to be kept white, such as globe artichokes. The flour acts as a bleaching agent and prevents the food discolouring.

| 1 litre | | 5 litres |
|---|---|---|
| 1 litre | **Cold water** | **5 litres** |
| 100 g | **Plain flour** | **500 g** |
| 3 | **Juice of fresh lemons** | **15** |
| 25 g | **Salt** | **120 g** |

1.  Mix the flour to a smooth paste using a small amount of the cold water.
2.  Mix the paste with the rest of the water.
3.  Add the lemon juice, stir well and strain to remove any lumps.
4.  Add the salt and bring the blanc to the boil over a high heat. Stir all the way to boiling-point, using a wooden spoon.
5.  The blanc is ready to use once boiling-point is reached.

# Soups

### Introduction to soups

The purpose of soups is to act as an appetiser, stimulating the customer's gastric juices ready for the main meal, and so portions do not want to be too large. Most soups are light and delicate in flavour and texture leaving the diner ready to enjoy the rest of the meal. If the soup is too heavy in texture and flavour he/she may be too full to enjoy the remainder of the meal.

Soups may be placed in two classifications, thickened and unthickened, which are then divided into different varieties.

### Thickened soups

1.  *Bisques*: smooth shellfish soups, thickened with rice, and finished with wine or liqueur and cream.
2.  *Brown soups*: smooth soups made from brown stock and thickened with a brown roux.
3.  *Cream soups*: smooth soups made in one of three ways:
    (a) purée soup finished with cream or milk;
    (b) equal quantities of béchamel and vegetable purée (adjusted with stock);
    (c) velouté soup finished with cream or milk.
4.  *Purée soups*: smooth soups thickened by their main ingredient or with the assistance of a starch additive, forced through a sieve or liquidiser.
5.  *Velouté soups*: smooth soups made with a blond roux and white stock, finished with a mixture of egg yolks and cream known as a liaison.

### Unthickened soups

6.  *Broths, bouillons*: high quality basic stocks made from beef, chicken or mutton bones, with the addition of diced vegetables and a corresponding garnish of beef, chicken or mutton; pearl barley or rice is also often added to broth.

7. Consommés; clear soups made from refined stock, often garnished with finely cut vegetables, meats, egg or rice.

## Unclassified soups

Unclassified soups are soups which do not easily fit into predetermined categories due to their composition. They include the following:

*Chowders:* thick fish soups heavily garnished with diced fish or shellfish, and with added bacon and crackers, finished with cream. Best known is clam chowder.

*Cold soups:* (excluding fruit soups) found chiefly among clear soups, e.g. consommé, bortsch. Soups such as vichysoisse and gazpacho are also classified in this group.

## The place of soups on the menu

Soups can be found on lunch menus, dinner menus and supper menus. Heavier and thicker-bodied soups are usually served at lunchtime whilst lighter and clear soups are served on more extensive menus and at the end of late evening functions just prior to the guest's departure, such as supper balls.

## Purée soups

### Basic recipe for pulse-based soups

Pulses are vegetables with a high starch content, which acts as a natural thickening agent. Dried pulses are best when they have been soaked overnight in clean cold water and then rinsed before use. They should be weighed before soaking.

| *1 litre* | | *5 litres* |
|---|---|---|
| 250 g | Main pulse ingredient | 1250 g |
| 50 g | Carrot ⎫ cut | 250 g |
| 50 g | Onion ⎪ for | 250 g |
| 50 g | Celery ⎬ mirepoix | 250 g |
| 50 g | Leek ⎭ | 250 g |
| 50 g | Streaky bacon (optional) | 250 g |
| | Bouquet garni | |
| | Salt and pepper | |

It is permissible to use any white stock, such as vegetable, lamb, chicken, beef, for pulse soups.

1. Select a pan of appropriate size for the volume of soup to be made, add mirepoix, pulse vegetables, bacon and stock to the pan.
2. Place the pan on a fierce heat and bring quickly to the boil.
3. Reduce the heat and allow the soup to simmer.

4. Skim the surface of the soup at regular intervals to remove scum and other impurities thrown to the surface during cooking.
5. Add the bouquet garni, cover the pan with a lid and simmer for approximately 1 hour, or until the main pulse vegetable is cooked.
6. Pass through a drum sieve or through a soup blender until smooth, finish with any required garnish and serve croûtons as an accompaniment.

### Croûtons for soup

These are small dice of bread, approximately ¼ cm in size, shallow fried in oil, clarified butter or margarine to a deep golden brown colour.

*Soups made using the recipe for basic pulse-based purée soups*

| | |
|---|---|
| **Purée of split green pea** | *Purée St Germain* |
| **Purée of lentil** | *Purée de lentilles* |

### Purée soup recipe for fresh vegetable purée soups

| | | |
|---|---|---|
| 1 litre | White stock, (vegetable, meat or poultry may be used as required) | 5 litres |
| 400 g | Main vegetable ingredient (sliced or shredded roughly) | 2 kg |
| 50 g | Sliced onion ⎫ | 250 g |
| 50 g | Diced celery ⎬ Mirepoix | 250 g |
| 50 g | Sliced leek ⎭ | 250 g |
| 100 g | Sliced potato | 500 g |
| 50 g | Butter or margarine | 200 g |
| | Bouquet garni | |
| | Salt and pepper | |

The 100 g of sliced potato may be replaced with 50 g patna rice as an alternative aid to thickening. Use 200 g of patna rice to 5 litres of soup.

1. Select a suitably sized saucepan for the volume of soup to be made. Add the butter or margarine, mirepoix and the main vegetable ingredient; cover with a lid and sweat, that is cook without allowing the food to colour.
2. Season and add the hot stock; bring quickly to the boil over a fierce heat.
3. Skim the surface to remove any surface impurities (scum), add the sliced potato or patna rice and bouquet garni, and re-boil.
4. Simmer gently for approximately 1 hour or until all ingredients are cooked; keep the soup covered to reduce excess evaporation of liquid.
5. Remove the bouquet garni and pass the soup through either a drum sieve or soup blender until smooth.
6. Finish by passing through a conical strainer (chinois) into a clean pan,

re-boil quickly, adjust seasoning and consistency and add appropriate garnish.

Serve with croûtons.

*Soups made using the recipe for basic fresh vegetable purée soups*

**Purée of celery**                    *Purée de céleri*
**Purée of carrot**                    *Purée de carottes*

The above soups are finished with finely chopped parsley.

**Purée of cauliflower**                    *Purée Dubarry*

Finish with 50 g of small sprigs of cauliflower, which should be pre-boiled and refreshed, to 1 litre of soup and finely chopped parsley.

*Broths*                    *Potages — Bouillons*

Broths are basically unthickened soups, which have flavour added by the addition of other ingredients and are garnished with combinations of vegetables, cereals, meat or seafood. The majority of broths contain a cereal, commonly barley or rice. Broths occasionally look like thickened soups, because of the starch content found in the barley or rice. There are three categories of broth:

1. When vegetables are added to the stock which already contains the meat ingredient for that particular soup.
2. When the vegetables are prepared and sweated and then the stock is added to the vegetables.
3. Fish broths which are known as chowders; these are also commonly finished with cream or milk.

**Basic recipe for broth I**

| 1 litre | White meat or vegetable stock | 5 litres |
|---------|-------------------------------|----------|
| 250 g   | Raw meat ingredient           | 1¼ kg    |
| 50 g    | Onion                         | 250 g    |
| 50 g    | Carrot                        | 250 g    |
| 50 g    | Celery                        | 250 g    |
| 50 g    | Leek                          | 250 g    |
| 30 g    | Barley                        | 150 g    |
|         | Chopped parsley               |          |
|         | Bouquet garni                 |          |

1. Blanch the raw meat ingredient in water and refresh to remove any impurities.
2. Place the meat into a pan of suitable size for the volume of soup being

made, add the stock and bring rapidly to the boil. Skim regularly to remove any scum.
3. Add the barley and seasoning and the bouquet garni.
4. Simmer until the meat and barley are almost cooked through.
5. Add the prepared vegetables and simmer until cooked.
6. Remove the meat and cut into small pieces and remove the bouquet garni.
7. Replace the diced meat, correct the seasoning and consistency.
8. Garnish with finely chopped parsley at service time.

*Broths made using basic recipe for broth I*

**Beef broth**                                    *Bouillon de boeuf*

Use stewing beef as the main ingredient.

**Chicken broth**                                 *Bouillon de volaille*

Use boiling fowl as the main ingredent.

**Scotch broth**                                  *Potage écossais*

Use stewing mutton as the main ingredient.

**Basic recipe for broth II**

| 1 litre | White chicken or vegetable stock | 5 litres |
|---|---|---|
| 500 g | Main prepared vegetable ingredient cut as required for specific soup | 2½ kg |
| 50 g | Vegetables required for garnish | 250 g |
| 25 g | Margarine or butter | 125 g |
|  | Bouquet garni |  |
|  | Chopped parsley |  |

1. Select a pan of suitable size for the volume of soup being made.
2. Add the margarine or butter and vegetables, place over a moderate heat and sweat.
3. Season and add the hot stock, bring the soup rapidly to the boil, skim to remove any surface scum.
4. Reduce the heat to a simmer and add the bouquet garni.
5. Simmer until the vegetables are just cooked.
6. Remove the bouquet garni, add the additional cooked garnish and correct the seasoning and consistency.
7. Finish with chopped parsley.

*Broths made using basic recipe for broth II*

## Minestrone                                               *Minestroni*

Cut all the vegetables in paysanne using 100 g each of onion, carrot, leek, potato, swede, turnip and green cabbage as part of the main ingredient for each litre of soup. Garnish with 25 g of tomato concassé, 25 g broken spaghetti, and a small amount of tomato purée to colour.

## Cockie-leekie

Use julienne of leek for main ingredient with the addition of 50 g of cooked julienne of chicken, 25 g cooked julienne of prunes and finely chopped parsley to each litre of soup.

*Shellfish broths*                                          *Chowders*

### Basic shellfish chowder recipe

| 1 litre | | 5 litres |
|---|---|---|
| 250 g | Fish stock | 1¼ kg |
|  | Cooked shellfish including |  |
|  | cooking liquor |  |
| 100 g | Paysanne of leek | 500 g |
| 100 g | Paysanne of potato | 500 g |
| 100 g | Blanched, diced belly pork | 500 g |
| 100 g | Tomato concassé | 500 g |
| 1 dl | Single cream | 4 dl |
| 25 g | Margarine or butter | 100 g |
|  | Bouquet garni |  |
|  | Finely chopped parsley |  |

1. Select a pan of suitable size for the volume of soup to be made.
2. Place the vegetables, blanched pork and butter in the pan and sweat.
3. Lightly season and add the hot stock, shellfish and cooking liquor.
4. Bring the soup quickly to the boil, skim to remove any surface scum and add the bouquet garni.
5. Reduce the heat and allow the soup to simmer until the vegetables are cooked.
6. Add the tomato concassé and remove the bouquet garni.
7. Correct the seasoning and consistency and add the cream and chopped parsley.

Serve perhaps with fresh moist breadcrumbs added to soup to act as a thickener. Broken or crushed water biscuits may also be used.

*Brown soups*                                               *Potage brun*

These soups are made from brown stock and meat and have a mirepoix and brown roux base.

## Recipe for basic brown soups

| 1 litre | | 5 litres |
|---|---|---|
| 1 litre | Brown stock | 5 litres |
| 250 g | Diced selected meat ingredient | 1¼ kg |
| 50 g | Diced onion | 250 g |
| 50 g | Diced carrot | 250 g |
| 50 g | Diced celery | 250 g |
| 50 g | Diced leek | 250 g |
| 30 g | Tomato purée | 125 g |
| 50 g | Dripping | 250 g |
| 50 g | Plain flour | 250 g |
| | Bouquet garni | |

1. Melt the dripping in a pan of suitable size for the volume of soup being made.
2. Add the meat and vegetables which have been cut for mirepoix.
3. Season and cook to a deep brown colour, add the flour and cook to a brown roux.
4. Remove from the heat and allow to cool slightly, then add the tomato purée; mix in well using a wooden spoon.
5. Add the hot brown stock a little at a time, mixing in well to avoid any lumps of flour.
6. When all of the stock has been mixed in, add the bouquet garni and bring the soup to the boil quickly and then reduce the heat to a simmer for 2½ to 3 hours, skimming regularly to remove any surface scum. Cover with a lid to reduce the level of evaporation.
7. Remove the meat content and the bouquet garni from the soup and pass the remainder of ingredients through a soup blender and then through a fine chinois.
8. Finely dice the meat and add to the soup, adjust the seasoning and consistency, using brown stock.

Suggested main meat ingredient would include oxtail, kidney or game flesh.

## *Clear soups*                                                    *Consommés*

Clear soups are best defined as refined stocks which have been clarified and flavoured by the addition of other foods. Consommé should be a clear amber colour when ready for service.

It is the coagulation of the protein in the egg whites and mince which causes the clarification of the consommé to occur; during cooking the coagulated protein rises to the surface as a crust and brings with it all the impurities, leaving a clear stock of consommé underneath.

## Notes for making a successful consommé

1. Make sure that you thoroughly mix the egg whites with the rest of the ingredients.
2. Always remove the grease from the top of the stock and consommé.

3. As soon as the consommé has come to the boil, turn it down to a simmer so as not to disturb the crust, which could result in a cloudy consommé.
4. Never use a lid when making consommé as this will make it difficult to control the cooking.

## Basic consommé recipe

| 1 litre | | 5 litres |
|---------|-----------------------|---------|
| 1 litre | Cold brown stock | 5 litres |
| 250 g | Minced shin beef | 2½ kg |
| 50 g | Brunoise of carrot | 250 g |
| 50 g | Brunoise of onion | 250 g |
| 50 g | Brunoise of celery | 250 g |
| 50 g | Brunoise of leek | 250 g |
| 50 g | Egg whites | 250 g |
| | Bouquet garni | |

The vegetable content acts as a mirepoix and gives flavour.

1. Mix all of the ingredients together in a pan of suitable size for the volume of soup being made and leave to stand in the refrigerator for at least 30 minutes.
2. Place over a moderate heat and bring slowly to the boil. As soon as the soup reaches boiling-point, reduce the heat so that the soup is only simmering gently. Do not stir or agitate as this will hamper the forming of a crust.
3. Allow to simmer for 1½ hours and then strain gently through a tammy or muslin cloth.
4. Allow the soup to settle and then remove all the grease from the surface of the soup.
5. Adjust the seasoning and then re-heat and add any garnish required for service.

Consommés are generally served with cheese straws as an accompaniment.

## Consommé cup                                    *Consommé en tasse*

As for the basic recipe and served in a consommé cup.

## Consommé with diced vegetables          *Consommé brunoise*

Allow 25 g carrot, 25 g turnip, 25 g leek and 25 g celery, all cut into brunoise and cooked before adding as a garnish, to each litre of soup.

### Cream soups

The majority of cream soups are made from a roux base in the form of béchamel sauce, the main flavour of the soup being the principal ingredient.

However, it should be noted that the term 'cream soup' can mean another smooth soup which has an addition of cream or milk in the final stages of preparation. These are commonly purées of velouté-based soups.

### Basic recipe for cream soups

| 1 litre | | 4 litres |
|---|---|---|
| | White stock | |
| | (usually vegetable or chicken) | |
| 350 g | Main vegetable ingredient | 1750 g |
| 50 g | Sliced onion ⎫ Mirepoix | 250 g |
| 50 g | Sliced leeks ⎬ | 250 g |
| 50 g | Diced celery | 250 g |
| 2 dl | Béchamel sauce | 1 litre |
| 50 g | Butter or margarine | 200 g |

1. Select a saucepan of suitable size for the volume of soup being made.
2. Add the butter or margarine and place the pan on a high heat.
3. Add the mirepoix and main vegetable ingredient, reduce the heat and allow to sweat, covered with a lid.
4. Add the hot stock and bring rapidly to the boil.
5. Skim to remove any scum from the surface of the soup.
6. Reduce heat and allow soup to simmer for approximately 1 hour or until the vegetables are well cooked and tender.
7. Pass the soup through a drum sieve with the vegetables or through a soup blender and add to a clean pan containing the hot béchamel sauce.
8. Mix thoroughly together and pass through a chinois into another pan.
9. Bring rapidly to the boil, adjust the seasoning and consistency and garnish as required.

It is permissible to replace the béchamel with 20 g of plain wholemeal flour to 1 litre of stock at the end of stage 3 and then finish the soup with fresh cream or replace half the stock with milk.

*Soups made using the basic recipe for cream soups*

### Cream of carrots                                      *Crème de carottes*

Garnish with finely chopped parsley and if required you may also garnish with 50 g of fine cooked julienne of carrot to each litre of soup.

### Cream of cauliflower                                   *Crème Dubarry*

Garnish with finely chopped parsley and 50 g of small sprigs of boiled cauliflower to each litre of soup.

Other cream soups would include cream of mixed vegetable, watercress and green pea.

## Cream of chicken                                    *Crème de volaille*

| | | |
|---|---|---|
| 1 litre | Chicken stock | 5 litres |
| 60 g | Margarine or butter | 300 g |
| 60 g | Plain flour | 300 g |
| ½ kg | Chicken carcass (chopped) | 2½ kg |
| 1 dl | Single cream | 4 dl |
| 50 g | Cooked julienne of white chicken | 250 g |

1. Melt the margarine or butter in a pan of suitable size for the volume of soup being made.
2. Add the flour and cook to a blond roux.
3. Remove from the heat and allow to cool slightly.
4. Add the hot stock a little at a time to avoid any lumps, mixing with a wooden spoon.
5. Bring quickly to the boil and add the chicken carcass, re-boil and allow to simmer for approximately 1 hour.
6. Strain into a clean pan and bring rapidly back to the boil.
7. Adjust the seasoning and consistency and add the cream.
8. Heat the julienne of chicken and add to the soup for service.

This soup can be converted into a velouté soup by adding an egg yolk to 1 dl of cream to make a liaison to add to the soup.

## Cream of tomato                                    **Crème de tomate**

| | | |
|---|---|---|
| 1 litre | White chicken or vegetable stock | 5 litres |
| 50 g | Butter or margarine | 250 g |
| 50 g | Streaky bacon bits | 200 g |
| 100 g | Diced carrot | 400 g |
| 100 g | Diced onion | 400 g |
| ½ | Bay-leaf | 3 |
| Small sprig | Thyme | Large sprig |
| 100 g | Tomato purée | 400 g |
| 50 g | Plain flour | 300 g |
| 1 dl | Single cream | 4 dl |

1. Melt the margarine or butter in a pan of suitable size for the volume of soup being made.
2. Dice the bacon and add to the pan and fry to a light brown.
3. Add the carrots, onion, bay-leaf and thyme and sweat for 15–20 minutes.
4. Add the flour and mix well in, allow the roux to cook to a blond stage, remove from the heat and allow to cool slightly.
5. Add the tomato purée and mix in well, making sure to avoid any lumps.
6. Add the hot stock, a little at a time, again to avoid any lumps. When all of the stock is added bring the soup to the boil and allow to simmer for at least 1 hour, skimming the surface at regular intervals to remove any impurities.
7. Strain the soup or put the soup through a soup blender and strain

through a fine chinois into a clean pan and bring back to the boil rapidly.

8. Adjust the seasoning and consistency and add the cream.

Served with croûtons. The bacon may be omitted to create a vegetarian soup.

## Miscellaneous soups

### Mulligatawny

| 1 litre | Chicken stock | 5 litres |
|---------|---------------|----------|
| 100 g | Brunoise of onion | 500 g |
| 50 g | Brunoise of apple | 200 g |
| 50 g | Margarine or butter | 200 g |
| 50 g | Plain flour | 250 g |
| 25 g | Mild curry powder | 125 g |
| 25 g | Tomato purée | 125 g |
| 25 g | Finely chopped chutney | 125 g |
| 25 g | Boiled patna rice | 125 g |
| 1 clove | Garlic paste | 3 cloves |

1. Select a pan of suitable size for the volume of soup to be made.
2. Place the butter or margarine in the pan along with the onion and apple and cook gently until soft; do not allow to colour.
3. Add the curry powder and allow to cook gently for 5 to 10 minutes and then add the flour and mix in well using a wooden spoon, to make a roux.
4. Remove the pan from the heat when the roux has cooked, and allow to cool slightly.
5. Add the tomato purée and mix in well.
6. Add the stock a little at a time, mixing in so as to avoid leaving any lumps of roux.
7. Bring quickly to the boil, reduce the heat and simmer for 15 minutes, skimming regularly to remove any surface scum.
8. Add the chutney and garlic paste and simmer for a further 45 minutes.
9. Pass through a soup blender and strain into a clean pan, adjust the seasoning and consistency and garnish with the plain boiled rice at service time.

This soup may be finished with 1 dl of single cream or plain yoghurt to each litre of soup as it is served.

Wholemeal flour may be used in place of plain and vegetable stock can be used in place of chicken stock.

## French onion soup                                         *Soupe à l'oignon française*

| 1 litre | Brown stock | 5 litres |
| 500 g | Shredded onions | 2½ kg |
| 50 g | Butter or margarine | 200 g |
| 1 clove | Garlic paste | 3 cloves |
| 25 g | Plain or wholemeal flour | 125 g |
| | Cheese toasted flutes | |
| | Grated parmesan in sauce-boat | |

1. Select a pan of suitable size for the volume of soup being made.
2. Place the margarine or butter in the pan with the shredded onions and garlic paste.
3. Sweat over a moderate heat until lightly browned and season with salt and milled black peppercorns.
4. Mix in the flour and allow to cook for 5–10 minutes.
5. Add the stock a little at a time so as not to leave any lumps of flour.
6. Bring quickly to the boil and skim to remove any surface scum.
7. Simmer for 30 minutes and serve in a petite marmite dish with a lid.
8. Garnish with cheese toasted flutes and a sauce-boat of grated parmesan.

**Note:** This soup can be made without the addition of flour if required.

## Cold leek and potato soup                                      *Vichyssoise*

| 8 dl | Chicken stock or vegetable stock | 4 litres |
| 350 g | Sliced leeks | 1750 g |
| 200 g | Sliced potato | 1 kg |
| 1 dl | Single cream | ½ litre |
| 50 g | Butter | 200 g |
| | Bouquet garni | |
| | Finely chopped chives | |

1. Select a pan of suitable size for the volume of soup being made.
2. Add the water, leeks and potato and sweat for 10–15 minutes. Season lightly.
3. Add the hot stock, bring quickly to the boil, skim to remove any surface scum and add the bouquet garni.
4. Reduce the heat and allow the soup to simmer for 1 hour covered with a lid.
5. Remove the bouquet garni and strain the soup or pass through a soup blender and finally through a chinois into a clean bowl.
6. Adjust the seasoning and stir over a bowl of iced water until cold.
7. When cold add the cream and garnish of finely chopped chives; serve well chilled.

### *Velouté soups*                                               *Veloutés*

These are soups made using a blond roux or velouté flavoured by different types of stocks. Velouté soups have a velvety texture which is created by adding a liaison of egg yolks and cream immediately before service. Once the liaison has been added to the soup it must not be allowed to re-boil or it will curdle or crack due to the coagulation of the egg yolk.

### Basic recipe for meat, fish and poultry veloutés, method I

| 1 litre | White meat, chicken or fish stock | 5 litres |
|---------|-----------------------------------|----------|
| 50 g | Diced onion | 250 g |
| 50 g | Diced celery | 250 g |
| 50 g | Diced leek | 250 g |
| 50 g | Plain flour | 250 g |
| 50 g | Margarine or butter | 250 g |
| 1 | Egg yolk | 4 |
| 1 dl | Cream | 3 dl |
| | Bouquet garni | |

1. Melt the butter or margarine in a pan of suitable size for the volume of soup being made.
2. Add the prepared vegetables and allow to sweat until tender.
3. Add the flour and cook to a blond roux.
4. Remove from the heat and allow to cool slightly before adding the hot stock a little at a time using a wooden spoon.
5. Bring rapidly to the boil and skim regularly to remove any scum.
6. Add the bouquet garni and simmer for at least 1 hour.
7. Strain or pass through a soup blender and then strain through a fine chinois into a clean pan.
8. Re-boil quickly, adjust the seasoning and consistency and remove from the heat, allowing the soup to cool slightly.
9. Add the liaison immediately before service, making sure not to allow the soup to re-boil.

### Basic recipe for vegetable velouté soups, method II

| 8 dl | White stock | 4 litres |
|------|-------------|----------|
| 350 g | Main vegetable ingredient | 1750 g |
| 50 g | Diced onion | 250 g |
| 50 g | Diced celery | 250 g |
| 50 g | Diced leek | 250 g |
| 40 g | Margarine or butter | 200 g |
| 2 dl | Chicken velouté | 1 litre |
| 1 | Egg yolk | 4 |
| | Bouquet garni | |

1. Melt the butter or margarine in a pan of appropriate size for the volume of soup being made.
2. Add all of the vegetables and sweat until cooked.
3. Add the stock and bring to the boil quickly, skim and add the bouquet garni.
4. Simmer for approximately 30 minutes.
5. Add the velouté and remove the bouquet garni, re-boil the soup and

pass through a soup blender and finish by passing through a fine chinois into a clean pan.

6. Re-boil and remove from the heat, allow to cool slightly and finish with the liaison immediately before service. Do not permit the soup to boil once the liaison has been added as this will cause the soup to curdle and spoil its presentation.

## Shellfish soups                                          Bisques

Shellfish soups are basically thickened, passed seafood soups made from fish stocks and specific shellfish. To assist with bringing out the natural flavours, wine, brandy or sherry can be added. The thickening agent used in biques is rice starch. Shellfish soups are usually very expensive to produce and very rich in flavour. Because of these factors, bisques are normally found on dinner menus.

### Basic shellfish soup recipe

| 1 litre | | 5 litres |
|---|---|---|
| 500 g | Fish stock | 2½ kg |
| 50 g | Live shellfish | 200 g |
| 50 g | Brunoise of carrot | 200 g |
| 50 g | Brunoise of onion | 200 g |
| ½ dl | Brunoise of celery | 2½ dl |
| 1 dl | Brandy | 5 dl |
| ½ dl | Dry white wine | 2½ dl |
| 50 g | Single cream | 200 g |
| 50 g | Butter or margarine | 250 g |
| 30 g | Rice | 150 g |
| | Tomato purée | |
| | Bouquet garni | |

1. Melt the butter or margarine in a pan of suitable size for the volume of soup being made.
2. Add the shellfish and sweat until cooked, e.g. lobster turns red. Note that for extra flavour when making crab or lobster bisque add the shells to the fish stock and simmer.
3. Add the brunoise of vegetables which acts as a mirepoix and sweat until cooked.
4. Add the dry white wine and simmer until reduced by two-thirds. Flame with the brandy and at this stage lightly season the ingredients in the pan.
5. Add the strained fish stock, bring to the boil rapidly and skim to remove any surface scum. Reduce the heat and simmer with the bouquet garni for 20 minutes.
6. Remove the bouquet garni and shellfish from the soup. Separate shellfish from the shells, cut the flesh for garnishing the soup and place on one side. Crush the shells and return to the soup. Re-boil for 10–15 minutes and then strain into a clean pan.
7. Add the rice and tomato purée and proceed to simmer the soup for 20–30 minutes or until the rice is well cooked.
8. Pass through a soup blender and then strain through a fine chinois to

form a smooth thick red bisque.

9. Re-boil quickly, adjust the seasoning and consistency, add the cream and garnish.

Serve with melba toast and butter.

# Sauces

## Introduction to sauces

Sauces are used to add moisture to dryer foods in order to aid digestion, and to cook foods so adding flavour to the food being prepared, such as casseroles or braisings.

Sauces are best defined as liquids which have been thickened by one of the following six methods:

1. A roux.
2. Cornflour, fécule or arrowroot.
3. Beurre manié.
4. Egg yolks.
5. Coulis.
6. Blood.

A sauce should be smooth in texture and glossy in appearance, have a well-defined flavour and be free-flowing in consistency.

## Thickening agents for sauces and soups

1. *Roux:* the mixing over heat of fat and flour, which is cooked together. There are three grades of roux, the grade used being dependent upon the sauce to be made.

(a) *White roux*: white sauces, e.g. béchamel sauce.
(b) *Blond roux*: veloutés, e.g. chicken velouté.
(c) *Brown roux*: brown sauces, e.g. espagnole sauce.

When making a roux, melt the fat, add the flour and allow to 'cook out', which allows the flour to cook in the fat, to the degree required. For a *white roux* do not allow the flour to colour; for a *blond roux* allow the flour to cook until a light brown colour; for a *brown roux* allow the flour to cook to a deeper brown colour.

*White and blond roux*: Use equal quantities of flour and margarine or butter.

*Brown roux*: Use slightly less fat to flour, e.g. 100 g fat to 125 g flour. The fat and flour for a brown roux must be cooked together slowly. Too rapid cooking may cause the roux to overcook, which would result in a chemical reaction in the starch known as 'Dextrinisation', which means in effect that the roux would lose a percentage of its thickening ability. Dextrinisation is when the fat separates from the roux and after having made the sauce the fat will rise to the surface and float on top. Another effect would be that due to the amount of flour needed to achieve the required thickness of sauce, the flavour of the finished sauce would be impaired and produce a bitter taste.

2. *Cornflour, fécule or arrowroot*: Used to thicken sauces and gravies (jus lié). All of these thickening agents need to be mixed to a smooth paste with a small amount of cold liquid, water, milk or stock, and then poured into the *boiling* liquid, stirring all the time, until the liquid has re-boiled. It should be noted that the sauce will not finish thickening until the liquid has re-boiled and continued to boil for a short time. Failure to stir the sauce continously whilst thickening will result in a lumpy sauce.

3. *Beurre manié*: Used in the production of fish sauces, but may be used to rescue other sauces which are too thin in consistency. Made from equal parts of butter and sieved plain flour, kneaded to a very smooth paste (it is essential that there are no lumps of flour in the paste), and then added in the form of small pellets to a *boiling* liquid, being whisked or stirred until thickening is completed.

4. *Egg yolks*: Used in the production of custards and emulsions such as mayonnaise and hollandaise. The egg yolks are used in various forms, e.g. whisked over heat, blended with sugar or blended with cold oil, dependent on the sauce being produced.

5. *Coulis*: This is a purée of fruit and vegetables, e.g. strawberry coulis or spinach coulis. No further thickening agent is used. Often used to decorate plates for Nouvelle Cuisine style presentations.

6. *Blood*: The one use of blood as a thickening agent for a sauce is for jugged hare, when the blood is poured into a gently *boiling* sauce, which must then not be re-boiled or the sauce will separate and curdle.

*Basic white sauce*                                                        *Béchamel*

| *1 litre* | | *5 litres* |
|---|---|---|
| 100 g | Butter or margarine | 500 g |
| 100 g | Plain flour | 500 g |
| 1 litre | Hot milk: skimmed, semi-skimmed, full fat or powdered | 5 litres |
| 1 | Onion clouté: onion studded with cloves | 2 |

1. Melt the margarine or butter over a gentle heat in a thick-based pan of appropriate size.
2. Sieve the flour and add to the pan: mix in well using a wooden spoon or spatula.
3. Allow to cook gently for a short time; do not allow the roux to colour.
4. Remove the pan from the heat and allow the roux to cool slightly.
5. Add the milk, which should be hot, a little at a time, stirring well into the roux.
6. Add the onion clouté to the sauce.
7. Cover the sauce with a cartouche and simmer gently for 20 minutes.
8. Remove the onion clouté from the pan and proceed to strain the sauce through a conical strainer into a clean container.

If the sauce is for immediate use place on to stove, re-boil and keep hot in a bain-marie, covering with a cartouche to stop a skin forming.

If the sauce is to be stored, cover with a cartouche and put to cool before refrigerating.

### Derivatives of béchamel sauce

These are sauces made using the basic white sauce as their foundation. The following are a selection of common derivatives.

**Cheese sauce** *Sauce mornay*

| 1 litre | Béchamel sauce | 5 litres |
|---|---|---|
| 100 g | Grated cheese | 500 g |
| 2 | Egg yolks | 10 |
| | Salt and pepper | |

Add grated cheese to boiling sauce, remove from heat and allow to cool slightly before adding egg yolks and seasoning. Do not allow the sauce to re-boil or it may split the sauce.

Served with boiled and poached fish, eggs and vegetables.

**Cream sauce** *Sauce crème*

| 1 litre | Béchamel sauce | 5 litres |
|---|---|---|
| 2 dl | Double cream | ½ litre |
| | Salt and pepper | |

Boil the béchamel sauce, add the cream and stir in well with a wooden spoon, season as required.

Serve with boiled fish and poached fish, eggs and boiled vegetable dishes.

### Onion sauce

*Sauce aux oignons*

| 1 litre | Béchamel sauce | 5 litres |
| 250 g | Brunoise of onion | 1 kg |
| 50 g | Butter or margarine | 150 g |
| | Salt and pepper | |

Sweat the brunoise of onion in the butter or margarine and then add to the boiling béchamel, stir in well with a wooden spoon, season as required.
Serve with roast mutton and egg dishes.

### Parsley sauce

*Sauce persil*

| 1 litre | Béchamel sauce | 5 litres |
| 2 tablespoons | Finely chopped parsley | 10 tablespoons |
| | Salt and pepper | |

Boil the béchamel sauce and add the chopped parsley and season as required.
Re-boil the sauce and allow to simmer while covered with a cartouche for 15 minutes before use.

### Velouté-based sauces

A velouté is a sauce made from a white stock such as chicken or fish and which is added to a blond roux. The principles are the same as when making béchamel sauce, only the milk used for béchamel is replaced with stock and the roux is cooked for slightly longer until a light sandy texture and colour is reached. The basic velouté sauce is then used as a base for a selection of other sauces. These are known as derivatives.

The following is a basic velouté sauce recipe which in turn is followed by sauces made using the basic recipe as their base.

### Velouté sauce

*Sauce velouté*

| *1 litre* | | *5 litres* |
| 100 g | Butter or margarine | 500 g |
| 100 g | Plain flour | 500 g |
| 1 litre | Hot white stock: Fish, chicken, lamb, veal stocks are suitable dependent on the dish being created | 5 litres |

1. Melt the margarine or butter over a gentle heat in a thick-based pan of appropriate size.
2. Sieve the flour and add to the pan. Mix in well using a wooden spoon or spatula.
3. Allow the roux to cook gently to sandy texture.
4. Remove the pan from the heat and allow the roux to cool slightly before adding stock.
5. Add the hot white stock a little at a time, mixing into the roux with a

wooden spoon or spatula, making sure there are no lumps.
6. When all of the stock has been added, stir to the boil.
7. Leave to simmer gently for 1 hour, covered with a cartouche to help prevent a skin forming.
8. Finally, pass through a conical strainer, with the assistance of a metal ladle (never use a wooden spoon in any form of sieve or strainer as splinters may get into the sauce). If the sauce is to be stored for future use pour into suitable containers, cover with a cartouche and allow to cool before refrigerating. If for immediate use strain into a clean pan and re-boil before using.

## Derivatives of veloutés

These derivatives are sauces which are made from a velouté-based sauce.

### Supreme sauce
*Sauce suprême*

| | | |
|---|---|---|
| 1 litre | Chicken velouté | 5 litres |
| 50 g | White mushroom trimmings | 250 g |
| 1 dl | Single cream | ½ litre |
| 2 | Egg yolks | 10 |
| | Lemon juice to taste | |
| | Salt and pepper | |

1. Allow the chicken velouté and mushroom trimmings to simmer for ½ hour.
2. Pour through a fine conical strainer into a clean pan.
3. Re-boil, remove from the heat, allow to cool slightly.
4. Mix the egg yolks and cream together (making what is known as a liaison) in a basin. Add a little of the sauce and mix into the liaison.
5. Add the liaison to the main pan of sauce; do not allow the sauce to re-boil after adding the liaison as the sauce will curdle.
6. Finally, add the lemon juice to give a hint of sharpness to the sauce and season as required.

Served with boiled chicken dishes, as the base for chaud-froid and in vol-au-vent fillings.

### Mushroom sauce
*Sauce aux champignons*

| | | |
|---|---|---|
| 1 litre | Chicken velouté | 5 litres |
| 250 g | Sweated, sliced white button mushrooms | 1½ kg |
| | Salt and pepper | |

Add the sweated, sliced white button mushrooms to the velouté after straining, finish with a liaison and lemon juice as for sauce suprême, season as required.
Served with boiled chicken and sweetbread dishes.

**Caper sauce**                                   *Sauce aux câpres*

| 1 litre | Mutton velouté | 5 litres |
|---------|----------------|----------|
| 50 g    | Capers         | 250 g    |
|         | Salt and pepper |         |

A basic mutton velouté to which you add the capers and simmer for 30 minutes with a cartouche cover, before use.

Served with boiled leg of mutton.

### Basic brown sauce

This is the basic brown sauce which is usually refined into a sauce known as demi-glace, making it smoother in taste and texture before using to make a wide selection of other sauces, known as derivatives.

The following is a recipe for basic brown sauce, which in turn is followed by sauces made using basic brown sauce as their base.

**Basic brown sauce**                             *Espagnole*

| 1 litre | Brown stock   | 5 litres |
|---------|---------------|----------|
| 50 g    | Dripping      | 250 g    |
| 60 g    | Plain flour   | 300 g    |
| 25 g    | Tomato purée  | 125 g    |
| 100 g   | Carrot        | 500 g    |
| 100 g   | Onion         | 500 g    |
| 50 g    | Celery        | 250 g    |

1. Melt the dripping in a thick-based pan of appropriate size.
2. Add the plain flour, allowing to cook slowly over a gentle heat to a light brown colour; stir at regular intervals to prevent the roux burning while cooking.
3. Allow to cool slightly and then mix in the tomato purée.
4. Add the stock to the roux, a small amount at a time, mixing the stock well into the roux.
5. Allow the sauce to simmer gently while you prepare the next stage.
6. Wash, peel and re-wash the vegetables.
7. Cut them into a rough dice (mirepoix).
8. Fry to a golden brown in a small amount of dripping and well drain before adding all the vegetables to the sauce.
9. Allow the sauce to boil and then reduce the heat and simmer for 4–6 hours; stir regularly to prevent burning. Skim before stirring, to remove any scum from the surface of the sauce.

**Note:** Do not allow the roux to colour too quickly or the starch content of the roux (which is the thickening agent for the sauce) may burn; if this happens the starch will lose a considerable amount of its thickening ability. In addition, over-browning and burning will result in a very bitter taste to the espagnole.

## Demi-glace

Reduce equal quantities of espagnole and brown stock by half. Skim well, and pass through a fine strainer. Re-boil and correct the seasoning. Cover with a buttered paper known as a *cartouche*.

## Chasseur sauce                               *Sauce chasseur*

| | | |
|---|---|---|
| 1 litre | Demi-glace | 5 litres |
| 50 g | Butter or margarine | 200 g |
| 250 g | White button mushrooms | 1 kg |
| 100 g | Brunoise of shallots | 500 g |
| 250 g | Tomato concassé | 1 kg |
| 1 teaspoon | Fresh chopped tarragon | 4 teaspoons |
| 2 dl | Dry white wine | 1 litre |
| | Salt and pepper | |

1. Melt the butter gently in a suitable sized sauteuse.
2. Add the brunoise of shallots and tarragon and sweat for 3–5 minutes
3. Finely slice the button mushrooms and add them to the pan.
4. Cook without allowing the shallots to colour for a further 5 minutes.
5. Drain off the butter.
6. Add the dry white wine and simmer until reduced in volume by half.
7. Add the demi-glace and simmer for 10–15 minutes. Add the tomato concassé and season as required.

Served with chicken, lamb and steaks, fried or grilled.

## Brown onion sauce                            *Sauce lyonnaise*

| | | |
|---|---|---|
| 1 litre | Demi-glace | 5 litres |
| 500 g | Finely sliced onion | 2 kg |
| 100 g | Margarine or butter | 400 g |
| 1 dl | Malt vinegar | 4 dl |
| | Salt and pepper | |

1. Melt the margarine or butter in an appropriately sized sauteuse.
2. Add the finely sliced onion and sweat covered with a cartouche for 10–15 minutes or until onions are soft.
3. Remove the cartouche and allow the onions to gain a light brown colour.
4. Add the malt vinegar to the pan and simmer until the vinegar has totally evaporated.
5. Add the demi-glace, bring quickly to the boil and then reduce the heat to simmer for 10–20 minutes.
6. Skim regularly to remove any scum from the surface.
7. Season as required.

Served with fried liver, sausages, Vienna steaks, burgers.

## Piquant sauce

### Sauce piquante

| | | |
|---|---|---|
| 1 litre | Demi-glace | 5 litres |
| 250 g | Brunoise of shallots | 1 kg |
| 2 dl | Malt vinegar | 8 dl |
| 100 g | Brunoise of gherkins | 400 g |
| 50 g | Finely chopped gherkins | 200 g |
| 2 tablespoons | Finely chopped tarragon, chervil, parsley | 6 tablespoons |

1. Add the shallots and vinegar to a sauteuse of appropriate size and simmer until vinegar has reduced by half in volume.
2. Add the herbs and simmer for a further 5–10 minutes.
3. Add the demi-glace, bring quickly to the boil and reduce the heat and simmer for 15–20 minutes.
4. Skim at regular intervals to remove any scum from the surface.
5. Season as required and add the finely chopped gherkins.

Served with Durham cutlets, bitoks and Vienna steaks.

## Reform sauce

### Sauce réforme

| | | |
|---|---|---|
| 1 litre | Demi-glace | 5 litres |
| 50 g | Butter or margarine | 200 g |
| 75 g | Brunoise of carrot | 350 g |
| 75 g | Brunoise of onion | 350 g |
| 75 g | Brunoise of celery | 350 g |
| 1 | Bay-leaf | 4 |
| Small sprig | Fresh thyme | Large sprig |
| 1 dl | Malt vinegar | 4 dl |
| 10 | Crushed black peppercorns | 2 dessertspoons |
| 50 g | Redcurrant jelly | 200 g |
| 25 g | Julienne of boiled ham | 200 g |
| 25 g | Julienne tongue | 100 g |
| 25 g | Julienne beetroot, boiled | 100 g |
| 25 g | Julienne of boiled egg white | 100g |
| 25 g | Julienne gherkin | 100 g |
| 25 g | Julienne white mushroom | 100 g |
| 10 g | Julienne of truffle | 50 g |
| | Salt and pepper | |

1. Melt the butter or margarine in a sauteuse of appropriate size.
2. Add the carrot, celery, onion and herbs and cook to a light golden brown colour.
3. Drain off the fat from the pan.
4. Add the peppercorns and vinegar and reduce by two-thirds.
5. Add the demi-glace and bring quickly to the boil; reduce the heat to simmer the sauce for 30–40 minutes.
6. Skim at regular intervals to remove any scum from the surface of the sauce.
7. Add the redcurrant jelly and mix in well.
8. Re-boil the sauce and strain through a conical strainer (chinois) into a clean pan.

9. Add all of the julienne garnish to the sauce, or if required reserve a quarter of the julienne garnish to decorate the food on the service dish.

Served with lamb cutlets réforme.

## Miscellaneous sauces and gravies

These are sauces and gravies which do not fit into any of the three categories already covered, e.g. béchamel, velouté or demi-glace sauce-based.

### Apple sauce                                      *Sauce aux pommes*

| | | |
|---|---|---|
| ½ kg | Cooking apples | 10 kg |
| ½ dl | Water | 8 dl |
| ½ | Lemon, juice of | 4 |
| 25 g | Castor sugar | 350 g |
| 15 g | Butter or margarine | 200 g |

1. Wash, peel, core the apples, slice roughly and add to a deep, thick-based pan.
2. Add the water, lemon juice and sugar, cover with a cartouche and cook quickly until reduced to a pulp.
3. Either pass through a conical strainer aided with a small ladle or finish with a short burst in the food processor and then pass through a fine sieve.
4. Pour into a clean pan and re-heat rapidly.
5. Using a wooden spoon, mix in the butter just before service.

Served with roast goose, duckling and most commonly roast pork.

### Orange sauce (savoury)                          *Sauce bigarade*

| | | |
|---|---|---|
| 1 litre | Duck stock, thickened with | 5 litres |
| 25 g | Arrowroot | 120 g |
| 1 dl | Pure orange juice | 5 dl |
| ½ dl | Pure lemon juice | 2½ dl |
| 3 oranges | Julienne of orange skin | 12 oranges |
| 1 lemon | Zest of lemon skin | 3 lemons |
| | Salt and pepper | |
| 1 dl | Curaçao or Grand Marnier | 3 dl |

1. Place the liquor into a sauteuse and reduce by half.
2. Add the duck stock and fruit juice, reduce by a third.
3. Strain through a conical strainer and then tammy.
4. If the sauce is too sharp a small amount of sugar may be added at this stage.
5. Re-boil the sauce, add the julienne and zest of orange and lemon, adjust the seasoning and consistency.

Served with braised and pot roasted (poêlé) duck.

## Bread sauce

*Sauce pain*

| | | |
|---|---|---|
| *1 litre* | | *5 litres* |
| 8 dl | Milk | 4 litres |
| 1 | Onion clouté | 2 |
| | (small onion studded with a small number of cloves and a bay-leaf) | |
| 275 g | Soft white breadcrumbs | 1250 g |
| 50 g | Butter or margarine | 200 g |

1. Bring the milk to the boil in a suitable sized thick-bottomed pan with the studded onion.
2. Reduce the heat and cover with a cartouche. Leave to stand for 15–20 minutes, to give the onion clouté time to infuse flavour with the milk.
3. Remove the onion clouté.
4. Sprinkle and stir in the breadcrumbs using a wooden spoon.
5. Stir in the butter, using a wooden spoon, just prior to service.

If to be held for service, place into a bain-marie to prevent the sauce burning, and cover with a cartouche.

Served with roast turkey, chicken and game birds.

## Cranberry sauce

*Sauce airelles*

| | | |
|---|---|---|
| 1 kg | Cranberries | 5 kg |
| 100 g | Castor sugar | 400 g |
| 3 dl | Water | 1 litre |
| 1 | Pinch of salt | 3 |

1. Rinse the cranberries under running cold water.
2. Place into a pan of suitable size and add the sugar, water and salt.
3. Bring quickly to the boil, covered with a cartouche.
4. Simmer for 10–15 minutes.
5. Pass through a drum sieve.

Served with roast game and poultry; may be served hot or cold.

## Mint sauce

*Sauce à la menthe*

| | | |
|---|---|---|
| 1 litre | Malt vinegar | 5 litres |
| 125 g | Finely chopped mint | 650 g |
| 30 g | Castor sugar | 125 g |
| ½ lemon | Lemon juice | 2 lemons |

1. Remove the leaves from the stalks and chop very fine with the sugar.
2. Add the mixture of sugar and mint to the vinegar and leave to stand in a cool place for at least 1 hour.
3. Add the lemon juice and stir in.
4. Store in sealed jars.

Served with roast lamb.

If dried mint is used, use 50 g to 1 litre of vinegar, boil the dried mint with the vinegar and allow to go cold before using.

## Curry sauce                                              *Sauce kari*

| | | |
|---|---|---|
| 75 g | Butter or margarine | 350 g |
| 100 g | Brunoise of onion | 500 g |
| 1 | Cloves of garlic | 4 |
| 35 g | Curry powder | 175 g |
| 50 g | Plain flour | 250 g |
| 50 g | Tomato purée | 200 g |
| 1 litre | Brown stock | 5 litres |
| 50 g | Brunoise of cooking apple | 200 g |
| 30 g | Chopped mango chutney | 150 g |

1. Melt the margarine or butter in a sauteuse of suitable size.
2. Add the onion and garlic and cook over a gentle heat until a light golden brown colour.
3. Add the curry powder and plain flour, mix in and cook as for a roux.
4. Add the tomato purée to the roux, mix in well using a wooden spoon.
5. Add the hot stock, a little at a time, mixing in well to ensure that there are no lumps of roux.
6. Bring to the boil, skim to remove any scum from the surface.
7. Add the apple and chutney, simmer for 45–60 minutes, skimming at regular intervals.
8. The sauce may then be served as it is, adjusting the seasoning as required, or if a smooth sauce is required then pass through a fine conical strainer (chinois) before seasoning.

**Notes:**
1. The sauce may be finished with a small amount of single cream or plain yoghurt.
2. Check on the strength of the curry powder; if very strong, adjust the amount used.

Served with poultry, meat, eggs and shellfish.

## Provincial sauce                                      *Sauce provençale*

| | | |
|---|---|---|
| 1 dl | Virgin olive oil | 4 dl |
| 1 | Clove of garlic cut brunoise | 4 |
| 1 kg | Tomato concassé | 5 kg |
| 2 dl | Dry white wine | 1 litre |
| 5 dl | Tomato sauce | 2½ litres |
| | Salt and pepper | |

1. Pre-heat the virgin olive oil in a sauteuse of suitable size.
2. Add the brunoise of garlic and cook over a low heat, taking care not to allow the garlic to brown.

3. Add the tomato concassé, add seasoning and the dry white wine.
4. Simmer until reduced by just over half in volume.
5. Add the tomato sauce, bring to the boil and simmer for 10–15 minutes.
6. Adjust the seasoning.

Served with poached eggs, omelettes, poached fish and shellfish dishes.

**Sweet and sour sauce**

| 1 litre | Jus lié | 5 litres |
|---|---|---|
| 100 g | Brunoise of onion | 500 g |
| 100 g | Julienne of red pimento | 500 g |
| 100 g | Julienne of green pimento | 500 g |
| 100 g | Butter or margarine | 500 g |
| 100 g | Moist brown sugar | 500 g |
| ½ dl | Malt vinegar | 2½ dl |
| 50 g | Julienne of carrot | 250 g |
| ½ dl | Pure lemon juice | 2½ dl |
| 25 g | Tomato purée | 125 g |

Additional ingredients which may be added to alter the taste to suit individual preference include caraway seeds, cinnamon stick, root ginger, orange zest, soy sauce, diced pineapple.

1. Place the brunoise of onion, julienne of pepper and carrots into a thick-based pan of suitable size and allow to sweat in the butter or margarine.
2. Add the moist brown sugar and allow to lightly caramelise.
3. Add to the pan the lemon juice and vinegar, simmer until reduced by half volume.
4. Add the tomato purée and mix well in using a wooden spoon.
5. Add the jus lié, mix in well and bring to the boil; skim to remove any scum.
6. Add any flavourings and seasonings required and simmer for 10–20 minutes.

Served with kebabs, chicken, prawns, pork, deep-fried foods.

**Tomato sauce** *Sauce tomate*

| 75 g | Butter or margarine | 350 g |
|---|---|---|
| 50 g | Diced bacon bits | 250 g |
| 100 g | Diced onion | 400 g |
| 100 g | Diced carrots | 400 g |
| 50 g | Diced celery | 200 g |
| 1 | Bay-leaf | 3 |
| 1 small sprig | Thyme | 1 large sprig |
| 1 | Clove garlic | 3 |
| 100 g | Plain flour | 400 g |
| 100 g | Tomato purée* | 500 g |
| 1 litre | White stock | 5 litres |
| 10 g | Castor sugar | 50 g |

1. Melt the butter or margarine in sauteuse of suitable size.
2. Add the bacon, onion, celery and carrot, fry to a light golden brown colour.
3. Add the bay-leaf, thyme and garlic and cook together for a further 5 minutes.
4. Add the flour and mix in well, making sure there are no lumps.
5. Cook to a blond roux stage and allow to cool slightly.
6. Add the tomato purée and mix in well.
7. Add the hot stock, a little at a time, using a wooden spoon or spatula, making sure there are no lumps.
8. Bring to the boil, stirring regularly, and skim to remove any scum.
9. Add the sugar and leave the sauce to simmer for 1 hour or longer; stir at regular intervals to prevent sticking and skim at regular intervals.
10. Adjust the seasoning, strain through a chinois and cover with a cartouche.

* **Note**: The quality of the tomato purée used will determine the exact amount required for correct colour and flavour to be achieved.

Served with deep-fried fish and made up dishes, such as cromesquis and savoury croquettes.

## Thickened gravy                                                      *Jus lié*

| | | |
|---|---|---|
| 25 g | Dripping | 75 g |
| 1 kg | Veal bones (chopped small) | 3 kg |
| 2 | Chicken carcasses (roasted) | 6 |
| 100 g | Diced carrots | 300 g |
| 100 g | Diced celery | 300 g |
| 100 g | Diced onions | 300 g |
| Small piece | Bay-leaf | 1 |
| Sprig | Thyme | Small bunch |
| 2 litres | Brown stock | 6 litres |
| 75 g | Tomato purée | 200 g |
| 75 g | Mushroom trimmings | 200 g |
| 40 g | Arrowroot | 120 g |

1. Roast the veal bones to a nice golden brown in the oven and drain well.
2. Fry off the diced vegetables in the remainder of the dripping to a good brown colour and also drain well.
3. Place all the ingredients (except the arrowroot) in a suitable size pan and bring to the boil.
4. Simmer gently for about 2 hours and skim during this time.
5. Dilute the arrowroot with a little water or sherry and stir into the simmering stock. Allow to cook for a further 15 minutes.
6. Correct the seasoning and consistency and strain through a fine chinois (without any pressure).

The finished jus lié should be a rich, reddish brown colour and quite transparent.

**Note:** Any surplus mushroom trimmings and/or soft cooking tomatoes can be added to the jus lié to enhance the richness of the finished gravy.

It is often used as a base for all brown sauces in preference to demi-glace and provides a much lighter sauce.

**Roast gravy**                                                         *Jus rôti*

**2½ dl**                    **Brown stock**                    **6 dl**

1.  Decant off the fat from the roasting tray, leaving any sediments in the base.
2.  Sit the tray on the stove top, put in the brown stock and bring to the boil.
3.  Using a wooden spatula, scrape around the base of the tray while the stock is boiling.
4.  Simmer for 10 minutes and strain into a clean saucepan.
5.  Allow to stand for 5 minutes and skim to remove any surface grease and scum.
6.  Season and re-boil, use as required.

### *Hot emulsion sauces*

These sauces are generally served with poached fish, e.g. salmon; vegetables, e.g. asparagus; and grilled or baked meats, e.g. steaks or beef Wellington. They add a rich smooth texture with a slight sharpness in the flavour to aid digestion. They are based on a blending together of eggs and clarified butter.

When making a sauce with egg and butter there are basic guidelines which need to be followed.

1.  Always use thin wire whisks in clean stainless steel or well-tinned sauteuse.
2.  Only add enough melted butter to enable the yolks to be liquid enough to whisk up to a fluffy stage.
3.  Do not allow the eggs to become too hot or the eggs will curdle, i.e. they should not be allowed to heat over 85°C.
4.  The butter must be clarified and skimmed before use.
5.  When sauces are made they should be strained through a tammy cloth into a warm container and held for service at 30–35°C.
6.  If too hot the sauce will split, if too cold the sauce will set.
7.  If the sauce should split, use the sauce in place of clarified butter, starting with fresh egg yolks in a clean bowl.

The two recipes following are the most common of the hot emulsion sauces used in the catering industry today.

## Hollandaise sauce                           *Sauce hollandaise*

| *1 litre* | | *5 litres* |
|---|---|---|
| 1 kg | Clarified butter | 5 kg |
| 1 tablespoon | Crushed white peppercorns | 4 tablespoons |
| ½ dl | Malt vinegar | 2½ dl |
| 10 | Egg yolks | 50 |
| 1 | Lemon, juice of | 4 |

1. Pour the vinegar and crushed peppercorns into a sauteuse and reduce until almost all the vinegar has evaporated.
2. Allow to cool slightly and add ¼ dl of warm water.
3. Whisk the egg yolks with the vinegar and water to a light fluffly stage over a bain-marie (bath of hot water). This stage is known as a *sabayon*.
4. Remove from the heat and allow to cool slightly whilst still whisking.
5. Whisk in the clarified butter in a steady stream, whisking all the time.
6. Strain the sauce through a fine muslin and adjust the seasoning, using salt only.
7. Finish the sauce by adding the lemon juice.

If necessary a little warm water can be added to adjust the consistency of the sauce to enable it to coat foods.
   Served with boiled and poached foods, e.g. vegetables and fish.

## Béarnaise sauce                             *Sauce béarnaise*

| 1 kg | Clarified butter | 5 kg |
|---|---|---|
| 50 g | Brunoise of shallots | 250 g |
| 15 g | Finely chopped tarragon, chervil stalks | 75 g |
| 1 tablespoon | Crushed white peppercorns | 4 tablespoons |
| 1 dl | Malt vinegar | 4 dl |
| 12 | Egg yolks | 55 |
| 15 g | Finely chopped tarragon and chervil leaves. | 75 g |

1. Place the brunoise of shallots, tarragon and chervil stalks, peppercorns and vinegar into a sauteuse of suitable size with the addition of ½ dl of water to 1 kg of butter; reduce until almost all the liquid has evaporated.
2. Add the egg yolks and whisk until cooked and light and fluffy in texture (sabayon).
3. Remove from the heat and allow to cool slightly, still whisking.
4. Whisk in the clarified butter in a slow steady stream.
5. Strain the sauce through a muslin and correct the seasoning with salt only.
6. Gently fold in the tarragon and chervil leaves and hold for service at 30-35°C.

The sauce should be thicker than hollandaise and as such is more likely to split if held for too long. To combat this, whisk periodically during service.

Served with grilled and shallow-fried meats and fish.

# Boiling shellfish

### Introduction to boiling shellfish

Shellfish should be cooked by dropping into a pan of rapidly boiling water (or court-bouillon), simmered for a specific length of time, removed from the cooking liquor and drained. The shellfish is either left to go cold for later use or used straight away. There are two categories of shellfish — *molluscs*, such as mussels, oysters and scallops, and *crustaceans* such as lobster, crab, prawns and crayfish.

Molluscs are more commonly cooked with very little water and a few finely chopped onions and butter on the stove top in a pan with a tight-fitting lid for 10-12 minutes and then served straight away.

Note that scallops are often removed from the shell before cooking and may be poached or shallow fried.

### Cooking time for crustaceans

| | | |
|---|---|---|
| Shrimps | *Crevettes grises* | 5–8 minutes |
| Prawns | *Crevettes roses* | 5–8 minutes |
| Crayfish | *Écrevisse* | 8–10 minutes |
| Scampi | *Langoustine* | 8–12 minutes |
| Crab | *Crabe* | 18-25 minutes |
| Crawfish | *Langouste* | 20-25 minutes |
| Lobster | *Homard* | 20-25 minutes |

**Mussels with white wine**      *Moules marinières*

| 1 litre | | 2½ litres |
|---|---|---|
| | **Fresh mussels** | |
| | **Finely chopped parsley** | |
| | **Salt and pepper** | |
| 1 dl | **Fish stock** | 2 dl |
| 30 g | **Brunoise of shallots** | 75 g |
| ½ dl | **Dry white wine** | 1¼ dl |
| ¼ lemon | **Fresh lemon juice** | 1 lemon |
| 30 g | **Beurre manié** | 70 g |

1. Make sure that all the shells are tightly closed: this indicates that the mussels are fresh. Throw away any open shells.
2. Scrape the mussel shells to remove barnacles, wash the shells in cold running water, and then drain.
3. Select a suitable size of thick-based saucepan with tight-fitting lid.
4. Add the brunoise of shallots, finely chopped parsley and dry white wine and bring to the boil.

5. Add the mussels and cover with a lid.
6. Bring back to the boil and continue to cook over high flame until all the shells have opened, 5–7 minutes.
7. Strain the cooking liquor into a stainless steel bowl and stand.
8. Scrape the mussels out of their shells and discard the beard and any sand from the mussels.
9. Place the mussels back into the shells and keep hot in a suitable bowl with a lid.
10. Decant the cooking liquor into a sauteuse, leaving any sediment in the bowl to be discarded later.
11. Bring the liquor to the boil and thicken by whisking in the beurre manié and simmer until thickened.
12. Season and add finely chopped parsley.
13. Pour the liquor over the mussels and serve straight away on a hot flat with a dish paper.
14. Accompany with wedges of crusty French bread to soak up the liquor.

# Boiling eggs

*General information on egg cookery*

Eggs have a great variety of uses in the catering industry. They can be served as dishes on their own, usually as a starter or salad, or cooked by a wide range of methods. They can also be used to aid the finishing of other dishes. Listed below are a few examples.

1. To aid the glazing or colouring of foods, as in eggwash or egg yolks in sauces.
2. As a base for emulsified sauces, such as mayonnaise and hollandaise.
3. To assist with thickening and enriching finished sauces, soups and white stews.
4. As a method of assisting coatings such as breadcrumbs to stick to foods before cooking.
5. To bind foods, helping them hold together for cooking, such as potato dishes or stuffings.
6. To aid the dispersal of air through foods — aeration, as in batters, sponges and soufflés.

In this book the egg dishes have been classified under their method of cookery. If more than one method of cookery is involved in the cooking the dish will be under the predominant method used.

**Boiled eggs**                                    *Oeufs bouillis*

1. Place the eggs into a wire basket and place into a deep pan of simmering water.
2. Bring the water back to the boil quickly and then allow to simmer until the eggs are cooked to the required degree.

Timing of the cooking should start when the water has come back to the boil.

*Degrees of cooking for boiled eggs*

**Soft boiled eggs served in the shell**          *Oeuf à la coque*

Cooking time 3–4 minutes. Served in the shell.

**Soft boiled eggs served out of the shell**        *Oeuf mollet*

Cooking time 3–4 minutes. When cooked, place into cold water to refresh, remove the shell and then replace into simmering water for 30 seconds. Serve as for any of the poached egg dishes (see poaching).

**Hard-boiled eggs**                               *Oeuf dur*

Cooking time 8–10 minutes. May be served with or without its shell.

**With white onion sauce**                         *Oeuf à la tripe*

| | | |
|---|---|---|
| 4 | Hot hard-boiled eggs | 10 |
| 3 dl | White onion sauce | 8 dl |
| 1 tablespoon | Very finely chopped parsley | 3 tablespoons |

1. Cut the hot hard-boiled eggs in half lengthways and place into a hot dish yolkside down.
2. Coat lightly with hot white onion sauce and sprinkle with very finely chopped parsley.

# Farinaceous dishes

*Introduction to farinaceous dishes*

The term 'farinaceous dishes' covers a wide range of products such as pasta, rice and gnocchi. All farinaceous dishes are savoury and may be served either as a starter or as an entrée (a middle course between the starter and main course).

## Gnocchi Paris style — *Gnocchi parisienne*

| | | |
|---|---|---|
| 500 ml | Milk | 1250 ml |
| 100 g | Butter | 250 g |
| 250 g | Strong flour | 625 g |
| 50 g | Grated parmesan cheese | 125 g |
| 5–6 | Eggs | 12–15 |
| | Salt to taste | |
| 1 litre | Thin béchamel sauce | 2.5 litres |
| 100 g | Grated cheese | 250 g |

1. Boil the milk in a thick-based pan with the butter and salt.
2. Stir in the sieved flour and cook until the mixture leaves the sides of the pan clean.
3. Allow the mixture to cool slightly.
4. Beat in the eggs singly to a smooth consistency, stir in the grated parmesan cheese, flavour with a little grated nutmeg if desired.
5. Place some of the mixture into a piping bag with a 1 cm plain tube. Have ready a shallow pan of simmering, salted water, and with the nozzle just over the edge of the pan, pipe out 2 cm lengths cutting each piece with a sharp knife.
6. Allow the gnocchi to poach gently until cooked, about 10 minutes.
7. Remove with a perforated spoon and drain well on a sieve or in a colander.
8. To serve, coat the base of a fireproof dish with a thin layer of béchamel sauce, bind the gnocchi gently with the béchamel and adjust the seasoning to taste.
9. Place the gnocchi in the dish and sprinkle with grated cheese.
10. Brown under a hot salamander.

## Potato dumpling — *Gnocchi piémontaise*

| | | |
|---|---|---|
| 200 g | Purée of potato | 500 g |
| 50 g | Sieved plain flour | 125 g |
| 25 g | Beaten whole egg | 60 g |
| 25 g | Butter | 60 g |
| 25 g | Grated parmesan | 60 g |
| | Grated nutmeg | |
| | Seasoning | |
| | Finely chopped parsley | |
| 2 dl | Tomato sauce | 5 dl |

1. Place the purée of potato in a stainless steel or earthenware mixing bowl.
2. Add the egg, butter, parmesan, nutmeg and seasoning.
3. Mix well and then mix in the flour to form into a firm mixture suitable for moulding.
4. Allow to cool enough to handle.
5. Divide into small pieces; allow four pieces to a portion.
6. Mould into the shape of small dumplings and depress the top slightly.

7. Place the dumplings into simmering, seasoned water and poach for approximately 5 minutes, that is until the dumplings float.
8. Remove from the pan and drain well.
9. Place neatly into buttered oven-proof dishes; sprinkle with parmesan and a few drops of clarified melted butter.
10. Place in a hot oven for 7–10 minutes to gratinate, or finish under a salamander if required.
11. To serve surround with a cordon of tomato sauce.

**Note:** This dish may also be coated with mornay sauce before gratinating if required.

### Roman style dumplings                                    *Gnocchi romaine*

| | | |
|---|---|---|
| 25 g | Grated parmesan | 60 g |
| ½ | Crushed clove of garlic | 2 |
| | Grated nutmeg to taste | |
| | Seasoning | |
| 25 g | Beaten egg yolk | 62 g |
| 25 g | Butter | 62 g |
| 120 g | Semolina | 300 g |
| 5 dl | Milk | 12¼ dl |
| 2 dl | Tomato sauce | 5 dl |
| | Finely chopped parsley | |

1. Select a firm shallow tray of suitable size for the volume of gnocchi romaine being produced.
2. Cut a sheet of greaseproof paper to fit the tray and grease the paper with butter or oil.
3. Line the bottom of the tray with the paper, place on one side until required.
4. Put the milk, nutmeg, garlic and seasoning in a suitable thick-based saucepan and bring to the boil.
5. Sprinkle on the semolina, whisking in with a piano wire whisk until back to boiling temperature.
6. Using a wooden spoon stir until the mixture has completed thickening and is of a smooth consistency.
7. Remove the pan from the heat and allow to cool slightly.
8. Using a wooden spoon, beat in the butter, egg yolk and grated parmesan and adjust the seasoning.
9. Put the mixture into the prepared tray and spread evenly. The mixture should be no more than 2 cm deep.
10. Leave the mixture to go cold and refrigerate until set.
11. When set turn on to a clean board and peel off the paper.
12. Cut into small discs or crescents and arrange neatly in a buttered oven-proof dish.
13. Sprinkle liberally with parmesan and a few drops of melted butter.
14. Place the dish in a hot oven for 7–10 minutes or until heated through

and a golden brown colour on top. Finish under the salamander if necessary.

15. Surround with a cordon of hot tomato sauce.

## Savoury rice (Italian style)                                   *Rizotto*

| | | |
|---|---|---|
| 200 g | Washed patna rice | 500 g |
| 50 g | Brunoise of onion | 125 g |
| 30 g | Margarine or butter | 60 g |
| | Seasoning | |
| | Bouquet garni | |
| 6 dl | Fresh chicken stock | 1½ litres |
| 25 g | Fresh grated parmesan | 60 g |

1. Select a pan of suitable size for the volume of rice being cooked.
2. Melt the margarine or butter in a pan, add the onions and sweat without colouring.
3. Add the patna rice and allow to sweat with the onions for a few minutes.
4. Add the bouquet garni, stock and a little seasoning.
5. Bring to the boil, reduce the heat to a simmer.
6. Simmer until the rice is soft and cooked and all of the stock has evaporated.
7. If more stock needs to be added during cooking, make sure the stock is boiling.
8. Stir frequently during cooking to help prevent sticking.
9. When cooked stir in the parmesan, using a fork, and then adjust the seasoning.
10. Remove the bouquet garni and serve.

## *Pasta*

### General points on pasta cookery

1. Pasta should always be cooked in plenty of boiling salted water.
2. Olive oil and herbs may be added to the water. The oil helps to prevent the pasta sticking together during cooking and the herbs improve flavour.
3. Stir gently during cooking.
4. Do not allow pasta to be overcooked.
5. If not being used straight away, refresh the pasta in cold running water.
6. Re-heat gently in boiling flavoured and seasoned water and drain well in a colander for service.
7. Grated cheese should be served with pasta in a separate dish.
8. Allow 10–15 g of pasta for a portion if used as a garnish.
9. Allow 25–50 g of pasta for a main course portion.
10. Pasta may be served as starters, entrées or main courses.

## Spaghetti with cheese     *Spaghetti italienne*

| 100 g | Spaghetti | 250 g |
|---|---|---|
| 25 g | Butter | 75 g |
| 25 g | Grated parmesan cheese | 75 g |
| | Milled salt | |
| | Milled pepper | |

1. Boil the pasta in a pan of boiling water with salt and olive oil, stirring regularly with a wooden spatula.
2. Allow to cook until al dente (firm but tender and cooked), approximately 12–15 minutes.
3. Drain well in a colander and return to a dry, clean, hot pan.
4. Mix in the butter and parmesan, season with salt and pepper and serve.

## Spaghetti with tomato sauce   *Spaghetti napolitaine*

| 100 g | Spaghetti | 250 g |
|---|---|---|
| 25 g | Butter | 75 g |
| 2½ dl | Tomato sauce | 7½ dl |
| 100 g | Tomato concassé | 250 g |
| | Milled salt | |
| | Milled pepper | |
| | Grated parmesan to accompany | |

1. Cook the spaghetti as for spaghetti italienne, omitting the cheese.
2. Drain and return to a clean dry pan.
3. Add the tomato sauce and seasoning.
4. Add tomato concassé and serve in a hot entrée dish accompanied with parmesan cheese.

## Spaghetti Milanaise     *Spaghetti milanaise*

| 100 g | Spaghetti | 250 g |
|---|---|---|
| 25 g | Butter | 75 g |
| 1½ dl | Tomato sauce | 3½ dl |
| 25 g | Julienne of tongue, ham and cooked mushroom | 75 g |
| | Milled salt | |
| | Milled pepper | |
| | Grated parmesan to accompany | |

1. Prepare as for spaghetti napolitaine up to and including stage 3.
2. Season and mix the julienne of tongue, ham and cooked mushroom.
3. Serve in a hot entrée dish accompanied with grated parmesan.

## Spaghetti bolognese                                    *Spaghetti bolonaise*

| | | |
|---|---|---|
| 25 g | Butter or olive oil | 75 g |
| 50 g | Brunoise of onion | 125 g |
| 1 | Clove of garlic | 2 |
| 100 g | Minced beef | 250 g |
| 1¼ dl | Demi-glace | 3 dl |
| 100 g | Tomato purée | 250 g |
| 100 g | Brunoise of mushroom | 250 g |
| | Milled salt | |
| | Milled pepper | |
| 100 g | Spaghetti | 250 g |
| | Oregano or marjoram to taste | |
| | Grated parmesan to accompany | |

1.  Heat the butter or oil in a sauteuse or frying-pan.
2.  Add the chopped onion, crushed garlic and cook gently for 5 minutes, do not allow to colour.
3.  Add the minced beef and cook for 10 minutes, allowing to colour slightly.
4.  Add the tomato purée and herbs.
5.  Add the demi-glace and simmer for 15 minutes.
6.  While the sauce is simmering boil the spaghetti as for italienne omitting the parmesan.
7.  Add the mushrooms and seasoning to the sauce and simmer for a further 5–10 minutes.
8.  Drain the spaghetti and dress on the service dish.
9.  Pour the sauce into the centre and accompany with a bowl of parmesan cheese.

## Macaroni cheese                                        *Macaroni au gratin*

| | | |
|---|---|---|
| 100 g | Macaroni | 250 g |
| 25 g | Butter | 70 g |
| 100 g | Grated cheese | 250 g |
| ½ litre | Thin béchamel | 1½ litres |
| ½ teaspoon | Diluted English mustard | 1 teaspoon |
| | Milled salt | |
| | Milled pepper | |

1.  Boil the macaroni as for spaghetti italienne omitting the parmesan.
2.  After draining the pasta return to the clean dry pan with the butter and add half the grated cheese.
3.  Add the béchamel and mustard.
4.  Season with salt and pepper.
5.  Pour into a dish and sprinkle with remainder of grated cheese.
6.  Brown under a salamander and serve.

# Boiling of meats

### Introduction to boiled meats

Although we refer to boiled meats as a specific method of cookery, in reality, the actual boiling-point is only maintained for a matter of several minutes. The temperature is then lowered and kept below boiling-point till cooking is complete. If boiling-point is maintained throughout the cooking time, the connective tissues (collagen, an insoluble protein) will be turned into gelatine. This, together with the rapid movement of the cooking liquor, will break the fibres apart. The result can be a stringy, flavourless meat.

The skill required to produce a near perfect French-style boiled beef together with its attractive variety of vegetables (garnish) is as great as in any other classicial form of cookery. It demands much care and attention.

### Weights for portion control

When boiling meats allow 150 g per portion for meat off the bone and 250 g per portion for meat on the bone.

### Cooking times for boiled meats

Ham, gammon and tongue require 20 minutes per ½ kg and an extra 20 minutes at the end of cooking (20 minutes over).

Beef and mutton require 25 minutes per ½ kg and an extra 25 minutes at the end of cooking (25 minutes over).

| **Boiled beef English** | | *Boeuf bouilli à l'anglaise* |
|---|---|---|
| 600 g | Pickled beef off the bone | 1½ kg |
| 250 g | Boiled and glazed turned carrots | 650 kg |
| 4 | Small whole boiled onions | 10 |
| 8 | Small suet dumplings | 20 |
| | Finely chopped parsley | |
| | Diluted arrowroot | |

1. Place the meat into a pan of cold water, bring to the boil and simmer until cooked, allowing 25 minutes per ½ kg and 25 minutes over. Skim regularly to remove any surface scum.
2. Cook the garnish with the meat by adding the onions 30 minutes and the carrots 20 minutes before the meat is due to be ready.
3. Add the dumplings 15 minutes before the meat is finally cooked.
4. When cooked remove the garnish and meat from the liquor.
5. Slice the meat through the grain and lay on a hot service dish.
6. Surround with the garnish.

7. If required thicken the cooking liquor with a little diluted arrowroot.
8. Nap the cooking liquid over the meat, then brush the vegetables with a little melted butter.
9. Sprinkle the dish with finely chopped parsley.

**Boiled gammon**                                                   *Jambon bouilli*
**Boiled ham**

| | | |
|---|---|---|
| 600 g | Ham or gammon off the bone | 1½ kg |
| | Finely chopped parsley | |
| 3 dl | Parsley sauce | 7½ dl |

1. Note that ham and gammon have been soaked in brine and need to be soaked overnight in cold water.
2. To boil, start in fresh cold water. Simmer until cooked.
3. If required, thicken the cooking liquor with a little arrowroot before napping over the sliced meat.
4. Finish with finely chopped parsley.
5. Serve with a sauce-boat of parsley sauce.

**Boiled leg of mutton**                                            *Gigot de mouton*

| | | |
|---|---|---|
| 600 g | Mutton off the bone | 1½ kg |
| | Picked parsley | |
| 3 dl | Caper sauce | 7½ dl |
| | Bouquet garni | |
| 3 | Whole carrots | 6 |
| 2 | Whole onions | 6 |

1. Place the prepared meat into simmering salted water.
2. Bring back to the boil, skim and allow to simmer.
3. Add the whole carrots, onions and bouquet garni.
4. When the meat is cooked, remove and keep warm.
5. Strain the liquor and check the seasoning.
6. For service: slice the meat through the grain and serve with a little of the liquor.
7. Garnish with a sprig of picked parsley and accompany the meat with a sauce-boat of caper sauce.

# Boiled vegetables

### Introduction to boiled vegetables

Vegetables may be cooked in three mediums: water, acidulated water or a blanc. Acidulated water and blanc are used when vegetables need to be kept white. Vegetables grown above ground and frozen or dehydrated vegetables are started in a boiling medium. Vegetables grown below ground are started in cold water and brought gently to the boil and simmered until cooked.

When the vegetables are cooked they should be refreshed if they are not to be used straight away (see notes on blanching and refreshing). Vegetables should be cooked to a stage known as 'al dente', which is when the vegetables are cooked but still firm and slightly crisp.

Blanched and refreshed vegetables must be stored in the refrigerator until required.

Re-heating or 'rechauffing' of vegetables can be achieved by various methods of cooking, such as sauté or by dipping into a 'chauffant', a pan of boiling salted water.

Allow 500 g of vegetables to 4 people.
Allow 500 g of potatoes to 4 people.

**Note:** While all the recipes given include some form of accompaniment with each vegetable or potato dish, the vegetables and potatoes may all be plain boiled and served without any form of accompaniment; this is known as 'au naturel'.

### Boiled potato dishes

Allow 500 g of peeled potatoes to 4 portions.
Allow 1250 g of peeled potatoes to 10 portions.
Start old potatoes in cold water, new potatoes in boiling water.
Cooking time: 20–25 minutes from reaching boiling-point.

### Preparation of new potatoes                    *Pommes nouvelles*

1. Wash, lightly scrub and rinse.
2. Place into a pan of suitable size and cover with boiling salted water.
3. Simmer gently until cooked, about 20 minutes.
4. Drain and serve brushed with butter in a hot service dish.

### New potatoes with mint              *Pommes nouvelles à la menthe*

Cook and serve as above, with the addition of fresh mint to the water at the start of cooking.

Serve garnished with the addition of blanched mint leaves.

### Preparation of old potatoes                    *Pommes de terre*

1. Wash, peel and re-wash the potatoes.
2. Cut into even-sized pieces or turn into the required shape. This is to make sure of an even cooking.
3. Place in a pan of suitable size and cover with cold salted water.
4. Bring steadily to the boil and simmer for 20–30 minutes, until tender.
5. Drain and serve in a hot service dish brushed with melted butter or use

as required for any of the following recipes.

## Mashed potatoes *Pommes purées*

| | | |
|---|---|---|
| ½ dl | Hot milk | 1¼ dl |
| 30 g | Butter | 75 g |
| | Salt and white pepper to taste | |

1. Proceed as for the basic method up to stage 4.
2. Pass the potatoes through a ricer into a clean pan or mix in a food mixer.
3. Add the hot milk, seasoning and butter.
4. Serve in hot service dishes, either domed or quenelle shaped.

## Delmonico potatoes *Pommes delmonico*

| | | |
|---|---|---|
| 4 dl | Milk | 1 litre |
| 1 dl | Double cream | 2½ dl |
| 40 g | Fresh white breadcrumbs | 100 g |
| 40 g | Clarified butter | 100 g |

1. Cut the potatoes into 6 mm cubes.
2. Place into a pan of suitable size and almost cover with milk.
3. Season with salt and white pepper, bring to the boil and simmer for 40 minutes or until cooked.
4. Transfer to a suitable size oven-proof service dish and sprinkle the sieved fresh white breadcrumbs on top of the potatoes.
5. Pour on the clarified butter and brown in a hot oven or under a salamander.
6. Serve in the oven-proof dish on a hot flat with a dish paper.

## Duchesse potato mixture *Pommes duchesse*

| | | |
|---|---|---|
| 400 g | Peeled potatoes | 1 kg |
| 1 | Egg yolk | 3 |
| 25 g | Butter | 60 g |
| | Salt and pepper | |
| | Ground nutmeg to taste | |
| | Eggwash | |

1. Cut the peeled potatoes into pieces of an even size and place into cold salted water.
2. Bring them to boiling-point and simmer until cooked, 20–30 minutes.
3. Drain into a colander and return the potatoes to the pan.
4. Return to heat to evaporate any excess moisture.
5. Put the potatoes through a ricer into a clean hot pan.
6. Season, add a little ground nutmeg and the egg yolks, mixing in well, over a gentle heat. Add the butter.
7. Place the mixture into a piping bag with a large star nozzle and pipe spiral shapes 2 cm wide × 4 cm high on to lightly greased baking trays.
8. Place into a hot oven for 3–4 minutes, that is until the surface of the

duchesse potatoes has hardened.

9. Remove from the oven and brush lightly with a little eggwash.
10. Return to the oven to brown or finish under a salamander.
11. Allow 2 per portion and serve in a hot service dish garnished with picked parsley.

**Note:** The duchesse potato mixture has many other uses, e.g. as a border garnish for flats and dishes and as a base for other potato dishes.

## Asparagus spears
*Asperges en branche*

| 24 | Sticks of asparagus | 60 |
| 2 dl | Melted butter or hollandaise sauce | 5 dl |

1. Using the back of a knife gently scrape the stem towards the root end.
2. Wash the asparagus and tie into bundles of no more than 12 spears.
3. Plunge into gently boiling salted water and simmer for between 12 and 20 minutes, depending upon the age and thickness of the spears.
4. To test if cooked gently squeeze the middle of the spear; if tender then the spear is cooked.
5. Serve straight away, dressed in a folded napkin on a suitable service dish.
6. Serve accompanied with a sauce-boat of melted clarified butter or hollandaise sauce.

## Globe artichoke
*Artichaut en branche*

| 8 | Slices of lemon | 20 |
| 4 | Globe artichokes | 10 |

1. Cut the stems off the artichokes to the base, so that the artichoke sits flat.
2. Slice the top off the artichoke about 3 cm down from the tip.
3. Trim the rest of the leaves with scissors or a sharp knife.
4. Place a slice of lemon on the base and top of the globe artichokes and tie on with a piece of string.
5. Plunge the artichokes into a simmering blanc or acidulated water and simmer for 20–30 minutes until tender.
6. Refresh in cold running water.
7. When cold cut the string and remove the lemon.
8. Using a small spoon scoop out the centre of the artichoke and remove the choke, leaving the inside clean.
9. Replace the centre leaves upside down.
10. Réchauffe in a pan of boiling salted water for 3–5 minutes.
11. Drain well and serve on a napkin accompanied with a sauce-boat of hollandaise.

**Note:** The dish may be served cold with vinaigrette.

## Jerusalem artichokes with butter          *Topinambours au beurre*

| | | |
|---|---|---|
| 600 g | Jerusalem artichokes | 1½ kg |
| 25 g | Clarified butter | 60 g |
| | Finely chopped parsley | |

1. Wash, peel and re-wash the artichokes.
2. Cut as required.
3. Just cover with acidulated water.
4. Bring gently to the boil and simmer until just cooked, 10–15 minutes.
5. Drain well.
6. Place into a heated service dish, brush with clarified butter and sprinkle with finely chopped parsley.

## Broccoli with butter          *Brocolis au beurre*

| | | |
|---|---|---|
| 500 g | Broccoli | 1¼ kg |
| 1 dl | Clarified butter | 2 dl |

1. Prepare the broccoli by trimming off the excess leaves and the excess stem.
2. Plunge into boiling salted water and simmer until cooked al dente, 8–12 minutes.
3. Drain and serve brushed with clarified butter in a service dish.

## Broccoli with hollandaise          *Brocolis hollandaise*

| | | |
|---|---|---|
| 1 dl | Hollandaise sauce | 2 dl |

Proceed as for broccoli with butter, substitute for the butter the hollandaise sauce.

## Brussel sprouts with butter          *Choux de bruxelles au beurre*

| | | |
|---|---|---|
| 500 g | Brussel sprouts | 1¼ kg |
| 1 dl | Clarified butter | 2 dl |

1. Trim the sprouts by removing any decaying leaves.
2. Make a small cut in the base of each sprout and wash in cold water.
3. Plunge the sprouts into boiling salted water.
4. Bring back to the boil and simmer until cooked al dente, 5–10 minutes.
5. Drain well and place into a hot service dish.
6. Brush with clarified butter and serve.

## Cabbage with butter

*Chou au beurre*

| | | |
|---|---|---|
| **500 g** | **Cabbage** | **1¼ kg** |
| **1 dl** | **Clarified butter** | **2 dl** |
| | **Salt** | |
| | **White pepper** | |

1. Cut the cabbage into quarters, cut out the core and remove the outer leaves.
2. Shred the cabbage and wash under running water.
3. Plunge into boiling salted water and simmer until cooked, for about 10-15 minutes.
4. Drain in a colander and place back into the pan over heat to help excess liquid to evaporate.
5. Add the butter and seasoning, mix gently using a wooden spoon.
6. Serve in hot service dishes garnished with picked parsley.

## Spring cabbage

*Choux de printemps*

| | | |
|---|---|---|
| **500 g** | **Spring cabbage** | **1¼ kg** |
| **1 dl** | **Clarified butter** | **2 dl** |
| | **Salt** | |
| | **Pepper** | |

1. Trim the cabbage leaves from the stalks.
2. Roll and shred the leaves.
3. Wash under cold running water.
4. Place into a little boiling salted water and simmer until cooked, 8–12 minutes.
5. Drain in a colander and place back into a pan over heat to evaporate any excess water.
6. Add the butter and seasoning, mix gently using a wooden spoon.
7. Serve in a hot service dish.

## Buttered carrots

*Carottes glacées*
*Carottes au beurre*

| | | |
|---|---|---|
| **500 g** | **Carrots** | **1½ kg** |
| | **Salt, sugar (to taste)** | |
| **25 g** | **Butter** | **75 g** |
| | **Finely chopped parsley** | |

1. Wash, peel and re-wash the carrots.
2. Cut into neat, even pieces or turn barrel shape.
3. Place into a suitable size pan with the salt, sugar and butter.
4. Barely cover with cold water and a buttered paper, and bring to boiling-point.
5. Simmer until cooked and all the water has evaporated.
6. At this stage, allow the carrots to take on a glaze.

7.  Remove from the heat and serve in a suitable dish; sprinkle with chopped parsley.

## Mashed carrots

| 500 g | Carrots | 1¼ kg |
|---|---|---|
| 25 g | Butter | |
| | Salt and white pepper | |
| | Finely chopped parsley | |

1.  Wash, peel and re-wash the carrots.
2.  Cut into fairly small pieces.
3.  Place into a suitable saucepan and just cover with water.
4.  Add the salt and bring to the boil, simmer until cooked.
5.  Drain and pass through a drum sieve or blender.
6.  Return to a clean pan, re-heat and add the butter.
7.  Add the pepper and stir well with a wooden spoon.
8.  Serve in a suitable service dish either domed or in the form of quenelles.
9.  Sprinkle liberally with finely chopped parsley.

## Cauliflower with butter                    *Chou-fleur au beurre*

| 500 g | Cauliflower | 1¼ kg |
|---|---|---|
| 25 g | Butter | 60 g |
| | Finely chopped parsley | |

1.  Trim the length of the stem and remove the outer leaves.
2.  If the stem is thick, hollow out using a peeler.
3.  Wash in cold running water.
4.  Place into plenty of boiling salted water and simmer for 15–20 minutes.
5.  Drain and serve as required, either whole or divided into portions.
6.  Nap with butter and sprinkle with finely chopped parsley.

## French beans with butter                   *Haricots verts au beurre*

| 500 g | French beans | 1¼ kg |
|---|---|---|
| 25 g | Butter | 60 g |

1.  Top and tail the beans and wash well in cold running water.
2.  Plunge into boiling salted water and simmer until cooked al dente, 8–10 minutes.
3.  Drain well and serve in a hot service dish brushed with butter.

## Leeks with butter                          *Poireaux au beurre*

| 500 g | Leeks | 1¼ kg |
|---|---|---|
| 25 g | Butter | 60 g |

1. Trim and remove any discoloured leaves and trim the tops.
2. Shave the root lightly.
3. Split the leek lengthways, leaving the root intact, so as to hold the leek together.
4. Wash well under cold running water.
5. Tie into small bundles, folded in half, and plunge into boiling salted water.
6. Simmer until cooked al dente, about 12–18 minutes.
7. Strain well to remove all excess moisture.
8. Remove the string and set the neatly folded bundles of leek in hot service dishes.
9. Brush with butter and serve.

**Note:** Leeks may also be served as mornay or with cream sauce.

## Runner beans

| | | |
|---|---|---|
| **500 g** | **Runner beans** | **1¼ kg** |
| **25 g** | **Butter** | **60 g** |

1. Top and tail the beans, making sure to remove the string that runs down the length of the bean edges.
2. Rinse well in cold running water.
3. Slice the beans into diagonal strips and plunge into boiling salted water.
4. Simmer for 10–15 minutes until cooked.
5. Drain well and serve in a suitable hot service dish brushed with butter.

## Leaf spinach                                   *Épinards en branche*

| | | |
|---|---|---|
| **1 kg** | **Leaf spinach** | **2¼ kg** |
| **25 g** | **Butter** | **60 g** |

1. Strip the leaves from the stalks.
2. Wash the leaves in cold running water and plunge into boiling salted water.
3. Simmer for about 5–8 minutes until tender.
4. Refresh in cold water and squeeze into small balls, extracting as much moisture as possible.
5. To finish for service, melt the butter in a sauteuse and add the spinach.
6. Season with salt and pepper and mix in the pan with a fork until the spinach is heated through.
7. Serve in a suitable hot service dish.

## Spinach purée                                   *Épinards en purée*

1. Proceed as for stages 1 to 4 above.
2. Pass the spinach through a drum sieve or food blender to make into a smooth purée.

3. Season and re-heat as above stage 5.
4. Serve in a hot service dish either domed or formed into the shape of quenelles.

## Parsnips with butter                    *Panais au beurre*

| 50 g | Parsnips | 1¼ kg |
| 50 g | Butter | 100 g |
|      | Finely chopped parsley | |

1. Wash, peel and re-wash the parsnips.
2. Cut the parsnips into four lengthways.
3. If required cut the parsnips into smaller pieces.
4. Place into pan and just cover with cold salted water.
5. Bring to the boil and simmer for 15–25 minutes.
6. Drain well and serve in hot service dishes brushed with butter and sprinkled liberally with finely chopped parsley.

**Note:** Parsnips may be served bound with cream sauce or parsley sauce or puréed.

## Swede with butter                       *Rutabaga au beurre*
## Turnip with butter                      *Navets au beurre*

| 500 g | Swede or turnip | 1¼ kg |
| 50 g | Butter | 125 g |
|      | Finely chopped parsley | |

1. Wash and trim the ends of the swede to give flat surfaces.
2. Peel the outer skin using a sharp knife.
3. Cut the swede to the required shape, e.g. batons, cubes or turned barrel shape.
4. Cook and serve as for buttered carrots.

## Sweetcorn                                          *Maïs*

There are three forms of sweetcorn available:

1. Corn on the cob.
2. Baby sweetcorn.
3. Sweetcorn niblets — frozen or tinned.

### Corn on the cob

Allow 1 cob per portion with 50 g of butter.

1. Remove the outer leaves and husk.
2. Rinse in cold running water and trim the ends as required.

3. Plunge into boiling salted water and simmer until tender, approximately 12–20 minutes.
4. Drain well and serve with a sauce-boat of melted butter.

### Baby sweetcorn

| | | |
|---|---|---|
| 400 g | **Baby sweetcorn** | 1 kg |
| 50 g | **Butter** | 125 g |

1. Rinse the corn under cold running water.
2. Plunge into boiling salted water.
3. Simmer until tender, about 8–12 minutes.
4. Drain and serve in a hot service dish, nap with melted butter.

**Note:** Baby sweetcorn may also be served mixed with warm double cream.

### Dried pulses

| | | |
|---|---|---|
| 250 g | **Dried pulses** | 650 g |

1. Soak the dried pulses overnight in cold water.
2. Drain and rinse thoroughly under cold running water.
3. Cover with fresh cold salted water, bring gently to the boil and simmer for 1½–2 hours until tender.
4. Drain well and serve as required.

Examples of dried pulses: butter beans, haricot beans, green kidney beans, red kidney beans, lentils, chick peas, marrowfat peas.
   Marrowfat peas need cooking for between 45 minutes and 1 hour and should be allowed to fall, as in a rough purée.

### Humous

| | | |
|---|---|---|
| 260 g | **Chick peas** | 650 g |
| 1–2 | **Cloves of garlic** | 2–3 |
| 1½ dl | **Half-whipped cream or plain yoghurt** | 4 dl |
| | **Juice of fresh lemon to taste** | |
| | **Salt and white pepper** | |
| | **Finely chopped parsley** | |
| | **Paprika** | |

1. Soak the chick peas overnight in cold water.
2. Rinse the chick peas under cold running water and place into a saucepan.
3. Re-cover with fresh cold water and add the crushed garlic.
4. Bring quickly to the boil and skim to remove surface scum.
5. Reduce the heat and simmer for 45 minutes or until the chick peas are tender, adding more water during cooking if required.

6. Drain the peas when cooked, purée to a smooth paste and allow to go cold.
7. When cold mix in the half-whipped cream or yoghurt and season.
8. Mix in the finely chopped parsley and lemon juice to taste.
9. Serve in a pot, sprinkled with paprika.

**Note:** Serve with hot toast or granary bread. May also be used as a dip or spread.

# Boiled pâtisserie dishes  *Pâtisserie bouilli*

## Introduction to boiled pâtisserie

This section deals with the basic preparation and finishing of sweet dishes which use boiling as their predominant method of cookery. Bavarois are light cream and milk dishes flavoured in various ways and set with gelatine. They are often used as the base for dishes, examples of which follow the basic recipe.

**Bavarois, basic mixture**

| 570 ml | Fresh milk | 1 litre 140 ml |
|---|---|---|
| 4 | Eggs | 8 |
| 115 g | Castor sugar | 230 g |
| 30 g | Leaf gelatine (soak in cold water) | 60 g |
| | *or* | |
| 30 g | Powdered gelatine | 60 g |
| 285 ml | Fresh cream | 570 ml |

1. Whisk the egg yolks and castor sugar together in a bowl.
2. Bring the milk to boiling-point, pour on to the yolk/sugar mixture and stir well.
3. Return to the pan and cook carefully over moderate heat until the mixture coats the back of the spoon.
4. Be careful at this stage to avoid the mixture boiling, otherwise it will curdle.
5. Remove from the heat and stir in the gelatine. In the case of leaf gelatine, squeeze out the surplus water first.
6. Stir until melted and strain through a fine strainer into a clean bowl.
7. Allow to cool in the refrigerator, stir occasionally.
8. Just on setting-point, carefully fold in the whipped cream and pour into suitable moulds.
9. The mixture may be lightened in texture with the addition of the egg whites whisked to a firm snow and folded in at the end.
10. Bavarois can be made in single flavourings, i.e. vanilla, coffee, chocolate, etc.

## Variations of bavarois

*Vanilla*: With the addition of a vanilla pod or a few spots of vanilla essence to the milk when heating.

*Chocolate*: With the addition of 85 g of grated plain chocolate (or 170 g) to the milk when heating. A few spots of chocolate colour will help to brighten the finished texture.

*Coffee*: With the addition of a small spoonful of soluble coffee granules (to taste) to the heated milk.

*Lemon*: With an infusion of lemon rind when heating the milk (which should be removed when straining the mixture).

*Orange*: As for lemon. The finished bavarois can be dressed with prepared orange segments if desired.

*Praline*: With the addition of 60–85 g of crushed praline to the basic mixture. Fold in at the cream stage. The larger formula will require approximately 150 g.

## Royal bavarois                                           *Bavarois royale*

1. Line (chemise) a round timbale mould with red jelly 5 mm thick on bottom and sides. Allow to set off in the refrigerator.
2. Line again with thin slices of swiss roll (mini swiss rolls are quite nice for this task).
3. Fill the mould with vanilla flavoured bavarois, and then set firm in the refrigerator.
4. For service: unmould and decorate around the base with a border of whipped cream.
5. The lined mould(s) may also be filled with a strawberry bavarois if desired, such as *charlotte aux fraises royale*.

## Charlotte russe

1. Line the charlotte mould with biscuits à la cuillère on the bottom and sides. The base biscuits should be trimmed fan shaped with pointed ends to fit neatly into the round base of the mould with the points towards the centre in the form of a rosette. The side biscuits should be trimmed to fit closely with the rounded biscuit surface facing the mould.
2. Fill with vanilla bavarois and allow to set off in the refrigerator.
3. Serve on a doily-covered round silver dish.

**Note:** the bavarois filling may be alternated with other flavours such as strawberry or raspberry. The name is changed accordingly: *charlotte russe aux fraises*, or *charlotte russe aux framboises*.

## Choux paste

| | | |
|---|---|---|
| 140 ml | Cold water | 700 ml |
| 56 g | Butter | 225 g |
| pinch | Salt | 15 g |
| pinch | Castor sugar | 15 g |
| 85 g | Strong flour | 350 g |
| 2–3 (approx.) | Eggs | 8–18 (approx.) |

1. Bring the water with the butter, salt and sugar to the boil.
2. Sieve the flour and when the butter and water have completely amalgamated, stir in the flour.
3. Cook (stirring with a wooden spatula) until the mixture leaves the sides of the pan.
4. Remove from the heat and allow to cool slightly.
5. Gradually beat in the eggs singly to a smooth texture. The paste should be of a firm piping consistency.

This mixture may be used for cream buns by piping the choux paste through a coarse star nozzle; also for éclairs, profiteroles, beignets soufflés (sweet and savoury) and spritzkuchen.

The correct consistency is of great importance, hence the flexibility in the egg content. If too slack, the piped shapes will tend to flow and lose their volume. Once the items have gone into the oven at the correct heat, no attempt should be made to open the oven door before they have had time to rise and set firm. The baking temperature is 215°C for about 20 minutes.

Other types of fat can be used, such as margarine, but butter produces a quality paste.

**Note**: For wholewheat choux paste, see page 78.

## Tom pouce filling

| | | |
|---|---|---|
| 250 ml (¼ litre) | Milk | 1 litre |
| 4 | Eggs | 16 |
| 170 g | Castor sugar | 680 g |
| 6 sheets | Leaf gelatine (soaked in cold water) | 24 sheets |
| 250 ml (¼ litre) | Double cream | 1 litre |
| 1 | Vanilla pod *or* | 1 |
| 4 spots | Vanilla essence | 16 spots |

1. Soak the leaf gelatine in cold water until soft.
2. Separate the eggs and beat the yolks with the sugar.
3. Bring the milk to boiling-point with the vanilla pod (if pod is used remove at this stage) and pour the hot milk on to the yolks and sugar mixture.
4. Return to the heat and cook gently until the mixture coats the back of the spoon. Do not allow to boil.

5. Remove from the heat and add the gelatine (squeezed out), stir until dissolved.
6. Pass through a conical strainer into a clean bowl and place in the refrigerator to cool. Stir occasionally and on setting-point fold in the lightly whipped cream.
7. Allow the filling to set off fairly well before using to sandwich the sheets of puff pastry.

## Pastry cream                                         *Crème pâtissière*

| | | |
|---|---|---|
| 75 g | Castor sugar | 150 g |
| 20 g | Cornflour | 40 g |
| 20 g | Flour | 40 g |
| 750 ml | Milk | 1½ litres |
| 6 | Egg yolks | 12 |
| 50 g | Butter | 100 g |
| 6 spots | Vanilla essence (or vanilla pod) | 12 spots |

1. Make a paste with a little of the milk, flour and cornflour.
2. Bring the remaining milk to boiling-point with the vanilla pod (or vanilla essence) and the sugar.
3. Remove pod if used, pour on to the flour mixture and whisk smoothly.
4. Return to the pan and bring carefully to the boil. Stir continuously.
5. Allow to cook gently for a few minutes and then remove from the heat.
6. Whisk in the egg yolks and pass through a conical strainer into a clean receptacle.
7. Add the butter and allow to cool.
8. Keep covered with a buttered greaseproof paper to prevent the cream skinning over.

## Filling for Danish pastries

| | | |
|---|---|---|
| 285 ml | Milk | 570 ml |
| 85 g | Castor sugar | 170 g |
| 45 g | Cornflour (diluted with 30–60 ml milk) | 90 g |
| 3 | Egg yolks | 6 |
| 1 | Vanilla pod | 1 |
| | *or* | |
| 6 spots | Vanilla essence | 12 spots |

1. Make a smooth paste with the cornflour and a little of the milk.
2. Bring the remaining milk to the boil with the vanilla pod or essence.
3. Whisk the egg yolks and sugar together and whisk in the hot milk.
4. Return mixture to the pan and add the diluted cornflour.
5. Stirring all the time, bring to boiling-point and cook out for 2 minutes.
6. Remove from the heat then pour into a basin. Cover with buttered paper.

## Apple conserve

| 450 g | Prepared cooking apple | 900 g |
|---|---|---|
| | (peeled, cored and sliced thinly) | |
| 60 g | Butter | 120 g |
| 85 g | Castor sugar | 170 g |
| 60 g | Apricot jam | 120 g |
| 1 | Lemon, juice of | 2 |

1. Use a thick-bottomed pan. Melt the butter, add the sugar and carefully cook to a nice golden colour.
2. Stir in the sliced apple, add the lemon juice and cook under cover until the apple falls into a soft mass.
3. Blend in the apricot jam and keep in a basin, covered. Use as required. Will keep for several days in refrigeration.

## Fresh egg custard sauce

| 5 dl | Milk | 1 litre |
|---|---|---|
| 50 g | Castor sugar | 100 g |
| 4 | Egg yolks | 8 |
| 2 drops | Vanilla essence | 4 drops |

1. Thoroughly mix together the egg yolks, sugar and vanilla essence in a stainless steel bowl of a size large enough to hold the volume of sauce being made.
2. Boil the milk and then whisk on to the egg mixture.
3. Pour into a thick-based pan of suitable size for the volume of sauce.
4. Place over a moderate heat and stir with a wooden spoon until the sauce has thickened to a stage where it coats the back of the spoon. On no account allow the sauce to boil as it will split.
5. Strain the sauce through a fine sieve into a clean pan.

## Chocolate sauce I                                    *Sauce chocolat*

| *1 litre* | | *5 litres* |
|---|---|---|
| 500 g | Grated plain chocolate | 2½ kg |
| 7 dl | Water or milk | 3½ litres |
| 125 g | Castor sugar | 600 g |
| 1 dl | Single cream | 5 dl |

1. Select a pan of suitable size for the volume of sauce being made and add the water or milk, sugar and grated chocolate.
2. Bring gently to the boil and simmer for 20–30 minutes.
3. Pour in the cream, stirring with a wooden spoon.

## Chocolate sauce II  *Sauce chocolat*

| *1 litre* | | *5 litres* |
|---|---|---|
| 8 dl | Thin béchamel | 4 litres |
| 125 g | Castor sugar | 600 g |
| 500 g | Grated chocolate | 2½ kg |
| 1 dl | Single cream | 5 dl |

1. Boil the béchamel in a pan of suitable size for the volume of sauce being made.
2. Add the grated chocolate and simmer for 15–25 minutes.
3. Add the single cream stirring in with a wooden spoon.
4. Serve hot.

## Lemon sauce  *Sauce au citron*

| 5 dl | Water | 1 litre |
|---|---|---|
| 2 | Fresh lemons | 4 |
| 100 g | Castor sugar | 200 g |
| 20 g | Arrowroot | 40 g |

## Orange sauce  *Sauce à l'orange*

| 5 dl | Water | 1 litre |
|---|---|---|
| 2 | Fresh oranges | 4 |
| 100 g | Castor sugar | 200 g |
| 20 g | Arrowroot | 40 g |

1. Select a thick-based pan of suitable size for the volume of sauce being made.
2. Add the water and sugar and bring it to the boil until the sugar is dissolved.
3. Remove the zest from the fruit and cut into a very fine julienne. Blanch in boiling water.
4. Squeeze the juice from the fruit and place on one side.
5. Mix the arrowroot to a smooth paste with a little cold water and pour into the boiling syrup, stirring all the time until the sauce has thickened.
6. Pass the sauce into a clean pan through a fine chinois.
7. Add the prepared fruit zest and juice.

Served mainly with steamed puddings.

## Melba sauce I  *Sauce melba I*

| 1 kg | Raspberries | 2 kg |
|---|---|---|
| 400 g | Icing sugar | 800 g |
| | Lemon juice | |

1. Pass the raspberries and icing sugar through a fine sieve to produce a smooth sauce.
2. Add a few drops of lemon juice to taste.

## Melba sauce II                                   *Sauce melba II*

| 800 g | Raspberries | 1600 g |
|-------|-------------|--------|
| 2½ dl | Water | 5 dl |
| 200 g | Castor sugar | 400 g |

1. Place all ingredients into a pan of suitable size for the volume of sauce being made.
2. Bring to the boil and simmer for 5 minutes.
3. Pass through a fine sieve.

If necessary thicken with a small amount of diluted arrowroot.

## Apricot sauce                                      *Sauce abricot*

| 400 g | Apricot jam | 800 g |
|-------|-------------|-------|
| 20 g | Arrowroot | 40 g |
| 2 dl | Water | 4 dl |

## Red jam sauce

| 400 g | Strawberry or raspberry jam | 800 g |
|-------|------------------------------|-------|
| 20 g | Arrowroot | 40 g |
| 2 dl | Water | 4 dl |

1. Select a thick-based pan of suitable size for the volume of sauce being made.
2. Add the jam and water, bring to the boil and dissolve the jam in the water.
3. Mix the arrowroot to a smooth paste with a little water and mix into the boiling sauce.
4. Stir with a wooden spoon until the sauce has cleared and finished thickening.
5. Pass the sauce through a fine chinois into a clean pan or double boiler.

## Apricot glaze

Allow 1 kg of apricot jam to 250 g of water.

1. Select a pan of suitable size for the volume of sauce being made.
2. Add the jam and water, bring to the boil and strain through a chinois into a clean pan.
3. Should the sauce need adjusting with either more jam or water, repeat the procedure from stage one.

A red glaze may also be made using this method. Substitute strawberry or red fruit jam for apricot.

## Bun wash

Allow equal quantities of castor sugar and water, e.g. 1 kg of sugar to 1 kg of water.

1. Place into a pan of suitable size for the volume of bun wash being made.
2. Boil together until a pale syrup has developed.

## Soaking syrup for savarin dough

| ½ litre | Water | 2 litres |
|---|---|---|
| 350 g | Castor sugar | 1½ kg |
| ½ | Cinnamon stick | 2 |
| 4 | Cloves | 12 |
| 6 | Coriander seeds | 20 |
| 1 | Orange zest and juice | 4 |
| 1 | Lemon zest and juice | 4 |

1. Select a pan of suitable size for the volume of syrup being produced.
2. Add the water and sugar and bring to the boil.
3. Add the rest of the ingredients and re-boil, allow to simmer for at least 15 minutes before using.
4. Strain the syrup and use for soaking cooked savarin rings, marignans, babas or other products made using savarin dough.

### *Boiled sugar*

### Stages of cooking:

| | |
|---|---|
| 102°C | The small thread |
| 105°C | The large thread |
| 113°C | The small ball |
| 120°C | The large ball |
| 140°C | The small crack |
| 157°C | The large crack |
| 182°C | Caramel |

As soon as the sugar solution begins to thicken in boiling, it is a definite sign that almost all of the water has been driven off. At this stage it is important to wash down the sides of the pan to remove any crystallized sugar.

Once the sugar reaches this degree of cooking, the various stages approach in rapid succession. A sugar boiling thermometer is indispensable, especially for the beginner. There are various 'hand tests' which can be applied. First immerse the forefinger and thumb in a bowl of iced water, then into the boiling sugar solution and back immediately *into the iced water*. The utmost speed is essential.

At the *small thread* stage, a spot of sugar solution held as described between the finger and thumb will form small strings.

At the *large thread stage,* the sugar strands become much stronger, and so on to the *small ball* and *large ball* stages when the sugar forms a kind of soft ball or hard ball accordingly. Thereafter, the sugar passes through various stages to the *large crack.* At this point a thread of sugar will crack between the teeth like glass. This is the final stage before the sugar rapidly turns to *caramel.* To check the cooking it is essential to immerse the base of the pan in very cold water.

For pulled sugar work use the following recipe.

## Pulled sugar work

| | |
|---|---|
| 500 g | Cube sugar |
| 100 ml | Water |
| 1 tablespoon | Liquid glucose |
| ½ | Lemon, juice only |

1. Place the sugar and water into a copper sugar boiling pan.
2. Bring to the boil and wash down the sides of the pan with a clean pastry brush dipped into warm water. Remove any scum as it arises using a metal spoon.
3. Cook the sugar to 154°C (hard crack) but add the glucose when the solution reaches 115°C and both the sugar and glucose are at the same consistency. Shake in the lemon juice at the end.
4. When cooked, cool immediately in cold water and then pour the solution out on to an oiled marble slab.
5. Add any colouring at this stage.
6. Using an oiled palette knife, turn in the edges of the sugar 'pool' towards the centre. As soon as the mass achieves suitable consistency, commence pulling and folding inwards towards the middle.
7. The sugar will soon take on a brilliant sheen. Note that it is important not to overpull the mass.
8. At this stage it is ready for weaving on to a basket frame or the making of leaves and flowers and other decorative items.
9. Any surplus sugar is kept malleable at the mouth of a warm oven or under a lamp.
10. Pulled sugar work requires a good deal of practice and close attention to the formation of flowers and other models. Initially, it is just enough to get the feel of the sugar and develop confidence.

## Dipped fruits

Stuffed dates (with marzipan filling), prepared orange segments, black and green grapes, and glacé cherry halves or walnut halves stuffed with marzipan are all suitable for dipping into boiled sugar.

Boil the sugar solution as above to 154°C following all the usual precautions to prevent crystallization. Carefully dip each item separately and place to dry on an oiled tray.

As with spun sugar, such fruits will not keep indefinitely and in any case should be kept in a warm dry atmosphere prior to service. When set, place each one into a petit-four case.

Sugar items for preservation, such as sugar baskets, fruits and flowers, will need to be kept in an airtight glass case or similar receptacle in which some silica gel (obtainable from the chemist) has been placed. Slaked lime can also be used although silica is more easily managed. Both work on the principle of extracting moisture from the surrounding environment and thus keep the sugar item 'dry'.

## Praline

| 230 g | Granulated sugar | 460 g |
| 230 g | Skinned almonds | 460 g |
| ½ | Lemon (juice only) | 1 |

1. Use a copper sugar boiler.
2. Add the sugar and lemon juice and cook over moderate heat until the sugar has melted.
3. Meanwhile, warm the almonds in the oven.
4. Raise the heat under the sugar and cook to a pale amber in colour. A deeper colour will give a stronger flavour.
5. Stir in the warmed almonds and remove from the heat.
6. Turn out the mixture on to an oiled marble slab and, using an oiled palette knife, turn the mixture over a few times.
7. Allow to go cold and set hard before breaking up and crushing to a fine powder with a heavy rolling pin.
8. Keep in an airtight container for future use.

**Note**: Crushed praline is a delicious flavouring for buttercreams, iced confections and gâteaux.

## Stock syrup

| 250 g | Granulated sugar | 500 g |
| 500 ml (½ litre) | Water | 1000 ml (1 litre) |

1. Bring the sugar and water to the boil and simmer until the sugar crystals are dissolved.
2. Carefully skim off any scum with a metal spoon.
3. Pour the syrup through a clean muslin into a suitable container and use as required.

**Note**: Stock syrup is always in demand in the pastry section and for this reason is part of the basic mise en place. It is used for a variety of items. The following are a few examples:

(a) thinning down fondant;

(b) splashing on torten and gâteaux bases;
(c) as a foundation syrup for fresh fruit salad;
(d) thinning down apricot jam for making an apricot glaze.

Keep covered when not in use and make frequently as part of the daily routine.

# Rice puddings

## Rice condé                                    *Riz condé*

| | | |
|---|---|---|
| 570 ml | Fresh milk | 1 litre 140 ml |
| 85 g | Carolina rice | 170 g |
| 2 | Egg yolks | 4 |
| 6 | Spots vanilla essence | 12 |
| | *or* vanilla pod | |
| 60 g | Castor sugar | 120 g |
| 140 ml | Fresh cream | 285 ml |

1. Bring the milk to the boil and add the well-washed rice.
2. Stir carefully into the boiling milk to prevent sticking on the bottom of the pan.
3. Add the sugar, vanilla (pod or essence) and cook gently under cover until the bulk of the milk is absorbed. Remove from the heat.
4. Beat in the egg yolks and allow the mixture to cool.
5. Fold in the whipped cream and pour the mixture into buttered flan rings (or other suitable shape) and spread level.
6. Allow to set in the refrigerator.
7. Meanwhile, prepare the chosen fruit, e.g. halved or quartered pears, apricot halves, pineapple slices or banana slices (the latter sprinkled with lemon juice to avoid discoloration).
8. Arrange the fruit neatly over the base, then glaze using the syrup from the fruit (or apricot glaze). Bring to the boil and thicken with diluted fécule (arrowroot); add a little granulated sugar whilst boiling to improve the clearness of the glaze.
9. In the case of fresh banana, always use boiling apricot.
10. If tinned fruit is being used, it should be well drained and dried on a clean kitchen cloth.
11. Allow to cool thoroughly before removing the ring and decorating with whipped cream, glacé cherries and diamonds of angelica.

**Note:** Alternatively, the condé may be put into individual dariole moulds or a large charlotte mould and set off in the refrigerator. Unmould on to a suitable dish or single plate, etc. and decorate as above.

The base of the moulds can be lined with jelly prior to filling (and set off); the individual condé may also be accompanied by a suitable sauce such as raspberry or apricot.

## Imperial rice                                     *Riz à l'impératrice*

Use the above recipe for rice condé and add an equal quantity of vanilla flavoured bavarois and a quantity of diced crystallized fruits (60 g small recipe; 120 g large amount).

1. Set a layer of red jelly in the bottom of some charlotte moulds.
2. Meanwhile, prepare the vanilla bavarois (see page 143) and the rice condé.
3. When the bavarois is on setting-point, fold into the prepared rice together with the crystallized fruits and fill up the moulds.
4. Place into the refrigerator to set.
5. Layer the base of a round dish with red jelly and set off.
6. For service, dip the mould(s) into hot water for 2–3 seconds and wipe dry. Shake gently to loosen and turn out on to the dish.
7. Decorate around the base perimeter with whipped cream.

## Rice pudding                                       *Pouding au riz*

| | | |
|---|---|---|
| 70 g | Carolina rice | 280 g |
| 70 g | Castor sugar | 280 g |
| 4 | Spots vanilla essence | ½ coffeespoonful |
| | *or* | |
| 1 | Vanilla pod | 1 |
| 15 g | Butter | 60 g |
| 600 ml | Milk | 2 litres 280 ml |

1. Bring the milk to the boil with the vanilla pod, then remove the pod.
2. Sprinkle in the washed rice and stir well to prevent sticking on the bottom of the pan.
3. Add the sugar and cook for 25–30 minutes until tender.
4. Flavour with vanilla essence (if used).
5. Pour into buttered pie dishes.
6. Add a little grated nutmeg on top, together with a knob of butter and brown lightly under a hot salamander.
7. Serve on a doily covered silver flat and wrap a pie collar around the dish.

**Note:** This method and recipe applies to pearl tapioca, macaroni, semolina, sago and ground rice, etc. A little fresh cream (single type), approximately 100 ml for the small recipe and 400 ml for the large amount, together with one or two egg yolks, can be beaten in before the browning stage. The cream and yolk(s) will help to enrich the finished pudding.

# Savouries

These dishes are commonly used as starters on menus or as snacks at receptions. They are also often found on buffet tables.

### Ham on toast                                    *Canapé yorkaise*

| | | |
|---|---|---|
| 150 g | Slices of boiled ham | 375 g |
| 2 dl | Thick béchamel sauce | 5 dl |
| 120 g | Butter | 25 g |
| 2 | Slices of toast | 5 |
| | Cayenne pepper | |

1. Cut 8 diamonds from the boiled ham.
2. Cut the remaining ham into brunoise and add to the hot béchamel sauce.
3. Simmer for 3–4 minutes and season with salt and cayenne.
4. Cut 2 round discs out of each slice of toast and butter.
5. Dome with the ham and béchamel mixture.
6. Top each canapé yorkaise with a ham diamond.
7. Serve on a hot flat with a dish paper and picked parsley.

### Ham and pickled walnuts on toast                *Croute Derby*

| | | |
|---|---|---|
| 100 g | Brunoise of cooked ham | 250 g |
| 1 dl | Thick béchamel | 2½ dl |
| 2 | Pickled walnuts | 5 |
| 10 g | Butter | 25 g |
| 2 | Slices of hot toast | 5 |
| | Cayenne pepper | |

1. Boil the sauce and add the brunoise of ham.
2. Simmer and season with salt and cayenne pepper.
3. Cut two round discs out of each slice of toast.
4. Dome with the ham filling and top with a slice of pickled walnut.
5. Serve on a hot flat with a dish paper and picked parlsey.

### Welsh rarebit

| | | |
|---|---|---|
| 150 g | Grated cheddar cheese | 375 g |
| 15 g | Plain flour | 35 g |
| 1 | Egg yolks | 2 |
| | Worcester sauce | |
| 25 g | Margarine | 60 g |
| 1 dl | Milk | 2½ dl |
| 4 | Tablespoons of beer | 10 |
| | English mustard | |
| 10 g | Butter | 25 g |
| 2 | Slices of toast | 5 |

1. Slowly melt the margarine in a saucepan, add the flour and stir in with a wooden spoon.
2. Cook out over a low heat for 3–4 minutes, do not allow to colour.
3. Add the milk a little at a time and mix to a very smooth sauce.
4. Simmer the sauce for 2–3 minutes and add the cheese.
5. Simmer for a further 3–4 minutes to melt the cheese.
6. Remove from the heat and allow to cool slightly.
7. Stir in the egg yolk.
8. In a separate pan, bring the beer to the boil and reduce until almost evaporated.
9. Add to the main mixture.
10. Add Worcester sauce and mustard to taste.
11. Butter the toast and spread on the mixture.
12. Cut the slices into 4 rectangles with crusts removed.
13. Place on a clean baking sheet and finish under a salamander until a golden brown colour.
14. Serve on a hot flat with a dish paper and picked parsley.

# Chapter 4
# Poaching                    *Pocher*

## The competency defined

The process of poaching can be described as the cooking of foods in the minimum amount of liquid (stock, syrup or milk), which, in most instances, remains just below boiling-point, i.e. at a stage referred to as simmering. Initially, items may, according to circumstances, be brought to boiling-point, after which the heat source is reduced and the poaching process commences. The temperature for poaching foods is 93–95°C (199–203°F).

## Reasons for poaching

The purposes of poaching as a food process are:

1. to cook the food item so that it becomes easily digested;
2. to produce food of a tender (and nutritious) texture and quality;
3. to render food safer to eat;
4. to ensure the food is pleasing to the eye and the palate.

## Methods of poaching

Poaching can be separated into two categories: shallow and deep.

Foods which are usually processed by the shallow method are cuts of chicken such as suprêmes (whole breasts), which are gently simmered in a well-flavoured chicken stock. Several cuts of fish are also shallow poached by the oven method. Folded fillets or paupiettes are barely covered with fish stock and a buttered paper; the cooking process is then completed in the oven set at about 180°C (356°F).

Forcemeat of chicken, fish or veal (quenelles) may also be poached in shallow stock. When poaching fish or chicken, the stock is never thickened during the poaching process. Instead, the cooking liquor is usually reduced to intensify the flavour, after which it is used to make any accompanying sauce. Sometimes, such stock, because of its succulence, is reduced down to a glaze and reserved as an essence with which to enhance other sauces as

157

required.

During the shallow poaching process, many foods (especially fish) are only partially covered with stock (not submerged), and because of this a cover or lid is required. This applies to items exposed to oven heat. In other cases, all that is needed is a cartouche, i.e. a sheet of buttered greaseproof paper which is torn or cut to fit the surface of the pan or dish. Such a covering ensures that there is an even distribution of heat during cooking and that the item does not dry out. This precaution applies especially when 'oven poaching'.

Deep poaching is generally used when poaching eggs; these are poached in 8–10 cm (3–4 in.) of simmering salted/acidulated water. Other examples of deep poaching are whole fruits such as apples or pears. In Britain, the term boiling is commonly used to describe what the French refer to as poaching. We describe menu items as boiled cod, or turbot, boiled salmon or boiled chicken, whereas in France such items would be refered to as poached in each and every case.

Products such as whole chicken and whole fish, such as salmon or turbot, are completely covered with cold liquid before being brought to boiling-point, and are then allowed to simmer gently until the cooking process is complete.

Conversely, cuts of meat and fish are placed into gently simmering liquid, and then poached until cooked.

# Organisation and preparation for poaching

In a full kitchen brigade, the following specialists would be involved in the poaching or preparation of foods for poaching:

| | |
|---|---|
| *Chef garde-manger* | Responsible for the intitial preparation of foods. |
| *Chef poissonnier:* | The poaching of all fish dishes and fish sauces. |
| *Chef saucier:* | The cooking and presentation of all entrées, such as poulet poché au riz, sauce suprême. |
| *Chef pâtissier:* | Poached fruits, gnocchi parisienne, rice-based dishes, such as riz condé and oeufs à la neige. |

For a fast and efficient service some foods, especially eggs, may be poached in advance and then carefully refreshed in cold water. The poached eggs are then held in water in the refrigerator until the time of service. The eggs are re-heated in gently simmering salted water as required. Much care must be exercised in the first instance not to over-cook the eggs prior to refreshing, otherwise the result will be a hard yolk and rubbery white.

Before placing the poached foods which are to be covered with a sauce on to the serving dish, the base of the dish should be lightly coated with a small amount of sauce; this will help to prevent the item sticking to the dish when being served.

When poaching fruits such as for a fruit compote, the fruit is covered with a hot stock syrup and then brought back to boiling-point, after which the pan is immediately removed from the direct heat. The surface is covered with a cartouche and the item is then allowed to poach gently. The benefit of the cartouche is two-fold. Firstly, it prevents excess evaporation of the cooking liquor (syrup), and secondly, it will help to keep the fruit items submerged beneath the syrup whilst cooking. The latter will ensure evenly poached fruit and also prevent fruit discoloration.

# Advantages of poaching

From a health point of view, poaching is an ideal method of food preparation. It renders many foods both succulent and nourishing and ensures that they are easily digestible for persons who are on a light diet (and one which is possibly fat free). It is a process which requires no fat or oil to be added to the food, and salt may be omitted from the cooking liquor if necessary. The result is a fat- and salt-free method of food preparation. In that sense, it is eminently suited to catering for persons with poor digestive systems such as the elderly, patients in hospitals, or those on low calorie diets.

# Effects of poaching on foods

Poached foods are cooked for the minimum amount of time and with much care in order to preserve the natural flavour and nutritional content of the items being prepared. Over-fast cooking will result in loss of shape in the form of shrinkage and a tough, dry and unpalatable product, and, of course, a loss of flavour and nutrients.

The poaching of food helps to make tender the fibres in the food's structural make-up, and in so doing, the texture of the food is rendered more edible.

# General rules for efficient poaching

1. During the poaching process, most foods should be covered completely by liquid throughout the cookery process. However, in the case of poached fish fillets, the fish is *barely* covered by fish stock, wine or milk, and is finished in the oven.

2. Whole food items such as fish, chicken and fruits should be started in cold liquid, then brought to boiling-point, after which they are allowed to simmer gently until cooked.

3. Cuts of fish, chicken and fruits should be started in gently simmering liquids, and allowed to continue simmering gently until cooked.
4. When poaching eggs, they should be added to the gently simmering acidulated water (i.e. water with added vinegar) one at a time, with the shallow pan tilted slightly; this will allow the egg to form a round shape.
5. The temperature of the cooking liquor must be carefully controlled so that it does not boil but only simmers gently.
6. Always make sure that foods are cooked through before removal from the liquid. The many types and quality of foodstuffs will affect the cooking times needed to ensure successful poaching of food items.

# General safety rules

1. Always make sure that you select a suitable size pan to prevent liquids spilling over, with the resulting possibility of scalding oneself or fellow workers.
2. Be most careful when moving pans which are being used for poaching, especially when they are full of hot liquid; tilting or jarring of such an item can result in spillage and the possibility of an accident.
3. Always add food items to the liquid in a careful and gentle manner to prevent splashing.
4. When removing a hot container from the oven to the table, always sprinkle the handle with flour so that other workmates are aware that it is a very hot dish!

# Techniques associated with poaching

There are many skills and techniques involved when preparing foods for poaching and when actually using the poaching process.

1. *Cutting and tying*: Certain foods need to be cut into even pieces and then tied to assist with retaining their shape; poached cod steaks are an example. Tying will also make certain foods easier to handle.
2. *Folding*: Foods such as fillets of fish are given a more pleasing appearance and made easier to handle when folded.
3. *Drying*: This process is carried out after certain food items have been cooked. It involves carefully removing surplus liquid from the item prior to coating with an appropriate sauce, such as poached fillets of sole with white wine sauce. Such foods need to be well drained, otherwise the retained liquid mixes with the sauce, spoiling the appearance and consistency of the sauce in question. Careful draining of excess moisture is best done using a clean kitchen cloth or absorbent paper.
4. *Reduction of cooking liquor*: This process involves removing the food

items when cooked (and keeping them warm), after which the cooking liquor is boiled rapidly until it reduces to the required degree. It may then be added to the accompanying sauce to enrich the sauce's flavour.

# Equipment used in poaching

Many types and sizes of utensils may be used for poaching, including shallow pans, such as plats à sauter and sauteuses, shallow trays and numerous fireproof dishes (ovenware) and oval plats à poisson.

The removal of poached items is assisted by the use of draining spoons, spiders and fish slices including broad-bladed palette knives.

All such items should be washed in hot soapy water after use, and then rinsed in clean hot water and thoroughly dried.

Pans and trays should be stored upside down on clean racks. Always check that the equipment is clean before use, and report any which is faulty.

# Self-assessment questions for poaching

1. Can you describe the process of poaching, and give examples of the two categories?
2. What is a cartouche, and what is its purpose?
3. Why is poaching as a method of food preparation a healthy process when catering for an invalid diet?
4. Normally, most foods are covered completely by liquid during poaching. There is, however, an exception. Can you name it?
5. There are several liquids which can feature in the poaching process; name three of them.
6. What is the approximate liquid temperature for poaching most food items?
7. One of the techniques associated with poaching is drying. What is its purpose?
8. Can you describe the reduction process as part of the poaching method?
9. Name three items of equipment used for the poaching of food items.
10. What safety precautions should be taken when removing very hot utensils from the oven?

When you have completed these questions check your answers with your fellow students and chef or lecturer.

# Poached egg dishes

## Introduction to poached egg dishes

Eggs may be poached in a variety of ways, either directly in the water or in a dish set in water (cocotte). The following recipes show how this may be achieved and give some examples of more common garnishes.

### Eggs cooked in a cocotte                    *Oeuf en cocotte*

This is the cooking of eggs in individual porcelain or glazed earthenware dishes known as cocottes. They are garnished in a wide variety of ways and usually served as starters or commonly these days as snacks at high tea. The method of cooking is similar to poached eggs au bain-marie, the difference being that the garnish is placed in the base of the cocotte dish and the finished product is served in the dish to the customer.

### General method for all cocotte recipes

1. Grease the cocotte dish with a little butter and season well with salt and milled pepper. This is to prevent the cooked egg sticking to the cocotte dish.
2. If a garnish is included in the recipe it should be placed into the base of the cocotte dish at this stage.
3. Break the egg into the cocotte dish so that it sits on top of the garnish.
4. Place the cocotte into a pan of shallow simmering water. The water should only come half-way up the side of the cocotte dish and should not be allowed to boil, as this may cause the water to spill into the cocotte.
5. Cover the pan with a lid and allow to simmer until the egg white is firm and the yolk is still soft, 6–10 minutes.
6. When the egg is cooked, pour off any water that may have gathered on the surface of the egg.
7. Finish with any sauce or cream as required in the recipe and garnish with parsley.
8. Serve immediately.

### Egg in cocotte                    *Oeuf en cocotte nature*

Allow 2 eggs per portion in individual cocottes for oeuf en cocotte nature. As with all cocotte dishes, remember to wipe the exterior of the dish before serving to the customer. Finish with a small piece of picked parsley.

**Egg with cream**                    *Oeuf en cocotte à la crème*

| | | |
|---|---|---|
| 4 | **Eggs** | 10 |
| 1 dl | **Double cream** | 2½ dl |

Proceed as for general method and finish with a cordon of hot double cream garnished with a piece of picked parsley.

**Egg garnished with**                *Oeuf en cocotte à la reine*
**brunoise of chicken**

| | | |
|---|---|---|
| 4 | **Eggs** | 10 |
| 1 dl | **Double cream or** | 2½ dl |
| | **sauce suprême** | |
| 50g | **Brunoise of cooked chicken** | 125 g |

1. Bind the chicken with a little cream or sauce suprême.
2. Proceed as for the general method and finish with a cordon of warm cream or sauce suprême.
3. Garnish with a piece of picked parsley.

**Poached eggs**                                 *Oeufs pochés*

**Method I**

1. Select a suitable pan or tray 10–15 cm deep.
2. Add approximately 6–8 cm of water with the addition of a little vinegar and salt.
3. Bring the liquor to the boil and then reduce the heat until just simmering.
4. Break the eggs into the liquor and simmer (poach) until the egg white has set but the yolk is still soft.
5. Remove the eggs from the liquor using a perforated spoon; allow the eggs to drain well before using.
6. The eggs may be used as soon as cooked or they may be refreshed to use at a later time. If they are to be refreshed, place into cold water and leave in the water until required. Re-heat by placing gently into simmering seasoned liquor, and leave in the liquor until it starts simmering again, 30 seconds to 1 minute.

**Method II**
**Poached au bain-marie (in a bath of water)**       *Oeufs en moules*

For this method of poaching, specially made pans can be purchased or individual moulds may be stood in a bath of water.

1. The pan (of a similar size to the pan used in method I) should be half

filled with water.
2. Bring the water to the boil.
3. Prepare the moulds by greasing lightly with a little butter and season with salt and pepper.
4. Crack the eggs into the mould and stand in the boiling water.
5. Cover with a lid and reduce the heat to a simmer.
6. Poach au bain-marie until the egg whites have set firmly but the yolk of the egg is still soft, 3–5 minutes.
7. When the egg is ready, turn out of the mould and serve as required.

**Variations**

Poached egg dishes may be prepared using either method I or method II. Usually 1 egg is allowed for a starter, although sometimes 2 eggs are given. Note that recipes for poached eggs may also be used for soft-boiled eggs served out of their shells (*oeufs mollets*).

**Poached egg with tongue and**                    *Oeuf poché bénédictine*
**hollandaise sauce served on**
**a toasted muffin**

| | | |
|---|---|---|
| 4 | Hot poached eggs | 10 |
| 2½ dl | Hollandaise sauce | 7 dl |
| 4 | Thin slices of ox tongue | 10 |
| 4 | Buttered toasted muffins | 10 |
| 4 | Slices of truffle for garnish | 10 |

1. Make sure that the hollandaise sauce is of a coating consistency.
2. Sit the buttered and toasted muffins on the service dish or plate.
3. Cut the tongue to fit neatly on the muffin.
4. Place the hot poached egg on top of the tongue and nap the muffin with the hollandaise sauce.
5. Finally garnish the top with a thin slice of truffle.

**Poached egg with spinach**                    *Oeuf poché florentine*
**and cheese sauce**

| | | |
|---|---|---|
| 4 | Hot poached eggs | 10 |
| 2½ dl | Sauce mornay | 7 dl |
| 100 g | Hot purée of cooked spinach | 250 g |
| | Grated parmesan cheese | |
| 4 | Warm short paste tartlet cases | 10 |
| | Picked parsley | |

1. Place the purée of hot seasoned spinach into the base of the tartlet case.
2. Sit the hot poached egg on the bed of spinach.
3. Making sure the sauce mornay is of coating consistency, nap the egg with a little sauce, to give a thin coating.
4. Flood the base of the service plate or a sur le plat with a thin coating of

the sauce.

5. Sprinkle the egg with a little grated parmesan and gratinate.
6. Sit the gratinated egg on to the service dish or sur le plat, garnish with a little picked parsley and serve.

**Poached egg on toast**

This is a typically English dish often served at breakfast or for afternoon or high tea service. Allow two eggs per portion and two slices of toast (muffins or crumpets may be used if preferred).

To serve, place two hot poached eggs on to trimmed buttered toast slices. Serve on hot plates to help keep the toast warm, garnished with a piece of picked parsley.

# Poached fish dishes     *Poisson poché*

### *Introduction to poached fish dishes*

On the menu, fish dishes are most commonly referred to as being poached. In practical terms the fish is simmered gently to prevent it breaking up during cooking.

Fish is cooked in court-bouillon, a flavoured stock.

The flesh of fish is not as tough to cook as meat. The delicate flesh of fish is held together by a fine connective tissue known as collagen, which turns to gelatin during the gentle cooking. As the collagen turns to gelatin the fish becomes more fragile and prone to flaking or breaking up. Whole fish are placed into cold water which is brought slowly to the boil and then the heat is reduced to a simmer. Cuts or portions of fish and small fish such as trout are started in simmering water. The action of starting fish in simmering water is to set the protein in the fish and speed the cooking process.

### *Basic methods for poached fish*

**Method I: Small cuts and small whole fish**

1. Lightly season the fish and leave to stand for 5–10 minutes.
2. Bring the court-bouillon to boiling-point and carefully add the fish.
3. Simmer until the fish is cooked. With portions of fish on the bone, a simple test is to try to lift out the bone. If it comes away clean the fish is cooked, if not, leave to cook a little longer.
4. When cooked, carefully lift out the fish and drain well.
5. Trim a darne of fish (see below) by removing the skin and bone before presenting. Whole fish would be trimmed in the restaurant.

**Method II: Large whole or pieces of fish**

1. Season the fish and allow to stand for 5–10 minutes.
2. Place into the cold court-bouillon.
3. Bring the court-bouillon gently to the boil, reduce the heat and simmer until the fish is cooked.
4. Drain the fish and remove any skin.
5. To serve, nap with a little of the cooking liquor and garnish with picked parsley and lemon wedges.

The cooking time for fish is a great deal shorter than for meat, as the flesh is much more tender and the collagen readily breaks down to gelatin. If serving the fish cold, remove the fish from the heat just before the fish is cooked and allow to go cold in the court-bouillon. This keeps the fish moist and full of flavour.

All hot fish dishes are served with an accompanying sauce and garnish. The garnish should always include sprigs of parsley and lemon wedges and may include plain boiled new or turned potatoes.

Suitable sauces include hollandaise, mousseline, anchovy, parsley, egg and shrimp.

*Cuts of fish (see diagrams on pages 52 and 53).*

| | |
|---|---|
| *La paupiette*: | A fillet of fish, such as plaice, lightly battered, spread with fish mousse and rolled; cooked by gently simmering and served with a sauce, e.g. bonne femme. |
| *La goujon*: | Thin strips of white fish, rolled and pané à l'anglaise: cooked by deep fat frying. |
| *Le délice*: | Trimmed and folded fillets of fish, usually plaice or sole, cooked by gentle simmering and served with a suitable sauce such as Dugléré. |
| *Le suprême*: | Cut from a larger fillet of fish such as turbot, on a slant, cooked by gentle simmering or grilling, accompanied by a suitable sauce like hollandaise. |
| *Le filet*: | Cut of fish without bone, cooked by various methods of cookery and served with an appropriate sauce. |
| *Le tronçon*: | Slice of flat fish cut on the bone. Served with a suitable sauce and cooked by grilling or gentle simmering. |
| *La darne*: | Cut as a slice on the bone through a round fish such as salmon or cod. Cooked by either gentle simmering or grilling. |

*Basic preparation for flat fish*

Allow 300 g of fish on the bone per person.
To prepare the fish tronçons:

1. Using a large solid chopping knife remove the head from the fish.
2. Trim off the skirt.
3. Starting at the tail end, cut down the centre of the fish and divide into two equal halves.
4. Cut each half into the required portions. A 4 kg fish will give approximately 8 to 10 portions.

| | |
|---|---|
| **Poached turbot** | *Tronçon de turbot poché* |
| **Poached brill** | *Tronçon de barbue poché* |
| **Poached halibut** | *Tronçon de flétan poché* |

1. Place the prepared and seasoned fish into a simmering court-bouillon.
2. Allow the court-bouillon to simmer gently and cover the fish with a lightly buttered cartouche. Simmer until the fish is cooked.
3. Remove the fish with a fish slice and trim the portion of fish for service.
4. Dress neatly on a service dish and garnish as required, e.g. wedge of lemon and picked parsley, new or turned boiled potatoes and hollandaise sauce.

| | |
|---|---|
| **Poached salmon** | *Darne de saumon poché* |
| **Poached cod** | *Darne de cabillaud poché* |

1. Cut through the bone to give a darne approximately 2 cm thick.
2. Cook as for basic method I.
3. Serve with a suitable sauce-boat of sauce, e.g. anchovy, egg or parsley. Salmon is more commonly served with hollandaise sauce.

| | |
|---|---|
| **Poached salmon trout** | *Truite saumonée poché* |

Allow ½ kg of unprepared salmon for 2 people. The average weight for salmon trout is 1 kg to 3½ kg. To cook follow the basic method I. To cook whole salmon, follow method II.

Salmon trout should be served with boiled new potatoes or turned potatoes, hollandaise sauce and fresh sprigs of parsley.

To prepare a salmon trout or salmon:

1. Wash the salmon under cold running water.
2. Using the back of a knife, scrape from tail to head and remove any scales.
3. Cut out the gills and wash under cold running water.

4. Cut up the belly of the fish and remove the intestines and blood from the backbone.
5. Using fish scissors, trim off all fins.
6. Give the fish a final rinse under cold running water and then proceed to cook.

**Appropriate cooking times for salmon trout and salmon**

| | |
|---|---|
| 1 kg to 3½ kg | 20 minutes |
| 4 kg to 6 kg | 25 minutes |
| 7 kg to 10 kg | 30 minutes |

**Fillets of plaice Bercy**                                    *Filets de plie Bercy*

| | | |
|---|---|---|
| 8 | Fillets of plaice | 20 |
| ½ dl | Dry white wine | 1½ dl |
| 50 g | Butter | 125 g |
| 30 g | Finely chopped shallots | 75 g |
| ½ dl | Fish stock | 1½ dl |
| 3 dl | Fish velouté | 7½ dl |
| ½ dl | Single cream | 1½ dl |
| ½ | Fresh lemon, juice of | 1 |
| 2 | Raw egg yolks | 5 |
| | Finely chopped parsley | |
| 500 g | Duchesse potato border | 1 kg |

1. Remove the skin from the fillets and trim the edges. Rinse in cold water.
2. Lightly butter and season suitable earthenware dishes.
3. Sprinkle the base of the dishes with the finely chopped shallots and parsley. Reserve a little finely chopped parsley to finish the fish.
4. Add the fillets of plaice folded into délices and lightly season.
5. Add the stock, lemon juice and wine and cover with a cartouche.
6. Poach in a moderate oven for 7–10 minutes.
7. Drain the fillets and arrange them neatly in a clean hot dish with a duchesse border.
8. Boil the cooking liquor in a sauteuse and add the velouté.
9. Strain into a clean sauteuse and finish with a liaison of the cream and egg yolk. Do not re-boil after adding the liaison.
10. Adjust the seasoning of the sauce.
11. Whisk in the butter.
12. Nap over the fillets, flame to a golden brown under a hot salamander and finish with finely chopped parsley.

## Fillets of plaice Duglèré          *Filets de plie Duglèré*

| | | |
|---|---|---|
| 8 | Fillets of plaice | 20 |
| 250 g | Tomato concassé | 600 g |
| ½ dl | Fresh fish stock | 1½ dl |
| 3 dl | Fish velouté | 7½ dl |
| ½ dl | Dry white wine | 1½ dl |
| ½ | Fresh lemon, juice of | 1 |
| 15 g | Finely chopped shallots | 35 g |
| | Finely chopped parsley | |
| 50 g | Butter | 125 g |
| 500 g | Duchesse potato border | 1 kg |

1. Skin the fillets and trim the edges.
2. Rinse in cold running water and then drain and dry.
3. Lightly butter and season suitable earthenware dishes.
4. Sprinkle the finely chopped shallots in the base of the dish.
5. Fold the fillets into délices and arrange neatly in the dish.
6. Sprinkle with finely chopped parsley and the tomato concassé; season lightly.
7. Add the lemon juice, wine and fish stock, cover with a cartouche.
8. Poach in a moderate oven for 7–10 minutes. Take care not to over-cook the protein in the fish, as this will spoil the texture of the dish.
9. Nap the bottom of a service dish with a little velouté and pipe a border of duchesse potato mixture around the dish.
10. Lift the fish out of the cooking liquor and arrange neatly in the prepared dish with the garnish.
11. Pour the cooking liquor into a sauteuse and add the velouté.
12. Bring to the boil and whisk in the butter.
13. Season and nap over the fish, finish with finely chopped parsley and serve.

The following recipes which specify plaice as the main protein are suitable for use with any other white fish, e.g. sole or lemon sole.

## Fillets of plaice in          *Filets de plie vin blanc*
## white wine sauce

| | | |
|---|---|---|
| 8 | Fillets of plaice | 20 |
| 1 dl | Dry white wine | 2½ dl |
| ½ | Fresh lemon, juice of | 1 |
| 50 g | Butter | 125 g |
| 15 g | Finely chopped shallots | 35 g |
| ½ dl | Fish stock | 1½ dl |
| 3 dl | Fish velouté | 7½ dl |
| ½ dl | Single cream | 1½ dl |
| 500 g | Duchesse potato mixture | 1 kg |
| 4 | Fleurons | 10 |
| | Finely chopped parsley | |

1. Remove the skin from the fillets of fish and trim the edges. Rinse in cold

running water.
2. Select an earthenware dish of suitable size for service.
3. Butter and season the dish.
4. Sprinkle the base of the dish with the finely chopped shallots.
5. Fold the fillets into délices and arrange neatly in the dish.
6. Add the wine, stock, lemon juice and seasoning.
7. Cover the dish with a cartouche and poach in a moderate oven for 7–10 minutes.
8. Drain the cooked délices and dress on a clean hot service dish with a border of glazed duchesse potato.
9. Place the cooking liquor from the fish into a sauteuse and bring to the boil with the fish velouté, season and then tammy into another clean sauteuse.
10. Whisk in the butter and then stir in the cream. Take care not to boil the sauce after adding the cream.
11. Nap the fish with the smooth sauce and garnish with the fleurons.

### Scallops with a cheese sauce  *Coquille St Jacques mornay*

| | | |
|---|---|---|
| 4 | King scallops | 10 |
| 50 g | Duchesse potato mixture | 250 g |
| 2½ dl | Mornay sauce | 6 dl |
| 50 g | Grated parmesan cheese | 125 g |
| | Picked parsley | |
| | Salt and ground white pepper | |

1. When purchasing fresh scallops, make sure that the shells are tightly closed; this ensures that they are fresh.
2. To open the shells place on to a hot stove top for a few seconds and then cut them out of the shell using a paring knife.
3. Rinse the scallops in cold running water and remove the trail.
4. Place the white flesh and orange roe into a little cold salted water, bring to the boil and skim to remove any surface scum.
5. Simmer for 7–10 minutes and refresh in cold running water.
6. Trim off any surface gristle and then slice the white flesh into escalopes.
7. Scrub the shells clean and bake dry in a hot oven.
8. Pipe a duchesse potato border around the edge of the scallop shells and line the base of the shells with mornay sauce.
9. Add the sliced white flesh and roe, nap with mornay sauce and sprinkle liberally with grated parmesan.
10. Gratinate the dish under a pre-heated salamander.
11. Serve on a hot flat with a dish paper and picked parsley.

### Scallops with white wine sauce  *Coquille St Jacques parisienne*

1. Proceed as for scallops with cheese sauce, replacing the cheese sauce with white wine sauce.
2. Glaze and finish with an additional garnish of julienne of truffle.

## Poached smoked haddock

*Aigrefin fumé poché*

| 4 × 150 g | Smoked haddock steaks | 10 × 150 g |
| 3 dl | Milk | 5 dl |
| 3 dl | Water | 5 dl |
| | Salt and pepper | |

1. Skin and trim the fish.
2. Bring the milk and water to the boil in a sauteuse.
3. Season and add the fish.
4. Allow the fish to simmer gently until just cooked, 10–15 minutes, covered with a cartouche.
5. When cooked drain and remove any bones from the fish.
6. Serve on a suitable service dish with a piece of picked parsley and nap with a little cooking liquor.

## Poached smoked haddock Monte Carlo

*Aigrefin fumé Monte Carlo*

| 4 × 150 g | Smoked haddock steaks | 10 × 150 g |
| 3 dl | Milk | 5 dl |
| 3 dl | Water | 5 dl |
| | Salt and pepper | |
| 5 | Poached eggs | 10 |
| 200 g | Tomato concassé | 500 g |
| 200 g | Mornay sauce | 1¼ litre |
| | Picked parsley | |

1. Cook the haddock as for poached smoked haddock.
2. Select a suitable service dish and place the hot tomato concassé on the base of the dish with a little sauce.
3. Sit the drained cooked haddock on the tomato concassé and top each piece of fish with a lightly poached egg.
4. Coat each portion with a layer of mornay sauce and garnish with a piece of picked parsley.

## Fish kedgeree

*Cadgery de poisson*

| 500 g | Smoked haddock | 1¼ kg |
| 2 | Hard-boiled eggs | 5 |
| 3 dl | Curry sauce | 7½ dl |
| 200 g | Cooked rice pilaff | 500 g |
| 50 g | Butter | 125 g |

1. Skin and poach the fish.
2. When cool enough to handle, remove all bones and flake the fish.
3. Dice the hard-boiled eggs and mix into the hot rice pilaff.
4. Gently fold in the flaked fish and heat in a suitably sized pan with the butter.
5. Adjust the seasoning.

6. Serve in a suitable service dish with a sauce-boat of curry sauce.

**Note:** As an alternative to smoked haddock, salmon is often used.

# Poached mousses     *Mousse pochée*

## Introduction to mousses

These are made with a mixture of cream and egg whites beaten with a main ingredient such as chicken or fish. The mixture is poached and served as either a starter or fish course. Mousses are easily digested and require little chewing so making them ideal for invalid cookery or elderly people.

## What is a mousse and how is it made?

There are hot and cold savoury mousses, and also cold sweet mousses. The latter variety resembles a lighter version of the bavarois or gelatinised Bavarian cream. Essentially, whichever type is produced, the most outstanding feature will be the texture, which will be of a light, slightly honeycomb nature.

Hot and cold savoury mousses are made from a purée of the main ingredient used: meat, poultry, game, ham or fish, *free from bone and sinews*. For hot mousses, the mixture is made from a purée of *raw flesh*, fresh cream, seasoning and egg whites. Cold savoury mousse is made from a purée of *cooked* meat, fowl, or fish, such as veal, chicken, game, ham, foie gras, salmon or lobster. The method of production differs in each case.

### Hot mousse

1. Reduce the main item to a purée by passing twice through the fine plate of a mincer or in a food processor.
2. Add seasoning to the raw purée, and gradually beat in the egg whites until the mixture takes on an elastic consistency.
3. Pass the mixture through a fine sieve into a clean bowl, then chill thoroughly in the refrigerator.
4. Finally, add the fresh cream gradually until the mixture is complete.
5. Well butter some small dariole moulds and fill each one with the mousseline mixture.
6. Place into a shallow tray of water. Cover the moulds with buttered greaseproof paper and oven poach until cooked.
7. The finished mousseline will feel firm to the touch when ready.
8. Turn out and serve with a suitable sauce and garnish.

## Cold savoury mousse

1. Reduce the main item to a purée by passing twice through the fine plate of a mincer or in a food processor.
2. Gradually add the cold velouté to the base mixture and then the cool melted aspic jelly.
3. Place the mixture on ice and continue stirring until just on setting-point. Immediately, remove away from the cold zone.
4. Check the seasoning before folding in the fresh cream (semi-whipped).
5. Finally, pour the mixture into suitable moulds which have been lined with a light coating of aspic jelly (and decorated on the base and sides if desired).
6. Place to set off in the refrigerator.
7. For service, unmould on to a dish and garnish with cut aspic jelly, or similar.

**Note**: see page 55, cold chicken, ham or fish mousse.

## Cold sweet mousse

Can be made from chocolate, lemon or fruit purée.

1. Soak the leaf gelatine in cold water until soft. Drain, and squeeze out any surplus water. Place to melt in a basin over low heat.
2. Meanwhile, sweeten the fruit purée with icing sugar and add any other flavouring and colouring.
3. Stir in the melted gelatine and allow the mixture to cool to setting-point.
4. Fold in the fresh cream (semi-whipped) and then the stiffly beaten egg whites.
5. Pour into lightly oiled moulds and place in the refrigerator to set.
6. Turn out on to suitable dishes and serve with an appropriate sauce and garnish. Such an example would be a raspberry mousse garnished with fresh raspberries and escorted by a fresh raspberry coulis.

## White fish mousse                                   *Mousse de poisson*

Made with whiting, plaice or sole flesh. Other fish suitable include pike and shellfish such as crayfish, crab and lobster.

Before poaching, the mousse mixture needs moulding into either quenelles or mousselines. *Quenelles* are made using teaspoons or by piping into very small balls before poaching in stock. *Mousselines* are made using tablespoons to mould the shapes before poaching in stock.

| | | |
|---|---|---|
| 240 g | Skinned and boned fillets of fish | 600 g |
| 1–2 | Egg whites | 2–3 |
| 2½ dl | Whipping cream | 6 dl |
| | Salt and ground white pepper | |

1. Pass the fish through a fine mincer twice.
2. Beat in the egg whites and season.
3. Push through a fine drum sieve and sit in a bowl over ice and water.
4. Beat until stiff and then beat in the cream; check the seasoning.
5. Cook in one of three ways:
   (a) En bain-marie — in a buttered mould, poach in a bain-marie, turn out and serve with a suitable fish-velouté-based sauce.
   (b) Mould into mousselines and poach in simmering fish stock, serve coated with a suitable fish-velouté-based sauce.
   (c) Mould into quenelles and poach either in fish stock or in a fish-based soup as garnish. May be served coated with a fish-based velouté sauce as a starter or fish course.

Suitable sauces include anchovy, vin blanc, Dugléré, Véronique.

## Hot ham mousse                                   *Mousse de jambon*

| | | |
|---|---|---|
| 240 g | Lean cooked ham | 600 g |
| 1–2 | Egg whites | 2–3 |
| 16 g | Frangipane panada | 40 g |
| 2½ dl | Whipping cream | 6 dl |
| | Pinch of paprika to taste | |
| | Ground white pepper to taste | |
| | Fresh grated nutmeg to taste | |
| 3 dl | Sauce suprême | 7½ dl |

1. Put the ham through a fine mincer twice and then through a fine drum sieve with the panada.
2. Beat over a bowl of ice and water, adding the egg whites and seasoning.
3. Beat in the cream and make into a smooth mousse.
4. Lightly grease a mould and pour in the mousse, tap the mould to level the mousse.
5. Poach slowly in a bain-marie, covered with a cartouche.
6. Allow to cool slightly and turn out of the mould.
7. Serve accompanied with sauce-boat of suprême sauce.

**Note:** Either individual or multi-portion moulds may be used for cooking and presentation of mousses.

## Hot chicken mousse                               *Mousseline de volaille*

| | | |
|---|---|---|
| 240 g | Raw chicken flesh | 600 g |
| 1–2 | Egg whites | 2–3 |
| 2½ dl | Whipping cream | 6 dl |
| | Salt and ground white pepper to taste | |
| 3 dl | Sauce suprême | 7½ dl |

1. Clean the chicken flesh of tendons and pass through a fine mincer twice.
2. Season to taste and beat in the egg whites over a bowl of ice and water.

3. Push through a fine drum sieve.
4. Beat in the cream to form a light mousse.
5. Lightly butter a mould or individual moulds and poach slowly en bain-marie.

# Poached pâtisserie

### Introduction to poached pâtisserie

Many sweets and sweet preparations involve poaching as a method of cookery. The following are a few examples of poached fruits and desserts.

**Snow eggs** *Oeufs à la neige*

| | | |
|---|---|---|
| 150 ml | **Fresh milk** | 1 litre 140 ml |
| 4 | **Eggs** | 8 |
| 140 g | **Castor sugar** | 280 g |
| | **Vanilla essence** *or* **pod** | |
| 60 g | **Flaked almonds** | 120 g |

1. Separate the eggs and whisk the whites to a firm snow, then whisk in half the amount of castor sugar to form a firm meringue.
2. Meanwhile, choose a shallow pan and three-quarters fill with barely simmering water.
3. Shape the meringue mixture into oval shapes using two dessert spoons, and poach in the gently simmering water until firm.
4. Half-way through the poaching, carefully turn over the shells to cook the reverse side.
5. Remove with a perforated spoon and allow to drain on a hair sieve. Blend the yolks with the remaining sugar and bring the milk and vanilla to the boil; whisk on to the sugar/yolk mixture. Remove the vanilla pod.
6. Return the pan and cook gently until the custard lightly coats the back of the spoon. *Do not allow to boil.*
7. Allow the custard to cool then pour into a suitable shallow dish. Cool thoroughly before placing the poached meringue shells on top.
8. Dust with castor sugar and colour very quickly under a hot grill to golden brown.
9. Garnish with a sprinkling of toasted almond flakes.
10. Serve very cold.

**Note:** A flat teaspoon of slaked arrowroot or cornflour added to the egg yolks will help to thicken the custard and prevent curdling. However, this is not really essential.

## Fresh fruits poached
*Compote des fruits fraises*

| 460 g | Fresh fruit | 2 kg |
| | (apples and pears, etc.) | |
| ½ litre | Stock syrup | 2 litres |
| ½ | Lemon | 2 |

1. Prepare the fruit by peeling, removing the cores and cutting into halves or quarters. Alternatively, pears may be left whole after peeling but with the stalk intact. Apples can be peeled and cored, and also poached whole. Fresh peaches and apricots usually have their skins removed (by blanching), and are then halved and de-stoned.
2. Use, if possible, a shallow pan for poaching. Place the prepared fruit in the bottom together with the syrup and lemon juice. Make sure that the fruit is covered by the syrup.
3. Cover the whole with greaseproof paper, and bring to simmering stage on the stove top.
4. Poach in the oven until just cooked.
5. Allow to cool, and serve well chilled in a suitable dish with the syrup.

Other stone fruits should be washed and poached as above, e.g. cherries, damsons, plums and greengages. Rhubarb sticks are trimmed of the leaves and end stalk, and cut into 5 cm lengths. Make sure to wash well before poaching.

## Dried fruits poached
*Compote des fruits*

1. Prunes, apricots, figs and apple rings, etc. should be well washed before covering with cold water and allowing to steep overnight.
2. Add 115 g of granulated sugar per ½ kg of dried fruit together with a piece of cinnamon stick, vanilla pod, lemon rind or one or two lemon slices.
3. Gently poach in the liquor (preferably in the oven) until tender, in the same manner as fresh, poached fruits.

Such fruits are generally served cold as a fruit compote for breakfast or luncheon.

**Note:** In the case of prunes, half the poaching liquid may be replaced by cold, strained tea. This, however is a matter of personal choice.

For soft fruits such as black and red currants and gooseberries, remove the stalks, then wash and drain and finish as for the stone fruits. Other soft fruits such as strawberries and raspberries are perhaps better prepared merely by removing any stalks, washing carefully and draining in a colander; such fruits do not really lend themselves to poaching.

# Poached savouries

See notes in Chapter 3 on boiled savouries.

### Smoked haddock on toast          *Canapé hollandaise*

| | | |
|---|---|---|
| 200 g | Smoked haddock | 500 g |
| 2½ dl | Milk and water | 6 dl |
| 1 | Hard-boiled eggs | 3 |
| 10 g | Butter | 25 g |
| 2 | Slices of toast | 5 |
| | Cayenne pepper | |

Trim the haddock and poach in the milk and water. Flake the fish into small pieces and discard any skin. Cut each slice of toast into two discs and butter. Dome each disc with flaked smoked haddock and top with a slice of hard-boiled egg. Sprinkle with cayenne pepper and serve on a hot flat with a dish paper and picked parsley.

### Smoked haddock with pickled walnut on toast          *Canapé Ivanhoe*

| | | |
|---|---|---|
| 200 g | Smoked haddock | 500 g |
| 1 dl | Thick béchamel | 2½ dl |
| 2½ dl | Milk and water | 6 dl |
| 4 | Pickled walnuts | 10 |
| 10 g | Butter | 25 g |
| 2 | Slices of toast | 5 |
| | Cayenne pepper | |

Trim the haddock and poach in the milk and water. Discard any skin and mix in with the béchamel. Season with cayenne pepper. Cut each slice into two discs and butter. Dome the haddock mixture on the discs and top with a slice of pickled walnut. Serve on a hot flat with a dish paper and picked parsley.

# Chapter 5
# Stewing                                    *Etuver*

## The competency defined

The principle of stewing as a method of cookery is the slow cooking of foods
in their own juices with the aid of a minimum amount of added moisture.
The latter can take the form of stock, wine, ale, sauce or butter (étuve au
beurre), the food being served with the sauce or cooking liquor as a complete
dish. During the cooking process the liquid is heavily flavoured by the juices
from the solid foods being cooked.

## Purpose of stewing

Because stewing is a slow, gentle method of cookery, it is suitable for the
cooking of the more economical and less tender cuts of meat, poultry and
game. The extended cooking action of stewing helps to tenderise the tougher
foods and make them more palatable and easier to digest.

## Methods of stewing

Stewed foods may be cooked in two ways, either in the oven or on the stove
top. However, it should be remembered that in each case the foods should be
cooked in a pan with a tight-fitting lid. This is to prevent excess evaporation
of the cooking liquid. During the stewing process, condensation forms on the
inside of the pan lid thus helping to keep the foods moist by the action of self-
basting. Any undue evaporation of the cooking liquid may result in burnt
food and an excessively dry product. A steady, controlled temperature is very
important. If necessary, liquid lost through evaporation can be replenished
during cooking. Such liquid should barely cover the food being stewed.

Foods which are suitable for stewing should be cut into small pieces before
cooking; these would include: meat, poultry, game, fish, vegetables and
fruits. Stewed food is always served complete with the sauce or cooking
liquor in which it has been cooked, hence the need to achieve the right
amount and consistency.

There are basically three types of meat stews, as follows:

1. Brown stews — usually described on the menu as a ragoût if beef based, navarin if lamb based. Brown stews are usually made with red meats.
2. White stews — generally described as blanquette if made with lamb or fricassée if made with chicken or veal.
3. Miscellaneous stews — i.e. those which cannot fit into either of the above categories. The miscellaneous stews include such examples as curries, goulash, chilli con carne, coq au vin, civet, Lancashire hot pot and Irish stew.

Not all stews are based on meat. Other foods also make excellent stews; examples of these are:

1. Fish stews — bouillabaisse, eel stew, lobster américain, lobster newburg, fish chowder, and moules marinières.
2. Vegetable stews — for example, stewed peas bonne femme style, or à la française; marrow or ratatouille (a mixed vegetable stew).
3. Stewed fruits – such as prunes, figs, apples, pears, apricots, plums, damsons and peaches.

# Organisation and preparation for stewing

In the traditional partie system the following staff would be responsible for stewed style foods:

| | |
|---|---|
| *Chef saucier*: | Meats, poultry, game dishes. |
| *Chef poissonnier*: | Fish dishes. |
| *Chef entremettier*: | Vegetable and potato dishes. |
| *Chef garde-manger*: | Initial preparation of meat, fish, poultry and game. |
| *Breakfast cook*: | Fruit dishes served at breakfast (otherwise, the chef pâtissier). |

All basic preparation of meats, poultry, fish and game would be carried out in the larder section then passed to the main kitchen.

# Advantages of stewing

There are a number of advantages to stewing, as follows:

1. The process of stewing produces a dish which is high in nutritional value, due to the food being cooked in the same sauce or liquor with which it is served. All the nutrients in the stewed food are contained by

the cooking liquor and served with the dish. Only a minimum amount of nutritional value is lost during cooking.
2. The process of stewing is ideal for cooking the cheaper and less tender cuts of meat, poultry and game.
3. Excluding the fuel cost for cooking, stewing is economical because of the cheap foods used, and the low labour cost owing to the ability to produce by simple methods large-scale quantities if required.

# Degrees of cooking

All foods which are cooked by stewing are well cooked. Careful control of the temperature is essential to the quality of the finished dish. The following rules need to be observed.

1. A tight-fitting lid should be used to retain steam and aid with maintaining temperature, as well as reducing undue evaporation.
2. The liquid (cooking liquor) should only simmer — never boil.
3. The time taken to cook a stew is dependent upon the structure of the foods being cooked.
4. The most suitable temperature for stewing is approximately 95°C (203°F) on the stove top or 150°C (302°) in the oven.

# Effects of stewing on foods

Due to the effects of stewing in a slow gentle heat the connective tissue in meats and poultry is changed into gelatine; this allows the fibres in foods to separate and as a result be more easily digested. The protein content is coagulated without becoming tough. However, over-cooking will result in meats becoming unpalatable and stringy in texture. The appearance is adversely affected and the colour and flavour of the finished dish would be spoiled. Slow gentle cooking is the rule!

# General rules for efficient stewing

Generally speaking, stews should not be too thick in consistency. Cooking may be carried out in a thin liquid, either water or stock, or the liquid may first be thickened with a starchy substance in moderation. Meat fibres become tender more rapidly in the absence of a thickening agent (flour, etc.), which can be added when the meat is cooked to adjust the final consistency of the sauce (see page 184).

# General safety rules

From the viewpoint of safety, it is essential that the right size of pan is used. If too small, spillage may occur during cooking, and there would be insufficient room to allow for the stirring of the food as and when necessary. If the pan is too large there may be excess evaporation due to the large surface area. Always exercise great caution when dealing with any hot liquid, and make sure to use a clean, dry oven-cloth to carry hot pans. Be careful when removing the lid or cover from a pan of hot liquid to avoid steam coming into contact with the skin.

Never leave pan handles over heat or sticking out from the stove as this may cause an accident.

# Techniques associated with stewing

*Blanching and refreshing:* This is the covering of foods with cold water, bringing rapidly to the boil, then rinsing under cold running water until all impurities (residue) have been removed. This procedure is used when making white stews, such as Irish Stew.

*Sealing and browning:* When producing a brown stew, the meat is first shallow fried in fat or oil to brown the meat, giving the stew a better colour and flavour. It also sets the surface protein and so retains the flavour in the meat.

# Equipment suitable for use when stewing

Equipment most commonly used and the most suitable would include stewing pans, bratt pans and oven-proof dishes when stewing in the oven. All the equipment used for stewing should be thoroughly washed in hot, soapy water, then rinsed in hot water and dried properly after use. Pans must be stored upside down on clean racks or shelving. Always check for loose handles, and if equipment is faulty in any way, report the fact to your superior immediately.

# Self-assessment questions for stewing

1. Define the principle of stewing as a method of cookery using your own words.
2. There are two ways of stewing. What are they?
3. Which type of meat is used in a ragoût? And which type of meat is used

in a navarin?
4. Name six miscellaneous stews based on meat.
5. What are the most suitable temperatures for stewing on the stove top?
6. Why is a stew (of meat) considered to be a fairly economical dish to prepare?
7. Name three thickening agents used for adjusting the consistency of a finished stew dish.
8. Describe the technique of blanching and refreshing.
9. What is the object of sealing and browning the meat when preparing a brown stew?
10. Can you name the ideal piece of equipment for the large-scale production of a brown stew?

When you have completed these questions check your answers with your fellow students and chef or lecturer.

# Fish stews                                          Poisson Etuvé

*Introduction to fish stews*

Fish stews are very nutritious and in some parts of the world form a major part of the diet. The following two recipes are classic examples, bouillabaisse from France and paella from Spain.

**Fish stew/soup**                                          *Bouillabaisse*

This dish is made with a combination of assorted fish, e.g. red mullet, John Dory, squid, crayfish, mussels and eel. Almost any fish or shellfish is suitable for use.

| | | |
|---|---|---|
| 400 g | Selected fish | 1 kg |
| 100 g | Shellfish in the shell | 250 g |
| 1 dl | Dry white wine | 2½ dl |
| 100 g | Brunoise of onion | 250 g |
| 100 g | Julienne of leek | 250 g |
| 100 g | Concassé of tomato | 250 g |
| ½ dl | Virgin olive oil | 1 dl |
| 1 | Bay-leaves | 2 |
| 10 | Crushed fennel seeds | 25 |
| 1 | Crushed clove of garlic | 2 |
| | Saffron to taste | |
| | Finely chopped parsley | |
| | Milled sea salt | |
| | Milled white pepper | |
| 5 dl | Fish stock | 1¼ litre |
| ½ stick | French bread | 1 stick |

1. Select a stew pan of suitable size and heat the oil.

2. Sweat the onion and leek without colour.
3. Add the selected fish which should have been filleted and any bones removed.
4. Add garlic, bay-leaf, fennel, parsley and season.
5. Cover with a cartouche and sweat for 5 minutes.
6. Add the wine and enough fish stock to just cover the fish.
7. Bring to the boil, skim and add the shellfish.
8. Add the saffron to give colour and flavour to the stew.
9. Cover with a tight-fitting lid. Stew until cooked, 20–30 minutes.
10. Adjust the seasoning and serve in hot soup bowls with thick slices of warm French bread.

**Notes:**
1. The bread may if required be flavoured with garlic.
2. If being served as a soup, use more stock.

**Spanish stewed rice**                                   *Paella*

The paella is actually a two-handled, shallow, cast iron pan in which this particular dish is cooked and served to the customer.

The ingredients for traditional paellas in Spain will vary from region to region and so the recipe given here is very general and can be altered to suit the fish available.

| | | |
|---|---|---|
| 200 g | Patna rice | 500 g |
| 250 g | Raw chicken flesh pieces | 600 g |
| 150 g | Prawns | 350 g |
| 150 g | Bearded cooked mussels in half shell with cooking liquor | 350 g |
| 100 g | Fillet of red mullet | 250 g |
| 2 | Crushed cloves of garlic | 4 |
| 60 g | Brunoise of onion | 150 g |
| 60 g | Tomato concassé | 150 g |
| 60 g | Cooked brunoise of pimento | 150 g |
| 50 g | Cooked peas | 125 g |
| ¼ dl | Olive oil | 1¼ dl |
| | Fresh thyme | |
| | Fresh tarragon | |
| | Oregano or basil | |
| | Saffron | |
| | White chicken stock | |
| | Finely chopped parsley | |

1. Infuse the saffron strands and then add to the onions.
2. Sweat the onions in the olive oil.
3. Add the chicken, pimento, herbs and garlic and cook until the chicken takes a light brown colour.
4. Add the rice and stir well, using a wooden spoon.
5. Add twice the volume of stock to rice, bring to the boil and then simmer covered with a cartouche and lid until the rice is half cooked.

6. Using forks or perforated spoons gently blend in the rest of the ingredients.
7. Finish cooking and adjust seasoning, sprinkle liberally with chopped parsley.

# Meat stews                              *Viande Etuvé*

### Introduction to meat stews

This is a long, slow method of cookery, which allows the cheaper and therefore tougher cuts of meat to be used. The long, slow cooking breaks down the collagen in the food, the white connective tissue which dissolves when cooked slowly in moist heat and turns into gelatine.

After cooking a stew it may be necessary to adjust the consistency. This is done in one of three ways:

1. Simmering the sauce until it has reduced in volume and so thickened in consistency.
2. Whisking into the simmering sauce either beurre manié or diluted arrowroot or cornflour. The sauce must be reboiled until it has finished thickening, which will not occur until the starch has been cooked.
3. Adding very thick Béchamel or demi-glace or velouté to the dish.

Meat stews are common throughout the world. From India to England meats are stewed in many ways, in thick spicy sauces or in thin stocks with onions and potatoes. Because all of the stock or sauce is served with the meat, the dish is very nutritional, since none of the soluble nutrients are thrown away in the liquid.

### Cuts of meat for stewing

| English | French | Approx. weight |
|---------|--------|----------------|
| *Beef* | | |
| Topside | *La tranche tendre* | 10 kg |
| Thick flank | *La tranche grasse* | 12 kg |
| Thin flank | *La bœvette* | 10 kg |
| Chuck rib | *Les côtes du collier* | 15 kg |
| Sticking piece | *Le collier* | 9 kg |
| Plate | *La poitrine* | 10 kg |
| Leg of mutton cut | *Le talon du collier* | 11 kg |
| | | |
| *Lamb* | | |
| Shoulder | *L'épaule* | 2 × 3 kg |
| Breast | *La poitrine* | 2 × ½ kg |
| Middle neck | *Le cou* | 4 kg |
| Scrag end | *Le cou* | 1 kg |

*Pork*

| | | |
|---|---|---|
| Shoulder | *L'épaule* | 3 kg |

*Veal*

| | | |
|---|---|---|
| Shoulder | *L'épaule* | 5 kg |
| Neck end | *Le cou* | 2½ kg |
| Scrag end | *Le cou* | 1½ kg |
| Breast | *La poitrine* | 2½ kg |
| Knuckle | *Le jarret* | 2 kg |

**Hungarian goulash**                                    *Goulache hongroise*

A selection of meats may be used to make goulash, although the most common is beef.

| | |
|---|---|
| Veal goulash | *Goulache de veau hongroise* |
| Pork goulash | *Goulache de porc hongoise* |
| Mutton goulash | *Goulache de mouton hongroise* |
| Lamb goulash | *Goulache d'agneau hongroise* |
| Beef goulash | *Goulache de boeuf hongroise* |

All the above meats should be skinned, trimmed of excess fat and cut into 2 cm dice.

Never be tempted to use too much paprika as the flavour increases with cooking.

| | | |
|---|---|---|
| 600 g | **Prepared meat** | 1½ kg |
| 120 g | **Brunoise of onion** | 300 g |
| 30 g | **Plain or wholemeal flour** | 75 g |
| 30 g | **Dripping** | 75 g |
| 30 g | **Paprika** | 75 g |
| 15 g | **Tomato pureé** | 35 g |
| | **Milled salt** | |
| 6 dl | **White stock** | 1½ litre |

*Garnish*

| | | |
|---|---|---|
| 8 | **Turned potatoes or new potatoes par-boiled** | 20 |
| 12 | **Plain boiled gnocchi parisienne** | 30 |
| | **Finely chopped parsley** | |
| 1 dl | **Plain yoghurt** | 2½ dl |
| | *or* | |
| | **Single cream** | |

1. Season the meat and roll in the paprika.
2. Select a large thick-based saucepan with a tight-fitting lid and melt the dripping.
3. Add the meat and onions and seal quickly.
4. Add the rest of the paprika and reduce the heat to allow the paprika to

cook slowly for 4 minutes.
5. Add the flour and colour to a light brown.
6. Allow to cool slightly and then add the tomato pureé, mixing in well.
7. Add the stock a little at a time to make a smooth sauce.
8. Bring to the boil, skim to remove any surface scum.
9. Adjust the seasoning.
10. Cover with a tight-fitting lid and reduce the heat to allow the goulash to stew until tender, 1½–2 hours.
11. The pan may be placed into a moderate oven to cook if required.
12. Stir at regular intervals to prevent sticking.
13. When the meat is almost cooked, add the par-boiled potatoes and continue cooking until the potatoes are cooked.
14. Adjust the consistency of the goulash as required.
15. Adjust the seasoning and serve in a hot service dish garnished with the plain boiled gnocchi parisienne and finely chopped parsley.
16. Serve with plain yoghurt or single cream either in sauce-boats or lightly poured on to the dish of goulash.

## Chilli con carne

| | | |
|---|---|---|
| ¼ dl | Olive oil | ½ dl |
| 500 g | Minced beef | 1¼ kg |
| 120 g | Soaked red kidney beans | 300 g |
| 100 g | Brunoise of onion | 250 g |
| 1 | Cloves of crushed garlic | 3 |
| 100 g | Tomato concassé | 250 g |
| 2 | Finely chopped chilli peppers | 4 |
| | Milled salt to taste | |
| | Ground cumin to taste | |
| | Dried oregano to taste | |
| 1 | Bay-leaf | 2 |
| 4 dl | White stock | 1 litre |
| | (Use only enough stock to cover the meat) | |

1. Select a suitable thick-based saucepan with tight-fitting lid.
2. Heat the olive oil and add the onions and chillis; sweat without colour.
3. Add the meat, seal and colour quickly.
4. Add the cumin, oregano, bay-leaf and garlic, mix in well.
5. Add the tomato pureé and soaked red kidney beans.
6. Add sufficient stock to just cover the meat.
7. Add the tomato concassé and mix well.
8. Bring to the boil and cover with the lid.
9. Reduce the heat to allow the chilli to stew gently until cooked, 1-2 hours.
10. If required, the chilli may be cooked in a moderate oven.
11. Stir at regular intervals to prevent sticking.
12. When cooked, adjust the seasoning and remove the bay-leaf.

**Note:** Serve accompanied with 50 g of plain boiled rice per portion. Also often served with hot garlic bread or warm bread and garlic butter.

## Brown beef stew                                      *Ragoût de boeuf*

| | | |
|---|---|---|
| 400 g | Stewing beef | 1 kg |
| 100 g | Macédoine of carrots | 250 g |
| 25 g | Plain flour | 75 g |
| 7½ dl | Brown beef stock | 2 litres |
| | Salt and milled black pepper | |
| 100 g | Macédoine of onion | 250 g |
| 25 g | Beef dripping | 60 g |
| 10 g | Tomato pureé | 25 g |
| 1 | Crushed clove of garlic | 2 |
| 1 | Bouquet garni | 1 |
| | Finely chopped parsley | |

1. Trim the meat of excess fat and sinew, and dice into 2 cm cubes.
2. Select a suitable sized thick-based pan and heat the dripping.
3. Add the meat and brown quickly, sealing in the meat's own juices.
4. Add the macédoine of carrot and onion and fry until the vegetables are lightly browned.
5. Add the flour and cook out the flour on the stove top for about 5–7 minutes, mixing in well.
6. Add the tomato pureé and mix in using a wooden spatula.
7. Add the stock a little at a time, mixing carefully to avoid lumps of flour.
8. Bring to the boil and skim to remove any surface scum.
9. Add the bouquet garni and crushed garlic, cover and simmer gently until cooked, 1–2 hours.
10. When cooked, adjust the seasoning and consistency, and serve in a hot service dish, sprinkled with finely chopped parsley.

## Brown lamb stew                                      *Navarin d'agneau*

| | | |
|---|---|---|
| 800 g | Trimmed and boned stewing lamb | 2 kg |
| 25 g | Dripping | 60 g |
| 100 g | Macédoine of carrot | 250 g |
| 100 g | Macédoine of onion | 250 g |
| 30 g | Plain flour | 75 g |
| 25 g | Tomato pureé | 60 g |
| 8 dl | Brown mutton stock | 2 litres |
| 1 | Bouquet garni | 1 |
| 1 | Crushed clove of garlic | 2 |
| 8 | Turned potatoes | 20 |
| 8 | Button onions | 20 |
| | Finely chopped parsley | |

1. Select a frying-pan of suitable size and melt the dripping.
2. Cut the meat into 2 cm pieces, season and fry in the pan, browning the surface of the meat on all sides.
3. Transfer the meat to a braising-pan.
4. Fry the onion and carrot to a golden brown in the frying-pan and add to

the braising-pan.
5. Sprinkle the meat and vegetables with flour and gently shake it in, then cook in a moderate oven for 10 minutes.
6. Mix the tomato pureé and enough brown stock to just cover the meat.
7. Add the bouquet garni, garlic and seasoning.
8. Bring to the boil and skim, cover with a lid and cook in a pre-heated oven at 180°C for 1 hour.
9. Fry the button onions to a golden brown and add to the meat along with the turned potatoes.
10. Skim to remove any surface fat, adjust the consistency and seasoning.
11. Bring to the boil on the stove top and replace the lid.
12. Replace into a moderate oven at 180°C and cook for a further 45 minutes.
13. Serve in a hot service dish, sprinkled liberally with finely chopped parsley.

## White meat stews

There are two basic types of white meat stew, the fricassée and the blanquette.

For a fricassée the meat, e.g. veal, poultry or rabbit, is cooked in the thickened sauce, and the sauce is then served as part of the finished dish.

For a blanquette the meat, e.g. lamb, veal or poultry, is stewed in a white stock and the sauce is made using the stock at the end of cooking. The sauce is then served as part of the finished dish.

Both the fricassée and the blanquette should be finished by adding a liaison of cream and egg yolk to the sauce just before service. Remember not to boil the sauce after adding the liaison, as this will cause the sauce to curdle.

**White lamb stew**                                      *Blanquette d'agneau*

| 500 g | Boned and trimmed shoulder of lamb | 1¼ kg |
|---|---|---|
| 8 dl | White lamb stock | 2 litres |
| 1 | Studded onion | 2 |
| 30 g | Butter | 75 g |
| 30 g | Plain flour | 75 g |
| | Fresh lemon juice to taste | |
| 1 dl | Double cream | 2 dl |
| 2 | Egg yolks | 4 |
| | Finely chopped parsley | |

1. Dice the lamb into 2 cm cubes.
2. Place into a saucepan of suitable size and cover with cold water.
3. Bring quickly to the boil and simmer for 3–5 minutes, then refresh under cold running water and drain.
4. Put the lamb back into a clean pan and add enough stock to just cover.
5. Bring quickly to the boil and simmer, skim to remove any surface scum.

6. Add the studded onion and seasoning, simmer gently for 1–1½ hours until the meat is tender.
7. In a separate saucepan, prepare a blond roux with the butter and flour.
8. Remove the cooked lamb from the stock and strain the liquid.
9. Use the liquid to make a velouté, adding the stock a little at a time to the blond roux.
10. When all the stock has been added, simmer for 30 minutes.
11. Season and add the lemon juice.
12. Strain the sauce over the lamb and bring to the boil.
13. Remove from the heat and blend the cream and egg yolk together.
14. Add a little sauce to the liaison and then stir into the main pan.
15. Serve in a hot service dish, sprinkled liberally with finely chopped parsley.

### White lamb stew                                  *Fricassée d'agneau*

| | | |
|---|---|---|
| 500 g | Boned and trimmed shoulder of lamb | 1¼ kg |
| 40 g | Butter/margarine | 100 g |
| 30 g | Plain flour | 75 g |
| 8 dl | White mutton stock | 2 litres |
| | Bouquet garni | |
| 1 | Studded onion | 2 |
| 1 | Egg yolk | 2 |
| ½ dl | Cream | 1 dl |
| 4 | Heart-shaped croûtons | 10 |
| | Finely chopped parsley | |

1. Dice the shoulder of lamb into 2 cm cubes.
2. Select a sauteuse of suitable size and heat the butter or margarine.
3. Sweat the lamb lightly, do not allow to colour.
4. Sprinkle on the flour and gently shake into the meat and butter.
5. Cover with a lid and put to cook in an oven at 180°C for 10 minutes.
6. Remove from the heat and allow to cool slightly.
7. Add the stock a little at a time, mixing in gently until enough stock has been added to just cover the lamb.
8. Season and bring quickly to the boil.
9. Skim to remove any surface scum and add the bouquet garni and studded onion, replace the lid and simmer for 1½ hours or until tender.
10. Remove the bouquet garni and studded onion.
11. Lift out the meat and place into a clean pan.
12. Mix the egg yolk and cream in a basin to form a liaison.
13. Add a ladle of the sauce to the liaison and mix well.
14. Stir the mixture back into the main sauce, re-heating slowly and stirring all the time, until the sauce thickens slightly. Do not allow to boil.
15. Adjust the seasoning and add to the meat by pouring through a fine chinois.
16. Allow the meat to re-heat, without boiling the sauce.
17. Serve in a hot service dish, sprinkled liberally with finely chopped

parsley and garnish with shallow-fried heart-shaped croûtons.

## Irish stew

| 500 g | Skinned and boned shoulder of lamb | 1¼ kg |
|-------|-------------------------------------|-------|
| 400 g | Peeled potatoes | 1 kg |
| 100 g | Celery | 250 g |
| 100 g | Button onions | 250 g |
| 100 g | Macédoine of onions | 250 g |
| 100 g | Savoy cabbage | 250 g |
| 100 g | Leeks | 250 g |
|       | Bouquet garni | |
|       | Finely chopped parsley | |

1. Trim and dice the lamb into 2 cm cubes.
2. Blanch and refresh the lamb.
3. Put the lamb into a sauteuse and add enough water to just cover the lamb, bring quickly to the boil and skim to remove any surface scum.
4. Season and add the bouquet garni.
5. Turn the potatoes into barrel shapes.
6. Cut the onion, cabbage, celery and leek into evenly sized pieces and add to the meat.
7. Simmer for ½ hour.
8. Add the button onions and simmer for ½ hour.
9. Add the turned potatoes and simmer with a lid to prevent excess moisture loss until cooked.
10. Adjust the seasoning and skim to remove all surface fat.
11. Serve in a hot service dish, sprinkled liberally with finely chopped parsley.

**Note:** If a tougher cut of lamb is used, it should be simmered for ½ hour before adding any other ingredients.

## Meat curry                                    *Kari de viande*

Curries are traditionally very hot spicy dishes, the amount of spices and curry powder used altering the strength of the curry produced. Do not be tempted to add extra curry powder during cooking as the full flavour and strength of the curry will not be realised until cooking is completed.

Use any stewing meat for this curry, such as lamb, beef or boiling fowl. The meat should be skinned, trimmed of all excess fat, boneless and diced into 2 cm cubes.

| | | |
|---|---|---|
| 200 g | Plain boiled rice | 500 g |
| 500 g | Chosen meat | 1¼ kg |
| 40 g | Butter or margarine | 100 g |
| 200 g | Brunoise of onion | 500 g |
| 1 | Clove crushed garlic | 2 |
| 20 g | Curry powder | 50 g |
| 20 g | Plain flour | 50 g |
| 20 g | Tomato pureé | 50 g |
| 8 dl | Brown stock | 2 litres |
| 30 g | Chopped mango chutney | 75 g |

*Optional extras*

| | | |
|---|---|---|
| 60 g | Macédoine of apple | 150g |
| 25 g | Sultanas | 60 g |
| 5 g | Dessicated coconut | 10 g |

1. Select a suitable sized pan and melt the butter or margarine.
2. Season the meat and add to the pan, seal quickly and allow to brown slightly.
3. Add the onions and garlic, mix into the meat and allow to sweat.
4. Sprinkle in the curry powder and flour and mix well.
5. Place into a hot oven for 10 minutes.
6. Remove from the oven, mix in the tomato pureé.
7. Add the brown stock, a little at a time, and mix in well.
8. Bring to the boil, season and skim to remove any surface scum.
9. Add the mango chutney and any of the optional extras required.
10. Cover with a lid and place into a moderate oven for 1–1½ hours, or until the meat is tender.
11. Skim the sauce to remove surface fat and scum, adjust the seasoning.
12. Serve in a hot service dish, accompanied with plain boiled rice.

**Note:** The recipe given may be adjusted as required, e.g. made stronger by adding more curry powder or using a stronger curry powder.

Accompaniments to curry include the following examples:

| | |
|---|---|
| Plain yoghurt | Coconut |
| Cream | Onion |
| Finely chopped parsley | Apple |
| Poppadums | Chillies |
| Bombay duck | Lime pickle |
| Banana | Chapatis |
| Chutneys | |

## Chicken in red wine

*Coq au vin*

| | | |
|---|---|---|
| 1–1½ kg | Chicken cut for sauté | 2½–3 kg |
| 5 dl | Red wine | 12 dl |
| 1 dl | Chicken stock | 2½ dl |
| ½ dl | Oil or butter | 1 dl |
| 15 g | Meat glaze | 35 g |
| | Salt and pepper | |
| 50 g | Beurre manié | 125 g |

*Garnish*

| | | |
|---|---|---|
| 100 g | Button mushrooms | 250 g |
| 100 g | Button onions | 250 g |
| 100 g | Lardons of bacon | 250 g |
| 5 | Heart-shaped croûtons | 10 |
| | Finely chopped parsley | |

1. Select a sauteuse of suitable size and heat the oil or butter.
2. Season the chicken and seal quickly in the pan; allow the chicken to colour slightly.
3. Remove the chicken from the pan and sit in a cocotte or stewing-pan with the bouquet garni.
4. Sauté the onions in the pan with the lardons and mushrooms until browned.
5. Remove from the pan and place into a bowl on one side.
6. De-glaze (swill out) the pan with the red wine and stock.
7. Bring to the boil quickly, season and pour over the chicken with the meat glaze.
8. Cover the container with a tight-fitting lid and stew in a moderate oven until tender, 45–60 minutes.
9. Remove the chicken from the vessel and place into a clean cocotte dish for service.
10. Garnish with the onions, lardons and mushrooms.
11. Boil the cooking liquor and reduce by a third.
12. Thicken by whisking in the beurre manié and boil until finished thickening.
13. Adjust the seasoning and strain the sauce over the chicken.
14. Heat thoroughly in a moderate oven for about 25 minutes.
15. Serve garnished with croûtons and sprinkled liberally with finely chopped parsley.

# Stewed vegetables

# Légumes étuvés

*Introduction to stewed vegetables*

As with stewed fish and meat dishes, the cooking liquor is served as a part of the finished item. This is not only beneficial from a nutritional aspect but ensures an excellent flavour to the finished dish. The following are a selection of stewed vegetable dishes which you will commonly find on restaurant menus.

## Marrow in tomato sauce                    *Courge provençale*

| 400 g | Marrow (or pumpkin or courgettes) | 1 kg |
|---|---|---|
| 200 g | Tomato concassé | 500 g |
| 100 g | Finely sliced onion | 250 g |
| ½ dl | Olive oil | 1 dl |
| 1 | Crushed garlic | 2 |
| | Basil to taste | |
| 1 | Bay-leaves | 2 |
| | Milled sea salt | |
| | Milled black pepper | |
| | Finely chopped parsley | |

1. Select a suitable stew pan and heat the oil.
2. Sweat the onion and garlic without colour for 5 minutes.
3. Peel the marrow or pumpkin and dice into 2 cm cubes or slice the courgettes into ½ cm thick rondes.
4. Add the main vegetable ingredient and sweat for a further 5 minutes.
5. Add the tomato concassé, basil and seasoning.
6. Cover with a tight-fitting lid and stew gently for 20-30 minutes.
7. Adjust the seasoning, serve in a hot vegetable dish sprinkled liberally with finely chopped parsley.

## Stewed peas French style                 *Petit pois à la française*

| 200 g | Shelled peas | 500 g |
|---|---|---|
| 10 g | Button onions | 250 g |
| 50 g | Chiffonade of lettuce | 125 g |
| | Pinch of sugar | |
| | Salt | |
| 30 g | Beurre manié | 75 g |

1. Select a stewing-pan of suitable size and add the peas, onion and lettuce.
2. Just cover with water, season with the sugar and salt.
3. Cover with a tight-fitting lid and stew until all is cooked, about 20–30 minutes.
4. Form a beurre manié into small pellets and shake into the stew.
5. Simmer until finished thickening.
6. Adjust the seasoning and serve in a hot vegetable dish.

## Ratatouille                                          *Ràtatouille*

| 200 g | Courgettes | 500 g |
| 200 g | Aubergines | 500 g |
| 200 g | Blanched tomatoes | 500 g |
| 100 g | Red peppers | 250 g |
| 100 g | Green peppers | 250 g |
| 100 g | Macédoine of onion | 250 g |
| ½ dl | Virgin olive oil | 1 dl |
| 1 | Clove of crushed garlic | 2 |
| | Milled salt | |
| | Milled pepper | |
| | Finely chopped parsley | |

1. Select a suitable sized stew pan and heat the oil.
2. Cut the peppers in half and remove the seeds; cut into julienne.
3. Sweat the onion, peppers and garlic in the oil without colouring.
4. Slice the courgettes ½ cm thick and dice the aubergines into 1 cm cubes.
5. Add the courgettes and aubergines to the pan and season.
6. Cover with a tight-fitting lid and stew on the stove or in a moderate oven.
7. When half-way through cooking, quarter the skinned tomatoes and remove the seeds; add the tomato flesh to the pan.
8. Continue cooking until the vegetables are just cooked.
9. Serve in a clean hot dish, sprinkled liberally with finely chopped parsley.

**Note:** If required, additional herbs such as basil, bay-leaves, oregano or marjoram may be used to help flavour the ratatouille, adding them at stage 5.

# Chapter 6
# Braising                                   *Braiser*

## The competency defined

Braising is the long, slow cooking of food in a sealed container with liquid in the oven. The liquid is served with the food as part of the finished dish.

## Purpose of braising

The main purpose of cooking foods by the braising process is:

1. To make the tougher cuts of meat and poultry tender and therefore easier to digest.
2. To create a specific flavour, texture and consistency.
3. To give a further variety to the customer's diet.

## Methods of braising

There are two methods of braising: white braising and brown braising.

1. *White braising* is used for sweetbreads and a range of vegetables, such as celery, leeks, endive, lettuce, onions and fennel; before cooking in the oven, the majority of vegetables should be blanched in boiling water and refreshed. This is done to help the vegetable to keep its colour, and also to render the item easier to shape for braising, e.g. folded leeks.
2. *Brown braising* is used for braising joints of meat, poultry and game. Items such as venison are usually marinaded in wine and aromats and larded (with backfat) before quickly sealing on all sides in hot dripping. The process is designed to give the exterior of the joint a rich brown colour and promote flavour in the finished dish.
   Smaller cuts of meat, poultry and game may also be brown braised, and the process is basically the same as for brown braising of meat joints.

When being placed into the braising vessel, the prepared foods are put on to a bed of vegetables known as a mirepoix (diced carrots, onions and celery). When brown braising, the mirepoix shoud be sweated until a light golden brown in colour. For white braising, the sweating should be carried out without coloration.

# Organisation and preparation for braising

The following specialists would be involved in the process of braised foods in a traditional partie system.

| | |
|---|---|
| *Chef saucier:* | Butcher's meats, offal, poultry and game. |
| *Chef entremettier:* | Vegetable and potato dishes. |
| *Chef garde-manger:* | Responsible for the initial preparation of all meat products ready for braising. |

Braising is a long, slow method of cooking which is suitable for use with the cheaper cuts of meat, poultry and game, as well as vegetables and some potato dishes.

A high standard of careful preparation is essential to achieve a satisfactory end-product. Braisings are both succulent and nutritious.

# Advantages of braising

1. Braised foods offer a wide variety to the menu with styles of service and presentation differing from dish to dish.
2. The process allows for maximisation of flavour and retention of nutrients as the cooking liquor is usually served with the main food being braised. An exception is vegetables, when it is often advisable to make a separate sauce, as the cooking liquor may be too strong in flavour.
3. Because braising is a long, slow process, it is ideally suited to the less tender cuts of meat and the older type of bird or game.

# Degrees of cooking

Braising requires a slow, constant temperature; this will allow for the breakdown of the connective tissue (in meats) and therefore tenderise the food.

The liquid should be just simmering.

# Effects of braising on foods

The partial 'roasting' (by the oven's radiant heat) and gentle stewing by the hot liquid produces a tender, succulent dish, the flavour of which is enhanced by the addition of the sliced vegetables and herbs.

# General rules for efficient braising

1. Keep the evaporation of cooking liquor to a minimum by maintaining a steady, controlled cooking temperature. The best temperature for braised foods is 150°C (302°F). At this heat the food will be cooked to the best advantage without undue dehydration.
2. Always braise in a braising-pan or other suitable vessel which is complete with a tight-fitting lid to contain the heat and conserve moisture.
3. Remember that the recommended cooking times are governed by the quality of the foods being braised. The tougher the raw commodity, the longer it will take to cook.
4. Meats, poultry and game for brown braisings should be sealed and browned in hot shallow fat prior to braising.
5. Vegetables and sweetbreads for white braising should be blanched prior to being braised.
6. Always make sure that you choose a pan of appropriate size for the volume of food being processed; not too big and not so small that liquor spills over the edge whilst simmering.
7. The flavour of braised items is improved by the addition of a bed of root vegetables; for brown braisings these should be sweated and cooked to a golden brown colour; for white braisings, the procedure is carried out without coloration.
8. Do not add too much liquor to the braising-pan. The liquid should only come approximately half-way up the depth of the food item.
9. Never attempt to rush the braising process; it should be a long, slow procedure to achieve maximum tenderness and food flavour.
10. Usually, the cooking liquor is utilised in the end sauce when serving braised meat, poultry and game. However, this does not apply to some vegetables as the liquor is considered too strong in flavour. Instead, a separate sauce is made, e.g. *petits choux braisés*.
11. When braising a whole joint of meat, for example, braised topside or thick flank (of beef), or poultry or whole game bird, it is good practice to glaze the items ready for service. This is achieved by masking the joint or bird with some of the finished sauce and returning to the oven (moderate heat) to set. Repeat several times if necessary to get a good rich glaze. Essentially, this sort of enhanced finish is desirable for presentation at the table (in the restaurant).

# General safety rules

1. Always use a pan of suitable size and shape, with a tight-fitting lid and handles.
2. Always use dry, thick oven-cloths when removing pans from the oven. Wet cloths conduct heat rapidly and can cause a nasty burn.
3. Be aware of escaping steam when removing the cover from the braising-pan; make sure that your sleeves are correctly rolled down to give adequate arm protection.
4. After removing any hot utensil from the oven, it is a recognised trade practice to sprinkle it with flour; this acts as a warning to other workers that the pan/vessel is very hot.

# Techniques associated with braising

1. *Shallow frying*: before brown braising can commence, you have to use the method of shallow frying to seal and brown the foods. This applies mainly to cuts of meat, poultry and game, and the preparation of root vegetables known as a mirepoix.
2. *Sealing*: is the effect of severe heat on the surface of the meat to give colour and promote flavour in the finished dish.
3. *Larding*: refers to the insertion of strips of fat bacon (backfat) into and through the meat to aid with the tenderising and moistening of the joint. Cuts of meat such as topside are very lean, and will benefit from this technique.
4. *Marinading*: refers to the soaking of meats in an acid solution made up of wine (usually), vegetables, garlic and herbs/seasoning (salt and peppercorns). This technique gives colour and strengthens the flavour of the food being marinaded. The marinade is often used as part of the cooking liquor; the action of the acid in the wine helps to tenderise the meat during soaking.
5. *Sweating*: is the cooking of vegetables in a small amount of fat; butter or margarine for white braisings, and first-class dripping for brown braisings. The process is usually carried out in a pan with a lid if for white braising without allowing the vegetables to colour. However, if the sweated vegetables are required for a brown braise, then they are sweated and allowed to cook to a golden brown colour.
6. *Basting*: is the action of regularly spooning the cooking liquor of meat over the joint to keep it moist and succulent during cooking.
7. *Blending*: is the putting together of different flavours to create a finished sauce or dish. It is also the mixing of textures, such as adding a diluted starch (e.g. arrowroot or cornflour) to thicken the accompanying sauce.
8. *Refreshing*: refers to the rapid cooling of foods under running cold water immediately after the blanching of vegetables or sweetbreads prior to

being braised.

9. *Browning:* relates to the colouring of meats in hot fat before braising commences, the object being to contain as much as possible of the natural juices and to enhance the finished flavour of the dish.

# Equipment used for braising

Strictly speaking, the process of braising has always been understood to be one which is performed by oven cookery. However, modern technology has given us quite a number of innovatory pieces of large-scale cooking equipment — the *bratt pan* is but one such fairly recent introduction. The makers claim that it is a multi-purpose piece of equipment which is capable of performing many of the basic methods of food preparation including braising. It is pedestal mounted and can be gas or electrically operated. Because of its large capacity, it is ideal for large-scale catering. The main features will include a hinged cover and a handwheel facility for tilting and pouring. From the safety viewpoint, it is fitted with flame failure (for gas models) and also automatic cut-out devices. As stated, its uses are many and include: boiling, poaching, stewing, and deep and shallow frying.

However, for small-scale braising special braising-pans are used. They are generally rectangular in shape (braisière rectangulaire) with a tight-fitting lid, and made in heavy duty copperware for commercial usage. Naturally, casserole style vessels can also be used for braising purposes, such vessels being made of nickel-copper, stainless steel or enamelled cast-iron.

To clean the small-scale equipment, it may be necessary to soak the pans before they can be scoured clean in hot, soapy water. They should then be rinsed in clean, hot water and dried before storing. Pans should be stored upside down on clean racks.

Finally, as with all equipment, before using, check that it is clean and that handles are firm and in a safe position.

# Self-assessment questions for braising

1. Can you give a brief description of the braising process?
2. Describe 'white braising'.
3. Describe 'brown braising'.
4. Which quality of meat, poultry or game is suitable for braising?
5. What is the approximate temperature when oven braising, and which type of cooking vessel is generally recommended?
6. Can you name at least four vegetables which are suitable for braising?
7. Why is it inadvisable to use a wet oven-cloth for dealing with hot oven items?
8. Can you outline the technique of 'larding' and say why it is used on lean

cuts of meat, etc?
9. Some meats are 'marinaded' prior to braising. What are the main benefits of this technique?
10. Can you describe some of the main features of a *bratt pan?*

When you have completed these questions check your answers with your fellow students and chef or lecturer.

# Braised fish dishes      *Poisson braisé*

### Introduction to braised fish dishes

The cooking times for fish, no matter which method of cookery is involved, are always shorter. This is due to the structure of the fish, in that the collagen breaks down much more easily in fish than in meat. As with stews the cooking liquor is served with the fish or other foods being braised. It should be remembered not to over-braise fish as they will break up and look unsightly for service.

Whole fish such as bream, trout and carp are more commonly found braised, and usually stuffed before braising.

Cuts of round and flat fish may be braised but this is not very common.

**Basic recipe for braised fish**

Allow 1 small whole fish per portion.
Carp/bream: 2–4 portions per fish.
150 g for cuts of fish on the bone.

| 4 portions | Selected fish | 10 portions |
|---|---|---|
| 40 g | Brunoise of carrot | 100 g |
| 40 g | Brunoise of leek | 100 g |
| 40 g | Brunoise of onion | 100 g |
| 40 g | Brunoise of celery | 100 g |
| 1½ dl | Dry white wine | 4 dl |
| 30 g | Butter | 75 g |
| | Bouquet garni | |
| | Salt and milled pepper | |
| 50 g | Beurre manié | 125 g |
| ½ dl | White fish stock | 1 litre |

1. Select a suitable braising dish, line with butter and place the mirepoix of vegetables in the base.
2. Sit the prepared fish on the mirepoix, add the wine and enough stock to cover only two-thirds of the fish.
3. Bring the liquid to the boil, skim and add the bouquet garni.
4. Cover the fish with a buttered cartouche and tight-fitting lid.
5. Place into a moderate oven, 150°C, and braise until tender, basting at regular intervals.

6. When cooked carefully lift out the fish and drain.
7. Strain the cooking liquor and reduce by one-third.
8. Thicken slightly with the beurre manié (arrowroot may be used if a clear sauce is required).
9. Coat the fish with the sauce and sprinkle liberally with finely chopped parsley.

**Service of braised fish**

1. Whole fish should be carved at the table for maximum presentation.
2. A variety of garnishes are suitable for use, e.g.:
   Doria — glazed turned cucumber
   Julienne — strips of blanched vegetables
   Paysanne — thin slices of blanched vegetables

# Braised meats

## Introduction to braised meats

All meats used for brown braising should be sealed in hot fat to trap the juices and flavour before braising commences. As braising is a long, slow method of cooking, cheaper, tougher cuts of meat may be used. The slow cooking process breaks down the tough connective tissues in the meat making it tender and digestible. There are a few exceptions to the rules for brown braising, namely in respect of offal in the form of sweetbreads, which are white braised, i.e. blanched in boiling water and then braised in white stock. They take less time to cook than brown braising as offal (sweetbreads) are more tender than the cuts of meat used for brown braising.

## Cuts of meat for braising

| *English* | *French* | *Approx. weight* |
|---|---|---|
| *Beef* | | |
| Thick flank | *La tranche grasse* | 12 kg |
| Chuck ribs | *Les côtes du collier* | 15 kg |
| Leg of mutton cut | *Le talon du collier* | 11 kg |
| | | |
| *Lamb* | | |
| Shoulder | *L'épaule* | 2 × 3 kg |
| Chump | | |
| Tongue | *La langue* | |
| Heart | *La coeur* | |
| Sweetbreads | *Le ris* | |

*Veal*

| Shoulder | *L'épaule* | 5 kg |
| Cushion | *La noix* | 3 kg |
| Under cushion | *La sous noix* | 3 kg |
| Thick flank | *La quasi* | 2½ kg |

*Poultry*

| Duck | *Canard* |
| Turkey wings | |

*Game*

All feathered game
Rabbits
Hares
Wild duck

## Brown braising

## Basic recipe

| | | |
|---|---|---|
| 600 g | **Chosen meat** | 1½ kg |
| 50 g | **Carrots** | 125 g |
| 50 g | **Onion cut for mirepoix** | 125 g |
| 50 g | **Celery** | 125 g |
| 30 g | **Plain or wholemeal flour** | 75 g |
| 30 g | **Dripping** | 75 g |
| 15 g | **Tomato purée** | 35 g |
| | **Bouquet garni** | |
| | **Milled salt** | |
| | **Milled black pepper** | |
| 5 dl | **Brown stock** | 1¼ litre |

1.  Select a suitable frying-pan and heat the dripping.
2.  Season the meat and seal, allowing to brown.
3.  Transfer the meat to a braising-pan.
4.  Sweat the vegetables in the frying-pan and brown lightly.
5.  Add the flour and form a brown roux.
6.  Add the tomato purée.
7.  Stir in the stock a little at a time and bring to the boil.
8.  Skim to remove the surface scum.
9.  Add the bouquet garni and season; pour the sauce over the meat and cover with a lid.
10. Braise in a moderate oven, checking regularly for sticking.
11. Braise until tender, 1½–2 hours.
12. Remove the meat to a clean hot service dish and adjust the seasoning and consistency of the sauce.
13. Re-boil the sauce and pass through a fine chinois over the meat.
14. Garnish as for any of the given recipes.

*Examples of brown braises*

**Braised beef steaks**                                    **Bifteck braisé**

Use slices of braising steak, garnish with a liberal sprinkling of finely chopped parsley.

**Braised lamb chops**                              **Côte d'agneau braisé**

Use cuts of braising lamb, garnish as for beef steaks.

**Braised veal chops**                              **Côte de veau braisé**

As for lamb chops.

*Garnishes suitable for pre-portioned brown-braised meats*

All braised meat dishes may be garnished in many ways. Below is a list of common garnishes suitable for serving with the dishes already given in this section.

**In red wine**                                              *Au vin rouge*

As for the basic recipe replacing half of the stock with red wine.

| | | |
|---|---|---|
| 120 g | Glazed turned carrots | 300 g |
| 120 g | Glazed turned turnips | 300 g |
| 120 g | Glazed button onion | 300 g |

**Gardener's style**                                          *Jardinière*

| | | |
|---|---|---|
| 100 g | Jardinière of carrots | 250 g |
| 100 g | Jardinière of celery | 250 g |
| 100 g | Jardinière of turnip | 250 g |

Plain boil the vegetables and garnish around the meat. Finish by brushing with melted butter.

**Peasant style**                                              *Paysanne*

| | | |
|---|---|---|
| 100 g | Paysanne of carrots | 250 g |
| 100 g | Paysanne of celery | 250 g |
| 100 g | Paysanne of turnip | 250 g |

Plain boil and garnish around the meat. Finish by brushing with a little melted butter.

## Spring vegetables

*Printanier*

| | | |
|---|---|---|
| 120 g | Glazed turned carrots | 300 g |
| 120 g | Button onion | 300 g |
| 100 g | Glazed turned turnip | 250 g |
| 100 g | Whole green beans | 250 g |

Glaze the vegetables in a little clarified butter. Plain boil the whole green beans and garnish around the dish. Brush the beans with melted butter.

*Common braised meat dishes*

## Beef braised in beer

*Carbonade be boeuf*

| | | |
|---|---|---|
| 600 g | Lean braising steak | 1½ kg |
| 300 g | Sliced onion | 750 g |
| 3 dl | Brown ale | 7 dl |
| 40 g | Plain or wholemeal flour | 100 g |
| 30 g | Dripping | 75 g |
| 1 | Crushed clove of garlic | 2 |
| 50 g | Castor sugar | 125 g |
| | Milled salt and peppercorns | |
| 5 dl | Brown stock | 1¼ litres |
| | Finely chopped parsley | |

1.  Slice the beef into small escalopes.
2.  Select a frying-pan of suitable size and heat the dripping.
3.  Pass the small escalopes of beef through the seasoned flour and seal quickly in the hot dripping.
4.  Remove the meat and reserve in a bowl.
5.  Sweat the onions in the frying-pan to a light brown colour with the garlic.
6.  Select a suitable braising dish and layer the meat and onions, sprinkling a little sugar, salt and pepper between each layer.
7.  Pour the brown ale over the meat and add enough brown stock to just cover the meat.
8.  Cover with a tight-fitting lid and braise slowly in a moderate oven, 180°C, for 1½–2 hours or until the meat is tender.
9.  Skim to remove surface grease and wipe the edge of the dish clean for service.
10. Serve sprinkled liberally with finely chopped parsley.

## Braised lamb chops

*Côte d'agneau braisé*

| | | |
|---|---|---|
| 4 × 200 g | Lamb chops | 10 × 200 g |
| 25 g | Dripping | 60 g |
| 100 g | Diced carrots | 250 g |
| 100 g | Diced onions | 250 g |
| 30 g | Flour | 75 g |
| 25 g | Tomato purée | 60 g |
| ½ | Clove crushed garlic | 1 |
| 1 | Bouquet garni | 1 |
| 8 dl | Brown lamb stock | 2 litres |
| | Finely chopped parsley | |

1. Select a frying-pan of suitable size and melt the dripping.
2. Season the lamb chops and fry to a light brown on both sides; remove from the pan and place into a suitable dish for braising.
3. Fry the diced vegetables to a light golden brown in the same frying-pan and add to the braising dish; mix in the flour.
4. Add the tomato purée and stir enough stock into the dish to almost cover the chops.
5. Add the garlic and bouquet garni, season, bring to the boil and cover with a lid.
6. Place into an oven at 180°C for 1–1½ hours to cook.
7. When cooked, remove the chops from the braising dish and set in a clean dish.
8. Skim the fat off the sauce and adjust the seasoning and consistency as required.
9. Strain the sauce over the chops in a hot service dish and sprinkle liberally with finely chopped parsley.

**Note:** This dish may be served with a suitable vegetable garnish, e.g. jardinière of vegetables.

## Lancashire hot pot

| | | |
|---|---|---|
| 800 g | Middle neck of lamb | 2 kg |
| 30 g | Dripping | 75 g |
| 600 g | Peeled potatoes | 1½ kg |
| 400 g | Shredded onions | 1 kg |
| 8 dl | White mutton stock | 2 litres |
| 30 g | Clarified butter | 75 g |
| | Finely chopped parsley | |
| | Salt and milled pepper | |

1. Select a frying-pan of suitable size for the volume of lamb and heat the dripping.
2. Season the lamb and lightly seal in the frying-pan, with just a little colouring to the flesh.
3. Slice the potatoes 3–4 mm on a mandolin.
4. Select a suitably sized earthenware oven-proof dish and place in a layer of onions and potatoes to cover the base.

5. Add the pieces of lamb and top with the remaining onions and sliced potatoes; the top layer of potatoes should be neatly overlapping for presentation.
6. Pour in enough stock just to cover the lamb and top layer of onions but not the potatoes.
7. Brush the potatoes liberally with clarified butter and put the dish to cook in an oven pre-heated to 180°C and cook for 1½–2 hours, or until the lamb is tender.
8. To serve brush the potatoes again with clarified butter and sprinkle liberally with finely chopped parsley.

## Braised liver and onion                    *Foie de boeuf braisé lyonnaise*

| | | |
|---|---|---|
| 400 g | Sliced and skinned ox liver | 1 kg |
| 200 g | Sliced onions | 150 g |
| 50 g | Dripping | 150 g |
| 30 g | Plain or wholemeal flour | 75 g |
| 1 litre | Brown stock | 2 litres |
| | Salt and milled black pepper | |
| | Additional seasoned flour | |
| | Finely chopped parsley | |

1. Heat the dripping in a suitable frying-pan.
2. Pass the meat through seasoned flour and seal quickly, allowing to brown.
3. Transfer the liver to the braising-pan.
4. Fry the onions to a golden brown in the frying-pan.
5. Add the brown stock a little at a time to form a sauce.
6. Skim to remove any surface scum and season.
7. Pour the sauce over the liver, cover with a lid and braise in a moderate oven until tender, 1½–2 hours.
8. Check during cooking to prevent sticking.
9. When cooked, skim to remove surface grease and adjust the seasoning.
10. Serve in hot service dish, sprinkled liberally with chopped parsley.

### Braised joints of meat

Joints differ from portions of meat in that joints have to be basted during cooking to give a glazed effect to the meat. When cooked the joint is then sliced into portions and served dressed with the thickened cooking liquor and a suitable garnish.

Cooking times for braised joints will differ according to the meat being braised. Some of the joints will need to be larded and marinaded before braising.

## Basic recipe for brown braised joints of meat

| | | |
|---|---|---|
| 1 kg | Prepared braising meat | 2½ kg |
| 60 g | Carrots | 150 g |
| 60 g | Onion | 150 g |
| 60 g | Celery | 150 g |
| 60 g | Leeks | 150 g |
| 40 g | Dripping | 100 g |
| 25 g | Tomato purée | 60 g |
| | Bouquet garni | |
| | Salt and milled black pepper | |
| | Finely chopped parsley | |
| 1 litre | Brown stock or wine | 2 litres |
| | Arrowroot for thickening | |

1. Select a braising-pan of suitable size and heat the dripping.
2. Add the mirepoix of vegetables and seasoned meat, seal and brown in a very hot oven or on the stove top.
3. Add enough stock or wine to reach two-thirds of the meat's depth and bring to the boil.
4. Skim to remove any surface scum and grease.
5. Add the tomato pureé, bouquet garni and season.
6. Cover with a tight-fitting lid, return to a moderate oven and braise until almost cooked.
7. Baste with the cooking liquor at regular intervals.
8. Remove the meat from the pan and slightly thicken the liquor with diluted arrowroot.
9. Adjust the seasoning and strain the sauce back over the meat.
10. Continue cooking until tender and serve as for any of the given recipes.

Total cooking time, 2–3 hours.

*White braised meats*                    *Viande blanc braisé*

Only white meats, e.g. veal, pork and offal such as sweetbread, are suitable for white braising due to the colour of their flesh.

### White braised veal                    *Pièce de veau braisé à blanc*

| | | |
|---|---|---|
| 1 kg | Cushion of veal | 2½ kg |
| 60 g | Macédoine of carrot | 150 g |
| 60 g | Macédoine of leek | 150 g |
| 60 g | Macédoine of celery | 150 g |
| 60 g | Macédoine of onion | 150 g |
| 40 g | Butter | 100 g |
| | Bouquet garni | |
| | Salt and white pepper | |
| 1 litre | White veal stock | 2 litres |
| | Fresh lemon juice to taste | |
| | Arrowroot to thicken the stock | |

1. Select a braising-pan of suitable size and heat the butter.
2. Add the mirepoix of vegetables and the veal, season and sweat without colouring.
3. Add enough stock to reach two-thirds of the depth of the veal.
4. Bring to the boil and remove any surface scum.
5. Add the bouquet garni and season.
6. Cover with a cartouche and a tight-fitting lid, place into a moderate oven to braise until tender, 1½–2 hours.
7. Baste the meat at regular intervals to give the meat a glaze.
8. When cooked lift out the veal and keep hot.
9. Boil the cooking liquor and thicken slightly with diluted arrowroot, add lemon juice, adjust the seasoning and strain through a fine chinois over the meat, which may be either carved and served or carved at the table.

## Braised sweetbreads                                   *Ris braisé à blanc*

| | | |
|---|---|---|
| 600 g | Sweetbreads | 1½ kg |
| 40 g | Macédoine of carrots | 100 g |
| 40 g | Macédoine of onion | 100 g |
| 40 g | Macédoine of celery | 100 g |
| 30 g | Butter | 75 g |
| | Bouquet garni | |
| | Finely chopped parsley | |
| | Fresh lemon juice to taste | |
| | Salt and white ground pepper | |
| 1 litre | White veal stock | 2 litres |
| | Arrowroot to thicken the stock | |

1. Soak the sweetbreads in cold running water to help remove any blood vessels.
2. Blanch and refresh the sweetbreads, remove the skin and ducts.
3. Select a suitable braising-pan and heat the butter.
4. Add the mirepoix of vegetables and sweat without colour.
5. Add the sweetbreads, season and add enough stock to just cover the sweetbreads.
6. Add the bouquet garni and bring to the boil and skim.
7. Cover with a cartouche and tight-fitting lid, place into a moderate oven to braise until tender, 1–1½ hours.
8. Lift out the sweetbreads and keep hot.
9. Boil the cooking liquor and reduce slightly.
10. Thicken with diluted arrowroot, adjust the seasoning and add the lemon juice.
11. Strain the sauce over the sweetbreads, which may be carved or left whole, and serve sprinkled liberally with chopped parsley.

# Braised vegetables   *Légumes braisés*

### Introduction to braised vegetables

A wide variety of vegetables and potatoes are suitable for braising, giving a good range of dishes for including in the menu. Braised vegetables and potatoes are served in their cooking liquor making them a very nutritious dish from a dietary aspect. All of their flavour is also retained and served in the cooking liquor.

### Berrichonne potatoes                    *Pommes berrichonne*

| | | |
|---|---|---|
| 400 g | Peeled potatoes | 1 kg |
| 100 g | Piece of streaky bacon | 250 g |
| 50 g | Macédoine of onion | 125 g |
| | Finely chopped parsley | |
| 30 g | Butter | 60 g |
| 2½ dl | White stock | 6 dl |

1. Turn the potatoes into barrel shape.
2. Select a sauteuse of suitable size and melt the butter.
3. Add the onion and cover with a lid.
4. Seal for 3–4 minutes on the stove.
5. Remove the rind from the bacon and cut the bacon into lardons.
6. Add the lardons to the sauteuse, replace the lid and cook for a further 3–5 minutes.
7. Add the potatoes and enough stock to reach half the depth of the potatoes.
8. Season and place into a hot oven 240–250°C, to cook.
9. Turn the potatoes gently after ½ hour's cooking.
10. Cook the pototoes for about 1 hour total.
11. When cooked they should be golden brown in colour and the majority of the liquid should have been absorbed by the potatoes.
12. Serve in a hot service dish liberally sprinkled with finely chopped parsley.

### Potatoes with bacon and onion               *Pommes au lard*

| | | |
|---|---|---|
| 400 g | Peeled potatoes | 1 kg |
| 100 g | Peeled button onions | 250 g |
| | Salt and milled black pepper | |
| 100 g | Piece of streaky bacon | 250 g |
| | Finely chopped parsley | |
| 25 g | Butter | 50 g |

1. Cut the potatoes in 1 cm cubes, rinse and dry in a clean cloth.
2. Remove the rind from the bacon and cut the bacon into lardons.
3. Select a sauteuse of suitable size and melt the butter.
4. Add the button onions and lardons to the sauteuse and fry to a light

golden brown.
5. Add the cubes of potato and enough stock to cover half the depth of the potatoes.
6. Season, cover with a lid and cook in the oven at 240-250°C for approximately 30 minutes.
7. Adjust the seasoning and serve in a hot service dish, sprinkled liberally with finely chopped parsley.

## Savoury potatoes                                    *Pommes boulangère*

| | | |
|---|---|---|
| **400 g** | **Peeled potatoes** | **1 kg** |
| **2½ dl** | **White stock** | **6 dl** |
| | **Salt** | |
| | **Milled pepper** | |
| **100 g** | **Finely sliced onion** | **250 g** |
| **30 g** | **Butter or margarine** | **75 g** |
| | **Finely chopped parsley** | |

1. Slice the peeled potatoes into discs using a mandolin to ensure even thickness; these discs should be no more than 3 mm thick.
2. Mix the sliced potatoes and onions together, season and place into a suitable sized buttered oven-proof dish.
3. Reserve enough slices of potato to make a neat topping of overlapping discs.
4. Add enough stock to almost cover the potatoes and finish by placing on top small pieces of butter or margarine.
5. Place the dish into a pre-heated oven set at 240–250°C until the top is a light golden brown colour.
6. Lower the heat and allow the savoury potatoes to cook gently; press occasionally with a fish slice.
7. When the potatoes are cooked, all the stock should be absorbed by the potatoes; this takes approximately 1½ hours.
8. Serve in a hot vegetable dish, garnished with a liberal sprinkling of chopped parsley.

## Fondant potatoes                                    *Pommes fondantes*

| | | |
|---|---|---|
| **400 g** | **Peeled potatoes** | **1 kg** |
| **5 dl** | **White stock** | **1½ litres** |
| **30 g** | **Clarified butter** | **75 g** |
| | **Finely chopped parsley** | |

1. Use evenly sized potatoes, and using a small paring knife turn the potatoes into a barrel shape, 4 cm × 1½ cm wide.
2. Allow 2 potatoes to a portion.
3. Sit the potatoes into an oven-proof dish of suitable size and depth.
4. Pour in enough white stock to reach half the depth of the potatoes.
5. Brush the tops with clarified butter.
6. Place into a pre-heated oven at 240–250°C and brush the potatoes at

regular intervals with a little clarified butter.
7. When the potatoes are cooked the stock should be completely absorbed by the potatoes.
8. Serve neatly arranged in a hot service dish, brush with melted butter and sprinkle liberally with finely chopped parsley.

## Basic preparation of braised vegetables

The majority of vegetables for braising are first blanched in boiling salted water and refreshed. This helps to retain the colour and allows for shaping of the vegetables.

### Cabbage/*Choux*
1. Remove the outer leaves and retain one large green leaf per person for shaping.
2. Quarter the remaining cabbage and blanch in boiling salted water, then refresh.
3. Season and wrap the cabbage quarters in the large green leaves.
4. Shape into balls by squeezing in a muslin cloth; this also removes excess moisture.

### Celery/*Céleri*
1. Trim the root and celery tops; use the tops for stews and soups, etc.
2. Cut in half lengthways and rinse under cold running water.
3. Blanch for 10 minutes in boiling salted water and refresh.
4. Proceed as for basic recipe.

### Stuffed cabbage/*Chou farcie*
As for the cabbage but stuff the centre of each ball with a little sausage meat stuffing.

### Belgian endive/*Endive belge*
1. Remove discoloured leaves, rinse under cold running water and leave whole.
2. Blanch for 10 minutes in boiling salted water and refresh for braising.

### Leek/*Poireaux*
1. Remove discoloured outer leaves.
2. Trim the tops for soups, stews, etc.
3. Trim the root and split the leeks in half lengthways, leaving the root intact.
4. Rinse under cold running water.
5. Blanch in boiling salted water for 5 minutes and refresh for braising.

### Lettuce/*Laitue*
1. Trim the base and remove any discoloured leaves

2. Rinse in cold water.
3. Blanch for 5 minutes in boiling salted water and refresh.
4. Drain and squeeze dry into an oval cigar shape.
5. Fold in half for braising.

Onions/*Oignons*
1. Trim the root and peel the onion.
2. Blanch in boiling water for 10 minutes, refresh and drain well.
3. If using small onions, leave then whole. Larger onions should be cut in half through the root.

Fennel/*Fenouil*
1. Trim the stems and tops.
2. Rinse under cold running water; if necessary cut the fennel into quarters or halves through the root.
3. Blanch in boiling salted water for 10 minutes and refresh ready for braising.

## Basic recipe for braising vegetables

| | | |
|---|---|---|
| 400 g | Main vegetable | 1 kg |
| 40 g | Macédoine of carrot | 100 g |
| 40 g | Macédoine of onions | 100 g |
| 40 g | Macédoine of celery | 100 g |
| 40 g | Diced leeks | 100 g |
| 20 g | Butter/margarine | 50 g |
| ½ litre | White meat or vegetable stock | 1 litre |
| | Arrowroot to thicken stock | |
| | Demi-glace or jus lié may be used if required | |
| | Salt and pepper | |
| | Bouquet garni | |
| | Finely chopped parsley | |

1. Select a suitable braising-pan and sweat the mirepoix vegetables, carrot, onion, celery and leek, in the butter.
2. Sit the prepared main vegetable on the mirepoix and season.
3. Add enough stock to half cover the main vegetable with stock and add the bouquet garni.
4. Cover with a buttered cartouche and a tight-fitting lid and place into a moderate oven, 150°C, and braise the vegetable until tender, 1–2½ hours.
5. When cooked lift out the vegetables and drain well.
6. Prepare the thickened sauce as required.
   (a) Reduce the liquor by one-third, thicken with arrowroot, season and nap over the vegetables after straining.
   (b) Reduce the cooking liquor to a glaze and add ½ litre of demi-glace or jus lié, season and strain the sauce, nap over the vegetables.
7. Finish for service by sprinkling liberally with finely chopped parsley.

## Stuffed braised peppers        *Piments farcis braisés*

| 4 | Small peppers | 10 |
|---|---|---|
| 200 g | Rice pilaff | 500 g |
| ½ dl | Meat or vegetable stock | 1 litre |
| | Picked parsley | |

1. Cut the tops off the peppers, scoop out the seeds and remove the skins.
2. Fill the cavity with rice pilaff and sit the tops back on the peppers.
3. Stand the peppers in a suitable braising pan or dish — it must hold the peppers in an upright position.
4. Add the stock so that it comes up to half the depth of the pepper.
5. Cover with a buttered cartouche and tight-fitting lid.
6. Braise in a moderate oven, 150°C, until the pepper is tender.
7. Serve in a clean braising-dish garnished with picked parsley.

**Notes:**
1. If only large peppers are available, proceed as for recipe given allowing half a pepper per portion. Cut the pepper in half lengthways after cooking and sprinkle with finely chopped parsley.
2. The stuffing can be varied depending upon the ultimate use of the pepper. If the pepper is meant as a main course or starter in its own right then any combination of the following ingredients could be added to the rice pilaff: crushed assorted nuts, prawns, brunoise of blanched vegetables, diced chicken or beef (pre-cooked), flaked cooked fish, peas, diced apricots and diced cooked lamb, parmesan cheese. If required brown rice or wild rice could be used in place of basic pilaff.

## Braised red cabbage Flemish style      *Chou-rouge flamande*

| 400 g | Shredded red cabbage | 1 kg |
|---|---|---|
| 10 g | Peeled and sliced cooking apples | 250 g |
| ½ dl | Cider vinegar | 1 dl |
| 30 g | Butter or margarine | 60 g |
| 30 g | Brown sugar | 60 g |
| | Salt and pepper | |
| | Finely chopped parsley | |

1. Trim any discoloured leaves from the cabbage, quarter and remove the centre stalks and shred.
2. Wash in cold running water.
3. Select a suitable earthenware dish and rub with the butter.
4. Add the cabbage, cider vinegar, brown sugar and seasoning.
5. Cover with a buttered cartouche and tight-fitting lid.
6. Braise in a moderate oven, 150°C, for 1½ hours.
7. Stir occasionally until two-thirds cooked.
8. Add the sliced apples and mix in.
9. Continue cooking until the apples and cabbage are tender.
10. Adjust the seasoning and serve in a clean hot dish sprinkled liberally

with chopped parsley.

**Note:** This dish should not be made in a metal container, especially aluminium, as the acid content of the food will cause pitting in the metal and discoloration.

# Chapter 7
# Steaming          *Vapeuriser*

## The competency defined

Steaming is the cooking of foods with moist heat under assorted degrees of pressure dependent upon which system is being used.

The lowest pressure used commercially is 0.16 kg/cm$^2$ (2½ lbs per square inch). At sea level the boiling point of water is 100°C (212°F). The temperature increases as the pressure is raised thus cooking foods faster. It is this principle that is used in pressure steaming and domestic pressure cookers.

During the steaming process heat is transferred from the steam or water vapour which then cooks and tenderises the food. Items which are suitable for steaming include fish, a wide range of vegetables, meat, offal and poultry. There is also an extensive selection of puddings, both sweet and savoury, to which this method will apply.

Steaming is an excellent method of cooking and is ideal for invalid cookery. Items such as meat can be made tender without causing indigestibility by prolonged cooking. As fish has a high percentage of water interspersed in the fibres it also cooks quickly. Such foods are more easily digested due to the protein content being just cooked, with the minimum loss of valuable nutrients and natural food flavours.

A method which is often used in preparing fish for an invalid diet is the *indirect* process. The food is placed between two plates and put on top of a pan of boiling water. The food does not come in contact with the water, and there is no loss of flavour from that cause.

## Purpose of steaming

The purposes of steaming are to:

1. render foods easier to digest;
2. create a more pleasing and edible texture;
3. render foods safe to eat;
4. complete the cooking process whilst maintaining a high nutrient level in the finished dish.

215

# Methods of steaming

There are two basic methods of steaming plus one other technique *(sous-vide)* which, whilst not generally referred to as steaming, nonetheless has the same effect of being cooked by the action of steam.

### Method I: Atmospheric or low pressure steaming

This is one of the most common methods of steaming. The food is cooked by either direct or indirect contact with steam. Direct contact would be in a steamer or suitable pan of boiling water.

In a steamer, steam is produced within the steaming chamber, or is fed into the chamber from a separate boiler. This exposure to moist steam will produce large amounts of water vapour, which in turn will create considerable surface water upon the items being processed. For this reason it is necessary to use perforated steamer trays to allow the condensation/water to drain off whilst in operation. In addition, such items as puddings must be covered, usually with buttered greaseproof paper circles and pudding cloths or cooking foil, which will prevent the condensation/water seeping into the pudding mixture.

The pan method will need a generous amount of boiling water to come at least two-thirds of the way up the side of the pudding basin, with a careful replenishment of boiling water to 'top up' that which is lost through evaporation during cooking. Adequate covering is necessary to prevent water soaking into the mixture, together with a tight-fitting pan lid to contain the steam. For small amounts, a perforated steamer can be fitted over the top of a pan of boiling water with the same precautions taken as described above.

The indirect method is as already mentioned in the reference to simple fish preparation for an invalid diet.

### METHOD II: High pressure steaming

This is a relatively new innovation and one which produces first-class results. Normal cooking times are considerably reduced, and because the steam generated is dry steam with a low moisture content, and from which the air has been expelled, there is a high retention of vitamins and trace elements. Large packs of frozen vegetables can be cooked to order (in 2–3 minutes) and the results in terms of taste and colour are superb. The same comments apply equally to other items such as fish and shellfish.

One high-speed steaming system produces steam in a separate generator which is then directed into the steaming chamber. The dry steam from which the air has been expelled is sprayed directly on to the food which reduces cooking times even more. The ultra-quick cooking time reduces shrinkage in meat products and is both time and fuel saving. Fresh vegetables cooked by this method, such as cauliflower and carrots, taste delicious and are far superior to those cooked by the conventional blanching and refreshing process.

### Sous-vide and vacuum cooking in a pouch

This is a fairly new technique, by which food is cooked in vacuum-sealed pouches in a convection steamer. Several items of specialist equipment are required, namely: a vacuum packaging machine; rapid chilling facilities; a pressureless steamer; and the special Cryovac plastic sachets.

The advantages are many: a minimum change in texture; less weight loss; no drying out of foods; and a good level of natural colour retention. Certain dishes are suitable for garnishing and decorating before cooking, with the foods being cooked in their own natural juices and flavour. The system achieves a high level of uniformity in terms of production output and the process is also labour saving.

A wide range of highly perishable food items can be bought and prepared in advance in single or multiple units as a basis for à la carte menus or banqueting service. Such a mise-en-place facility has its advantages in ironing out the peaks and troughs of production time, and enables the kitchen staff to maintain a steady throughput of dishes in a more orderly fashion. It will also assist the cost-effectiveness of strict portion control.

**Methods for sous-vide**

Raw foods such as breasts of chicken, duck and game, and cuts of fish such as salmon, turbot and brill, are placed into the vacuum pouches together with prepared vegetables, herbs, spices, stocks and wines. A special vacuum packaging machine then seals the pouches, after which they are cooked in a convection steamer. The temperature and cooking time have to be strictly controlled.

When cooked, the sealed pouches are rapidly cooled and stored at 3°C (37°F) until required for service.

At the time of service, the pouch is placed into a pan of boiling water or a steamer to re-heat.

# Organisation and preparation for steaming

In a traditional partie system the following chefs would be involved in this method of cookery.

| | |
|---|---|
| *Chef garde-manger*: | Concerned with the basic preparation of meats and fish. |
| *Chef saucier*: | Cooking of all butcher's meat and poultry/game (for entrées). |
| *Chef pâtissier*: | Production of sweet puddings and suet pastry. |
| *Chef poissonnier*: | Production of all fish dishes. |
| *Chef entremettier*: | Production of all vegetable and potato dishes. |

The preparation of meat for steaming would include lightly seasoning and tying the meat as required. If the meat is to be cooked without stock then it should be placed on to a perforated steamer tray. If it is to be cooked in stock, it should be placed into a deep steaming pan. Steamed meats are generally served with a similar type of garnish as boiled meat dishes.

The preparation of fish for steaming would include lightly seasoning and flavouring with lemon juice, and steaming as for meats. The dishes are garnished and served as for conventional boiled or poached fish dishes.

The preparation of vegetables for steaming would include placing the items into a perforated steamer tray, and steaming until cooked. The mode of service is usually as for boiled vegetables.

Eggs are also suitable for steaming in their shells to the hard-boiled stage. The steaming time at normal pressure is about 15 minutes.

# Advantages of steaming

1. Steaming is very economical as regards fuel costs.
2. When steaming fish it is possible to retain the natural juices with which to make an accompanying sauce.
3. High pressure steamers can be used for 'batch cooking' which allows such items as vegetables to be cooked à la minute (to order). Thus, it is possible to serve freshly cooked vegetables with a high retention level of colour, flavour and nutritional value.
4. Because the steaming process is suitable for large-scale cooking, it can also be labour saving.
5. Low pressure steaming at $0.16 \text{ kg/cm}^2$ (2½ lbs per square inch) makes it easy to control the degree of cooking and reduces the possibility of over-cooking the protein content of foodstuffs (ideal for invalid diets).
6. Careful steaming of foodstuffs will help to retain a fairly high level of the natural nutrients and flavour.

# Degrees of cooking

When foods are prepared by the steaming method they are usually cooked until they are just ready to eat. This is to avoid over-cooking the protein — which would tend to toughen the food and render it indigestible.

# Effects of steaming on foods

The effect of steaming on foods is that the basic structure and texture of the food is changed by a chemical reaction within the food item. The average weight loss in steaming is approximately 15 per cent.

218

# General rules for efficient steaming

1. This method of cookery is best suited to foods which can be cooked slowly without too much loss of colour, flavour and texture. The slower the process of cooking, the more digestible food becomes.
2. Root vegetables need to be placed on to trays which are perforated to allow the draining of condensed steam.
3. Puddings in basins need to be covered with greaseproof paper and foil or a cloth to prevent absorbing condensation/surface water into the mixture and becoming soggy.
4. When steaming foods over a pan of boiling waer, the vessel must be covered with a tight-fitting lid.
5. When using a high pressure steamer the door must be closed properly to trap all the heat and pressure.

# General safety rules

1. When using commercial steaming equipment always follow the maker's directions for operating and cleaning.
2. Always exercise great care when opening steamer doors. Never stand too close and always stand behind the door (using it as a shield) to avoid any escaping steam.
3. Always ensure that the water supply is turned on and at the correct level in the steamer tank.

# Techniques associated with steaming

*Greasing*: The inside of pudding basins or moulds should be lightly coated with a suitable fat or oil before adding the food to be steamed.
*Traying up*: This refers to the methodical filling of trays with prepared moulds or basins for ease of handling in bulk steaming.
*Covering/waterproofing*: Foods which are cooked in pudding basins should be protected by covering them with protective paper and foil/muslin to prevent condensation/surface water soaking into the food item.

# Equipment used for steaming

Foods may be steamed in basins or moulds (pudding sleeves), or between two plates, and then cooked on top of a pan of boiling water; in an atmospheric steamer; in a high compression steamer, or in a pressureless convection steamer.

All equipment used for steaming should be washed in hot detergent water, then rinsed and dried. Water chambers should be drained, rinsed and refilled. The steamer door should be left slightly ajar to allow a flow of air when the equipment is not in use. Door hinges should be oiled regularly.

## Self-assessment questions for steaming

1. What is the definition of steaming as a method of cookery?
2. What is the lowest pressure used commercially in low pressure moist steam equipment?
3. What sorts of foods are suitable for steaming?
4. High pressure steaming has certain advantages over atmospheric or low pressure steaming. What are they?
5. Sous-vide as a modern technique of food preparation has several advantages. Can you name three of them?
6. 'Batch cooking' using a high pressure steamer has certain advantages. What are they?
7. What precautions must be taken when cooking puddings by the low pressure steaming method?
8. What are the general safety rules to be observed when using any sort of steaming equipment?
9. Can you give a brief outline of two techniques associated with steaming?
10. What are the general procedures when washing steaming equipment?

When you have completed these questions check your answers with your fellow students and chef or lecturer.

## Steamed fish                    *Poisson vapeurisé*

*Guidelines for steaming fish*

Trout, bream, carp, salmon trout and turbot are all examples of whole fish suitable for steaming. Cuts of fish such as darnes of salmon, halibut, turbot, fillets of plaice and sole are also suitable for steaming.

Steaming may be used as an alternative to poaching and fish cooked by steaming may also be served with any of the garnishes given for poached fish dishes. Steaming is mainly used when bulk cooking foods in hospitals or homes for elderly persons.

Before steaming the fish it should be seasoned lightly and sprinkled with a little lemon juice and covered with greaseproof paper to protect the surface and help keep in flavour.

Cooking times for steamed fish are the same as for poached fish, except when using a high pressure steamer in which case the cooking times are greatly reduced and can prove to be as quick as cooking the fish in a microwave.

For recipe examples see Poached Fish dishes. Assemble the dishes as for poaching, but use steam as the method of cookery.

# Steamed meat                     *Viande vapeurisé*

## Introduction to steamed meat

Meats are only steamed in a pastry case, such as in the recipe given below for steak pudding.

### Steamed steak pudding

| | | |
|---|---|---|
| 500 g | Stewing steak | 1¼ kg |
| 100 g | Brunoise of onion | 250 g |
| 1 dl | Brown beef stock | 2½ dl |
| 1 | Teaspoon Worcester sauce | 2 |
| | Chopped parsley | |
| 15 g | Plain flour | 25 g |
| 250 g | Suet paste | 625 g |
| | Salt and pepper | |

1. Use two-thirds of the pastry to line greased pudding moulds. Individual or larger basins may be used.
2. Dice the meat into 1 cm cubes and mix with the onion and parsley and Worcester sauce and season.
3. Put the mixture into the lined basins.
4. Mix the plain flour to a smooth paste with a little cold water.
5. Boil the stock and thicken with the flour paste, stirring until thickening is completed.
6. Strain the sauce and use to moisten the meat in the basin.
7. Use the remaining suet paste to put a lid on the basins.
8. Seal the edges by moistening with a little water.
9. Cover with greaseproof paper and a pudding cloth and steam for a minimum of 3 hours.
10. When cooked remove the cloth and greaseproof paper.
    (a) If individual basins have been used, turn out on to a plate, split open and garnish with watercress.
    (b) If using larger multi-portion basins, leave in the basin and stand the basin on a flat inside a folded napkin.
11. Serve with extra gravy in a sauce-boat.

Variations on this would include the addition of kidneys, mushrooms or oysters.

# Steamed vegetables *Légumes vapeurisés*

### Introduction to steamed vegetables

Vegetables are easily steamed but usually only for bulk catering in hospitals or elderly people's homes. The following recipes are common examples.

### Potatoes steamed in their jackets     *Pommes en robe de chambre*

| | | |
|---|---|---|
| 500 g | Potatoes | 1¼ kg |
| | *or* | |
| 4 | Even-sized potatoes | 10 |

1. Wash and scrub the potatoes under cold running water.
2. Steam until tender, 20–30 minutes.
3. Serve split open in a folded napkin with a piece of picked parsley.

### Potatoes with cream     *Pommes à la crème*

| | | |
|---|---|---|
| 1 dl | Hot double cream | 2½ dl |
| 50 g | Butter | 125 g |
| 1 dl | Milk | 2½ dl |
| | Salt and pepper | |

1. Prepare and cook the potatoes as above.
2. When cooked, peel and slice ½ cm thick.
3. Layer in a suitable pan and add just enough milk to almost cover the potatoes.
4. Add the butter and bring to the boil.
5. Simmer for 3–5 minutes and serve in a hot service dish.
6. Finish with a cordon of hot double cream.

### Potatoes with cream and parsley     *Pommes maitre d'hôtel*

1. Proceed as for potatoes with cream.
2. Finish by sprinkling liberally with chopped parsley.

### Steamed potatoes     Pommes vapeur

| | | |
|---|---|---|
| 400 g | Peeled potatotes | 1 kg |

1. Prepare the potatoes as for plain boiling and season.
2. Place into steamer trays and cook in a steamer, the cooking time being dependent upon the type of steamer used.
3. Serve in hot service dishes with a lid.

### Steamed vegetable guidelines

Steaming is a good method to use when cooking large quantities of food, especially vegetables. Most vegetables are suitable for steaming. However, it should be noted that green vegetables, e.g. brussel sprouts or whole green beans, should be cooked in high pressure steamers, as when cooked in an atmospheric steamer the vegetables tend to lose their green colour and appear unappetising.

Before steaming foods they should be lightly seasoned and laid in perforated steamer trays allowing the water to drain off the food. Steamed vegetables should be served as for any of the boiled vegetable recipes. For examples, see Boiled Vegetables section.

The cooking times for steamed vegetables are the same as for boiled vegetables, except when using a high pressure steamer, in which case the cooking times are greatly reduced and prove to be as quick as cooking vegetables in a microwave.

# Steamed pâtisserie

### Introduction to steamed pâtisserie

The following recipes are a selection of dishes for which the predominant method of cookery used is steaming. Also included is some basic preparation, e.g. suet paste.

### Suet paste

| | | |
|---|---|---|
| 230 g | **Flour, medium strength** | 450 g |
| 60 g | **Fresh breadcrumbs**<br>  **(optional)** | 120 g |
| 115 g | **Shredded beef suet** | 230 g |
| 15 g | **Baking powder** | 30 g |
| 10 g | **Salt** | 25 g |
| 125 ml (approx.) | **Cold water** | 250 ml (approx.) |
| *For sweet puddings add:* | | |
| 50 g | **Castor sugar** | 100 g |

1. Sieve the flour and baking powder together into a suitable bowl.
2. Blend in the suet and breadcrumbs and make a bay.
3. Add the salt (and sugar if being used) and the cold water.
4. Mix lightly to a medium, firm dough.

Uses for plain dough: dumplings, meat puddings and savoury rolls. Sweet puddings: jam, syrup and fruit.

The introduction of breadcrumbs into the paste is not essential. However, it does help to produce a light textured dough whether it is being used in the making of sweet or savoury items.

## Jam roll

1. Roll out some suet paste to a rectangle approximately 25 × 20 cm.
2. Brush the edges with cold water and spread with jam.
3. Roll up swiss roll style after first tucking in the side edges to contain the filling.
4. Moisten the bottom edge to seal the roll, and wrap in a buttered greaseproof paper and a muslin pudding cloth.
5. Loosely tie both ends and steam for about 1½ hours.
6. Serve with jam or custard sauce.

## Apple roll

1. Proceed as above with the paste, and layer generously with thinly sliced cooking apples.
2. Sprinkle with moist soft brown sugar and some grated lemon zest.
3. Roll up and steam for about 1½ hours.
4. Serve with a custard sauce or fresh cream.

### Currant or sultana roll

1. Add a proportion of dried fruit (currants or sultanas) to the sweetened suet paste mix at the dry stage, about 100 g fruit per 400 g suet paste.
2. Bind the mixture with cold water, roll and tie up as above.
3. Steam for about 1½ hours and serve with custard or vanilla sauce.

These puddings can also be made in pudding sleeves, in which case, place the prepared roll in its buttered greaseproof wrapping and fit into the pudding mould. Steam as usual. Other fillings may be used in place of jam, for example: treacle or golden syrup, chopped dates, stoneless raisins and dried figs.

### Steamed apple pudding

*Pouding vapeur aux pommes*

| | | |
|---|---|---|
| 900 g | Cooking apples (Bramleys) | 2 kg |
| 170 g | Soft brown sugar | 350 g |
| 1 | Lemon, grated zest and juice | 2 |
| 85 g | Breadcrumbs | 170 g |
| 60 g | Butter | 120 g |
| 100 ml | Water | 200 ml |

1. Well butter a large pudding basin and coat fairly thickly with moist brown sugar (demerara type).
2. Line the basin carefully with thinly rolled suet paste. Reserve some for the lid.
3. Fry off the breadcrumbs to a golden brown in butter. Place to one side.
4. Peel and quarter the apples and remove the cores. Slice not too thinly.

5. Layer the pudding with the following:
   (a) layer of apples;
   (b) brown sugar;
   (c) grated zest and juice of lemon;
   (d) layer of breadcrumbs.
   Continue in this manner almost to the tip of the basin.
6. Add 1 or 2 small pieces of butter, and sprinkle the filling with water (do not be over-generous as the apples will also 'throw' some).
7. Wet the inner rim of suet paste and place on the lid.
8. Cover the top with buttered greaseproof paper and foil or muslin.
9. Steam for about 2 hours.
10. Serve with custard sauce or fresh cream.

The brown sugar coating on the basin will impart a lovely, rich biscuit flavour and colour to the pudding. Some pastrycooks also add a clove or two to the filling — this is optional.

### Steamed sponge pudding                                      *Pouding vapeur*

| | | |
|---|---|---|
| 140 g | Medium flour | 430 g |
| 115 g | Butter | 340 g |
| 115 g | Castor sugar | 340 g |
| 2 | Eggs | 6 |
| 60 ml | Milk | 180 ml |
| 10 g | Baking powder | 30 g |
| 85 g | Dried fruit (optional) | 260 g |

1. Sieve the flour and baking powder together on to greaseproof paper.
2. Cream the butter and sugar to a light consistency.
3. Beat in the eggs singly, then add the milk and fold in the sieved flour and baking powder.
4. Add dried fruit if desired, such as currants, sultanas and peel.
5. Place into buttered and sugared basins or individual dariole moulds.
6. Cover the tops with greaseproof paper, and steam for about 1 hour.
7. Serve with custard sauce.

### Variations:

### Chocolate

Substitute 30 g cocoa powder for 30 g of flour in the smaller recipe; 90 g of cocoa for 90 g of flour in the larger quantity. Serve with chocolate sauce.

### Syrup or jam sponge

Place a little syrup or jam in the bottom of each mould or basin, then add the pudding mixture. Steam as usual. Serve with syrup or jam sauce.

225

## Black cap sponge

Place a little syrup and some washed currants ino the bottom of each mould or basin and then add the mixture. Steam as usual. Serve with syrup or custard sauce.

## Christmas pudding                                           Pouding de Noël

| | | |
|---|---|---|
| 230 g | Shredded suet | 900 g |
| 130 g | Medium flour | 520 g |
| 170 g | Sultanas | 700 g |
| 170 g | Currants | 700 g |
| 170 g | Stoneless raisins | 700 g |
| 115 g | Cooking apple (prepared) | 450 g |
| 85 g | Stem ginger | 315 g |
| 230 g | Mixed peel | 900 g |
| 115 g | Citron peel | 450 g |
| 170 g | Barbados sugar | 700 g |
| 15 g | Mixed spice | 60 g |
| 5 g | Ground ginger | 20 g |
| 5 g | Grated nutmeg | 20 g |
| 1 | Orange, zest and juice | 4 |
| 1 | Lemon, zest and juice | 4 |
| 140 ml | Ale | 570 ml |
| 170 g | Breadcrumbs (brown or white) | 700 g |
| 1 measure | Rum | 4 |
| 1 measure | Brandy | 4 |

1. Mince very finely the stoned raisins, stem ginger, cut mixed peel and half the amount of sultanas.
2. Break this down with the fruit zest and juices.
3. Place the remainder of the fruit and dry ingredients including the spices into a large mixing bowl.
4. Add the fruit mass, and blend all together with the beaten eggs, brandy, rum and ale.
5. Well mix and divide into prepared pudding basins which have been greased with clarified butter and dusted with soft demerara sugar.
6. Cover with circles of buttered greaseproof paper and silver foil or muslin. Tie around with string.
7. Allow to stand overnight in a very cool place before steaming for 6–7 hours for a 1 kg pudding; larger 1½ kg puddings require about 8 hours.
8. Cool with the covers removed and then top with fresh greaseproof and foil or muslin covers.
9. Store for 3–4 weeks for best results.
10. Steam for about 2 hours when re-heating for service.

The puddings must be stored in a cool, damp-free environment; under such conditions they will keep for several months.

## Vegetarian Christmas pudding

| | | |
|---|---|---|
| 100 g | Wholemeal breadcrumbs | 200 g |
| 100 g | Wholewheat flour | 200 g |
| 1 teaspoon | Baking powder | 2 teaspoons |
| 50 g | Soft brown sugar | 100 g |
| ½ teaspoon | Ground ginger | 1 teaspoon |
| ½ teaspoon | Ground mixed spice | 1 teaspoon |
| ½ teaspoon | Ground cinnamon | 1 teaspoon |
| ½ teaspoon | Ground nutmeg | 1 teaspoon |
| 250 g | Raisins | 500 g |
| 150 g | Sultanas | 300 g |
| 50 g | Chopped mixed peel | 100 g |
| 50 g | Ground almonds | 100 g |
| 250 g | Grated peeled cooking apples | 500 g |
| 1 | Zest and juice of orange | 2 |
| 1 | Zest and juice of lemon | 2 |
| 1–2 | Eggs | 2–3 |
| ¼ dl | Milk | ½ dl |
| ½ dl | Brandy | 1 dl |
| 3 dl | Brandy or rum sauce | 7½ dl |
| | *or* | |
| | Brandy or rum butter | |

1. Mix the breadcrumbs with the flour, baking powder, soft brown sugar and all of the spices.
2. Blend in the dried fruits, mixed peel and ground almonds.
3. Add the peeled and grated apples, zest and juice of oranges and lemons.
4. Beat in the eggs, milk and brandy, mixing in well.
5. Lightly grease a litre or 2 litre pudding basin and fill three-quarters full with mixture.
6. Cover with greaseproof paper, allowing room for expansion of the pudding during cooking.
7. Wrap in muslin or tin foil and place into a steamer.
8. Steam for 4–5 hours.
9. Allow the pudding to go cold and then re-wrap in greaseproof paper and muslin.
10. Steam for a further 2 hours or re-heat out of the basin in a microwave for 4–5 minutes.
11. If steamed, turn out on to a hot service flat and serve with sauce-boats of the chosen sauce or topped with the chosen butter.

# Chapter 8
# Baking     *Boulanger*

## The competency defined

Baking is most clearly defined as the cooking of foods in an oven by convected dry heat which is modified by steam, produced by the moisture inside the food being processed. The volume of steam is dependent upon the nature of the item(s) being baked, since some foods possess more or less moisture than others.

## Purpose of baking

There are three main reasons for baking foods:

1. To produce an attractive product which is both visually pleasing to the eye and stimulating to the palate by the use of texture, colour and aroma.
2. To render foods both palatable and digestible and so safer to eat.
3. To provide a wider choice in the variety of foods available on the menu.

## Methods of baking

There are three main methods of baking, as follows.

### 1. Baking with modified heat

This is the placing of foods to be baked in a bath of water known as a bain-marie. Foods cooked by this method include many baked-custard-based sweets, such as crème caramel, crème renversée, bread and butter pudding. The full range of pâtés (for hors d'oeuvre) are also cooked in this style.

The presence of water around the outside of the dish, mould or container adjusts the heat, and compels the food to cook at a slower rate. This form of cooking for egg custard products will prevent over-heating, and the strong possibility of the mixture curdling. Pâté also will benefit from the precautionary method, with the extra moisture generated by the bain-marie helping to ensure a mellow textured item.

## 2. Increased humidity baking

This is the baking of products (usually bread and cakes) with the addition of extra steam. In the case of bread, some baker's ovens are specially fitted with a steam injector which floods the oven with steam as the bread items are set to bake. Failing this device, an alternative method is to place some containers of water in the oven: this will also provide extra moisture. Some bread items demand the steam treatment. Vienna bread is a good example. The steam is actually 'sprayed' on to the surface of the dough at the commencement of baking. The same principle would, of course, apply to crusty rolls as well.

## 3. Dry baking

This is the simple straightforward baking of foods as commonly practised in every kitchen. During baking, steam is produced from the water content of the food item which, combined with the dry heat of the oven, cooks the food being processed. Many foods can be cooked by the baking method including savoury items such as meat, fish, poultry, game, offal and raised pies, as well as various potato dishes and vegetables. However, because of the cellulose content of many vegetables (apart from very young ones), oven baking is not the most satisfactory method of preparation, an exception, of course, being potatoes which contain a large amount of water. The same will apply to most fruits which, when baked, will generate steam which softens their cellulose content.

As a process, perhaps the largest class of goods cooked by the baking method are those items which come under the heading of pâtisserie (pastries, sponges, cakes both large and small, soufflés and other baked puddings). The other aspect of pastry preparation is yeast goods, such as bread, buns, croissants, brioche and savarin paste.

### Oven heat

One of the most important attributes of the skilled pastry-cook or baker is to get to know an oven's capacity and capabilities. No two ovens are alike. Each one seems to have its own foibles — not the least of which is controlling the oven heat. Although the majority of commercial ovens will have a thermostat control fitted, nevertheless heat control can vary by several degrees. It is essential to pre-set the oven prior to baking, and there are few recipes which will omit details of the recommended baking temperature, as well as the approximate baking time.

Certainly, as far as *pastry work* is concerned, it is very important that the precise oven temperature is reached before placing such items as cakes or paste goods such as puff pastry, short pastry and choux pastry in to bake. Failure to observe this basic requirement will almost certainly end in disappointment if not disaster.

In the examples quoted above, what happens is that, once the heat cooks the starch grains in the flour, they absorb the fat content of the items, and the liquid in the form of steam, and the air expands on heating. The gluten also expands and sets to retain its shape. Therefore, if the initial oven heat is insufficient, the desired results will not be obtained.

Puff pastry, which is very rich in fat content, requires more heat at the commencement of baking than any other pastry. The aim in any laminated pastry is to keep the layers even. Air and steam raise the pastry; consequently, the starch in the flour must burst quickly so that the increased amount of fat will be absorbed. Even rolling is vital to ensure well-shaped goods. That is why it is important to keep the layers of fat and pastry even and straight-sided during the make-up stages and avoid breakages. If the latter should occur, the air and steam will escape during baking, and the pastry will not rise evenly. It is quite common practice to splash the surface of the baking tray with water before placing puff pastry items in the oven. This helps to generate extra steam.

Although most choux pastry items are piped out on to greased trays and then baked off with quite satisfactory results (and again oven temperature is of great importance), goods such as choux buns are much improved if the items are covered by a '*bonnet*' whilst baking.

'Bonnets' can take the form of a metal cover some 20 cm (10 in.) deep made to fit the baking tray. The cover slows down the setting of the gluten and allows for greater expansion of the air inside the bun. The technique can almost double the volume of the article being processed. However, much care must be exercised in the timing and temperature employed, and under no circumstances should the cover be raised during the baking process. This would allow the steam to escape and the choux paste to collapse. There is no way for the operator to recover such a situation.

### Ovens

There are many types of ovens which will lend themselves to successful baking, such as general purpose ovens, roasting ovens, forced convection ovens and specialist pastry ovens. There are several features about the last named which are designed especially to assist with the baking of pastry goods. They are often multi-tiered, each drop-down door being fitted with a glass observation panel. Thermostatic controls are standard, and quite often each tier will be serviced by a steam injector device. The more usual form of heating is either gas or electricity, with the apparatus being mounted on rollers (castors) for easy movement.

# Organisation and preparation for baking

In the traditional partie system the following chefs would be responsible for the baking of specific products.

| | |
|---|---|
| *Chef poissonnier:* | Baked fish items. |
| *Chef saucier:* | Baked meats, poultry and game dishes, e.g. relevés and entrées. |
| *Chef entremettier:* | Vegetables, potatoes and cheese soufflés. |
| *Chef pâtissier:* | Dough and pastry items including sponge-based goods. |
| *Chef garde-manger:* | The raw preparation of all fish, meat, poultry and game. |

The general rules for efficient organisation and preparation are as follows:

1. Always ensure that the oven is pre-heated to the required temperature for the food to be baked. Naturally, temperatures will vary according to what is being processed.
2. When using pastry as a covering, e.g. fruit pies, etc., never stretch the pastry to fit — it will only shrink during cooking. Instead, allow the rolled-out pastry to fit naturally over the pie dish before securing and notching the outer edge with tweezers. When trimming off excess pastry, always angle the knife outwards to allow for slight shrinkage whilst cooking.
3. Before baking pastry products, it is necessary to allow the item to relax for a period of time after the initial preparation. This applies especially to puff pastry. The same ruling will apply when making up basic puff pastry. It is essential that the pastry should be covered and placed to one side to relax – preferably in the refrigerator — before being utilisted. An overnight resting is a good policy to be on the safe side.

    Any attempt to short-cut a resting period, whatever the pastry, will inevitably result in shrinkage and distortion of the finished appearance, be it fruit or savoury pie, flan case or puff pastry item.
4. Dry-baked goods are usually served on a dish paper or doily (according to the class and type of item). A deep-dish chicken pie would be set on a dish-paper-covered flat, whereas mille-feuilles are served on a doily on a silver dish. Each style will enhance the appearance of the foods served.

# Advantages of baking

1. Baking provides an opportunity to produce a wide variety of savoury and sweet products.
2. Bakery items (yeast goods and pastries) are readily saleable due to their visual appeal and also aroma when freshly baked.
3. Baked goods are fairly easily processed in batches, and a good standard of uniformity of colour, size and degree of finish is readily achieved.

# Degrees of cooking

Baking pastry or dough products should generally be cooked to a nice golden brown colour or until the foods are thoroughly cooked.

# Effects of baking

The chemical changes in specific foods brought about by the use of raising agents alters the basic structure of raw foods, and creates a more easily digestible product.

### Chemical raising agents

*Baking powder*: Made from a blend of bicarbonate of soda and cream of tartar with a starchy substance (rice flour) added to absorb moisture from the atmosphere and prevent gas from being given off during storage.

This mixture, when combined with moisture and heat, will react to produce carbon dioxide gas. Used as a raising agent in numerous pastry items, it helps to aerate the product and thereby lighten the texture.

*Ammonium carbonate*: This is another chemical which is used commercially. On heating, a large amount of gas is generated. Although it it is the cause of a strong smell of ammonia at the time of baking, the articles produced, when cold, lose all trace of the odour. It is very much a product of the bakery industry.

All such chemicals should be stored in an airtight container when not in use.

### Yeast

Conversely, yeast is a living organism which grows by budding when provided with suitable conditions, namely moisture, food and warmth. The nature of yeast and its use in baking is discussed in detail on pages 255–6.

# General rules for efficient baking

1.  Accuracy in the measuring and weighing of commodities to be used in the composition of dishes to be baked is essential if the end-product is to be of the highest standard. This requirement is most important when making formulae for bakery and confectionery goods. With pâtisserie, the item is either correct or incorrect. In almost every case, once an item has been made up and processed, the possibility of rectifying errors is

well-nigh non-existent.

2. The oven must always be pre-heated to the required temperature in advance of production, and the temperature controlled and monitored throughout the cooking process.
3. All baking trays and small equipment, such as tins and moulds, should be prepared in advance of making up recipes.
4. The constant opening and slamming of oven doors should be avoided at all times, as this allows hot air to escape and be replaced by draughts of cold air. The latter will naturally cause a drop in oven temperature, and could impair the cooking/baking of any foods being processed.
5. Always use oven space efficiently, and make maximum use of the space available. Fuel is an expensive commodity!
6. Never knock or jar products such as sponges or soufflés prior to baking, as this action could cause air to be knocked out and impair the quality of the finished product. Place such items into the oven carefully, and do not slam the oven door. This too can have a detrimental effect upon volume and texture. The same ruling applies to the full range of yeast goods.

# General safety rules

1. Jackets with long sleeves are essential for baking and the sleeves should always be kept rolled down to protect the arms from burning on hot trays or oven doors.
2. Always use thick, dry oven-cloths when removing trays from a hot oven. The cloths should not be torn or threadbare as they may snag and cause an accident.
3. Never be tempted to overload trays, or try to remove heavy trays without assistance.
4. Always be very careful when handling hot trays and be mindful for other people who may be working within close proximity.

# Equipment used for baking

*Baking sheets*: These are usually made from black wrought iron, which should be wiped clean after use. If they are washed too often, this will cause the foods to stick. Baking sheets acquire a veneer or thin film (almost non-stick) through constant use. Undue washing will remove it.

New baking sheets should be *seasoned* by being heated in a hot oven, then wiped and lightly oiled before being used to bake off trayed goods.

If baking trays need to be washed (and they do from time to time), they should be washed in hot soapy water to remove any burnt-on residue, after which they require rinsing in hot water and drying in a hot oven.

All forms of moulds should be treated in the same manner as baking trays. *Food mixers*: These are available in varying sizes and capacities including those with a computer programme which are able to carry out mixing instructions according to the time schedule required. They are beautifully engineered and will last a lifetime if taken care of and serviced on a regular basis by qualified agents. Each machine is equipped with a range of attachments including whisking, beating and kneading appliances.

Another important feature of the large-scale food mixer is its mobility factor. Machines are mounted on rollers which enable them to be moved as required to any convenient part of the production room. It is then a simple matter of plugging into a power source and proceeding with the production schedule.

*Mobile equipment:* We have already mentioned large commercial style bakers/pastry ovens which are also capable of being moved within the production area by the means of castors, and this too has many advantages — not the least being the improved cleaning facility which such mobility affords. To be accurate, a great deal of commercial kitchen equipment is designed with an in-built facility that enables the operator to move the pieces around, not merely as an aid to cleaning/hygiene, but also as a means of meeting alternative production situations.

Practical room layouts are no longer the subject of the 'set piece'. In the past, once the layout of production facilities had been determined, that was, broadly speaking, the option for the rest of its natural life. Not so today. All manner of heavy duty pieces are 'roller mounted' and can be relocated as required. The result is that a production area can be changed around at will. Naturally, the service facilities, gas, electricity and water, are installed to meet appropriate needs. Obviously, not everything is capable of being moved at will, nor is this really necessary. There are still many pieces of equipment which are placed *in situ* and remain permanently sited, such as bench-mounted small and medium-size food mixers, open-topped boiling tables and steaming ovens, to name but three pieces appropriate to pastry work and confectionery. Nevertheless, the blend of static and mobile equipment is now part of modern kitchen planning.

# Techniques associated with baking

*Greasing*: This is the preparation of trays, tins or moulds prior to baking. The equipment is brushed with fat or oil in order to prevent foods from sticking to equipment.

*Marking*: Certain foods may be marked prior to baking as a form of decoration or perhaps to indicate portion size.

*Brushing*: This practice may occur at any of the three stages prior to baking off.

1. Before: items may be glazed with egg wash to give colour to the finished article.

2. During: sometimes breadrolls are brushed with milk whilst baking to enhance the finished appearance.
3. After: at the end of baking, it is usual to brush an assorted variety of yeast buns with sugarwash to give the items a nice shiny finish.

*Cooling*: After baking, it is good practice to place the articles on to cooling wires so that air can circulate around the goods and prevent the bases from becoming soggy.

*Finishing*: This is the final stage for numerous baked products, such as when bun wash is brushed on to hot cross buns, or coarse sugar is sprinkled on to sweet puff pastry goods: the latter are then returned to the oven to allow caramelisation to occur, resulting in an attractive glossy finish. This last procedure is also known as glazing.

*Recovery time*: This refers to the time given to allow the oven to re-heat in between cooking batches of food.

*Resting period*: This is the time allowed for freshly rolled out pastry items to recover prior to baking off. It applies to both sweet and savoury short pastry, and also puff pastry. The main object is to give the gluten content of the flour time to relax after rolling, and thus avoid distortion in the finished item.

*Dusting*: This is the light coating of foods with flour prior to baking; it can occur at three stages in the preparation, such as when rolling or moulding the pastry or dough; or on trays when cooking specific items; or actually dusting finished baked bread/rolls to give a floury appearance.

# Paper bag cookery

Paper bag cookery is becoming less common in the cooking of the 1990s. However, this method was at one time more popular in restaurants. The French term for paper bag cookery is '*en papillote*' and involves the cooking of individual portions of food inside a pocket or parcel of oiled greaseproof paper or more commonly today tin foil. The pocket is sealed to prevent the escape of excess steam and the maximum amount of natural flavour and nutrition is held by the food.

Larger pieces of food to be cooked by this method may be partially pre-cooked by grilling or shallow frying.

It is also permissible to add very finely chopped vegetables, herbs and spices to the bag.

The prepared bags are then placed on to lightly greased baking sheets, which must have a raised edge, and placed into a pre-heated oven.

When the food is cooked it is placed in front of the customer and opened by the waiter for maximum visual effect.

# Self-assessment questions for baking

1. Define the three main methods of baking.

2. What causes the 'lift' in puff pastry items when exposed to oven heat?
3. Why is it important to keep the layers of fat and paste even during the manufacturing (rolling out) of puff paste?
4. What is the purpose of a 'bonnet' when baking off choux buns?
5. What is the reason for 'resting' puff paste goods prior to baking off?
6. What are the three main constituents of commercially produced baking powder?
7. Which three requirements are necessary to activate the 'budding' process of yeast?
8. Can you name one of the benefits associated with mobile kitchen equipment?
9. Why is it good practice to allow baked items to cool on cooling wires?
10. What is meant by the term 'recovery time' when batch baking?

When you have completed these questions check your answers with your fellow students and chef or lecturer.

# Baked fish                                   *Poisson cuiré*

### Introduction to baked fish

This method is most suited to small whole fish or fillets. The fish may be stuffed before cooking with a suitable stuffing, such as lemon, parsley and thyme.

The fish should be served in its own juices or with a suitable garnish and sauce. Be careful not to over-cook the fish as this will result in the fish breaking up and spoiling the texture of the flesh.

### Steaks                                                *Darnes*

| | | |
|---|---|---|
| Cod | 1 × 150 g per portion | *Cabillaud* |
| Hake | 1 × 150 g per portion | *Colin* |
| Haddock | 1 × 150 g per portioin | *Aigrefin* |

**Baked fish (basic recipe)**                    *Poisson au four*

1. Lightly brush the base of the cooking dish with clarified butter.
2. Rub the fish with lemon juice and season lightly.
3. Place the fish in the prepared dish.
4. Brush the fish with clarified butter, cover with a cartouche and bake until cooked, about 15 minutes depending on the size of the fish portion.
5. Serve as required by the recipe. Always remove centre bone and skin from darnes for service.

**Baked fish steaks**  
**with beurre fondu**

*Darne de poisson*  
*au four beurre fondu*

| 100 g | Beurre fondu | 250 g |
|---|---|---|

1. After baking, remove the skin and bone from the darne and nap with the beurre fondu (lemon butter).
2. Garnish with picked parsley and lemon.

*Small whole fish*

| Herring | 1 × 200 g per portion | *Hareng* |
|---|---|---|
| Mackerel | 1 × 200 g per portion | *Maquereau* |
| Red mullet | 1 × 200 g per portion | *Rouget* |
| Trout | 1 × 200 g per portion | *Truite* |

**Baked stuffed red mullet**  
**with provençale sauce**

*Rouget farci au four*  
*sauce provençale*

| 200 g | Lemon, parsley and thyme stuffing | 500 g |
|---|---|---|
| 3 dl | Provençale sauce | 7½ dl |

1. Cut, trim and clean the fish.
2. Remove the backbone and fill the cavity with the stuffing.
3. Bake as for basic recipe.
4. Serve with a sauce-boat of provençale sauce.

**Note:** An alternative stuffing would be blanched julienne of vegetables with a little garlic for flavour.

**Baked stuffed trout**

*Truite farci au four*

| 200 g | Cooked brown rice | 500 g |
|---|---|---|
| 40 g | Broken shelled walnuts | 100 g |
| 60 g | Beurre maitre d'hôtel | 150 g |

1. Cut, trim and clean the fish.
2. Remove the backbone and fill the cavity with the well-seasoned mixture of brown rice and walnuts.
3. Bake as for the basic recipe.
4. Serve napped with beurre maitre d'hôtel.

## Trout in a paper bag
*Truite en papillote*

| | | |
|---|---|---|
| 4 | Trout | 10 |
| 20 g | Julienne of carrots | 50 g |
| 20 g | Julienne of celery | 50 g |
| 20 g | Julienne of onion | 50 g |
| | Salt and milled pepper | |
| 60 g | Clarified butter | 150 g |
| | Chopped parsley | |
| 1 dl | Dry white wine | 2½ dl |
| | Plain flour | |
| 4 | Heart-shaped pieces of greaseproof paper | 10 |
| | Oil | |

1. Trim and cut the trout.
2. Remove the backbone and rinse thoroughly.
3. Blanch the julienne of vegetables and stuff the trout with vegetables.
4. Brush the paper on both sides with oil.
5. Sit the trout in the centre of the paper, season and sprinkle with flour and chopped parsley.
6. Sprinkle with plenty of dry white wine and seal inside the paper.
7. Place into a hot oven in a tray with a little oil in the base and cook for 12–18 minutes, until the trout is cooked.
8. Serve with a suitable sauce, such as hollandaise or paloise.

## Seafood in puff cases
*Bouchées des fruits de mer*
*Vol-au-vents des fruits de mer*

| | | |
|---|---|---|
| 8 | Bouchée cases | 20 |
| | *or* | |
| 4 | Vol-au-vent cases | 10 |

1. Place the puff pastry cases on to lightly greased baking sheets and bake in a hot oven until a deep golden brown.
2. Remove from the oven and transfer on to wire cooling racks and allow to cool and set.
3. Remove the centre and place on one side for later use.

| | | |
|---|---|---|
| 50 g | Peeled prawns | 125 g |
| 50 g | Mussels | 125 g |
| 50 g | Cockles | 125 g |
| 50 g | Diced scallops | 125 g |
| 50 g | Diced button mushrooms | 125 g |
| 1 teaspoon | Finely chopped parsley | 1 tablespoon |
| 1½ dl | White wine sauce | 3½ dl |
| ¼ | Juice of fresh lemon | ¾ |
| 25 g | Butter | 60 g |

1. Select a saucepan of suitable size for the volume of filling being made.
2. Add the butter and melt gently.
3. Add the diced button mushrooms and lemon juice and sweat the

mushrooms.

4. Add the shellfish and sweat with the mushrooms for 4-5 minutes.
5. Add the finely chopped parsley and white wine sauce and seasoning.
6. Place the puff pastry cases into the oven to warm through and then fill each case with the filling and replace the tops.
7. Serve on a hot flat with a dish paper, garnish with picked parsley.

## Fish pancakes                                    *Crêpes de poisson*

| 8 | Pancakes | 20 |
| 400 g | Flaked cooked fish | 1 kg |
| | (salmon, haddock, whiting) | |
| 1 | Egg yolk | 2 |
| 5 dl | Fish velouté | 1¼ litre |
| ½ dl | Single cream | 1 dl |

1. Bind the flaked fish with a third of the sauce.
2. Divide the mixture between the crêpes, laying a strip down the centre of each crêpe and then rolling in a cigar shape, or spreading the filling on the crêpe and then rolling in a cigar shape.
3. Nap the base of an earthenware dish with a little sauce and sit the rolled crêpes in the dish.
4. Make a liaison by mixing the cream and egg yolk together.
5. Add a small amount of sauce to the liaison and then stir the liaison into the main sauce.
6. Adjust the seasoning and do not re-boil the sauce after adding the liaison.
7. Place the crêpes into a hot oven, covered with a piece of damp greaseproof to prevent them drying out.
8. When heated thoroughly, nap the crêpes with the sauce and glaze under a hot salamander.
9. Served garnished with a piece of picked parsley.

**Note**: The crêpes may be coated with any suitable sauce, such as bonne femme, Dugléré or Bercy.

Crêpes may be filled with a variety of fillings, such as mixed seafood, diced ham in velouté, curried meat or fish.

## Fish pie

| 250 g | Cooked fish | 625 g |
| | (without skin or bones) | |
| 1 | Hard-boiled eggs | 3 |
| 50 g | Mushrooms | 125 g |
| | Finely chopped parsley | |
| | Salt and pepper | |
| 250 g | Duchesse potato mixture | 625 g |
| 2½ dl | Thin béchamel sauce | 6 dl |

1. Bring the béchamel quickly to the boil and add the flaked fish and finely chopped parsley.
2. Finely chop the mushrooms and roughly chop the egg and add to the béchamel.
3. Season as required.
4. Lightly butter a deep pie dish.
5. Add the fish mixture, leaving 1 cm depth on the dish.
6. Using a large star nozzle and piping bag, pipe on the duchesse potato.
7. Brush with a little milk or eggwash and place into a hot oven to brown.
8. Serve on a hot flat with a dish paper.

Types of fish suitable include cod, haddock, salmon scraps and whiting. Serve with plain boiled or steamed vegetables.

### Russian fish pie                        *Coulibiac de saumon à la russe*

| | | |
|---|---|---|
| 300 g | Cold cooked salmon | 750 g |
| 80 g | Rice pilaff | 200 g |
| 80 g | Sliced sweated mushrooms | 200 g |
| 2 | Hard-boiled eggs | 5 |
| ½ dl | Thin fish velouté | 1 dl |
| | Chopped parsley | |
| | Salt and pepper | |
| 260 g | Puff pastry | 650 g |
| 3 dl | Hollandaise sauce | 7½ dl |

1. Roll out the puff pastry into either one large rectangle or individual portions.
2. Mix together the rice, mushrooms, diced hard-boiled eggs and finely chopped parsley.
3. Place half the mixture down the centre of the rectangle and layer the flaked salmon on top of the rice.
4. Nap the salmon with the velouté and place the remaining rice on top of the salmon.
5. Moisten the edges of the pastry and fold over the edges, sealing well.
6. Sit the coulibiac on a lightly greased baking tray with the seal underneath.
7. Decorate as required with strips of puff pastry and brush with eggwash.
8. Bake in a hot oven at 200°C until a deep golden brown.
9. Serve accompanied with sauce-boats of hollandaise sauce.

**Note:** Traditionally this dish is made using brioche paste in place of puff paste.

### Russian chicken pie                     *Coulibiac de volaille à la russe*

Proceed as for Russian fish pie, replacing the salmon with cooked sliced chicken and the fish velouté with chicken velouté.

# Baked eggs

*Introduction to baked eggs*

Baked egg dishes are found mainly as starters and occasionally as an intermediate course on a menu. More substantial baked egg dishes may be served at high tea as a snack meal. The following are two of the more common recipes used in today's menus.

**Eggs cooked in the dish**            *Oeufs sur le plat*

This is the cooking of eggs in buttered oven-proof china or cast iron dishes. The eggs may be garnished in a variety of ways and must always be cooked to order. Depending upon the dish being created, the garnish may be placed on top of or underneath the egg. When served as a starter one egg is sufficient; at other times two eggs may be used.

1. The sur le plat dish must be lightly greased with butter and seasoned with salt and milled pepper.
2. Place the dish on the edge of a solid top stove to heat through.
3. If the garnish is underneath the egg, now is the time to add the garnish.
4. Break in eggs one at a time and cook on the stove top until the white starts to set.
5. Transfer the sur le plat to a moderate oven to finish the cooking process.

**Note:** The yolk should still be soft but hot and the egg white firm but not dry.

6. If the garnish is to go on top of the egg, now is the time to add the cooked garnish.
7. If a cordon of sauce is to be added, it should be added at the end of cooking.
8. Finally, garnish with chopped or picked parsley and serve straight away in the dish.

**Egg with grilled chipolata**        *Oeuf sur le plat Bercy*
**sausage and tomato sauce**

| | | |
|---|---|---|
| 4 | **Eggs** | 10 |
| 8 | **Chipolatas, grilled** | 20 |
| 1½ dl | **Tomato sauce** | 3½ dl |
| | **Chopped parsley** | |

1. Follow the general method with the grilled chipolatas garnishing on top of the cooked egg.
2. Finish with a cordon of tomato sauce and chopped parsley.

**Egg with bacon** *Oeuf sur le plat au lard*

| | | |
|---|---|---|
| 4 | **Eggs** | 10 |
| 8 | **Rashers grilled back bacon** | 20 |
| | **Picked parsley** | |

1. Lay the rashers of grilled bacon in the base of the prepared sur le plat dish.
2. Cook as for the general recipe and finish with a piece of picked parsley.

# Baked farinaceous dishes

## Introduction to baked farinaceous dishes

These dishes include pasta, rice and pizzas, all of which are savoury dishes and may be served as either starters or main meals as required by the customer. Many modern restaurants, and pizza restaurants especially, offer the customer a choice on the menu of starter and main course portion and prices.

### Cannelloni

| | | |
|---|---|---|
| 350 g | **Cannelloni tubes** | 875 g |
| 50 g | **Fresh grated parmesan** | 125 g |
| *Filling* | | |
| 100 g | **Purée of spinach** | 250 g |
| 100 g | **Cooked minced beef** | 250 g |
| 75 g | **Brunoise of onion** | 130 g |
| 1 | **Egg yolk** | 3 |
| 20 g | **Butter** | 50 g |
| | **Salt and milled pepper** | |
| 1 | **Crushed glove of garlic** | 2 |
| *Sauce* | | |
| 4 dl | **Tomato sauce** | 1 litre |
| | **Rubbed basil to taste** | |
| 1 | **Crushed clove of garlic** | 2 |

1. Heat a large sauté pan and melt the butter for the filling.
2. Sweat the onion with the garlic without colour until tender.
3. Add the mince and spinach and cook for 10–12 minutes.
4. Remove from the stove, season and mix in the egg yolks.
5. If too moist add a few breadcrumbs to the mixture.
6. Pipe the mixture into cannelloni tubes and place the cannelloni in a deep earthenware oven-proof dish.
7. Cover with the sauce and place into a hot oven, 170°C–185°C, for 40-50 minutes, until the pasta is cooked.

8. Sprinkle with the parmesan and finish in the oven or under a salamander to a light golden brown.
9. Serve with salad and new potatoes.

**Note:** The filling may be changed for vegetarian fillings, see vegetarian cannelloni.

## Lasagne

| | | |
|---|---|---|
| ½ dl | Olive oil | 1 dl |
| 500 g | Lasagne | 1250 g |
| 500 g | Mozzarella cheese | 1250 g |
| 500 g | Ricotta cheese | 1250 g |
| 130 g | Fresh grated parmesan | 300 g |
| 4 dl | White sauce | 1 litre |

*Filling*

| | | |
|---|---|---|
| ½ dl | Olive oil | 1 dl |
| 100 g | Brunoise of onion | 250 g |
| 2 | Crushed cloves of garlic | 4 |
| 1 kg | Minced beef | 2½ kg |
| 4 dl | Tomato sauce | 1 litre |
| 600 g | Tomato concassé | 1½ kg |
| 70 g | Tomato purée | 160 g |
| | Salt and milled pepper | |
| | Rubbed basil to taste | |
| | Rubbed oregano to taste | |
| 2 | Bay leaves | 3 |
| 230 g | Sliced button mushrooms | 575 g |

1. Prepare the filling by heating the oil in a large saucepan, add the onion and garlic, sweat without colour until soft.
2. Stir in the beef and sweat for 10–15 minutes.
3. Mix in all the remaining ingredients for the filling with the exception of the mushrooms, bring to the boil and simmer for 1½ hours; stir regularly to prevent scorching.
4. Stir in the mushrooms and simmer for a further 30 minutes.
5. Remove the bay leaves and if necessary adjust the seasoning and consistency.
6. Half fill a large saucepan with water and the olive oil for cooking the lasagne.
7. Bring the water to the boil, add the lasagne sheets, one at a time, and cook for 12–16 minutes, or until al dente (just tender).
8. Refresh in cold running water and drain.
9. Place a layer of pasta in the base of an oven-proof dish and add a layer of the filling sprinkled with parmesan, mozzarella slices and ricotta cheese.
10. Finish with a layer of pasta topped with white sauce and the mixture of cheese.
11. Bake in a hot oven, 175–185°C for 45–55 minutes.
12. Serve with salad and new potatoes.

### Vegetarian lasagne

Proceed as for the basic recipe for lasagne, replacing the meat content with an equal quantity of paysanne of vegetables and flaked almonds, sweated in a little garlic butter.

Layer as for the basic recipe, napping each layer of vegetables with a little white sauce.

As an alternative to plain white pasta sheets try using spinach pasta (lasagne verdi) or wholemeal pasta sheets.

### Vegetarian cannelloni

Proceed as for the basic recipe for cannelloni, replacing the meat filling with chestnut stuffing, or lemon, parsley and thyme stuffing.

The cannelloni may also be stuffed with any of the vegetarian stuffings used for stuffed peppers.

### *Pizza topping*

Allow 250 g of pizza dough for 2–4 portions of pizza.

### Margherita

| *2–4 portions* | | *5–10 portions* |
|---|---|---|
| 400 g | Thinly sliced tomatoes | 1 kg |
| 180 g | Mozzarella cheese | 450 g |
| 5 g | Finely chopped fresh basil | 15 g |
| | Milled pepper | |
| ¼ dl | Olive oil | ½ dl |
| 100 g | Tomato concassé | 250 g |

1. Spread the base of the pizza with the tomato concassé.
2. Arrange the thin slices of tomato on the bed of concassé.
3. Cover with the slices of mozzarella cheese and season.
4. Sprinkle on the basil and dribble with the olive oil.
5. Place on to a lightly greased baking sheet and place into a hot oven, 200°C, for 15–20 minutes until the dough is cooked and the pizza is lightly coloured; serve straight away.

### Napoletana

| | | |
|---|---|---|
| 200 g | Tomato concassé | 500 g |
| 240 g | Mozzarella cheese | 600 g |
| 8 | Anchovy fillets | 20 |
| | Milled pepper to taste | |
| 1 teaspoon | Dried oregano | 2½ teaspoons |
| ¼ dl | Olive oil | ½ dl |

1. Spread the pizza base with tomato concassé.
2. Add mozzarella cheese and dried oregano and seasoning.

3. Criss-cross the top with a neat lattice-work of anchovy strips.
4. Dribble with a little olive oil and cook as for Magherita.

**Four seasons pizza**                                   *Quattrostagione*

Divide the pizza into four quarters, without cutting all the way through. Place one of each of the following fillings on to quarters and cook as for Margherita.

**Tomato topping**

| | | |
|---|---|---|
| 400 g | Tomato concassé | 1 kg |
| ½ teaspoon | Dried basil | 1 teaspoon |
| 8 | Strips of anchovy fillets | 20 |
| 24 | Halved and stoned black olives | 60 |

**Mushroom and pepperoni topping**

| | | |
|---|---|---|
| 139 g | Sautéed sliced mushrooms | 325 g |
| 180 g | Sliced pepperoni sausage | 450 g |

**Artichoke topping**

| | | |
|---|---|---|
| 100g | Smoked ham slices | 325 g |
| 180 g | Sliced artichoke hearts | 450 g |

**Shrimp or prawn topping**

| | | |
|---|---|---|
| 180 g | Sliced mozzarella cheese | 450 g |
| 180 g | Shelled shrimps or prawns | 450 g |
| 180 g | Cooked asparagus tips | 450 g |

Season to taste and dribble the pizza with olive oil before cooking.

**Note:** Foods for pizza toppings include the following: sweetcorn, diced peppers, mushrooms, tuna, julienne of cooked chicken, cockles, mussels, shrimps, prawns.

# Baked meat dishes

*Introduction to baked meat dishes*

Baked meat dishes need to be protected from drying out in the oven so they are protected with a coating of some kind, usually pastry of some description which also forms part of the finished dish.

**Fillet of beef in puff pastry**                    *Filet de boeuf Wellington*

| | | |
|---|---|---|
| 600 g | Beef fillet | 1½ kg |
| 140 g | Duxelle | 350 g |
| | Salt and milled pepper | |
| 60 g | Pâté de foie gras | 150 g |
| 450 g | Puff pastry | 1 kg |
| 2 dl | Madeira sauce | 5 dl |
| | Olive oil | |
| ½ bunch | Watercress | 1 bunch |

This dish may be produced as individual portions or as one large Wellington to be carved at the table.

1. Trim and season the fillet.
2. Heat the oil in a suitable sized sauté pan and seal the surface of the fillet.
3. Mix the duxelle with the foie gras.
4. Roll out the puff pastry into an oblong shape, large enough to wrap the fillet.
5. Spread the top of the fillet with the duxelle and foie gras mixture and wrap the fillet inside the puff pastry.
6. Moisten the edges of the puff pastry to seal the fillet inside.
7. Sit on a lightly greased baking tray with the seal underneath.
8. Decorate as required using strips of puff pastry.
9. Brush with eggwash and place into a hot oven, cooking the pastry to a deep golden brown. The meat should be medium rare when carved.
10. Serve on a hot service flat garnished with watercress and a sauce-boat of Madeira sauce.

**Steak pie**

| | | |
|---|---|---|
| 500 g | Stewing beef | 1250 g |
| 100 g | Brunoise of onion | 250 g |
| | Seasoned plain or wholemeal flour | |
| | Salt and milled pepper | |
| | Chopped parsley | |
| 200 g | Puff, short or wholemeal pastry | 500 g |
| 1 dl | Brown stock | 2½ dl |
| | Worcester sauce | |

1. Dice and trim the stewing steak into 2 cm cubes.
2. Season the meat and pass through the seasoned flour.
3. Mix the brunoise of onion and chopped parsley with the meat and place into a suitable sized pie dish.
4. Add enough stock to almost cover the meat.
5. Add a dash of Worcester sauce to taste.
6. Roll out the pastry to a depth of 4 mm and moisten the edge of the pie dish.
7. Line the edge of the dish with a thin strip of pastry.
8. Moisten the pastry edge and cover the pie with the rest of the pastry.

9. Seal and trim the edge, decorating as required.
10. Allow to rest for 30 minutes before baking: this is to avoid excessive shrinking of the pastry during cooking.
11. Brush with a little eggwash to glaze during cooking.
12. Place the pie into a hot oven to colour the pastry and set firm.
13. Reduce the heat to 140–150°C and continue cooking until the meat is tender, 2–2½ hours.
14. When the meat is tender, remove the pie from the oven and clean the edge of the dish.
15. Surround the dish with a pie collar for service.

**Notes:**
1. When rolling out the pastry do not over-stretch as this will result in shrinkage.
2. When the pastry has browned and set, cover with a sheet of damp greaseproof paper to avoid burning. Re-moisten the paper as necessary.
3. The filling may be pre-cooked by stewing.

**Shepherds pie**

| | | |
|---|---|---|
| 500 g | **Minced lamb** | 1¼ kg |
| 30 g | **Butter or margarine** | 75 g |
| 100 g | **Brunoise of onion** | 250 g |
| | **Finely chopped parsley** | |
| | **Salt and milled pepper** | |
| 1½ dl | **Demi-glace** | 4 dl |
| 600 g | **Duchesse potato mixture** | 1½ kg |
| 20 g | **Clarified butter** | 50 g |

1. Select a sauté pan of suitable size and heat the butter or margarine.
2. Sweat the onions without colouring.
3. Add the minced lamb and parsley and season.
4. Sweat without colouring for 15–20 minutes.
5. Add the demi-glace and simmer for a further 20 minutes.
6. Pour the mixture into oven-proof pie dishes.
7. Pipe on the duchesse potato mixture using a star nozzle.
8. Brush with the clarified butter and place into a hot oven until the potato crust is a light golden brown.

**Moussaka**

| | | |
|---|---|---|
| 500 g | Minced lamb | 1¼ kg |
| | Oregano or marjoram to taste | |
| 40 g | Brunoise of onion | 100 g |
| 1 | Crushed clove of garlic | 2 |
| 1 tablespoon | Finely chopped parsley | 2 tablespoons |
| 100 g | Finely chopped mushrooms | 250 g |
| 15 g | Tomato purée | 35 g |
| 1 dl | Demi-glace | 3 dl |
| 1 | Aubergines | 3 |
| 1½ dl | Olive oil | 4 dl |
| | Plain flour | |
| 2 | Tomatoes | 6 |
| 4 dl | Milk | 1 litre |
| 3 | Eggs | 8 |
| | Salt and pepper | |
| 75 g | Grated cheese | 200 g |
| | Parmesan cheese | |

1. Select a sauté or frying-pan of suitable size and heat a small amount of the olive oil.
2. Add the onion and mince, sweat together for 5–10 minutes.
3. Add the garlic and cook for 3–5 minutes; do not allow the mince to colour.
4. Add the oregano or marjoram, seasoning and mushrooms and sweat for 3–5 minutes.
5. Add the tomato purée and demi-glace, mix well and simmer for 15–20 minutes, or until the mixture has thickened slightly.
6. Adjust the seasoning and pour the mixture into suitable oven-proof earthenware dishes. The mixture should be no deeper than 4 cm.
7. Blanch the tomatoes and remove the skins.
8. Slice the tomatoes and layer on top of the meat.
9. Slice the aubergine into rings and sauté in the remaining olive oil and layer on top of the tomatoes.
10. Place into a moderate oven at 180°C for 20 minutes.
11. Beat the eggs and milk together, season and mix in the grated cheese and parmesan.
12. Pour on top of the aubergine to a depth of ½–1 cm and place back into the oven until set and a golden brown colour, 20-25 minutes.

**Cornish pasties**

| | | |
|---|---|---|
| 100 g | Raw minced beef | 250 g |
| 100 g | Brunoise of raw potato | 250 g |
| 100 g | Brunoise of raw swede | 250 g |
| 50 g | Brunoise of raw onion | 125 g |
| | Finely chopped parsley | |
| | Salt and milled pepper | |
| 200 g | Short or puff pastry | 500 g |
| | Eggwash | |

1. Roll out the pastry into 10 cm discs. The pastry should be no thicker than 4 mm.
2. Mix the remaining ingredients together and season well.
3. Moisten the filling with a little water and place a suitable amount on to one half of each disc of pastry.
4. Eggwash the edges of the pastry disc, roll over and seal, and neaten by fluting the pastry edges.
5. Brush with eggwash and place on to lightly greased baking trays. Allow to rest for 30 minutes.
6. Cook in a pre-heated oven at 200°C to a deep golden brown colour.
7. Serve on a hot service flat lined with a dish paper.
8. Serve accompanied with a suitable sauce, e.g. Madeira or plain jus.

## Sausage rolls

| | | |
|---|---|---|
| 100 g | Puff pastry | 250 g |
| 200 g | Sausage meat | 500 g |

1. Roll out puff pastry approximately 3 mm thick and cut into 7 cm wide bands. Roll sausage meat into ropes about 25 mm thick.
2. Eggwash the edges of pastry.
3. Place sausage meat on pastry.
4. Fold pastry over to enclose meat.
5. Crimp edges neatly.
6. Mark lightly on top with edge of knife and cut into desired lengths, usually 6 to 8 cm long.
7. Eggwash, tray up and rest before baking off at 205°C.

**Note:** A smaller version of the above can be made which are suitable for cocktail savoury sizes.

The baking process may be improved by splashing the tray with cold water. This helps to generate steam during baking, and is a tip which could be usefully applied to all puff pastry items.

## Game and poultry pies

| | | |
|---|---|---|
| 1½ kg | Poultry or game or rabbit | 4 kg |
| 100 g | Quartered button mushrooms | 250 g |
| 60 g | Brunoise of onions | 150 g |
| 8 | Rashers of streaky bacon | 20 |
| | Seasoned plain or wholemeal flour | |
| | Salt and milled pepper | |
| | Chopped parsley | |
| 200 g | Puff, short or wholemeal pastry | 500 g |
| 1 dl | White stock | 2½ dl |

**Note:** Cut the chicken for sauté. Cut pigeon in half and remove the carcass. Cut rabbit into joints.

1. Season the meat in the seasoned flour and wrap each piece in rindless bacon.

2. Roll the meat in the seasoned flour and set in a pie dish of suitable size.
3. Add the onions, mushrooms and parsley, add enough stock to almost cover the meat.
4. Roll out the pastry to 6 mm depth and moisten the edge of the pie dish; line with a strip of pastry.
5. Moisten the pastry and cover the meat with the rest of the pastry; seal the edge and trim.
6. Allow the pie to stand for 30 minutes; this is to reduce possible shrinkage of pastry during cooking.
7. Brush with eggwash and place the pie into a hot oven to set and brown the pastry.
8. Reduce the heat to 150°C and cover the pastry with damp greaseproof paper to prevent the crust from burning.
9. Cook until the meat is tender, 1½–2 hours.
10. When the meat is cooked, clean the edge of the pie dish, surround with a pie collar and serve.

## Chicken in paper bag                    *Suprême de volaille en papillote*

| 4 | Chicken suprêmes | 10 |
|---|---|---|
| 2 dl | Provençale sauce | 5 dl |
| 4 | Slices of boiled ham | 10 |
| 30 g | Plain flour | 75 g |
| 120 g | Clarified butter | 300 g |
| | Salt and milled pepper | |
| 4 | Large heart-shaped pieces greaseproof paper | 10 |
| | Picked parsley | |
| | Olive oil | |

1. Brush the greaseproof paper hearts on both sides with olive oil.
2. Pass the suprêmes through seasoned flour.
3. Heat the butter in a sauté pan and sauté the chicken to a light golden brown.
4. Place a slice of ham on each paper heart and sit the suprême on the ham.
5. Nap each of the suprêmes with provençale sauce.
6. Fold over the edges of the greaseproof and seal well.
7. Place into a hot tray with a little oil in the base and cook in a hot oven for 5–7 minutes.
8. Serve in the bags, garnished with a piece of picked parsley.

## Chicken pancakes                        *Crêpes de volaille*

| 400 g | Cooked diced chicken (without bone or skin) | 1 kg |
|---|---|---|
| 4 dl | Suprême sauce | 1 litre |
| 30 g | Butter | 75 g |
| 8 | Pancakes | 20 |
| | Chopped parsley | |

1. Heat the butter in a sauté pan of suitable size and toss with the chicken.
2. Season and add a third of the sauce, to form a salpicon.
3. Divide the filling between the pancakes and roll.
4. Set in earthenware service dishes with a little sauce napped on the base.
5. Place into a hot oven to heat through; when ready coat the pancakes with sauce and gratinate before service.

**Note:** If required the sauce may be finished with a sprinkling of grated parmesan before gratinating.

# Baked vegetable dishes *Légumes cuirés*

### Introduction to baked vegetables

Many baked vegetable and potato dishes are also suitable for serving as dishes in their own right and are increasingly found on menus as vegetarian dishes. In this section are popular baked vegetables and vegetarian dishes.

### Baked jacket potatoes *Pommes au four*

Allow one potato of about 150 g per person.

1. Scrub the potato in cold running water and score an incision round the potato skin, no deeper than 3 mm.
2. Place on to baking tray with a bed of salt and place into a hot oven at 240–250°C for 1–1½ hours.
3. Turn the potato during cooking, after ½ hour.
4. Remove from the oven when cooked.
5. To test if the potato is cooked, hold a clean dry cloth and squeeze gently; if cooked the potato will feel soft.
6. Serve on a hot flat in a folded napkin.
7. Served accompanied with butter.

### Baked jacket potatoes with cheese *Pomme gratinées*

| 4 | Even-sized baked potatoes | 10 |
|---|---|---|
| 100 g | Butter | 250 g |
| 30 g | Grated parmesan | 75 g |
| | Picked parsley | |

1. Cut the cooked potato in half lengthways.
2. Scoop out the flesh, leaving the skin intact.
3. Place the potato into a basin and mash with a fork.
4. Add the butter, salt and pepper and parmesan cheese and gently mix through with a fork. Hold back a little parmesan for gratinating.
5. Return the mixture to the skins.

6. Sprinkle liberally with the remaining parmesan cheese and heat through in an oven pre-heated to 200°C until the surface is a golden brown.
7. Serve on a hot flat with a dish paper garnished with a piece of picked parsley.

**Note:** Many items of food may be added to baked jacket potatoes in the same manner as above, e.g. for the parmesan substitute brunoise of cooked ham or mushrooms, etc.

## Marquis potatoes                                    *Pommes marquise*

| 400 g | Duchesse potato mixture | 1 kg |
| 80 g | Tomato concassé | 200 g |
| | Finely chopped parsley | |
| | Eggwash | |

1. Pipe the duchesse potato mixture, using a large star nozzle, on to lightly greased baking trays, in the shape of a nest 4 × 2 cm in size.
2. Allow two nests per portion.
3. Place the nests into a hot oven to set the surface of the potato, 3–4 minutes.
4. Remove the tray from the oven and brush the potatoes lightly with a little eggwash.
5. Fill the centre of the nests with tomato concassé and return to the oven to brown the potatoes or finish under a salamander.
6. Serve on a hot service dish, sprinkled with finely chopped parsley.

## Anna style potatoes                                    *Pommes Anna*

| 600 g | Peeled potatoes | 1½ kg |
| 60 g | Butter | 150 g |
| | Salt and white pepper | |

1. Heat the pommes Anna moulds in an oven or on the stove top.
2. Grease with a little butter.
3. Trim the potatoes into cylindrical shapes and slice as thinly as possible into discs on a mandolin.
4. Arrange a layer of neatly overlapping discs on the base of the Anna mould and season.
5. Build up the discs of potatoes seasoning as you build.
6. Arrange a neat layer of discs around the sides of the Anna mould as you build.
7. Add the last of the butter by brushing over the top layer of the potatoes.
8. Press well down and cover with a lid.
9. Cook in a hot oven, 240-250°C, for about 1 hour.
10. During cooking, press the potatoes at regular intervals to help them compact.

11. To serve, remove the lid and turn out on to hot service dish and serve whole or cut each Anna into 4 portions.

**Note:** For pommes Anna the potatoes must not be washed after cutting as the starch in the potatoes is required to bind the finished dish together for service.

## Stuffed aubergines                    *Aubergine farci au gratin*

| | | |
|---|---|---|
| 2 | Aubergines | 5 |
| 200 g | Duxelle | 500 g |
| 1 | Clove crushed garlic | 2 |
| 30 g | Fine white breadcrumbs | 75 g |
| | Salt and milled pepper | |
| ½ dl | Demi-glace | 1 dl |
| | Finely chopped parsley | |
| 1 dl | Olive oil | 2½ dl |

1. Cut the aubergine in half lengthways, score the flesh in a criss-cross.
2. Heat the olive oil in a sauté pan and shallow fry the aubergines, flesh side down, until the flesh becomes soft and lightly coloured.
3. Scoop out the flesh leaving the skin intact.
4. Cut the flesh into pieces and add the duxelle and garlic.
5. Continue to cook together in the sauté pan, add the finely chopped parsley and season.
6. Bind with a little demi-glace if required.
7. Re-fill the aubergine skins with mixture and sprinkle liberally with breadcrumbs.
8. Decorate with a criss cross pattern using the edge of a palette knife.
9. Set the aubergines in earthenware dishes and bake in a hot oven, 180°C, until hot.
10. Gratinate and serve with a cordon of jus lié.

## Baked tomatoes                    *Tomates au four*

| | | |
|---|---|---|
| 8 | Tomatoes | 20 |
| 30 g | Clarified butter | 60 g |

1. Blanch the tomatoes, removing the skin.
2. Lightly brush with clarified butter and season.
3. Bake in a moderate oven for 5–7 minutes.

## Stuffed tomatoes                    *Tomates farci au gratin*

| | | |
|---|---|---|
| 8 | Tomatoes | 20 |
| 200 g | Duxelle | 500 g |
| 40 g | Fine breadcrumbs | 100 g |
| | *or* | |
| | Grated parmesan cheese | |

1. Blanch and skin the tomatoes.

2. Remove the top of the tomatoes and scoop out the seeds.
3. Pipe in the duxelle and sprinkle with breadcrumbs or parmesan.
4. Brush the outside with a little butter, and bake in a moderate oven for 5–7 minutes.

## Mushroom and nut loaf

| | | |
|---|---|---|
| 260 g | **Brunoise of onion** | 650 g |
| 260 g | **Chopped mushrooms** | 650 g |
| 260 g | **Assorted finely chopped nuts** (brazils, almonds, walnuts, peanuts) | 650 g |
| ¼ dl | **Vegetable oil** | ½ dl |
| 120 g | **Fine breadcrumbs** | 300 g |
| 1–2 | **Eggs** | 2–3 |
| | **Salt and milled pepper** | |
| | **Worcester sauce to taste** | |
| 10 g | **Chopped parsley** | 20 g |

1. Select a suitable size saucepan and heat the oil.
2. Add the brunoise of onion and sweat without colour.
3. Add the chopped mushrooms and sweat for 2–4 minutes.
4. Remove the pan from the stove and mix in the finely chopped nuts and breadcrumbs (white or wholemeal).
5. Moisten by beating in a raw egg.
6. Add Worcester sauce to taste.
7. Mix in chopped parsley and season to taste.
8. Lightly grease a loaf tin or tins and press in the mixture, leaving 2 cm clearance at the top of the tin.
9. Place into a hot oven, 180–190°C, and bake for 1 hour until the loaf is lightly browned.
10. Remove from the oven and allow to stand for 10 minutes before turning out on to a hot service flat.
11. Carve into portions and serve with plain boiled or steamed vegetables or salad.

**Note:** A suitable sauce may also be served with the mushroom and nut loaf, e.g. tomato.

## Parsnip and tomato casserole with cheese

| | | |
|---|---|---|
| 800 g | **Peeled parsnips** | 2 kg |
| 280 g | **Tomatoes** | 700 g |
| 120 g | **Grated gruyère cheese** | 300 g |
| | **Salt and milled pepper** | |
| 1–2 | **Crushed cloves of garlic** | 2–3 |
| | **Pinch of oregano to taste** | |
| 2 dl | **Plain yoghurt** | 4½ dl |
| 200 g | **Wholemeal rice pilaff** | 500 g |

1. Slice the peeled parsnips.

2. Blanch the tomatoes, remove the skins and slice thinly.
3. Select a suitable deep earthenware casserole dish and rub with crushed garlic.
4. Sprinkle with rubbed oregano.
5. Layer the parsnips, tomatoes and grated cheese.
6. Add a thin layer of plain yoghurt and season.
7. Repeat the process until all the ingredients have been used, finishing with a top layer of yoghurt and gruyère cheese.
8. Place into a pre-heated oven at 180–200°C, covered with a lid, and cook for 40–50 minutes, or until the parsnips are tender.
9. Uncover the casserole dish and allow the cheese topping to colour, either in the oven or under a salamander.
10. Serve accompanied with a wholemeal rice pilaff.

**Note:** Wholemeal rice pilaff is made following the basic recipe for pilaff, substituting brown rice for patna rice.

# Baked flour products

## Introduction to baked flour products

The following pages are intended to introduce you to the subject of baking with flour and how yeast works within this field, and to culinary terms and techniques used in bakery work. The recipes which follow have been selected to allow you to develop skills and information found at the start of this section.

## The process of fermentation

### Nature of yeast

Yeasts are microscopic forms of plant life. There are two types of yeast:

1. The wild yeast floating about in the air.
2. Commercial yeast. This is the one used in bread making and other types of fermented goods, and is first prepared from wild yeasts freed from impurities.

A very small amount of yeast (28 g) contains thousands of cells. Many of these are not single; smaller cells either singly or in 3s and 4s are attracted to these. Growth takes place quickly — small cells grow to the size of parent cells and in time reproduce other small cells.

Yeast is a plant and grows by budding when provided with food — carbohydrates, protein and mineral matter, obtained from flour and sugar. Sugar, warmth and moisture are essential to the growth of the cells which is extremely rapid; extreme heat kills, while extreme cold retards their growth — and the presence of a high percentage of sugar hinders and poisons it. What happens is that too much sugar shrinks the yeast cells and prevents budding. Too much salt slows growth making it not so healthy, resulting in close textured mixtures.

We can see from the foregoing that it is of great importance to observe the basic rules of fermentation, and to use a correctly balanced recipe and method.

When the organism yeast is provided with food (flour), moisture (water or milk), and heat (controlled temperature), fermentation will take place, and this in turn produces the gas *carbon dioxide* and *ethyl alcohol*. It is the carbon dioxide which is responsible for increasing the volume of the dough, e.g. bread and buns, etc., while the ethyl alochol is the constituent which gives the product its special flavour.

The commercial yeast which is available in fresh compressed blocks of 450 g (1 lb) is the best for first-class work, and should be kept wrapped and under refrigeration when not being used. On no account should it be left out in the heat of the kitchen, otherwise deterioration is rapid. Fresh compressed yeast has a lovely smell and is crumbly in texture. When stale, it loses its nice fawn colour and goes brown and discoloured. It also turns very sticky. At this stage it is best discarded.

A 'long life' yeast is also available in dried form, with a shelf-life of several months. Used according to instructions, it can produce a worthwhile product. The usual amount required is about half that of fresh yeast. The dried product is reconstituted in warm water in order to activate the process of fermentation; the approximate temperature of the water should be 37°C (98.6°), much higher than that recommended for fresh yeast. Dried yeast is manufactured in granular, pellet or flake form, and is obviously very useful to have as a stand-by, or in those situations where the fresh commodity may not be so readily available.

### Flour

Flours which are capable of producing doughs with a high gluten content are necessary for all fermented goods. They are known as *strong* flour or sometimes referred to as bread flour. Strong flour is produced from Canadian and American wheats which have a protein content of about 16 per cent, whereas weak flour has a protein content of approximately 8 per cent. The aeration of the finished product, such as bread and buns, is directly related to the gluten factor which exists in the flour/liquid mixtures, the dough. The higher the gluten content, the stronger the gluten film and the greater the possible aeration.

### Method of mixing

If possible, all fermented doughs will benefit from working in a draught-free environment. An ambient temperature of about 21°C (70°F) is ideal for this work; not a problem during the summer months, but during the winter it means ensuring doors and windows are shut to keep out the cold air.

*Flour:* Should be at room temperature and always sieved before mixing.
*Fat:* Should be rubbed into the flour by hand or mixed on the machine using a dough hook.
*Water:* Should be at the right temperature, i.e. 21°C (70°F) — or warmer for dried yeast, see above. In the warmer months, the water can be taken straight from the tap and used. Part of the water will be used to dilute the yeast, and the remainder will have the sugar and salt content added so that both items are dissolved before adding to the flour and fat. If there is an egg content, this will be whisked into the water, salt and sugar.
*Mixing:* If by hand on the bench top, the flour and fat is drawn together with a bay in the centre, into which the yeast and other liquid is poured. If there is a fruit content in the recipe, this should be scattered around the perimeter of the flour before mixing takes place. The dough is kneaded until it attains a smooth, elastic consistency, at which stage it is placed into a suitable container, covered with a clean cloth and placed aside to prove.

It is important *not* to put the bowl over any sort of *direct* heat, such as a stove rack, but rather to leave it in a suitable part of the room away from draughts.
*BFT:* Refers to 'bulk fermentation time'; the length of time from when the dough is made and put to prove until it has doubled in size. Under normal conditions, BFT is about 1 hour for the dough to reach its full ripeness. Correctly proved dough has a lovely silky texture which is ideal for moulding.
*Knocking back:* At the full proving stage, the dough is knocked back, and then scaled off into the required weights, moulded and trayed up ready for the final proof. The pieces should roughly double their size before being taken to the oven. At all stages, keep doughs well covered to avoid skinning over.
*Baking:* There are marginal differences between baking times in which the sugar and fat content is relatively low, as in tinned bread rolls, and those fermented mixtures which are high in sugar and fat, such as savarin and brioche paste.

Bread and bread rolls require a good, solid oven temperature 232°C (450°F), while richer items are better baked at a lower temperature of 204°C (400°F) in a steady oven. A certain amount of steam is present during the baking process, and especially when the oven is full to capacity. Specialist pastry ovens are often fitted with a steam injector device; such steam will help to produce a loaf (or bread roll) with a slight glaze and pale golden top.

In the case of small batch baking, a pan full of water can be set in the oven beforehand — and this should generate sufficient steam to give moist baking conditions. These remarks apply equally to the baking of fruit cakes, especially those of the heavily fruited kind, such as Christmas and Wedding cakes.

**Large-scale production**

This will obviously involve the use of heavy duty mixing machines and proving cabinets which generate both warmth and steam. Machines may also be used for dividing and moulding the dough. Nevertheless, the basic rules will still apply.

The bulk fermentation time will vary marginally between small- and large-scale production; in the latter instance, the use of a special dough thermometer is advisable. Dough temperature is the controller of fermentation, and a thermometer will help to achieve consistent results.

# Self-assessment questions for fermentation

1. How many types of yeast are there?
2. How does yeast multiply?
3. What elements are essential to the growth of yeast cells?
4. What is the name of the gas which is responsible for raising yeast dough?
5. Which quality of flour is used in yeast work production?
6. What is meant by the phrase 'bulk fermentation time'?
7. Why are the rich fermented items, such as brioche and savarins, baked at a lower temperature than bread and bread rolls?
8. What is the purpose of generating extra steam whilst baking off bread rolls?
9. What is the approximate *protein* content of strong (bread making) flour?

# Baking bread dough

The following is a selection of basic bread recipes for making savoury bread dough products.

**Bread dough**

| | | |
|---|---|---|
| 800 g | Strong flour | 1½ kg |
| 15 g | Salt | 28 g |
| 28 g | Yeast | 56 g |
| 7 g | Lard | 15 g |
| 7 g | Castor sugar | 15 g |
| 500 ml | Water (approx.) | 1 litre |

1. Dissolve the yeast in the tepid water and add the sugar.
2. Rub the lard into the sieved flour and add the salt.
3. Mix all to a smooth elastic dough. Cover with a cloth and put to prove in a warm place for about 45 minutes until doubled in size.
4. Knock back, and scale off into desired weights. Mould up, and place the dough into greased (warmed) bread tins.

5. Allow to prove until the dough reaches the top rim of the tin.
6. At this stage, the top of the dough may be cut with the point of a very sharp knife to give an open effect; otherwise, leave it plain.
7. Set the bread in a fairly hot oven, 232°C (450°F) and bake for the following times:
   450 g (1 lb) loaf — about 35 minutes
   900 g (2 lb) loaf — about 45 mintues
8. After removal from the oven, immediately turn out of the tin on to a cake wire to cool.

## Bread rolls

| | | |
|---|---|---|
| 460 g | Strong flour | 920 g |
| 28 g | Milk powder | 56 g |
| 7 g | Salt | 15 g |
| 7 g | Castor sugar | 15 g |
| 15 g | Lard | 28 g |
| 28 g | Yeast | 56 g |
| 250 ml | Water (approx.) | 500 ml |

1. Dissolve the yeast in part of the tepid water, and whisk the milk powder, salt and sugar into the remainder.
2. Sieve the flour and rub in the lard. Mix all to a smooth elastic dough.
3. Cover and prove to double the size (about 45 minutes), then knock back.
4. Scale off at desired weights and mould up into plain or fancy shapes.
5. Place on to greased trays and cover with a damp cloth; prove to double the size.
6. Eggwash carefully, dust lightly with flour.
7. Bake at 232°C (450°F) for 12–15 minutes.
8. Whenever possible, to produce a nice crisp roll it is advantageous to bake on the sole of the oven.

## Brioche

Prepare a ferment from the following:

| | |
|---|---|
| 2½ dl | Water at 32°C (90°F) |
| 15 g | Castor sugar |
| 42 g | Yeast |
| 115 g | Strong flour |

Dissolve the yeast in the water, and whisk in the flour and salt. Allow the ferment to rise and drop; this takes about 30 minutes.

Meanwhile, prepare the following:

| | |
|---|---|
| 570 g | Strong flour |
| 28 g | Castor sugar |
| 7 g | Salt |
| 340 g | Butter |
| ½ litre | Egg at 32°C (90°F) |
| ½ dl | Milk |

1. Only slightly break the butter into the flour. Do not rub in.
2. When the ferment has dropped, mix all the ingredients to a smooth dough; well mix to toughen. Place into a suitable bowl and cover with a cloth. Keep in the refrigerator for not less than 12 hours.
3. The following morning, remove and knock back, then allow to recover at room temperature.
4. Scale off at required weights (usually 56 g; 2 oz), and shape up as for small cottage-style loaves.
5. Place into greased crinkled tins, and allow to prove in a little steam.
6. Snip the side of each one with scissors in three places, and eggwash carefully.
7. Bake at 191°C (375°F) for about 15 minutes to a nice golden brown.
8. Remove from the tins and cool on a wire rack.
9. Brioche paste can also be made into loaves 450 g (1 lb) in weight; bake the latter at 215°C (420°F) for about 20 minutes.

Brioche loaf slices (quartered) used in place of ordinary bread in bread and butter pudding is delicious.

## Bridge rolls

| | |
|---|---|
| 500 g | **Strong flour** |
| 42 g | **Yeast** |
| 35 g | **Lard** |
| 20 g | **Milk powder** |
| 7 g | **Salt** |
| 7 g | **Castor sugar** |
| 250 ml | **Water (approx.)** |

1. Dissolve the yeast in part of the water and whisk the milk powder, sugar and salt into the remainder.
2. Sieve the flour and rub in the fat. Blend all to a clear dough.
3. Cover and prove for 45 minutes until doubled in size.
4. Scale off at 28 g (1 oz) pieces, and mould finger shapes; place fairly close together on greased baking trays and prove to double the size.
5. Eggwash with half-strength eggwash and bake at 220°C (430°F) for 12–15 minutes.

## Wholemeal bread

| | | |
|---|---|---|
| 900 g | **Wholemeal flour** | 1 kg 800 g |
| 15 g | **Salt** | 28 g |
| 20 g | **Yeast** | 42 g |
| 500 ml | **Water (approx.) at 32°C (90°F)** | 1 litre |
| 15 g | **Lard** | 28 g |

1. Dissolve the salt in part of the water, and the yeast in the remainder.
2. Rub the fat into the flour and make a bay. Pour in the liquids and blend all to a well-mixed dough. Wholemeal dough needs to be on the slack

side in order to give a nice mellow eating texture.
3. Prove to double the size before knocking back. Scale off into individual rolls at 56 g (2 oz), or mould into loaf shapes (round or tinned) at 450 g (1 lb) size.
4. Place into greased tins and prove for a further 50–60 minutes to double the volume.
5. Bake in a solid oven at 235°C (475°F) for 40–45 minutes.
6. Turn out of the tins to cool.

**Note:** It is often very difficult to give precise liquid measurements for most fermented goods, the reason being that two sacks of flour are seldom alike! Certainly, with wholemeal flour, as opposed to the more refined white flour varieties, the amount of liquid that the flour takes up is such that too tight a dough will result in 'pinched' and under-sized goods which are lacking in volume and rather tough to eat.

A nice finish to this type of article is to dust the tops with wholemeal flour before taking to the oven. The baking heat can be reduced slightly once the goods have set, e.g. down to 232°C (450°F).

**Fancy shaped bread rolls**

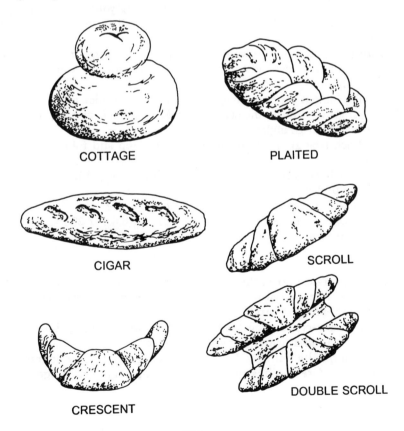

COTTAGE

PLAITED

CIGAR

SCROLL

CRESCENT

DOUBLE SCROLL

261

## Croissants

| | | |
|---|---|---|
| 450 g | **Strong flour** | 900 g |
| 15 g | **Salt** | 28 g |
| 28 g | **Castor sugar** | 56 g |
| 150 ml | **Cold water** | 300 ml |
| 15 g | **Yeast** | 28 g |
| 150 ml | **Milk (tepid)** | 300 ml |
| 285 g | **Butter** | 570 g |

1. Dissolve the yeast in half of the milk and the sugar and salt in the remainder.
2. Rub 56 g (112 g) of the butter into the sieved flour and make a bay.
3. Place the water and the milk into the centre and mix all to a smooth dough.
4. Wrap in greaseproof and allow to lie in the refrigerator for 1 hour.
5. Meanwhile, flatten out the butter to a thin layer; roll out the dough to a rectangle and place the flattened butter over one half. Fold the other half of the dough over the top to enclose.
6. Roll out the dough to another rectangle and fold into three; this constitutes one complete turn. Rest for ½ hour covered in the refrigerator.
7. Give a further roll (with the folded edge facing you) into a rectangular shape and again fold into three. Cover and allow to rest overnight if possible.
8. With the folded edge towards you, repeat the rolling and folding into three (this will now constitute three complete turns). Allow to rest for 20–30 minutes.
9. Finally, roll out the paste to approximately 6 mm thick and 35 cm wide.
10. Cut lengthways down the centre to make two bands of paste, then from each band cut triangles.
11. Roll each triangle up from the base to the top and fold into crescent shapes.
12. Place each crescent on to greased baking trays (with the tip of the triangle underneath).
13. Brush with eggwash and prove to double the size.
14. Brush again with half-strength eggwash and bake at 226°C (440°F) to golden brown.

**Notes:**
1. It is important to turn the croissant paste with the folded edge towards you each time, and also to mark exactly how many turns the paste has had (with a finger mark).
2. Some pastry-cooks eggwash the edges before rolling up into crescent shapes: it is all a matter of personal choice.
3. Use best quality butter and chill in the refrigerator before attempting to flatten out. Use a rolling pin for the latter operation and a light dusting of flour.

4. The baking off is important: avoid 'flash' heat and bake on the sole of the oven. In this way, both the tops and bottoms of the croissants will take on a nice golden brown, crisp exterior.
5. Finally, cool on wire racks.

# Baked pâtisserie products

### Basic bun dough

Bun dough is a sweet product, unlike bread dough which is savoury. This dough is suitable for the production of all yeast goods either plain or fruited, such as Chelsea buns, currant buns, hot cross buns, cream cookies, Swiss buns, doughnuts and many more varieties. It will produce a first-class article if the usual care is taken in the make up and baking procedures.

| | |
|---|---|
| 540 g | Strong flour |
| 15 g | Milk powder |
| 35 g | Yeast |
| 15 g | Egg |
| 70 g | White shortening or butter |
| 85 g | Castor sugar |
| ¼ litre | Water at 21°C (approx.) |
| 6 spots | Bun spice |
| 5 g approx. | Salt |

1. Break down the yeast in half of the tepid water, and blend the egg, sugar and salt in the remainder.
2. Sieve the flour and rub in the fat. Make a bay and add the yeast and egg mixtures to the flour. Blend all to a smooth dough.
3. Cover with a cloth and prove to double the size in a suitable place away from any cold draughts. Any cold air will retard the action of the yeast in the process of fermentation.
4. Knock back before using and keep covered.

### Chelsea buns

1. Roll out the basic dough to a rectangular shape. Avoid using too much flour for dusting when rolling out.
2. Brush the surface of the dough with melted butter, and sprinkle with dried mixed fruit, such as currants, sultanas and candied peel (about 70 g), and a liberal dusting of castor sugar (50 g). The dough can be flavoured with a little grated nutmeg if desired.
3. Eggwash the edges and roll up lengthwise (like a swiss roll) as tightly as possible. The diameter of the roll should be about 6 cm.
4. Brush the outside of the roll with melted butter, and cut downwards with a very sharp knife into slices 2 cm thick.
5. Place cut side downwards on to a greased baking tray in neat rows, allowing sufficient room for expansion during the final proof.

6. Cover with a cloth and prove in a warm, draught-free place until doubled in size.
7. Bake at 225°C (440°F) for about 15 minutes to a nice golden brown.
8. On removal from oven, brush the tops with melted butter and dust well with castor sugar.

## Butter buns

1. Scale the basic dough at 40 g pieces. Mould round and allow to rest for 10 minutes.
2. Roll out to 12–15 cm round.
3. Place a small amount of filling in the centre, and fold in half. Add a little more filling and fold over again to quarter size. Tray up on greased baking trays and prove to double the size.
4. Eggwash the tops with half-strength eggwash, and bake at 220°C (430°F) for 12–15 minutes.
5. Cool on a cake wire and dust with icing sugar.

## Butter bun filling

| | |
|---|---|
| 215 g | **Butter** |
| 330 g | **Castor sugar** |
| 6 spots | **Vanilla essence** |

Cream together the above ingredients. Keep in the refrigerator covered with foil. Use as required.

## Fruited tea cakes

1. Scale off fruited dough, i.e. 100 g mixed fruit (currants and sultanas) added to the basic recipe, into 150 g pieces and mould round; cover with a cloth.
2. Pin out (with a rolling pin) to 12 cm diameter rounds, and place not too close together on greased baking trays; docker well with the point of a knife.
3. Prove to double size, eggwash and bake at 226°C (440°F) for 12–15 minutes.

## Cream cookies

1. Scale off plain bun dough at 40 g pieces. Mould round and place on to greased baking trays. Cover and prove to double size.
2. Eggwash the tops with weak eggwash and bake at 220°C (430°F) for 12–15 minutes. Allow to cool on a cake rack.
3. When cold, cut through (half-way) laterally with a sharp knife and pipe in a generous spot of red jam, then a bulb of whipped cream.
4. Dust the tops with icing sugar.

## Swiss fingers

1. Scale off plain bun dough at 40 g pieces and mould round. Rest for 10 minutes then remould into finger shapes. Arrange fairly close together on greased baking trays and prove to double size.
2. Eggwash carefully and bake at 220°C (430°F) for approximately 12 minutes.
3. When cool, ice the tops with pink fondant or lemon water icing.

### Lemon water icing
Dilute sufficient icing sugar with water to a thick fluid consistency. Add a few spots of lemon juice to taste. Gently heat to 37°C (98°F) and use while still warm.

## Hot cross buns

1. Add 100 g of mixed fruit (currants, sultanas and cut mixed peel) and 4 spots of bun spice essence to the basic dough recipe at the mixing stage, and allow to prove to double size. Knock back and scale off at 50 g pieces.
2. Mould round and tray up on greased baking trays. Prove to double size.
3. Eggwash carefully with half-strength eggwash and pipe on crosses.
4. Bake at 225°C (440°F) for approximately 15 minutes.
5. Wash over with bun wash whilst still hot.

### Crosses for hot cross buns

Well mix the following to a smooth paste. Keep covered to avoid skinning over.

| | |
|---|---|
| 56 g | Cornflour |
| 56 g | Plain flour |
| 40 g | Nut oil |
| 2 dl | Water |
| | Small pinch of salt |
| 2 spots | Bun spice essence |

### Bun glazes (eggwash)

1. 2 parts egg and 1 part water whisked together.
2. 2 parts egg and 1 part castor sugar, and 1 part water whisked together.
3. 1 egg, 2 egg yolks, pinch of salt, pinch of castor sugar, whisked together.

### Sugar bun wash

| | |
|---|---|
| 250 ml | Boiling water |
| 115 g | Castor sugar |
| 30 g | Powdered gelatine |

1. Heat together until dissolved and strain before using.
2. Apply carefully to the tops of bun goods as soon as the latter come out of the oven.
3. The bun wash is best used when hot; it will keep for several days in a cool place.

## Savarin paste       Pâté à savarin

| | | |
|---|---|---|
| 230 g | Strong flour | 450 g |
| 15 g | Yeast | 30 g |
| 10 g | Salt | 20 g |
| 100 ml | Fresh milk | 200 ml |
| 3 | Eggs (medium size) | 6 |
| 15 g | Castor sugar | 30 g |
| 115 g | Melted butter | 230 g |

1. Sieve the flour and make a bay.
2. Warm the milk and eggs (beaten) to blood heat (about 37°C).
3. Dissolve the yeast in the tepid milk, and add to the flour with the salt, and the beaten egg.
4. Blend all to a smooth dough, giving a good beating either by hand or by machine.
5. Cover with a clean cloth and allow to rest in a warm place for about 30 minutes until the mixture has doubled in size. Do not place the savarin paste over or near direct heat.
6. When risen, beat in the melted butter, and then the sugar to produce a smooth, elastic dough. Use at once.
7. Using a large savoy bag and plain tube, pipe the mixture into greased savarin moulds. Only half fill each mould.
8. Allow to prove until the mixture reaches the rim of the mould.
9. Bake at 218°C for approximately 20 minutes to a nice golden brown.
10. Allow to cool for a few minutes before removing from the moulds.
11. Turn out on a cake wire and use as required.

## Rum baba       *Baba au rhum*

1. Grease some dariole moulds, and sprinkle a few washed currants in the bottom of each.
2. Half fill with savarin paste, and allow to prove until the mixture reaches the top edge of the mould.
3. Bake at 220°C for 20 minutes.
4. Turn out of the moulds and allow to cool.
5. Soak carefully in hot syrup (see page 150) and drain on a cake wire.
6. Sprinkle each one with rum and glaze with boiling apricot glaze.
7. Arrange neatly on a flat dish; decorate each one with a rosette of whipped cream and angelica diamonds and quartered glacé cherry.

**Savarins — large and small**

1. Grease some small savarin rings (or the large size) and half fill with savarin paste.
2. Prove until the mixture reaches the top edge of the mould(s) and bake at 220°C for 20 minutes for the individual size, and 30 minutes for the large savarin.
3. Turn out and allow to cool.
4. Soak carefully in hot syrup and drain on a cake wire.
5. Sprinkle with rum (optional) before glazing with boiling apricot glaze.
6. Set the savarin on to a suitable dish, and garnish accordingly.

Small savarins are usually finished with a whirl of whipped cream in the centre and angelica and glacé cherry.

Large savarins can be finished with fresh fruit salad or fresh strawberries, etc., then decorated with whipped cream.

**Marignans**                                        *Marignans chantilly*

1. Using the standard savarin paste, grease some oval/boat-shaped moulds, and one-third fill with the paste.
2. Allow to prove until the paste reaches the top of the mould.
3. Bake at 220°C for about 20 minutes to a nice golden brown.
4. Turn out and cool on wire racks.
5. Soak the marignans in hot syrup, and replace on to the rack.
6. Glaze each one with apricot glaze (use hot), and decorate with whipped cream.

After glazing, some pastry cooks make an incision along the side of each one and pipe the cream into the slit. The top is then decorated with angelica and glacé cherry.

**Note:** It is important to avoid soaking the savarin, baba or marginan too much, or the finished texture will be impaired with the item becoming soggy and unappetising. Always measure the syrup ingredients carefully so that the correct density is achieved. Finally, the syrup must be hot when soaking takes place.

# Baked pastry dishes

*Directions for lining a flan ring*

Mould a portion of flan paste into a round shape. Dust lightly with flour and roll out the paste first one way, then turn, turning again each time it is rolled. Measure the flan ring to the paste until the size required is obtained. Lightly grease both flan ring and baking tray. Pick up the paste on the rolling pin and lay over the top of the ring. Ease the paste into the ring gently without pulling or stretching, allowing the paste to take the form of the ring naturally. Roll over the top of the flan ring to remove surplus paste. Gently thumb up the sides, and mark the rim with pastry tweezers. Make a circle of greaseproof paper and place in the flan case. Fill this with dried pulses, such as haricot beans. Bake blind at 190°C for approximately 25 minutes. Remove the pulses and flan ring, eggwash the sides and return to the oven to glaze. When cooked, the crust should be golden brown and crisp.

Some, such as apple flan, frangipane flan, and similar flans will have a filling, which is placed into the lined flan ring prior to baking off.

## Apple flan                                            *Flan aux pommes*

Line a flan ring in the usual manner. Prepare an apple purée sufficient for the number of flans required based on the following proportions.

| | |
|---|---|
| **1 kg** | **Cooking apples** |
| **115 g** | **Granulated sugar** |
| **55 g** | **Butter** |

1. Peel, quarter, core and slice the apples in thick slices (reserve the peelings and core).
2. Melt the butter in suitable pan, add the sugar and apples plus a few drops of lemon juice and cover with a tight-fitting lid.
3. Cook over moderate heat to a thick purée.
4. Allow to cool.
5. Layer the prepared flan case with the apple purée.
6. Peel, quarter and core a nice cooking apple and cut into neat thin slices.
7. Arrange in overlapping pieces on top of the filling beginning at the outer edge of the flan. Proceed in circles working towards the centre of the flan. Dust the top with sugar and bake at 204°C until cooked and the apple slices have taken on a nice colour.
8. Towards the end, remove the flan ring, eggwash the sides of the flan and return to the oven to glaze.
9. Finally mask the top carefully with a glaze made from the apple trimmings prepared in the following manner:
10. Cover the peelings with cold water and add sugar to taste.
11. Flavour with lemon juice and bring to the boil. Simmer for approximately 15 minutes and strain through a fine chinois.
12. Reboil and thicken with diluted arrowroot.
13. Add a little more sugar if necessary to clarify glaze. Use boiling hot. The glaze will set nicely when cold.

Some pastry-cooks use apricot glaze but the above gives both good flavour and appearance.

## Bakewell tart

| | | |
|---|---|---|
| 170 g | Butter | 340 g |
| 170 g | Castor sugar | 340 g |
| 3 | Eggs | 6 |
| 85 g | Ground almonds | 170 g |
| 85 g | Cake crumbs | 170 g |
| 55 g | Medium flour | 115 g |

1. Cream the butter and sugar to a light consistency, and beat in the eggs in three lots.
2. Fold in the ground almonds, cake crumbs and sieved flour.
3. Line a flan ring(s) with a good quality sweet short paste.
4. Cover the base of the pastry with a thin layer of raspberry jam.
5. Three-quarters fill the flans with the Bakewell mixture.
6. Level off the tops and decorate with a lattice of pastry strips.
7. Eggwash the strips of paste and bake at 191°C for about 30 minutes.
8. When cooked, brush over the top with thin lemon-flavoured water icing or thinned down fondant.

## Pear bordaloue                              *Flan aux poires bourdaloue*

1. Line a greased flan ring with flan paste, and bake blind. Allow to cool.
2. Meanwhile, prepare a frangipane cream filling (see below).
3. Two-thirds fill the baked flan case with the frangipane cream which has been flavoured with 50 g of crushed praline (see page 152).
4. Smooth level and decorate the top with halved or quartered poached pears.
5. Mask with the same cream (slightly thinned down with a spoonful of double cream) and garnish lightly with toasted flaked almonds and granulated sugar.
6. Pass the flan under a very hot salamander to caramelise the sugar.

Apricot halves can be used in place of pears (flan aux abricots bourdaloue).

## Frangipane cream

| | | |
|---|---|---|
| 500 ml | Milk | 1 litre |
| 6 spots | Vanilla essence (or vanilla pod) | 12 spots |
| 5 | Egg yolks | 10 |
| 2 | Eggs | 4 |
| 50 g | Cornflour | 100 g |
| 75 g | Granulated sugar | 150 g |
| 10 g | Butter | 20 g |

1. Blend together the eggs, yolks, sugar and vanilla with the cornflour and a little of the milk to a smooth paste.
2. Bring the remainder of the milk to the boil, and pour on to the mixture.
3. Whisk well before returning to the pan. Re-boil and simmer gently for

about 10 minutes.
4. Pass through a fine strainer and beat in the butter.
5. Keep covered with a buttered paper to prevent skinning over. Use as required.

## Lemon meringue pie

| | | |
|---|---|---|
| 115 g | **Castor sugar** | 460 g |
| 30 g | **Butter** | 115 g |
| 1 | **Egg yolk** | 4 |
| 140 ml | **Cold water** | 570 ml |
| 20 g | **Cornflour** | 85 g |
| 1 | **Grated zest and juice of lemon** | 4 |

1. Boil the water and sugar together to dissolve.
2. Add the diluted cornflour, and whisk in quickly; cook for 2–3 minutes.
3. Remove from the heat and whisk in the butter.
4. Finally, add the lemon juice, grated zest and yolk(s) of egg.
5. Pour the mixture immediately into a previously baked flan case.
6. Allow to set, then cover the top with meringue and decorate with meringue whirls.
7. Place in a moderate oven to colour nicely and serve on a doily-covered silver flat.
8. The finishing heat for meringue is about 150°C for 10–15 minutes.

The above can be served as a tranche (slice) by preparing a rectangular shaped pastry case and finishing as for the pie method.

## Apple turnovers *Chausson aux pommes*

1. Peel, quarter and remove the core from 750 g of cooking apples, and cut into dices (1 cm).
2. Sprinkle with granulated sugar and lemon juice.
3. Meanwhile, roll out about 500 g puff paste to about 5 mm thick.
4. Cut out rounds of paste 12 cm in diameter, and roll an oval shape.
5. Moisten the edges with eggwash, and place a spoonful of prepared apples in the centre.
6. Dust with granulated sugar and a pinch of powdered cinnamon.
7. Fold over and seal the edges. Brush the top with eggwash or egg white, and dip in castor sugar — face side down.
8. Place upright on a greased and water-splashed baking tray, and allow to rest for 20 minutes.
9. Bake at 220°C for about 20 minutes to golden brown.

## Eccles cakes

*Filling*

| | |
|---|---|
| 200 g | Washed currants |
| 100 g | Soft brown sugar |
| 75 g | Mixed peel |
| 25 g | Melted butter |
| 25 g | Apricot jam |
| | Pinch of grated nutmeg |

1. Blend the butter with the remainder of ingredients.
2. Roll out some puff paste 3 mm thick, and cut out rounds using a 10 cm cutter. (Use approximately 500 g of puff pastry scraps.)
3. Eggwash the edges and place a spoonful of filling in the centre.
4. Draw in the edges to the centre, and seal in the mixture.
5. Invert on the table and lightly roll with the pin.
6. Make an incision in the centre, brush the top with egg white and dip into castor sugar.
7. Place sugar side up on a greased and water-splashed baking tray.
8. Rest for 20 minutes before baking at 220°C for about 15 minutes.

## Cream horns

1. Use puff paste or puff paste trimmings, and roll out fairly thinly.
2. Cut into strips approximately 2 cm wide and 35 cm long.
3. Moisten down one side and starting at the point of the cream horn mould, commence to roll up cone fashion with the paste slightly overlapping at each turn.
4. Secure the paste at the wide end with a little water or egg white.
5. Brush over with egg white and dip the upper surface into coarse granulated sugar.
6. Arrange sugar side up on a greased and water-splashed baking tray.
7. Rest for 20 minutes. Bake at 210°C to golden brown.
8. Remove from the tins carefully and allow to cool.
9. Pipe a spot of red jam, and fill with sweetened whipped cream.

## Mince pies

1. Roll out virgin puff paste, 3 mm thick, and cut out circles with a 9 cm cutter.
2. Invert on to a greased and water-splashed baking tray.
3. Eggwash the rims, and place a spoonful of mincemeat in the centre.
4. Invert a similar disc of puff paste on top, and secure the outer rim by lightly pressing on top with a smaller sized cutter about 8 cm diameter.
5. Make a small incision in the top with the point of a knife, and eggwash carefully.
6. Allow to rest for 20 minutes and bake at 216°C for about 15 minutes.
7. Dust with icing sugar before serving.

## Palmiers

1. Roll out virgin puff paste 36 cm wide, and 2–3 mm thick.
2. Brush all over with egg white, and dredge with granulated sugar.
3. Fold the two edges to the centre. Brush again with egg white and dredge with sugar.
4. Fold over once again, and lightly press down with a rolling pin.
5. Cut across with a sharp knife into ½ cm wide strips.
6. Place on prepared baking sheets *cut* surface downwards.
7. Allow to rest for 20 minutes before baking at 216°C.
8. Half bake, then draw to the mouth of the oven and turn each one carefully with a palette knife.
9. Finish baking to a crisp golden brown.
10. Serve plain, or join together with a spot of red jam and fill with whipped cream.

## Fleurons

1. Roll out puff paste 3 mm thick and using a 7 cm fluted cutter, carefully cut out half-moon shapes 5 cm wide.
2. Invert on to a water-splashed baking sheet, and allow to rest for 1 hour.
3. Eggwash the tops and bake at 210°C for 12–15 minutes to a nice golden brown.

**Note:** Fleurons are used as a garnish for many poached fish dishes, épinards aux fleurons (spinach purée served with puff paste crescents), and similar kitchen preparations.

## Gâteau Tom pouce

1. Roll out puff paste (as for mille-feuille) into a square or rectangle (trimmings will do) and cover the base of a water-splashed baking sheet.
2. Docker well, and allow to rest for 30 minutes before baking off at 204°C to a crisp, golden brown.
3. Cool, then cut into strips 10 cm wide. Brush the bottom layer with boiling apricot jam and cover generously with a thick layer of filling.
4. Finish with a top piece of pastry (inverted on to the flat side), and brush with boiling apricot jam.
5. Spread evenly with tempered white fondant. Pipe parallel lines of colour fondant (chocolate or pink) across the surface before the fondant sets, and using the point of a knife, lightly draw through to complete a 'feather' design.
6. Allow to set in a cool place before carefully cutting across with a sharp knife into portions approximately 6 cm wide.

**Note:** For filling, see page 145.

## Mille-feuille

1. Roll out puff paste trimming about 6 mm thick and cover the base of a water-splashed baking sheet. Well docker and allow to rest for 30 minutes.
2. Bake at 204°C to a crisp, golden brown. Allow to cool before cutting into strips 10 cm wide.
3. Spread the first two layers thinly with raspberry jam, then layer generously with best quality pastry cream and build three layers high. The top piece should be inverted to show a nice flat surface.
4. Press lightly together, and brush the top with boiling apricot jam.
5. Cover the top with tempered white fondant, and quickly pipe parallel lines of chocolate fondant across the surface.
6. Score with the point of a knife in opposite directions to complete a 'feather' design.
7. When set, cut across into portions 5–6 cm wide.

**Note:** For pastry cream (crème pâtissière), see page 146.

## Gâteau pithivier

| | | |
|---|---|---|
| 250 g | Puff pastry | |
| 50 g | Apricot jam | |
| 250 g | Frangipane | |

1. Prepare the frangipane in the usual manner (see below).
2. Roll out the paste about 3 mm thick.
3. Using a flan ring as a template, cut out two circles of paste, the top slightly larger than the base.
4. Spread carefully with jam on the base.
5. Layer with the frangipane.
6. Eggwash the edges.
7. Cover with the top circle and mark with a knife carefully.
8. Eggwash, rest and bake at 205°C for 25 minutes.

## Frangipane

Filling for tarts, flans, etc.

| 2 | Eggs | 6 |
|---|---|---|
| 100 g | Butter | 300 g |
| 100 g | Castor sugar | 300 g |
| 100 g | Ground almonds | 300 g |
| 25 g | Medium flour | 75 g |
| 2 spots | Lemon and almond essence | 6 spots |

1. Cream the butter and the sugar together to a light consistency.
2. Beat in the eggs singly to form an emulsion.
3. Finally, fold in the flour, almonds and the two flavourings.

4.  Allow to rest for 20 minutes, before using.

It is practical for economy purposes to replace half the quantity of ground almonds with sieved, stale cake crumbs. Naturally, the quality and eating properties of the finished goods are not of the same standard.

### Vol-au-vents

1.  Roll out virgin puff paste 6 mm thick.
2.  Remove centres with small cutter in regular equidistant lines.
3.  Roll out a second sheet of puff paste 7 mm thick.
4.  Docker well and eggwash all over (the base only).
5.  Place the first sheet on top of the second sheet.
6.  Cut out required size; glaze tops with eggwash.
7.  Tray up on water-splashed baking sheet and rest well before baking off at 220°C for 20 minutes.

### Notes:

1.  *Bouchées* may be made in the same way as vol-au-vents. They are usually 3–5 cm in diameter according to requirements.
2.  The above method is much quicker than the normal means of production whereby each vol-au-vent or bouchée is cut out separately and joined together. Both methods are, however, correct and it is a matter of choice.
3.  It is a good idea when placing the top sheet of puff paste on to the base to invert it first; i.e. after rolling out the sheet, turn it over. This will help to achieve straight sides on the bouchées or vol-au-vents. Certainly when making individual vol-au-vents, always invert both the bottom and top circles of paste.

## Sponges and cakes

There are several fairly simple rules to observe in the manufacture of sponge goods and the general range of cakes. Failure to do so will often result in disappointment.

The sponge cake in its various forms is probably the most popular cake item in this country and possibly in Europe. It comes in several types: savoy sponge fingers and sponge drops; plain and chocolate flavoured swiss rolls; sponge rounds and sheets, both of which usually form the basis of most gâteaux; and the wide range of torten.

1.  It is essential that all utensils are scrupulously clean and free from grease; in other words, they should be scalded in boiling water before operations begin.
2.  Naturally, the correct ingredients and a balanced formula are equally

important.

3. The temperature of the ingredients is also important (especially during the winter months); about 24°C is satisfactory, and during cold weather, it is a good idea to leave all ingredients (including the flour) to achieve room temperature before attempting to produce the final article.

## Production method

For large quantities the use of a machine is essential to achieve the correct amount of aeration when whisking the egg/sugar base batter. Set the machine to operate at top speed. It is a good idea to warm the sugar on a tray in the oven to speed up the whisking operation. After warming, simply tip on to the egg, and whisk well for about 10 minutes. The resultant batter should be light, and solid. Any glycerine and flavouring would be added at this stage.

The choice of flour is important; if possible try and obtain a quality cake flour for lightness of texture and tender eating consistency.

The flour should be folded in by hand with the fingers held apart, making sure to get right to the bottom of the bowl. Speed and lightness of hand are very important with care being taken not to over-mix at this stage.

Finally, the sponge batter should be deposited into the prepared tins or frames in one portion to avoid air holes. With large batches, the batter is generally weighed first then scooped from the scale pan straight into the mould.

In a few instances the eggs are separated with the whites being folded in at the end along with the flour. In this case the whites are whipped separately, e.g. savoy sponge fingers (biscuits à la cuillère). Whichever method of production is employed, the basic precautions are the same.

## Cake-making techniques

All the remarks pertaining to choice and care in processing the materials will apply to cakes, whether Madeira, fruit, birthday, wedding or whatever.

Before baking, make sure that the finished cake batter will be protected during the baking process. Cover the tops with damp tissue paper to prevent drying out and scorching. Give plenty of protection on the sides and bottom of the cake tin to preserve the cake's natural moisture.

Make sure that the oven is pre-set at the correct baking temperature, and that the time of baking is noted when baking commences.

Once the cakes have been placed in the oven, give them a chance to rise and set before attempting to open the oven door to check their progress. In any case, if the temperature and timing is right, such a check is hardly necessary until towards the end of the baking process.

## Christmas cake

| | |
|---|---|
| 230 g | Butter |
| 230 g | Soft brown sugar |
| 285 ml | Egg |
| 285 g | Medium flour |
| 25 g | Ground almonds |
| 315 g | Sultanas |
| 340 g | Currants |
| 140 g | Diced mixed peel |
| 5 g | Mixed spice |
| 1 | Grated zest and juice of lemon |
| 50 ml | Rum |
| 5 spots | Vanilla essence |

1. Blend the fruit together with the rum and zest and juice of lemon.
2. Allow to stand covered overnight.
3. Toast the ground almonds, and blend with the sieved flour and mixed spice.
4. Cream the butter and sugar to a light, fluffy consistency.
5. Add the eggs in several lots and the vanilla essence, to achieve a solid but light batter.
6. Fold in the flour carefully, and finally blend in the fruit.
7. Scale off at 700 g into a 20 cm lined cake tin, and level the top.
8. Bake at 182°C falling to 171°C for 1¾ hours taking all the usual precautions to avoid over-baking.
9. After cooling in the tin, wrap and keep in a cool place for at least 3 weeks before using.

The yield will be 2 × 20 cm cakes and 1 × 15 cm.

Give plenty of bottom and side protection during baking, and cover the top with a piece of silver foil to keep in the moisture. Remove the latter towards the end of baking. The cake will mature nicely over a three-week period.

## Madeira cake

| | | |
|---|---|---|
| 130 g | Butter | 500 g |
| 170 g | Castor sugar | 690 g |
| 3 | Eggs | 12 |
| 1 | Grated zest of lemon | 3 |
| 55 g | Scone flour | 230 g |
| 115 g | Cake flour | 455 g |

1. Cream the butter and castor sugar to a light consistency.
2. Beat in the eggs in four stages to a light batter.
3. Flavour with the zest of lemon.
4. Carefully fold in the sieved flours without over-mixing.
5. Divide the small mixing between 2 × 15 cm lined cake tins.
6. Bake at 177°C for 1¼ hours.

The larger mixing will yield 7–8 cakes.

## Almond sponge base for torten

| 200 g | Egg (liquid weight) | 800 g |
|-------|---------------------|-------|
| 130 g | Castor sugar | 520 g |
| 15 g | Glycerine | 60 g |
| 85 g | Medium flour | 340 g |
| 45 g | Cornflour | 170 g |
| 45 g | Roasted ground almonds | 170 g |
| 60 g | Melted butter | 230 g |

1. Heat the castor sugar on a tray in the oven.
2. Add to the eggs and glycerine and whisk to a full sponge on the machine.
3. Pour in the butter on slow speed (only about 4 turns), then blend in the ground almonds gently by hand.
4. Scale off to the desired weights into torten rings, and bake at 204°C for 20–25 minutes.
5. Allow to cool before removing from the torten rings.
6. Wrap and keep overnight to use the following day.

Allow 315 g of the mixture to a 25 cm diameter torten ring. Place the greased and floured rings on to a baking sheet, which should be lined with a double thickness of good quality greaseproof paper to give added protection during the baking. The tops can be protected with sheets of damp tissue paper.

## Butter sponge                                           *Genoese*

| 3 | Eggs | 12 |
|-------|---------------------|-------|
| 170 g | Castor sugar | 680 g |
| 55 g | Butter | 230 g |
| 30 ml | Hot water | 120 ml |
| 115 g | Medium flour | 460 g |

1. Whisk the eggs and sugar together over hot water to a full sponge.
2. Meanwhile, melt the butter and water together. Remove the egg/sugar mixture from the heat and continue to whisk until cool.
3. Stir the butter/water into the egg/sugar batter, and then fold in the sieved flour. Do not over-mix.
4. Pour the smaller mixing into two prepared 15 cm diameter sponge tins and level off with a plastic scraper.
5. Bake at 215°C for 15 minutes.
6. Turn out on to a cooling rack when ready.

## Chocolate Genoese

Use the above recipe but substitute 30 g of cocoa for the same amount of flour. The colour can be brightened with the addition of a few spots of chocolate colour if desired.

### Sponge tin preparation

1. Brush the inside of the tins carefully with melted butter (clarified), dust with flour (shake out the surplus), and finally, dust with castor sugar.
2. Alternatively, use the special sponge grease:

| | |
|---|---|
| 115 g | **White vegetable shortening** |
| 115 g | **Medium flour** |
| 6 spots | **Vanilla essence (optional)** |

Cream the fat and flour together with vanilla, and use to brush the tins. Dust with castor sugar before adding the sponge mixture.

# Baked sweet dishes (cold)

### Swiss roll

| | | |
|---|---|---|
| 1 | **Egg yolk** | 4 |
| 3 | **Eggs** | 12 |
| 85 g | **Castor sugar** | 340 g |
| 70 g | **Medium flour** | 280 g |
| 1–2 spots | **Vanilla essence (optional)** | 8 spots |
| 15 ml | **Glycerine** | 60 ml |

1. Prepare a swiss roll tin by lining with greaseproof paper.
2. Whisk the yolk, eggs, sugar and vanilla to the ribbon stage over warm water — at which point remove from the heat.
3. Continue to whisk until cool, then add the glycerine.
4. Shake in the sieved flour, and tip the mixture out on to the tin.
5. Gently spread level, and bake in a hot oven at 238°C for 7 minutes. It is important not to over-bake the sponge.
6. When baked, tip out on to a sugar-dusted sheet of greaseproof paper, and spread thinly with red jam.
7. Roll up and leave aside for several minutes to set.
8. Trim the ends with a sharp knife before serving.

### Chocolate swiss roll

Use the above recipe but substitute 15 g of cocoa for the same amount of flour. Flavour with a few spots of chocolate compound and colouring. When cool, spread with vanilla or chocolate buttercream and roll up.

### Victoria sponge

| | | |
|---|---|---|
| 2 | **Eggs** | 16 |
| 85 g | **Castor sugar** | 690 g |
| 30 g | **White vegetable fat** | 230 g |
| 55 g | **Butter** | 460 g |

| 15 ml | Milk | 115 ml |
| 130 g | Medium flour | 1 kg |
| 5 g | Baking powder | 30 g |

1. Cream the fats with the sugar until light and fluffy.
2. Beat in the eggs in several lots and fold in the flour and baking powder (sieved together).
3. Any flavourings (vanilla essence, etc.) should be added when beating in the egg.
4. Finally, add the milk to achieve a nice dropping consistency.
5. The amount of milk will vary acording to the particular strength of flour used.
6. Meanwhile, prepare some 15 cm diameter sponge tins by greasing and dusting with flour.
7. Drop in 200–230 g of the mixture into each tin and spread level.
8. Bake at 191°C for 15–20 minutes to a nice golden brown.
9. When cool, split through and layer with raspberry jam and dust the tops with icing sugar.

The above mixture will make a nice, tender eating sponge. Take all the usual precautions with the basic ingredients: make sure that all ingredients are at room temperature, especially during the colder months of the year. Cold fats, etc. will not emulsify to the required degree and the finished product will be 'tight' and lacking in volume. These remarks are appropriate to all cake and sponge making recipes.

### Gâteau Macmahon

*Sweet paste base*

| 25 g | Medium flour |
| 170 g | Butter |
| 115 g | Icing sugar |
| 85 g | Ground almonds |
| 50 g | Beaten egg |
| 1 teaspoon | Lemon juice |

1. Sieve the flour on to the table and make a bay in the centre.
2. Place the butter and icing sugar in the middle and cream together.
3. Add the egg and lemon juice and begin to draw in the flour.
4. Mix to a smooth paste, then wrap in greaseproof paper and rest in the refrigerator for 15 minutes until firm.
5. Use one-half of the paste and divide the half into two pieces. Roll out into two 20 cm diameter circles. Docker well and cut one of the discs into eight segments.
6. Bake until crisp and golden brown in an oven at 193°C.
7. Spread with red jam on the base disc and place inside a paper-lined 20 cm hoop.

Make a *strawberry bavarois* from the following:

| | |
|---|---|
| 170 ml | **Milk** |
| 60 g | **Castor sugar** |
| 2 | **Yolks** |
| 250 ml | **Cream** |
| 15 g | **Leaf gelatine** |
| 250 ml | **Strawberry purée** |

1. Make the basic bavarois in the usual manner, and add the fruit purée when the custard is cool and before folding in the whipped cream.
2. Pour on the prepared bavarois into the lined hoop and spread level.
3. Set off in the refrigerator.
4. Coat four of the top segments with red glaze and dredge the other four with icing sugar.
5. Arrange the pieces on top alternately red and white.
6. Finally, carefully remove the hoop and band of paper and serve on a doily-covered silver flat.

## Chocolate éclairs

1. On to lightly greased baking sheets, pipe with a savoy bag and 12 mm plain tube, finger-shaped pieces of choux paste 10 cm long.
2. Bake in an oven at 215°C for 18 minutes. Do not open the oven door during the baking process.
3. When ready, cool on wire racks; make a slit in the side of each one and fill with whipped cream or a mixture of half whipped cream and half pastry cream.
4. The icing for the top should be fondant flavoured with plain chocolate. Temper the fondant first, then blend in the melted chocolate to taste. If necessary, adjust the coating consistency with a little stock syrup.
5. When completed, set in paper éclair cases.

## Coffee éclairs

Make as for chocolate éclairs and fill in similar fashion. Ice the tops with coffee-flavoured fondant icing.

## Almond choux buns

1. Using the basic choux paste mix, and a 1 cm plain tube, pipe out on to greased baking sheets bulbs 4–5 cm in diameter.
2. Eggwash the tops and strew with flaked almonds.
3. Bake at 220°C for 15 minutes until firm and golden brown.
4. Allow to cool then fill with whipped cream (flavoured with crushed praline).
5. Brush the tops carefully with boiling apricot glaze and ice with thin

vanilla fondant.

## Cream buns                                  *Choux à la crème*

1. Pipe out bulbs of choux paste through a 1 cm coarse star tube, or a 1 cm plain tube, as desired, on to greased baking sheets; the bulbs should be approximately 5 cm in diameter.
2. Bake at 220°C for 15 minutes. When firm and golden brown, remove from the oven and allow to cool on a cooling wire. Fill with whipped cream and dust heavily with icing sugar.
3. Alternatively, the tops may be iced with chocolate or coffee-flavoured fondant.

For a choux bun of much greater volume the baking sheet may be covered with a special cream bun cover 15 cm deep before baking. The cover traps the steam generated during the baking process and thereby enhances the volume. Some pastry-cooks add a small pinch of 'vol' or ground ammonium carbonate to the basic mixture. This has a stabilising effect during baking. Once under cover, the choux buns are baked at 225°C for 25 minutes.

However, the first method will produce quite satisfactory results.

## Profiteroles                               *Profiteroles au chocolat*

1. Prepare miniature choux buns about 2 cm in diameter and bake at 220°C for 15 minutes to golden brown. Allow to cool.
2. Fill with whipped cream and dress in pyramid form in a deep glass dish.
3. Dust heavily with icing sugar.
4. Serve accompanied by a hot chocolate sauce.

**Note:** Very tiny profiteroles, about the size of a pea, are sometimes served as a garnish with consommé (consommé aux profiteroles).

## Almond cream barquettes and tartlets

1. Line the chosen moulds (greased) with sweet paste.
2. Pipe a spot of red jam into the bottom of each mould.
3. Half fill with almond cream and allow to rest before baking off at 190°C for 15–20 minutes to a nice golden brown.
4. Allow to cool before finishing off as desired.

## Tartlet finishes

1. Cover the top with praline-flavoured chocolate buttercream then garnish with chocolate shavings. Dust the top with icing sugar.
2. Cover the top with vanilla-flavoured buttercream and garnish with

broken meringue pieces. Finally, dust the top with chocolate powder.
3. Brush the top with boiling apricot glaze, then garnish with some toasted flaked almonds. Finally, dust the top with icing sugar.
4. Almond cream barquettes can be finished in a similar fashion, with care being taken not to make them appear too bulky — especially when being served as an afternoon tea pastry.

## Brandy snaps

| | | |
|---|---|---|
| 250 g | Medium flour | 500 g |
| 5 g | Ground ginger | 10 g |
| 5 g | Mixed spice | 10 g |
| 60 g | Butter | 120 g |
| 60 g | White shortening | 120 g |
| ½ kg | Castor sugar | 1 kg |
| 375 g | Golden syrup | 750 g |

1. Sieve together the flour, ginger and mixed spice.
2. Rub the fats into the flour and add the sugar and golden syrup.
3. Mix to a smooth paste, and divide into 25 g portions; mould round into balls.
4. Place on to greased baking trays, leaving sufficient room for the items to flow during baking.
5. Flatten slightly with the hand.
6. Bake at 176°C to golden brown. Remove from the oven.
7. Cool slightly then mould over greased or oiled rolling pins or suitable size dowelling and allow to set firm.
8. Serve plain or filled with whipped cream.

The mixture is best made up overnight and moulded up the following day. The diameter of the rolling pin or dowelling will obviously determine the size of the finished article.

## Shortbread

| | | |
|---|---|---|
| 140 g | Medium flour | 570 g |
| 34 g | Cornflour | 112 g |
| 112 g | Butter | 450 g |
| 60 g | Castor sugar | 230 g |

1. Work the butter and sugar together, but do not cream.
2. Lightly draw in the sieved flours and rub down to a smooth paste.
3. Roll out to 12 cm thickness and cut into desired shapes.
4. Tray up on lightly greased baking trays and well docker.
5. Bake at 210°C to pale golden brown — about 15 minutes.
6. Dust with castor sugar on removal from the oven.

If desired, 100 g nibbed almonds or 100 g chopped walnuts may be added to the mix when drawing in the flour.

## Viennese whirls

| | | |
|---|---|---|
| 230 g | Butter | 460 g |
| 60 g | Castor sugar | 112 g |
| 112 g | Medium flour | 230 g |
| 1 | Small egg (size 3) | 1 plus 1 egg yolk |
| 4 | Spots vanilla essence | 8 |
| 140 g | Medium flour | 280 g |
| | Small pinch baking powder | 10 g |

1. Cream to a light consistency the butter, sugar, flour, egg and vanilla essence and continue to beat.
2. Sieve the second lot of flour and baking powder together and add to the creamed mixture; give another good beating.
3. Line some tartlet moulds with paper cut linings and using a savoy bag and a large star tube, half fill the moulds, piping in rosette fashion. Allow to rest for 30 minutes before baking off at 200°C for 15 minutes. Dust heavily with icing sugar when baked.

## Basic scone dough

| | |
|---|---|
| 450 g | Medium flour |
| 25 g | Baking powder |
| 30 g | Milk powder |
| 10 g | Salt |
| 85 g | Butter or margarine |
| 85 g | Castor sugar |
| 60 ml | Egg |
| 285 ml | Water (approx.) |

1. Sieve well together the flour, baking powder, milk powder and salt.
2. Rub in the butter or margarine and make a suitable bay.
3. Whisk well together the sugar, egg and water and add to the rubbed in fat/flour mix. Blend to a light scone dough.
4. Add 85 g of dried fruit (sultanas, currants, etc.) per 460 g of flour. Fruited scones will generally take about 30 ml water extra per 450 g flour.
5. The mixture should be on the soft side to produce a tender eating scone; and, of course, freshly made.
6. Roll out the scone dough to 30 cm thickness and cut out with a 5 cm round cutter.
7. Invert and place on to greased baking trays. Pack fairly close together on the tray to conserve steam when baking.
8. Eggwash and bake at 215°C for 15 minutes until just baked and golden brown.
9. Avoid 'flash' heat otherwise over-baking will occur.
10. Cool on wire racks.

### Simple cold meringue mixture

| 4 | Egg whites |
|---|---|
| 200 g | Castor sugar |

1. Stiffly beat the egg whites to a peak.
2. Carefully sprinkle on the castor sugar, mixing in all the time.
3. Line the baking sheets with good quality greaseproof paper.
4. Pipe out the meringue shells through a savoy bag using a 12 mm plain tube into even oval shapes.
5. Bake at 93°C until firm and pale fawn in colour. This can take 2–3 hours.
6. Correctly baked meringues will keep crisp and firm for quite a long time if kept in a warm, dry atmosphere.

### Meringue chantilly

Sandwich together two meringue shells with whipped cream, and garnish with glacé cherry and angelica diamonds.

### Meringue glacée chantilly

Sandwich two meringue shells with dairy ice cream and pipe a rosette of whipped cream on top.

### Small and large vacherins

1. Using a 7 mm plain tube, pipe out bouchées no more than 8 cm diameter.
2. Bake in usual manner and finish as desired, filled with fruit and whipped cream.
3. For large vacherins, 15–20 cm diameter, it is first of all necessary to outline the required shape (round or oval) in pencil on greaseproof paper.
4. Using a 12 mm plain tube, pipe the outline and fill in for the base.
5. Pipe further outline rings of similar diameter and bake off as usual.
6. To assemble: place the meringue base on a suitable baking tray and build up the vacherin by superimposing several meringue rings one on top of the other — joining each one with a little fresh meringue mixture.
7. For advance preparation these products may be returned to the oven to dry out, and then used as required.
8. For service, fill with chosen fruit, such as fresh strawberries, raspberries, tinned fruit if desired and glaze the top with thickened fruit syrup. Finally decorate with whipped cream. Vacherins are sometimes veiled with spun sugar to enhance the visual effect.
9. If the vacherins have to stand for any length of time before being

served, brush the interior of the cases with melted chocolate before filling. This helps to keep the meringue crisp and dry.

## Swiss meringue

| | |
|---|---|
| 350 ml | Egg white |
| 450 g | Castor sugar |
| 2 spots | Acetic acid |

1. Place the sugar and whites in a suitable mixing bowl, and add the acetic acid.
2. Place the bowl over a bain-marie of warm water and whisk until the mixture doubles in bulk and is of a firm consistency.
3. Remove from the heat and beat until cool.
4. Use as a topping for flans, or pipe out into various shapes and dry off in a cool oven to make small petits fours.

## Meringue italienne

| | | |
|---|---|---|
| 290 g | Granulated sugar | 580 g |
| 100 ml | Cold water | 200 ml |
| 140 ml | Egg white | 285 ml |
| 60 g | Castor sugar | 120 g |

1. Cook the sugar and the water to boiling-point.
2. Meanwhile, whisk the egg white to a firm foam and whisk in the castor sugar. Pour on the sugar solution on slow speed, then whisk to full volume. Use as required.

# Baked sweet dishes (hot)

### Apple charlotte                    *Charlotte aux pommes*

| | |
|---|---|
| 900 g | Russet style apples |
| 60 g | Butter |
| 1 | Grated zest of lemon |
| 112 g | Soft brown sugar |
| | Pinch of powdered cinnamon |

1. Melt the butter, add the sugar and stir over a moderate heat to a light caramel.
2. Add the peeled and quartered apples, lemon zest and cinnamon.
3. Cover with a lid and allow to cook gently until the apples are just tender.
4. Meanwhile, line a timbale mould on the bottom and sides neatly with slices of bread cut into fingers 40 mm wide and soaked in melted butter.
5. Well fill with the prepared apple, and cover the top with a crust of bread to protect it while cooking.

6.  Bake in an oven at 200°C to a nice, crisp golden brown (about 1 hour).
7.  Allow to rest a little before turning out on to a hot round dish.

The base of the mould should be lined with a tight-fitting circle of bread divided into segments (and soaked in butter) for ease of service.

If using cooking apples such as Bramleys add about 90 g fresh white breadcrumbs to the filling for binding purposes. Serve the charlotte with hot apricot sauce apart.

### Apple dumplings

1.  Roll out apple dumpling paste (see page 71) 7 mm thick, and cut into 12 cm squares. Eggwash the edges.
2.  Peel and core some medium-size cooking apples, and place on the squares of paste.
3.  Fill the centres of apples with sugar and a pinch of powdered cinnamon.
4.  Brush all round the apple with beaten eggwash, and bring each corner of the paste up and over the fruit to meet at the centre at the top of the apple.
5.  Seal the edges by pinching them together with thumb and forefinger.
6.  Place a cut-out circle of paste on top (using paste trimmings), and tray up on a greased baking sheet.
7.  Eggwash all over, and bake in a moderate oven at 182°C for approximately 30 minutes to a nice brown.
8.  Dust heavily with a mixture of castor and icing sugar when baked.
9.  Serve with a custard sauce or semi-whipped cream.

### Baked apples                                    *Pommes bonne femme*

1.  Choose medium-sized cooking apples, and remove the cores with the point of a sharp knife or apple corer. Then score through the skin around their circumference. Place into a shallow baking dish.
2.  Fill the centre with a mixture of brown sugar, sultanas and cinnamon, and a small knob of butter on top.
3.  Just cover the bottom of the dish with water and cook until tender in a moderate oven (177°C) for about 35 minutes.
4.  Serve in a shallow dish with a little of the liquor. May be accompanied by fresh cream, sauce anglais, etc.
5.  The final appearance can be improved by brushing the apples over with a thin boiling apricot glaze.

### Fruit crumble

Use any fresh fruit as available, such as apples, rhubarb, plums or gooseberries. After preparation, blanch the fruit by covering with cold water and bringing to near boiling-point. Drain immediately in a colander and allow to cool. Meanwhile, prepare the crumble topping:

| | | |
|---|---|---|
| 230 g | **Medium flour** | 900 g |
| 115 g | **Butter or margarine** | 460 g |
| 140 g | **Castor sugar** | 485 g |

1. Sieve the flour, and rub in the chosen fat to fine crumbs.
2. Blend in the sugar.
3. Place a generous depth of blanched and drained fruit into a greased pie dish or other suitable receptacle. Add a good layer of granulated sugar to sweeten.
4. Carefully spread a thick layer of crumble topping over the fruit, and bake at 177°C to a nice golden brown, about 1 hour.
5. Remove from the oven and clean around the rim of the dish.
6. Place on to a doily-covered silver flat and surround the pie dish with a pie collar.
7. Serve with fresh cream or custard sauce.

**Baked jam roll**

1. Use a good quality sweet paste.
2. Roll the paste into a rectangular shape 15 cm × 30 cm, and eggwash the extreme edges.
3. Spread lightly with stoneless jam, e.g. raspberry, etc.
4. Fold over the two short sides about 1 cm, and roll up swiss roll fashion.
5. Eggwash the final edge to seal the roll.
6. Place sealed edge down on to a greased baking tray and allow to rest for 15 minutes before baking at 182°C for about 40 minutes.
7. Eggwash the top surface whilst resting.
8. For service, dust the top with icing sugar and serve on a doily-covered silver flat.
9. Serve accompanied by a custard or red jam sauce.

# Egg and milk-based puddings

**Bread and butter pudding**

1. Sprinkle a few washed sultanas into the bottom of a greased pie dish and cover with a layer of slices of buttered bread (cut triangular shaped with crusts removed), each piece slightly overlapping.
2. Sprinkle with castor sugar and more sultanas, and finish with a neat layer of triangular slices of bread, butter side uppermost.
3. Cover with an egg custard made from:

| | | |
|---|---|---|
| 3 | **Eggs** | 9 |
| 85 g | **Castor sugar** | 260 g |
| 570 ml | **Fresh milk** | 1½ litres |
| 4 spots | **Vanilla essence** | 1 teaspoon |
| | (or vanilla pod) | |

4. After filling the dish with the custard, allow to soak for 15 minutes.
5. Add more custard to top up and dust the top with grated nutmeg.
6. Cook bain-marie style in a shallow tray of water in a moderate oven at 177°C to a pale golden brown for about 45 minutes.

A more sophisticated version can be made using slices of brioche or milk rolls in place of standard sliced sandwich bread.

### Baked egg custard                                          *Crème renversée*

| | | |
|---|---|---|
| 570 ml | **Fresh milk** | 1 litre 140 ml |
| 3 | **Eggs** | 6 |
| 60 g | **Castor sugar** | 120 g |
| 4 spots | **Vanilla essence** | 8 spots |

1. Whisk the eggs and sugar together and also 140 ml of the milk.
2. Bring the remainder of the milk to boiling-point and add the vanilla essence (or a vanilla pod).
3. Slowly whisk on to the eggs and sugar, and strain into a suitable pie dish. Dust the top with grated nutmeg.
4. Place the dish in a shallow tray of water and bake in the oven at 180°C until set.
5. Remove and clean off the edges of the dish before surrounding with a pie dish collar.
6. Set on a doily-covered silver flat.

This pudding is often served accompanied by a dish of poached fruits, such as pears or apples.

### Cabinet pudding                                          *Pouding de cabinet*

| | | |
|---|---|---|
| 570 ml | **Fresh milk** | 1 litre 140 ml |
| 85 g | **Castor sugar** | 170 g |
| 140 g | **Stale sponge cake** | 280 g |
| 3 | **Eggs** | 6 |
| 4 spots | **Vanilla essence** | 8 spots |
| | (or vanilla pod) | |
| 60 g | **Currants and sultanas** | 120 g |
| 60 g | **Glacé cherries** | 120 g |

1. Dice the sponge and mix with the chopped glacé cherries and dried fruit.
2. Place into greased and sugared dariole moulds (half full).
3. Warm the milk, and whisk on to the eggs and sugar and vanilla essence.
4. Strain and fill up the moulds with the custard.

5. Place into a shallow tray, half full of water, and allow to stand for 15 minutes.
6. Cook in a moderate oven at 177°C for about 45 minutes until set.
7. Allow to stand for a few minutes before turning out on to a round silver flat or individual dishes.
8. Serve with a custard or apricot sauce apart.

**Diplomat pudding**                                    *Pouding diplomate*

Proceed as for cabinet pudding but serve cold with a light raspberry sauce. Replace the currants and sultanas with dried, crystallised fruits, e.g. pineapple, glacé cherries, etc.

**Burnt cream**                                          *Crème brulée*

| | | |
|---|---|---|
| 285 ml | Fresh cream | 1 litre 140 ml |
| 285 ml | Fresh milk | 1 litre 140 ml |
| 5 | Eggs | 20 |
| | Vanilla pod | |
| 115 g | Castor sugar | 460 g |
| 30 g | Icing sugar | 120 g |

1. Infuse the vanilla pod in the milk, and bring to the boil with the cream.
2. Remove the vanilla pod, and pour the milk/cream on to the beaten eggs and castor sugar.
3. Strain the custard, and pour into suitable fire-proof dishes.
4. Stand the dishes in a tray of water, and bake in a slow oven, 135°C, for about 1 hour until just set.
5. Allow to cool.
6. Dredge the tops heavily with the icing sugar, and place under a very hot salamander until the sugar has caramelised.
7. Serve very cold with whipped or double cream.

A richer version of the 'burnt cream' may be made from the following:

| | | |
|---|---|---|
| 570 ml | Fresh cream | 1 litre 140 ml |
| | Vanilla pod | |
| 115 g | Castor sugar | 230 g |
| 30 g | Icing sugar | 60 g |
| 6 | Egg yolks (size 1) | 12 |

Method as above. The smaller mixture will make 5–6 china ramaquins; the larger formula double that amount.

## Cream caramel                                      *Crème caramel*

| | | |
|---|---|---|
| 570 ml | **Milk** | 1 litre 140 ml |
| 4 | **Eggs** | 8 |
| 85 g | **Castor sugar** | 170 g |
| 60 g | **Granulated sugar** (for caramel) | 120 g |
| 4 spots | **Vanilla essence** (or vanilla pod) | 8 spots |

1. Whisk the eggs, castor sugar and one-quarter of the milk together.
2. Bring the remainder of the milk to the boil with the vanilla.
3. Whisk slowly on to the first mixture, and strain into a clean bowl.
4. Meanwhile, place the caramel sugar into a suitable pan with one or two teaspoons of cold water; boil to a light caramel colour. Remove from the heat and add one or two spots of cold water to check the heat.
5. Pour a little caramel into each dariole mould, and allow to set.
6. Add sufficient custard to fill each mould to the top.
7. Place the moulds in a shallow tray with sufficient water to come three parts up the sides of the moulds.
8. Cook in the oven at 177°C until set, about 40 minutes.
9. Remove from the heat and allow to cool.
10. For service, loosen carefully around the top edge of the mould and shake gently to loosen the caramel cream.
11. Invert on to a silver dish or individual platter, and allow *all* the caramel to run down the sides.

## Queen of puddings                                   *Pouding à la reine*

| | | |
|---|---|---|
| 60 g | **Castor sugar** | 120 g |
| 570 ml | **Milk** | 1 litre 140 ml |
| 3 | **Egg yolks** | 6 |
| 2 spots | **Vanilla essence** | 4 spots |
| 122 g | **Fresh breadcrumbs or** cake crumbs | 225 g |
| 30 g | **Apricot jam** | 60 g |
| 30 g | **Red jam** | 60 g |
| 60 g | **Butter** | 120 g |
| 3 | **Egg whites** ⎱ Meringue | 6 |
| 60 g | **Castor sugar** ⎰ | 120 g |

1. Bring the milk to boiling-point with the butter.
2. Beat the yolk, sugar and vanilla together, and pour on the hot milk/butter.
3. Place the crumbs in a buttered pie dish, and strain on the custard. Set the dish in a shallow tray of water (bain-marie) and bake in a moderate oven until set, about 30 minutes.
4. Use the middle shelf of the oven at 177°C.
5. Allow to cool, then spread the red jam (warmed) over the custard base.
6. Meanwhile, make the meringue by whisking the whites to a firm foam and folding in the sugar.

7.  Using a savoy bag and large star tube, pipe the top lattice-work style.
8.  Fill the cavities with the warmed apricot jam,
9.  Dredge with icing sugar, and finish in a moderate oven to a golden brown. Use the top shelf for the final stage.
10. Serve on a doily-covered silver flat.

**Baked rice pudding**                                   *Riz à l'anglaise*

| | | |
|---|---|---|
| 70 g | Carolina rice | 280 g |
| 70 g | Castor sugar | 280 g |
| 4 spots | Vanilla essence | ½ coffeespoonful |
| 15 g | Butter | 60 g |
| 600 ml | Milk | 2 litre 280 ml |

1.  Wash the rice and put into a buttered pie dish with the milk, sugar and vanilla. Mix gently with a fork.
2.  Add a generous knob of butter and some grated nutmeg to taste, make sure that the rim of the dish is clean, and bake in a slow oven for a minimum of two hours. The top should be nicely coloured and the rice tender.
3.  Serve on an oval dish covered with a doily.
4.  A pie collar should be placed around the dish.

# Baking flour and eggs (soufflés)

Soufflés require a certain amount of skill to prepare, and involve the blending of beaten egg whites with a sauce. The air trapped in the mixture in the eggs causes the mixture to expand during baking.

*What are soufflés and how are they made?*

Soufflés may be sweet or savoury products. The foundation is usually a light sauce mixture, e.g. béchamel or crème pâtissière with the egg content providing the stabilisation and aeration during the cooking process.

The egg proteins coagulate with the proteins present, e.g. flour and milk, to form a structure. The whipped egg white foam is a colloidal system of air surrounded by albumen. The whisked egg whites must be folded in carefully to form a homogenous mass, with care being taken not to over-mix and thereby break down much of the aeration. The elastic nature of the albumen is very important to the finished nature of the soufflé, as it allows incorporated air to expand on heating without breaking the foam, and it coagulates (or sets) so losing its liquid nature but retaining its shape. The result is a light textured batter of well-risen proportions and flavoured according to its basic constitutent — sweet or savoury. Because of the lightness of the finished item, it is advisable to waste no time in transporting the cooked soufflé from oven to table.

During the baking stage, which must be carefully controlled and timed, the oven allows steady, even rising of the mixture, so giving maximum volume and stability to the fragile foam. Water, eggs and milk are converted to steam which exerts pressure causing air in the foam to expand. The albumen stretches and the mixture rises. Gluten in the flour expands, the starch grains, partially gelatinised in the panada making, finally burst and gel. The egg proteins form a new bonded structure and coagulate. Because of the high proportion of albumen (egg white) to flour, this structure is not rigid, and the soufflé eventually collapses as steam escapes, hence the need for speed in service!

**Basic soufflé mixture**

| | | |
|---|---|---|
| 60 g | Butter | 240 g |
| 60 g | Castor sugar | 240 g |
| 60 g | Medium flour | 240 g |
| 300 ml | Milk | 1 litre 250 ml |
| 4 | Egg yolks | 16 |
| 6 | Egg whites | 24 |

*Method*
1. Butter and sugar the sides of the soufflé mould (not the base).
2. Melt the butter and stir in the flour to form a roux.
3. Bring the milk and sugar to boiling-point with the vanilla.
4. Pour on to the roux base slowly, and blend to a smooth consistency over a moderate heat until mixture thickens.
5. Transfer to a clean bowl and beat in the yolks singly.
6. Finally, semi-whisk the egg whites and fold carefully into the mixture.
7. Two-thirds fill the mould(s) and gently level off with plastic scraper or palate knife.
8. Place on a baking tray and cook at 210°C for 15–20 minutes until firm to the touch.
9. Remove from the oven and dust the top with icing sugar.
10. Serve immediately, as the soufflé will start to collapse shortly after being removed from the oven.

*Alternative method*
1. Bring three-quarters of the milk to boiling-point together with the butter.
2. Blend the remainder of the cold milk with the flour, egg yolks and sugar to a smooth paste, and add slowly to the boiling milk mixture.
3. Reduce the heat and stir until the mixture thickens.
4. Remove from the heat and add the chosen flavouring.
5. Fold the whisked whites into the warm soufflé mixture but do not over-mix.
6. Three-quarters fill prepared, buttered soufflé dishes and smooth the top(s) level.
7. Bake carefully until well risen and golden brown. Serve immediately.

**Note:** Whichever method is used, there is no reason why a soufflé should not be successful given attention to detail and a balanced recipe. Always use egg whites which are about a week old, and fold into the base whilst the mixture is still hot.

### Coffee soufflé                                                   *Soufflé moka*

Flavour the milk with 1–2 teaspoons of soluble coffee crystals. Dust with icing sugar before serving.

### Orange soufflé                                              *Soufflé à l'orange*

Add the grated zest of an orange to the base mixture before folding in the whipped egg whites. Finish as for basic soufflé.

### Lemon soufflé                                               *Soufflé au citron*

Proceed as for orange soufflé substituting the grated zest of one lemon to the basic mixture.

### Chocolate soufflé                                         *Soufflé au chocolat*

1. Add 30 g of cocoa powder or 50 g of melted chocolate to the basic mixture before beating in the yolks and other ingredients.
2. The appearance of the soufflé may be brightened with the addition of 3–4 spots of chocolate compound colouring if required.
3. Finish as before and dust the top with icing sugar before serving.

### Cheese soufflé                                            *Soufflé au parmesan*

| | | |
|---|---|---|
| 45 g | Butter | 170 g |
| 60 g | Flour | 230 g |
| 140 ml | Milk | 570 ml |
| 3 | Egg yolks | 12 |
| 4 | Egg whites | 16 |

1. Butter 4 small individual soufflé dishes or one large dish, and sprinkle well with grated parmesan cheese.
2. Make a roux with the butter and flour, pour on the hot milk, stir out any lumps to form a smooth consistency.
3. Simmer for 10 minutes on the side of the stove. Remove from the heat.
4. Add the grated cheese, stir in, add the yolks one at a time, and season to taste with the salt and a pinch of cayenne pepper.
5. Finally, fold in the whisked egg whites, fill the mould to just below the top edge, and cook at 210°C for 15–20 minutes to a nice golden brown.
6. Serve immediately.

**Note:** A savoury soufflé can also be made using the alternative method described earlier. Add any seasoning to the milk and butter. The flavouring, such as cheese or spinach, is blended in prior to folding in the whisked egg whites.

# Chapter 9
# Roasting                                    *Rôtir*

## The competency defined

The simplest definition is to say that roasting is the cooking of foods by dry heat with the aid of a small amount of fat or oil in an oven or on a spit (à la broche).

Spit cooking involves radiant heat. Oven roasting is a mixture of radiant and convected heat.

The dryness of the heat inside the oven is modified by the presence of steam, which is generated by the moisture content of the foods being roasted. Originally, roasting was performed on a spit over an open fire, with the moisture produced during the process being dispersed into the air. A continuous turning of the carcass took place, and the meat was continually basted.

## Methods of roasting

There are two basic methods of roasting, as follows:
1. *Oven roasting*: This is the most common method used in everyday commercial catering. The process involves placing prepared foods into a pre-heated oven.
   There are three types of oven which may be used.
   (a) Conventional gas or electrically heated domestic or commercial ovens.
   (b) Forced air convection ovens.
   (c) Forced air convection ovens combined with a microwave facility.
2. *Spit roasting*: This is the original method of roasting, and is becoming increasingly rare in the catering industry of the 1990s. That is not to say that it never happens—at county shows and fêtes, whole carcass roasting is very often a major attraction, and one which requires a great deal of skill. The Guildhall in London has often been the venue for the presentation of very impressive roasts such as the traditional Baron of Beef. Roasting was an art at which the English cook excelled. Traditionally, in the brigade structure in large kitchens, the chef rôtisseur was invariably of English extraction. Nowadays, such large kitchen brigades are restricted to the

minority of very big establishments.

However, the modern electronically operated spits which are a feature of many delicatessens and other take-away food shops spit-roast their chicken by popular demand, and very good they are too.

# Organisation and preparation for roasting

In the traditional partie system the following chefs would be directly involved in the preparation and organisation of foods for roasting.

| | |
|---|---|
| *Chef garde-manger*: | Preparation of all meats, poultry and game. |
| *Chef entremettier*: | Preparation of all vegetables and potatoes for roasting, and also the actual roasting of vegetables and potatoes. |
| *Chef rôtisseur*: | Actual roasting of meats, poultry and game. |

When oven roasting, the oven should be pre-heated to a sufficient degree which will be hot enough to seal the outside of the food. Once sealed, the temperature should be adjusted to the required level according to what is being roasted. The sealing of the surface of meats, poultry and game is achieved by the coagulation of the surface protein which is known as albumen.

Even with good sealing, a proportion of the natural juices will escape during cooking, and these juices are used in making the accompanying roast gravy.

Before roasting commences, it is necessary to season the meat, poultry or game, and in some instances herbs are also added. Certain joints of meat, poultry and game may also be stuffed prior to roasting, to enhance the flavour of the food being cooked.

When arranging joints of meat in roasting trays, they should be raised up from the bottom of the tray to prevent 'frying' on the base of the joint. The bones of the meat being processed usually form a 'trivet' for this purpose. In the case of poultry, the bird is first laid on its side, then turned over to the opposite side before finally being set upright for the end of the roasting period. In this way, the bird's natural juices will aid in retaining the succulence of the flesh, and the meat will be evenly browned all over. Since the legs will take longer to cook than the breast, the practice of turning also ensures that the heat will penetrate the leg joints evenly and at the same time protects the breast of the bird.

When roasting vegetables, such as potatoes, they are first blanched and then started on the stove top in very hot fat and coloured evenly all over. Finally, they are oven roasted to a nice golden brown at a temperature of approximately 205°C (401°F). They should have a nice crisp exterior.

*Roast gravy*

Generally speaking, in first-class cookery, roast gravy is thin in consistency. It is made in the following manner.

After removal of the joint, the excess fat is carefully decanted into a separate container, and the roasting tray is heated on top of the stove in order to set the remaining meat sediment in the bottom of the tray. This will have a natural brown colour so there should be little need to add colouring, artificial or otherwise. A good quality brown stock is then added to dissolve the sediment, stirred, and brought to the boil; seasoned to taste and strained through a medium fine strainer (chinois). Any surplus fat can be removed with absorbent kitchen paper, although some cooks prefer to serve it as it is. In the latter case, it is known as 'broken gravy', and should have a nice natural colour and flavour. An important point to note is—never make more gravy than is necessary; aim for quality rather than quantity! Half a litre (18 fl. oz) should serve approximately 9–10 persons.

# Degrees of cooking

It is general practice to serve roast beef slightly underdone, although this is not to every person's taste. Conversely, roast pork should always be well cooked and without any trace of pinkness when carved.

Roast lamb is usually served slightly pink, but, as with roast beef, much depends upon the individual palate. Both roast veal and roast mutton should be cooked right through without any sign of pinkness.

The average roasting time for most meats is 20–25 minutes per ½ kg (1 lb) and 20 minutes over. To test if cooked, press the joint firmly to see if any juices are released which show any signs of blood—bearing in mind the above comments relating to each sort of meat being processed.

After removal from the oven, the joint should be allowed to rest for at least 15–20 minutes before serving. This will help to avoid undue shrinkage and curling of the sliced portions. Carve the meat against the grain, with lamb and mutton cut slightly thicker than roast beef.

Usually, a separate sauce-boat of gravy will accompany the portioned joint.

# Advantages of roasting

1. After roasting, good quality joints are made tender and have a superb flavour.
2. The juices which escape from meat, poultry and game during roasting are used in the making of accompanying gravies, so maximising the use of natural flavours and essences.
3. When spit roasting, the visual impact of the process can be used to great

commercial advantage by creating a focal attraction for customers.

4. The flavour of spit-roasted foods is very individual, and is improved by continual basting. Much of the flavour achieved by this method is dependent upon the type of fuel used to cook the food, such as charcoal.

# Effects of roasting on food

By placing the meat into a hot oven or over a spit to roast, the action of the heat seals the protein on the surface of the meat. It also helps to retain some of the natural juices, and impart its own special flavour. Initially, the roasting temperature needs to be kept at a high level until the outer surface begins to take on a good colour. The temperature can then be reduced to allow the interior of the joint to cook steadily and without over-cooking the surface of the meat.

## General rules for efficient roasting

1. Make sure that the oven is pre-heated to the required degree of heat.
2. Ensure that items of game, poultry and meat are of the highest quality, and that meats have a good distribution of fat (known as marbling) through the flesh.
3. Always season foods prior to roasting.
4. Always raise joints off the base of the roasting tray to prevent the bottom of the joint 'frying'. The meat can be set on a bed of bones, a trivet or a bed of root vegetables (cut into thick slices).
5. When roasting vegetables, always start them off in very hot fat and drain them well before service.

The actual temperature for oven-roasted meats can only be of an approximate nature. After the initial sealing of the joint at approximately 220°C (430°F) for some 20 minutes, the heat is turned down to between 170°C and 150°C (340°F) and cooked according to the required degree. The lower temperature will account for less shrinkage, and is therefore more economical. On the other hand, certain small items such as some game (grouse, for example) and best end of lamb will feature on the à la carte menu as dishes which are cooked to order. In that case, a higher oven temperature will prevail, about 200°C (430°F). Similarly, prime cuts of beef such as the boned out strip loin (contrefilet de boeuf) and whole fillet of beef which are usually served underdone will also merit the higher temperature.

# Safety rules for roasting

1. When handling hot roasting trays, always use a strong, dry oven-cloth; and for large trays, use two.
2. Always choose a roasting tray of appropriate size for the amount of food to be roasted. Too large a tray can result in the fat and sediment burning. Conversely, if the tray is too small, it will be difficult to gain access to the fat for basting purposes.
3. Before trying to remove joints of meat, poultry or game from the roasting trays, make sure that you have a firm retaining hold on the roasted item, usually with a roasting fork.
4. After usage, as always, if still hot, sprinkle the roasting tray(s) with flour as a warning to others.

# Techniques associated with roasting

*Singeing*: A technique used prior to roasting poultry and feathered game—after plucking, the birds are held over a naked flame to singe off any remaining stubble.

*Boning*: Involves the removal of the bones from joints of meat to facilitate stuffing and carving.

*Tying*: Holding meat joints with string to help maintain the shape of the meat whilst cooking.

*Trussing*: Securing the legs and body with string (using a trussing needle) prior to roasting.

*Trivet*: A metal stand used to raise a joint of meat off the bottom of the roasting tray and clear of the fat: this will prevent the joint becoming too crisp on the underside through being allowed to stand in the hot fat. The bones of the meat being cooked can also be utilised in this fashion.

*Basting*: Involves the regular coating of the meat, poultry or game with the hot fat from the bottom of the roasting tray. This is done to help keep the food moist, and encourage the development of a rich, brown surface on the food.

*Barding*: Layering of certain meats and game birds with thin slices of pork backfat; this helps to produce moisture and prevents the meat from drying out whilst roasting. It can also reduce the amount of shinkage because of the added protection.

*Larding*: Basically serves the same purpose as barding. However, in this instance, the fat is cut into thin strips (lardons) and, with the aid of a special larding needle, the strips are threaded through the flesh. It is a technique which is very much applicable to the leaner cuts of meat, such as veal and fillet of beef.

*Turning*: When oven roasting, it is necessary to turn large joints of meat, poultry and game to facilitate even colouring and cooking of the food.

# Equipment used for roasting

For notes on the types of ovens available, see above under Methods of Roasting. In modern-day cookery, spits are often built into ovens and are electrically powered. They are also available in the form of spits built over fires of wood, gas and charcoal.

Meat probes are special thermometers which can be stuck into joints to register internal temperatures. This helps to make sure that foods are cooked sufficiently to destroy harmful bacteria.

Trays used for roasting have to be very strong and have firm handles. They should be washed in hot soapy water, rinsed in clean hot water and thoroughly dried.

All equipment for roasting should be checked before and after use for any faults. Defects should be reported immediately to the person in charge.

# Self-assessment questions for roasting

1. Define roasting as a method of cookery.
2. What are the two basic methods of roasting?
3. In the traditional 'partie' system, which specialist chefs would be involved in the roasting process?
4. What is the usual consistency of roast gravy (with one or two exceptions), and how does it derive its colour?
5. Can you name the accompaniments for the following roast meats: beef, lamb, pork, mutton and veal?
6. Why should roast joints be allowed to rest before carving?
7. What is the action of heat on the surface of roasted meat joints?
8. Why is it beneficial to raise joints off the bottom of the tray whilst roasting?
9. Can you give a brief description of at least five techniques which are associated with the roasting process?
10. What is the advantage of using a modern meat probe with which to test roast meat joints?

When you have completed these questions check your answers with your fellow students and chef or lecturer.

# Cuts of meat for roasting

Before meats can be roasted they need to be cut into joints of suitable sizes to facilitate cooking and carving. The different joints are listed below.

## *Cuts of beef suitable for roasting*

### Sirloin (on the bone) *Aloyau de boeuf*

1. Saw through the chine bone, remove any sinew, string back on to the bone.
2. The fillet should be removed for use as steaks or as required.

### Sirloin (off the bone) *Contrefilet de boeuf*

1. Lift the sirloin off the bone and remove the fillet.
2. Remove any sinew and excess fat.
3. Roast flat or rolled and tied with string.

### Ribs (on the bone) *Côte de boeuf*

Wing rib, fore rib and middle rib are all suitable for roasting.

1. Saw through the chine bone, remove the nerve and saw through the base of the ribs on the underside.
2. Tie well with string, to hold the shape.

### Fillet (head and centre) *Filet de boeuf chateaubriand*

1. Trim the fillet, lard and season well.
2. Roast on a trivet.

## *Cuts of veal suitable for roasting*

### Breast of veal *Poitrine de veau* (2nd quality)

1. Bone out the breast, trim and stuff.
2. Season and roll the breast.
3. Tie with string to secure the shape.

### Best end of veal *Carré de veau* (1st quality)

1. Remove the chine bone and trim the ribs.
2. Scrape the end of the rib bones and season before roasting.

### Legs of veal (small) *Cuissot de veau* (1st quality)

1. Remove the aitch bone
2. Trim the knuckle and lard.
3. Season and tie with string for roasting.

**Loin of veal**                    *Longe de veau* (**1st quality**)

1. Trim the meat and loosen from the chine bone.
2. If required the meat may be removed from the bone.
3. Season and proceed to roast.

### Cuts of pork suitable for roasting

**Spare ribs**                    *Échine de porc* (**2nd quality**)

1. Trim the ribs, secure the rind and rub with a little salt.
2. If necessary secure with string.
3. Roast and, as required, brush with a suitable sauce.

**Shoulder of pork**              *Epaule de porc* (**2nd quality**)

1. Bone out the shoulder and if required fill with a suitable stuffing.
2. Score the rind and rub with a little salt.
3. Tie with string to hold shape.

**Legs of pork**                  *Cuissot de porc* (**2nd quality**)

1. Remove the aitch bone and trotter and score the ring.
2. Rub with a little salt.

**Loin of pork**                  *Longe de porc* (**1st quality**)

Loin of pork may include the chine bone if required.

1. Trim the loin, remove the kidney if present.
2. Loosen the meat from the bone.
3. Score the rind and rub in a little salt.
4. Tie the meat back on to the bone and proceed to roast.

### Cuts of lamb suitable for roasting

**Legs**                          *Gigot d'agneau* (**1st quality**)

1. Trim the knuckle and aitch bone.
2. Tie well with string to hold shape.
3. Remove the aitch bone to facilitate carving.

**Shoulder**                      *Epaule d'agneau* (**2nd quality**)

1. Trim the knuckle or bone out completely.
2. Season and if boned out, stuff, roll and tie with string.

**Best end**                           *Carré d'agneau* **(1st quality)**

1. Skin the lamb, remove the chine bone, trim the ribs and score the fat.
2. Season well and cook on a trivet.
3. Roast and serve with cutlet frills on the exposed ribs.

**Breast**                           *La poitrine d'agneau* **(2nd quality)**

1. Remove the skin and bone out.
2. Stuff, roll, tie with string and season.

**Loin**                                 *Longe d'agneau* **(1st quality)**

1. Bone out the loin, season and roll.
2. Tie with string.

Loin may be stuffed if required.

**Long saddle (includes chump)**          *Selle d'agneau* **(1st quality)**

1. Skin the saddle, trim the flaps and remove excess fat.
2. Remove the kidneys.
3. If required, bone out or roast on the bone.
4. Secure the flaps with string.
5. Season and roast.

**Short saddle (chump removed)**          *Selle d'agneau* **(1st quality)**

Proceed as for long saddle.

*Feathered game for roasting*

**Pheasant**                                              *Faisan*
(October–January)

1. Clean out the innards (eviscerate), singe and remove the wishbone to facilitate cutting.
2. Season and truss to hold its shape.
3. Bard by covering with rashers of streaky bacon.
4. Roast for 30–45 minutes per pheasant; the bird should be just done.
5. Serve on a deep-fried croûton spread with pâté.

**Partridge**                                          *Perdreau*
(September–January)

1. Proceed to prepare and roast as for pheasant, allowing 20–25 minutes

per bird.
2. The partridge should be served just done.

## Grouse
(August–December)

1. Proceed to prepare and roast as for pheasant, allowing 20–25 minutes per bird.
2. The grouse should be served pink to medium.

## Quail                                                    *Caille*
(Available all year)

1. Proceed as for pheasant, allowing 10–12 minutes per bird.
2. Serve the bird just done.

## Guinea fowl                                            *Pintade*
(Available all year)

1. Proceed as for pheasant, allowing 40–50 minutes per bird
2. Serve the bird just done.

### Furred game for roasting

## Saddle of hare                                  *Râble de lièvre*
(August–March)

1. Trim the saddle, remove all sinew, lard and season.
2. Seal quickly at the start of roasting.
3. Cook rare to medium, allow 25–30 minutes per saddle.

## Saddle of venison                            *Selle de venaison*
(June–January)

1. Proceed as for saddle of hare, allowing 30 minutes per kg and 30 minutes over.
2. Should be served underdone.

## Haunch of venison                          *Hanche de venaison*
(June–January)

Proceed as for saddle of venison.

### Poultry for roasting

| Chickens | Baby | *Poussin* | 300 g | 1 per portion |
|---|---|---|---|---|
| | Small | *Poulet de grain* | 1 kg | 3 portions |
| | Medium | *Poulet reine* | 1–2 kg | 4–6 portions |
| | Large | *Poulard* | 2–3 kg | 6–8 portions |
| Capon | | *Chapon* | 3–5 kg | 8–12 portions |
| Duck | | *Canard* | 2–3 kg | 4–6 portions |
| Duckling | | *Caneton* | 1½–2 kg | 2–4portions |
| Goose | | *Oie* | 6 kg | Allow 200 g per portion |
| Gosling | | *Oison* | | Allow 200 g per portion |
| Turkey | | *Dinde* | 3½–20 kg | Allow 200 g per portion |
| Young turkey | | *Dindonneau* | | Allow 200 g per portion |

1. Prepare all of the above by cleaning out the inside, singeing off any feathers and trimming.
2. Remove the wishbone to facilitate carving.
3. Stuff if required, but increase the cooking time slightly to allow for the extra density of the stuffing.
4. Season and truss well.

When roasting turkeys the legs may be removed and sinew cut out. The legs may then be roasted separately.

# Accompaniments for roasting

Roasted foods are always dry in texture. To combat this dryness, roast foods are served with extensive accompaniments, which are listed below.

### Accompaniments for roasted game

**Saddle of hare**                                    *Râble de lièvre*

Serve with roast gravy, redcurrant jelly, sausagemeat stuffing balls, and watercress.

**Venison**                                           *Venaison*

Serve with roast gravy, redcurrant jelly, sauce poivrade and watercress.

## All other game

All other game which has been roasted is traditionally served with the following accompaniments.

1. If the roast game is a bird, it is sat upon a fried croûton of suitable size, which is spread liberally with pâté. The croûton may be oblong, round or heart-shaped.
2. Accompaniments for all roasted game include the following:

Roast gravy                  *Jus rôti*
Fried brown breadcrumbs      *Chapleure*
Game chips                   *Pommes chips*
Bread sauce                  *Sauce pain*
Watercress
Grilled bacon
These accompaniments are also served with roast chicken.

*Accompaniments for roasted meats and poultry*

**Roast beef English style**                  *Bouef rôti à l'anglaise*

Serve with watercress, sauce-boats of horseradish sauce, roast gravy and Yorkshire pudding. English mustard may also be served.

**Roast chicken English style**               *Poulet rôti à l'anglaise*

Serve with game chips, grilled streaky bacon rashers, sauce-boats of roast gravy and bread sauce and garnish with bread sauce.

**Roast chicken with stuffing**               *Poulet rôti farcie*

Serve with sauce-boats of roast gravy, accompany with lemon, parsley and thyme stuffing and watercress.

**Roast duck/duckling**                       *Canard/caneton rôti*

Serve with sauce-boats of roast gravy, balls of sage and onion stuffing, watercress and sauce-boats of apple sauce.

**Roast gosling/goose**                       *Oison/oie rôtie*

Serve with the same accompaniments as for duck.

**Roast Guinea fowl**                         *Pintade rôtie à l'anglaise*

Serve in the same manner as for roast chicken English style.

**Roast lamb** *Agneau rôti*

Serve with sauce-boats of roast gravy, mint sauce and redcurrant jelly, garnish with watercress.

**Roast mutton** *Mouton rôti*

Serve with sauce-boats of white onion sauce, roast gravy, mint sauce, redcurrant jelly and garnish with watercress.

**Roast pork** *Porc rôti*

Serve with sauce-boats of roast gravy, apple sauce and accompany with sage and onion stuffing and watercress.

**Roast turkey** *Dindonneau/dinde rôti*

Serve with roast gravy, bread sauce, grilled chipolatas, chestnut stuffing, grilled rashers of streaky bacon, cranberry sauce and watercress.

**Roast veal**

*Veau rôti*

Serve with thickened gravy and sage and onion stuffing, and garnish with watercress.

## Carving of roasted foods

Wherever possible meat should be carved through the grain to make sure that it is not stringy. If cut along the grain the fibres will be long, which may result in the meats becoming tough to eat.

Carving may be performed in the restaurant or in the kitchen depending on the style of presentation.

When carving poultry or feathered game, where possible serve a combination of leg and breast.

Smaller birds may be served halved or whole depending on their size.

When carving legs or shoulders on the bone, always carve in and across the grain, going down towards the bone.

## Stuffings *Farcies*

Stuffings have a variety of uses in food preparation. They may be used to stuff vegetables such as tomatoes; rolled into balls to accompany jugged hare; and used for stuffing meats prior to cooking such as beef olives, chicken, turkey, shoulder of lamb to give but a few examples.

## Sage and onion stuffing

| | | |
|---|---|---|
| 100 g | White breadcrumbs | 250 g |
| 100 g | Brunoise of onion | 250 g |
| 50 g | Butter | 120 g |
| 1 teaspoon | Finely chopped parsley | 1 tablespoon |
| | Rubbed sage to taste | |
| | Milled sea salt | |
| | Milled pepper | |
| | Stock of appropriate flavour to moisten *or* | |
| 1 | Beaten egg | 2 |

1. Select a pan of suitable size and sweat the brunoise of onion with the butter, sage, parsley and seasoning.
2. Mix the breadcrumbs to form the stuffing; adjust the seasoning as required.
3. If the stuffing is to be cooked separately, lightly moisten with a little stock and place into a greased earthenware dish, cover with a cartouche and bake in a moderate oven at 150°C for about 20 minutes.
4. If the stuffing is to be used to stuff meat before cooking, moisten with beaten egg, which will coagulate during cooking and thus hold the stuffing together when carving.

## Parsley, lemon and thyme stuffing    *Farcie de persil et citron*

| | | |
|---|---|---|
| 100 g | White breadcrumbs | 250 g |
| 50 g | Finely chopped suet | 120 g |
| ¼ dl | Zest and juice of lemon | ¾ dl |
| | Thyme to taste | |
| 1 teaspoon | Finely chopped parsley | 1 tablespoon |
| | Milled sea salt | |
| | Milled pepper | |
| | Suitable stock | |
| 1 | Beaten egg | 2 |

1. Mix the breadcrumbs, suet, lemon, thyme and parsley.
2. Season and proceed as for sage and onion stuffing.

**Note**: The suet may be replaced with butter or margarine for vegetarian use.

## Sausagemeat stuffing    *Forcemeat*

| | | |
|---|---|---|
| 100 g | Pork sausagemeat | 250 g |
| 50 g | White breadcrumbs | 125 g |
| 50 g | Finely chopped suet | 120 g |
| 25 g | Beaten egg | 60 g |
| | Milled salt | |
| | Milled pepper | |
| | Mixed herbs to taste | |

1. Put all ingredients into a bowl and mix well.

2. Use to stuff vegetables before braising. Alternatively, roll into balls and deep fry coated pané à l'anglaise to accompany game stews.

### Chestnut stuffing
*Farcie de marrons*

*Recipe 1*

| | | |
|---|---|---|
| 100 g | **Sausagemeat stuffing** | 250 g |
| 50 g | **Chopped, peeled chestnuts** | 125 g |

1. Mix stuffing and chestnuts together.
2. Seal in a cartouche wrapping and muslin, and steam for 45 minutes at atmospheric pressure.

*or*

Stuff into a turkey and cook with the turkey.

*Recipe 2*

| | | |
|---|---|---|
| 100 g | **Parsley, lemon and thyme stuffing** | 250 g |
| 50 g | **Chopped, peeled chestnuts** | 125 g |

Mix well together and use as above.

**Note**: This recipe is also suitable for use in vegetarian cannelloni.

### Apricot stuffing
*Farcie d'abricot*

| | | |
|---|---|---|
| 100 g | **White breadcrumbs** | 250 g |
| 50 g | **Brunoise of onion** | 125 g |
| 1 teaspoon | **Finely chopped parsley** | 1 tablespoon |
| 50 g | **Butter or margarine** | 120 g |
| 50 g | **Macédoine of apricots** | 125 g |
| | **Milled salt** | |
| | **Milled pepper** | |

1. Select a suitable pan and sweat the onion in the butter with the parsley and season.
2. Add the apricots and mix well.
3. Mix in the breadcrumbs and adjust the seasoning.
4. If necessary add a little apricot juice or beaten egg to moisten.
5. Cook according to ultimate use: commonly used as a stuffing for shoulder of lamb; or rolled into balls, pané à l'anglaise and deep fried, to serve with a brown lamb stew.

# Roast vegetables        *Légumes rôtis*

### Introduction to roast vegetable dishes

Few vegetables are suitable for roasting with the main course. The only roasted vegetables are root varieties and potatoes as they are sturdier and hold their shape when cooked. Care should be taken not to over-cook roast vegetables as they will become dry and almost indigestible.

**Roast potatoes**                                              *Pommes rôties*

| | | |
|---|---|---|
| **400 g** | **Peeled potatoes** | **12 kg** |
| **50 g** | **Dripping or oil** | **125 g** |

1. Cut the potatoes into evenly sized pieces allowing 3 to 4 pieces per portion.
2. Rinse in cold running water and dry in a clean cloth.
3. Select a roasting tray of suitable size and add the dripping or oil.
4. Heat on the stove top or in the oven until the fat starts to smoke.
5. Add the potatoes and bring the fat back up to temperature on the stove top before putting the tray into the oven. This is to help prevent the potatoes sticking to the tray.
6. Season with a little salt and cook in a hot oven at 240–250°C until a deep golden brown.
7. Turn the potatoes after 30 minutes cooking, to ensure an even colour.
8. When cooked remove from the oven (about 1 hour total cooking time) and drain well.
9. Serve in a hot service dish.

**Château potatoes**                                          *Pommes château*

| | | |
|---|---|---|
| **400 g** | **Peeled potatoes** | **1 kg** |
| **50 g** | **Dripping or oil** | **125 g** |

1. Turn the potatoes into barrel shapes as for fondant potatoes.
2. Place into a saucepan of boiling salted water, bring back to the boil and simmer for 5 minutes.
3. Refresh and dry in a clean cloth.
4. Roast as for roast potatoes and serve in the same manner.

**Roast parsnips**                                                 *Panais rôtis*

| | | |
|---|---|---|
| **400 g** | **Parsnips** | **1 kg** |
| **50 g** | **Dripping or vegetable oil** | **100 g** |
| | **Salt** | |

1. Top the parsnips and peel.
2. Cut into quarters.
3. Heat the fat in a suitable roasting tray and add the parsnips.
4. Proceed as for roast potatoes.

**Note:** With older parsnips, it is necessary to remove the coarse core which will be tough and fibrous in texture.

## Yorkshire pudding

| | | |
|---|---|---|
| 2½ dl | Milk and water | 6 dl |
| 100 g | Plain flour | 250 g |
| 50 g | Beaten egg | 125 g |
| 30 g | Dripping | 75 g |
| | Salt | |

1. Sieve the flour and salt into a bowl of suitable size for the volume of batter being produced.
2. Form a well in the centre and mix the egg with half of the liquid. Pour the liquid into the well.
3. Beat the liquid and flour together, adding the rest of the liquid a little at a time, to form a smooth batter.
4. Allow to stand for 20–30 minutes before use.
5. Place the dripping into the pudding moulds and heat in hot oven at 200°C to smoking-point.
6. Take the trays out of the oven and drain off any excess dripping. Fill the trays with batter.
7. Return to the top shelves of the oven and cook until a deep golden brown colour, at which stage the pudding should have risen.
8. Serve straight away, with roast beef or on their own with onion gravy as a starter course.

# Recipe for Sour Cream Coffee Cake

(6 03)

2 Sticks butter ⎤
2 cups sugar  ⎦ cream together

2 cups sugar
2 beaten egg
1 cup sour cream
1/2 tsp. vanilla
2 cups flour
1/4 tsp. salt
1 tsp. baking powder

Add, mix and pour into floured and greased tube pan. Pour in half of batter. — Sprinkle with half of topping then remaining batter and remaining topping. Bake 350° 50 minutes, let cool

Topping ⎤ 4 Tbs. brown sugar
        ⎦ 1 Tbs. cinnamon

*Notes.*

# Chapter 10
# Pot Roasting          *Poêler*

## The competency defined

Items to be dry braised (pot roasted) must be of first-class quality. Only the choicest cuts of meat such as strip loins (from the boned-out sirloin of beef), cushion veal (noix de veau), whole fillet of beef, and young birds of poultry and game, etc. will lend themselves to this process.

Such foods are first placed upon a base of stewed vegetables made up of finely cut onions, carrots and celery, together with lean ham, fresh thyme, a bayleaf and a glass of dry sherry or Madeira wine. Only butter is used in the cooking, and the process is carried out in a suitable size braising-pan with a lid. Whilst cooking, the item should be basted frequently with the butter and natural juices; towards the end of the process, the lid is removed to allow the food to take on colour. The French term for this method of cookery is *poêler*. It is used extensively in high-class cookery.

## Purpose of pot roasting

The reasons for pot roasting are:

1. To provide the customer with variety of flavour and a texture which is pleasing to both the eye and the palate.
2. To add choice and nutritional value to the customer's diet.

## Method of pot roasting

Strictly speaking, this is not a real method of roasting as described in the section on roasting. The item is cooked in a covered container which naturally generates an amount of steam. However, one of the benefits of the conserved moisture is the delicious tenderising effect upon the commodity.

The cooking juices are used to enhance the finished sauce which will accompany the poêlage. Some cooks cover the joint or bird with buttered greaseproof paper before placing on the lid—it is all a matter of personal choice.

311

The final process is to drain off the fat carefully without discarding the vegetables and cooking juices (sediment) in the bottom of the pan. Meanwhile, keep the meat warm. Add a little stock to deglaze the sediment and sufficient jus lié for the amount of sauce needed. Bring to the boil and simmer gently. Correct the seasoning and consistency, then pass through a fine strainer (chinois); keep hot. The dish and garnish can then be presented as required.

# Organisation and preparation for pot roasting

In a traditional partie system the following chefs would be involved with the production of pot roasted items:

| | |
|---|---|
| *Chef garde-manger*: | Responsible for the preparation of all meats, poultry and game for pot roasting. |
| *Chef saucier*: | Responsible for the actual cooking and presentation of such items. |

# Advantages of pot roasting

Items which are pot roasted (poêlé) are served in the dish in which they are cooked, and all the ingredients are served as an integral part of the presentation, as in chicken en cocotte. This also means that none of the flavour is lost and nutrients remain in the accompanying sauce.

# Degrees of cooking

Generally speaking, all foods which are pot roasted are cooked through until tender, but definitely not over-cooked.

# General rules for efficient pot roasting

1. Foods suitable for pot roasting include meat, poultry and game, all of which should be of first-class quality.
2. The vessel used for pot roasting should be of an appropriate size for the commodity being processed, and should be covered with a tight-fitting lid.
3. Allow sufficient butter to ensure adequate basting of the food. No other medium (liquid) is involved during the cooking process.

4. Pot roasting is usually carried out at a slightly higher temperature than normal roasting, and the cooking time is marginally longer.
5. Two-thirds of the way through pot roasting, the lid of the vessel should be removed to allow the dry heat to colour the item.
6. Apart from butter, the only other commodity employed is the base of stewed vegetables (in butter) made up of finely cut onions, carrots and celery together with lean ham, fresh thyme, a bayleaf, and dry sherry or Madeira wine; the whole being referred to as a *matignon*.

# Effects of pot roasting

These are similar in most respects to normal roasting, although the effect of exposing the food to moist heat in a covered container and the high quality of each commodity used may result in a more succulent texture.

# General safety rules

The main safety rules will apply as for roasting. However, when using pot or earthenware dishes for pot roasting, never place the hot dish straight into water or on to a cold surface, as this could cause the dish to crack.

# Equipment used for pot roasting

This will include oval and round casseroles (fairly deep), cocottes and braisières all of which must have tight-fitting lids. Such items should, after use, be washed in hot, soapy water, rinsed in clean hot water and dried thoroughly.

# Self-assessment questions for pot roasting

1. Which quality of foods will lend themselves to the pot roasting process?
2. Can you describe the main difference between pot roasting and normal roasting?
3. What is a matignon and how is it prepared?
4. What is the French term for this method of cookery?
5. How is the finished sauce made which accompanies the main commodity?
6. Can you name at least three general rules for efficient pot roasting?
7. Name three vessels which are suitable for carrying out the pot roasting process?
8. To what degree are pot roasted items normally cooked?

9. In your own words describe the method of pot roasting.
10. Describe the advantages of pot roasting foods.

When you have completed these questions check your answers with your fellow students and chef or lecturer.

# Foods suitable for pot roasting

Foods suitable for pot roasting include meat, poultry and game of all kinds. Pheasant, sirloin of beef, rabbit and chicken are the most common foods for pot roasting. The juices are served as part of the finished dish, to retain all nutrients and flavour.

### Pot roast (basic recipe) *Poêler*

| 4 portions | | 10 portions |
|---|---|---|
| | Chosen meat<br>e.g. chicken, beef, or veal | |
| 5 dl | Demi-glace or jus lié | 1¼ litres |
| 200 g | Carrot, onion, celery, leek<br>cut for mirepoix | 500 g |
| 50 g | Butter<br>Salt and milled pepper<br>Herbs as required<br>e.g. tarragon or basil | 100 g |

1. Select a cooking vessel of suitable size, with a tight-fitting lid.
2. Brush the interior lightly with butter, add the mirepoix of vegetables and herbs.
3. Season the chosen meat and sit on top of the mirepoix.
4. Brush the meat with the rest of the butter.
5. Cover with the lid and pot roast in a pre-heated oven at 175°C until required for serving.
6. Baste the meat every 20 minutes during cooking.
7. When the meat is cooked, remove from the pot and keep hot until required for service.
8. Swill out (deglaze) the cooking pot with a wine or spirit and reduce over heat on the stove top.
9. Add the demi-glace and reduce until the required consistency has been achieved. *Note* that if the meat has been cooked in an earthenware cocotte dish the sauce should be finished in a sauteuse so as not to damage the cocotte dish.
10. Strain the sauce through a fine choinois, de-grease the top of the sauce, adjust the seasoning.
11. Remove any string from the meat and cut into portions.
12. Return to the cocotte dish or if using beef or veal, which is sliced, serve on a hot service flat.
13. Coat or surround with the sauce and garnish as given in the following recipes.

**Note:** It is also permissible to serve the meat whole and carve at the table.

### Pot roasted sirloin of beef niçoise

*Contrefilet de boeuf en cocotte niçoise*

| | | |
|---|---|---|
| 8 | Château potatoes | 20 |
| 8 | Small grilled or baked tomatoes | 20 |
| 200 g | Boiled whole green beans | 500 g |
| ½ dl | Madeira | 1¼ dl |
| ¼ bunch | Watercress | ½ bunch |

1. Pot roast the beef as for the basic recipe.
2. Simmer the Madeira for one minute and add to the strained demi-glace.
3. Garnish the meat with the above, brushing the potatoes, tomatoes and beans lightly with clarified butter.

### Pot roast chicken with onions and ham

*Poulet en cocotte bonne femme*

The chicken should be cleaned, trimmed and trussed before cooking, remembering always to remove the wishbone to facilitate carving.

| | | |
|---|---|---|
| 100 g | Button onions | 250 g |
| 100 g | Lardons of ham | 250 g |
| 100 g | Cocotte potatoes | 250 g |
| | Finely chopped parsley | |
| 25 g | Butter | 60 g |

1. Par-boil the button onions and blanch the lardons.
2. Cook the cocotte potatoes as normal.
3. Finish the button onions by shallow frying in a little butter to a light golden brown.
4. Add the lardons to the pan and allow to colour lightly.
5. Use to garnish the basic recipe.
6. Finish with finely chopped parsley.

### Pot roast duckling with orange

*Caneton poêlé à l'orange*

| | | |
|---|---|---|
| 200 g | Orange segments | 500 g |
| 1 dl | Orange juice | 2½ dl |
| ½ dl | Lemon juice | 1¼ dl |
| ¼ dl | Orange curaçao | ½ dl |
| | Julienne of orange zest | |
| ¼ bunch | Watercress | ½ bunch |

1. Blanch the orange zest in boiling water, refresh and place on one side.
2. Mix the orange and lemon juice with the orange curaçao.
3. Simmer for one minute, add the blanched zest.
4. Add the mixture to the demi-glace after it has been strained.
5. Coat the duckling with the sauce and sprinkle liberally with orange

315

segments.
6. Serve on a hot dish with watercress garnish.

## Pot roast pheasant                              *Faisan en cocotte*

| | | |
|---|---|---|
| 100 g | Quartered button mushrooms | 250 g |
| 100 g | Button onions | 250 g |
| ½ dl | Madeira | 1¼ dl |
| | Finely chopped parsley | |
| 25 g | Butter | 60 g |

1. Par-boil the button onions and sauté to a light golden brown colour to finish cooking.
2. Add the mushrooms and sauté until cooked.
3. Drain off any butter from the pan, remove the mushrooms and onions, keeping them hot.
4. Deglaze the pan (swill out) with the Madeira and simmer until reduced by half volume.
5. Add the Madeira to the strained demi-glace and coat the pheasant with the sauce.
6. Garnish with the button onions and mushrooms.
7. Finish with a liberal sprinkling of finely chopped parsley.

# Chapter 11
# Grilling                         *Griller*

## The competency defined

Grilling is a fast method of cooking which uses *radiant heat*. It is one of the dry methods of cooking (along with roasting, baking and frying), which requires no added moisture, the main reason being that it is a method which is particularly suited to first-class cuts of meat, poultry and game.

Only the best quality foods are suitable and the cuts of meat should be of the short-fibred variety. Such foods are placed close to the source of heat which seals the exterior and cooks the item very quickly. It is this initial sealing at the start of the operation which helps food to retain its own juices and thereby contributes towards both the texture and the natural flavour, be it meat, fish, poultry or shellfish.

## Purpose of grilling

1. To make foods palatable and digestible.
2. To give foods a distinctive colour, flavour and texture.
3. To provide the diet with a range of grilled items which, correctly prepared, can be relatively low in fat content.

## Methods of grilling

There are three methods of grilling foods:

1. The 'silver grill' whereby meat, fish, poultry and shellfish are cooked on bars over fierce heat, such as gas, charcoal/barbecues.
2. Under radiant heat, e.g. gas or electric salamanders.
3. Between two electrically pre-heated ribbed plates, such as a rima grill or a sandwich toaster.

When using the first method, i.e. over radiant heat, the grill bars need to be pre-heated and brushed with oil beforehand, otherwise the food items will stick to the bars.

A great deal of care and attention to detail is required when grilling meats since different items will require different degrees of heat. Initially, it is usual to start foods cooking on the hottest part of the grill, and then move them to a less fierce heat to finish cooking. Very thick cuts of meat (5 cm) will need quick browning on each side before being drawn to a more moderate part of the grill to ensure gradual penetration of the heat.

Most items for grilling are confined to smaller cuts of meat such as steaks, chops, cutlets, and kebabs. The grilling in such cases is usually fairly rapid and sufficient to meet most people's tastes. Poultry items should be cooked right through and will need moderate heat to effect this state.

# Grilling of fish and vegetables

There is more moisture in fish than in meat. However, unlike meat, there is no fat in the fibres of white fish. After being well brushed with a fat, such as clarified butter or oil, the fish should be grilled over moderate heat to ensure a moist finish and an attractive appearance.

Apart from the foods already mentioned, one or two other items may be cooked by grilling, e.g. tomatoes (a fruit) and mushrooms (a fungus). In general, however, most vegetables require moist heat to soften the cellulose content and are therefore not suitable for grilling purposes.

# Organisation and preparation for grilling

In a traditional kitchen brigade, the following staff are involved in the process of preparing and grilling of foods.

*Chef garde-manger:*　　Basic preparation of fish, meat and poultry.
*Chef entremettier:*　　Basic preparation of vegetable items.
*Chef grillardin:*　　The actual grilling of most of the foods.

To ensure a fast and efficient service, all food items including garnishes are organised well in advance (on a mise-en-place basis), prior to the commencement of the actual service. The aim is to avoid delays and to keep in line with the usual practice of stated menu times for different dishes. As grilled items are cooked to order, the client likes to know in advance approximately how long a certain dish will take to execute.

During the actual grilling process, the grillardin (grill cook) will, in the interests of personal safety, use a large pair of grill tongs to move items of food being prepared; this is to avoid having to expose hands, arms or other parts of the body to excess heat by reaching over (or under) the heat source.

# Advantages of grilling foods

1. Charcoal grilled foods have a distinctive appearance and flavour.
2. The actual speed of the grilling process allows for fast cooking and service.
3. There is ease of control during the cooking process due to the open access to the foods being grilled (as part of the mise-en-place system).
4. The large variety of suitable foods for grilling purposes allows for an extended choice of menu.
5. Elaborate 'silver grills' may be positioned in full view of the clients in order to achieve maximum sales and visual eye appeal.

# Degrees of cooking

| *English* | *French* | *Description* |
|-----------|----------|---------------|
| Rare | Au bleu | Very underdone with plenty of blood visible |
| Underdone | Saignant | Deep pink/red colour |
| Just done | À point | Light pink in colour |
| Well done | Bien cuit | Cooked through (brown outside) with no visual trace of blood |

# Effects of grilling on foods

Due to the speed of cooking by grilling, there is a very little loss of nutrients or flavour. When grilling meats, the intense heat of the surface of the meat causes it to coagulate and seal the surface protein, consequently trapping the meat juices and the flavour inside the food. However, over-exposure to excessive heat will result in over-coagulation of the protein which becomes hard, giving an unpalatable surface to the meat. If the meat is shrunken and firm, it is over-cooked. When the latter stage is reached, the over-heated protein shrinks and liberates the natural liquid content. The result: a hard piece of meat.

Fish can be grilled in pieces or cooked whole. Pieces are generally mounted on skewers (en brochette) or otherwise cooked in steak or fillet form. When cooked whole, fish need to be gutted and trimmed (of fins, etc.). Small round fish such as herring, mackerel, trout and whiting are sometimes lightly scored (ciseler) in order to assist in the cooking process and to allow heat penetration. It will also help to prevent the outer skin blistering and bursting which would spoil the visual presentation of the dish.

Various methods can be applied when preparing dish for grilling:

1. Dry the fish on a clean kitchen cloth, lightly season and rub with lemon juice. Pass through melted butter and fresh white breadcrumbs. Pat

lightly with a palette-knife to remove any excess crumbs. Place on a greased grill tray, sprinkle with melted butter and grill to a nice golden brown. Generally, fillets or suprêmes of any white fish may be prepared in this manner. After grilling, the fish is again sprinkled with melted butter and served on a hot oval silver dish. This particular form of presentation is known as St Germain.

2. Dry the fish, season and sprinkle with lemon juice; pass through seasoned flour, then good quality oil or melted butter. Place the fish on to well-greased trays ready for grilling. The latter preparation is best done just prior to grilling. After grilling, brush again with melted butter and serve on a hot oval dish.

3. When grilling live lobster, split them lengthways and remove the sac from the head, and the waste cord (the trail) from the tailpart. Crack the claws, then season lightly, sprinkle with melted butter somewhat generously, place over moderate heat and grill. A 1 kg (2¼ lb) lobster will take about 25–30 minutes. Alternatively, place the lobster on grill trays and grill. It is preferable, however, to cook the lobster partially, in a good court-bouillon first so that the flesh does not become quite so tough as when grilled from the raw state.

In general terms, when grilling fish, it should be brushed or sprinkled with melted butter or oil to retain moisture and achieve an evenly cooked article.

Whole or large pieces of fish need to be cooked on both sides to ensure a thorough and even cooking. However, thin cuts or small pieces of fish do not require grilling on both sides because the intensity of the heat will soften and cook the fibres right through. Grilled plaice fillets are a good example.

Grilled fish items are generally accompanied by a sprig of freshly washed and picked parsley, dressed lemon wedges (free from pips) and, according to designation, an appropriate sauce or savoury butter. Grilled fish steaks should always have the centre bone carefully removed together with the outer skin and any trimmings. The fish is then presented on the hot dish or plate.

# General rules for efficient grilling

1. Small items should be cooked quickly but with care.
2. Larger items, after being coloured and sealed on the hottest part of the grill, should be moved to a slightly cooler zone to complete the cooking process. Remember that over-cooking will result in shrinkage (and undue weight loss) and subsequent loss of natural moisture.
3. Similarly, items which are cooked for a prolonged length of time tend to dry out with a resulting loss of flavour.
4. During the grilling process, the regular basting of foods and the oiling of grill bars will prevent sticking, and also drying out of the item.
5. Always use special tongs, palette knives or fish slices for lifting and turning foods on the grill. Never use a cook's fork to pierce the meat, as the result will be a loss of natural juices (and flavour).

# General safety rules

1. Great care should be taken when moving grill bars whilst they are still hot.
2. Only use grill trays which have adequate raised edges, and never overload the tray(s).
3. Never place trays or other items of equipment on top of a salamander; not only will they get extremely hot, but also an unsuspecting colleague may be drenched with boiling hot fat or other liquids.
4. Great care should be exercised when removing foods from under the salamander during the grilling operation. Trays get very hot and it is most important to use a handling cloth which is sufficiently thick to withstand the heat.
5. At the end of the service all taps should be turned off and the heat source extinguished, be it gas or electricity.

# Techniques associated with grilling

*Flouring*: This is the passing of fish through seasoned flour in preparation for grilling. This process should only be carried out just prior to cooking as the flour attracts moisture from the fish if left for any length of time. The end result then is that a crust is formed which mars the appearance.

*Oiling, basting and greasing*: Grill bars need to be oiled prior to usage, otherwise the food items will stick to the bars during cooking. All trays which are being used for grilling purposes must be greased before use. Food items are also coated with oil or fat (clarified butter or best quality beef dripping) in preparation for the cooking process. During grilling, it is advisable to brush the food items with a suitable fat; this is referred to as basting, which will assist in moisture retention. Some grilled goods may also be basted with special sauces in order to add flavour, such as shish kebab which is marinaded beforehand; or skewered meats (en brochette) which are served at barbecues with a special barbecue sauce.

*Crumbing*: Fish is sometimes crumbed (with fresh breadcrumbs) prior to grilling and may be passed through one of two methods:

1. Seasoned flour, eggwash and dry breadcrumbs.
2. Melted butter and fresh breadcrumbs, then placed on greased trays and cooked under a salamander.

*Charring or searing:* This refers to the dark brown markings found on foods which have been grilled—usually whole fish or steaks. The marks are caused by contact with very hot grill bars, or they may be made with a special branding iron.

# Equipment used for grilling

The *salamader* grill which cooks from above is powered by gas or electricity. The salamander bars and drip tray should be cleaned in hot detergent water, then thoroughly rinsed in hot water and all parts replaced. Finally, the salamander should then be lit for a short time to make sure that all parts are quite dry.

Electric toasters should be kept clean and free from debris (crumbs) at all times in the interest of safety and efficiency.

*Under-fired grills* are heated in several ways, by charcoal, gas or coke. Much care must be taken when cleaning the grill as the fire bricks with which the grill is lined are easily broken. After using the grill, all the burned remnants of charcoal or coke should be removed. In the case of gas, the supply should be turned off. The grill bars should then be thoroughly cleaned and oiled ready for use again.

Small equipment used for grilling should be cleaned in hot detergent water then thoroughly rinsed and dried. All of the above equipment needs to be checked and regularly maintained in a clean and safe condition. Any faults should be reported immediately to the person in charge. Finally, gas and electrical equipment should be serviced by experts on a regular contract basis.

When grilling by the 'over radiant heat' method (silver grill), whereby the items are cooked on oiled bars, the foods sometimes slip between the bars and are difficult to extricate—especially fish. To avoid this problem, fish items such as whole sole or plaice are 'sandwiched' between two wire grids made from tinned steel wire, hinged one side and made especially for use over charcoal and other forms of under-fired radiant heat. The grids tend to stabilise the item being held and reduce the risk of the food breaking up. The whole fish remains encased within the grid whilst turning during the grilling process. Fish slices and large broad-bladed palette knives are also used to assist the turning of foods.

Certain items require cooking on a *grill tray*. This is a shallow tray with an edge on all four sides to top the foods slipping off, and also to prevent the spillage of liquids and fats from the items during grilling. A grill tray would be suitable for bacon, sausages, lambs' kidneys, tomatoes and mushrooms.

The salamander type grill can also be used for the browning, gratinating and glazing of foods. Examples are: au gratin dishes such as cauliflower au gratin; duchess potato borders; and foods coated with a sauce which require browning/glazing, such as glazed fish dishes like sole vin blanc glacée or sole Bercy.

Foods which are being cooked by grilling should never be pierced with a fork when turning; use a pair of grill tongs to avoid the potential loss of valuable juices and preserve the flavour and natural moisture level of the item.

When cooking by the 'between heat' method (between electrically heated elements) the plates need to be pre-heated and oiled beforehand. This method is more commonly used for the smaller cuts of meats and to make toasted sandwiches.

# Safe hygiene practices

This aspect of food preparation is of the utmost importance, especially in view of the 'prepared to order' principle of most of the grill process items. Under no circumstances should raw meat, fish, poultry and similar foodstuffs be left lying around in the heat of the kitchen during the service. Instead, whatever items are on order should be obtained direct from the refrigeration/cold store where the temperature should be 1°C to 4°C (34°C to 39°F). Contrast this with the ambient temperature of a busy hot kitchen which can easily reach 29°C (85°F) or more on occasions.

Uncooked meat or fish will rapidly deteriorate if exposed for any length of time in such conditions, and thus become a health hazard.

It is very important to keep uncooked and cooked foods apart, before, during and after service, and to handle such foods as infrequently as possible. Such rules will help to minimise the problems of cross-contamination which is an ever-present danger when dealing with cooked and raw foods together. For the same reasons, the working surfaces should be kept quite separate. These same rules will also apply during storage.

In a 'front of house' situation where the grilling process is on public view, the usual practice is to have all the food items displayed in a refrigerated display unit. All items should be set out on suitable trays (usually plastic which is impervious) and where possible handled with food tongs rather than by hand.

Finally, because of the frequency of handling of food items during the grilling operation, frequent hand washing/scrubbing is essential to maintain good standards of food hygiene.

# Self-assessment questions for grilling

1. What method of heat is commonly associated with the grilling process?
2. Can you name the three methods of grilling?
3. How would you describe steak which is 'au bleu'?
4. Why are most vegetables unsuitable for grilling?
5. Name two members of a traditional kitchen brigade who are involved in the preparation/grilling of foods (give the French terminology).
6. Can you briefly describe two advantages of the grilling process?
7. Why is it advisable to use a wire fish grid when grilling whole flat fish such as plaice or Dover sole?
8. Name three items of food which are usually cooked on a grill tray.
9. Why should meats never be pierced with a cook's fork during the grilling process?
10. Why do over-cooked meat items (steaks) tend to be hard and dry?
11. Why are small round fish often scored (ciseler) prior to grilling?
12. Can you describe the St Germain preparation process for fish?

13. Why is it advisable to partially cook lobsters prior to grilling them?
14. Outline three general rules for efficient grilling.
15. Describe briefly three safety rules when grilling food items.
16. Why should fish for grilling not be 'floured' too far in advance?
17. Briefly describe the terms *charring* or *searing*.
18. Can you name three fuels used for heating *under-fired grills*?
19. Why are grill bars pre-heated and brushed with oil before use?
20. Give a brief outline of the method of cleansing small equipment items which have been used for grilling.

When you have completed these questions check your answers with your fellow students and chef or lecturer.

# Grilled fish dishes

*Introduction to grilled fish dishes*

Remember to use only the best quality fish for grilling, especially if cooking small whole fish such as herrings or sardine. The better the quality of the raw fish, the better the cooked dish will look and taste. *See* Effects of grilling on foods.

**Grilled cod steaks**              *Darne de cabillaud grillé*

1. Wash, drain and dry the steaks.
2. Pass through seasoned flour.
3. Brush well with melted clarified butter, oil or margarine.
4. Place on to lightly greased grill tray (with a raised edge).
5. Grill on both sides under a salamander, brushing occasionally with a little melted fat.
6. If cooked, the centre bone will come away easily. Also remove the outer skin and neatly trim the edges.
7. Serve on a hot dish and garnish with a sprig of picked parsley, and lemon wedges along the sides.
8. Serve any of the savoury butters, e.g. maitre d'hôtel, or a suitable sauce, e.g. sauce diable.

**Grilled herring**              *Hareng grillé*

1. Remove the scales from the fish using the back of a small knife.
2. Remove the head and clean out the intestines (reserving the roe, if required).
3. Trim off all the fins and trim the tail. Wash, drain and dry the herring.
4. Make 3–4 light incisions about 3 mm deep on either side of the fish.
5. Pass through seasoned flour and carefully shake off any surplus.

6. Brush with melted butter, oil or margarine.
7. Place on to a greased grill tray, and grill on both sides taking care not to burn the tail. (The latter can be protected during the grilling process with a slice of potato.)
8. When cooked, dress on a suitable hot dish and brush with melted butter.
9. Garnish with a sprig of parsley and a lemon wedge.
10. Serve with a sauce-boat of sauce moutard (mustard sauce) separately.

### Grilled mackerel         *Maquereau grillé*

1. Cut off the head, remove the intestines and clean the inside of the fish.
2. Cut down each side of the backbone and remove the bone entirely.
3. Trim off all the fins and trim the tail; also remove the rib bones.
4. Wash well, drain and dry. Pass through seasoned flour and remove any surplus.
5. Place cut side down on a greased grill tray; brush with melted butter, oil or margarine.
6. Grill on both sides under a salamander and serve presentation side upwards on a hot dish.
7. Garnish with parsley sprigs and lemon wedges.

### Fillets of grilled plaice       *Filets de plie grillés*

Both fillets of sole and fillets of plaice are prepared and cooked in the following manner.

1. Fillet the fish and remove the skin. Wash, drain and dry each fillet.
2. Pass through seasoned flour and shake gently to remove surplus.
3. Lightly score the fish on the 'skin side' to prevent curling whilst being grilled.
4. Place on a greased grill tray (presentation side down) after having brushed the fish with oil or melted butter.
5. Grill on both sides under a salamander. Thin plaice fillets may require grilling one side only to cook through.
6. Serve the fillets on a hot dish garnished with a sprig of parsley and lemon wedges.
7. Serve any of the savoury butters or a suitable sauce, e.g. sauce anchois, apart.

### Grilled salmon steak       *Darne de saumon grillé*

1. Pass the salmon steaks through seasoned flour, then shake gently to remove any excess.
2. Place on to greased grill trays, and brush with oil.
3. Grill on both sides (about 5 minutes on each side); brush at regular

intervals with oil whilst grilling.

4. Remove the centre bone and serve on a hot dish; garnish with sprigs of parsley, lemon wedges, and a separate dish of sliced cucumber together with a suitable sauce, such as sauce verte, or a savoury butter.

**Grilled whole sole or plaice**                    *Sole grillée, petite plie grillée*

1. Scale the white side of the plaice, and remove the head and skirt from round the fish.
2. Clean the stomach cavity of congealed blood. In the case of sole, remove the black skin. Wash, drain and dry the fish.
3. Pass through seasoned flour and shake gently to remove any excess flour.
4. Place on a greased grill tray, white skin down. Brush the fish with oil or melted butter.
5. Grill on both sides under a salamander for 4–5 minutes each side.
6. Serve presentation side upwards on a hot dish, and garnish with a sprig of parsley and lemon wedges. The fish may be accompanied by any of the savoury butters or a sauce.

**Note:** The removal of the dark skin of the plaice is a matter of discretion.

# Grilled meats                    *Viande grillé*

*Introduction to grilled meats*

All the better quality cuts of meat are suitable for grilling due to their tender make-up. The connective tissue breaks down easily and quickly in steaks, unlike shin or other cheaper cuts which take much longer to cook.

*Grilled cuts of beef*

As already stated, only the tenderest cuts of meat are suitable for grilling, and this rule still applies to beef. The cuts of beef suitable for grilling come from the sirloin, the rump and the fillet.
The cuts from the rump include the following:

| | | |
|---|---|---|
| Point steak | (No French name) | 1 × 200 g per person |
| | | Cut from the point of the rump |
| Rump steak | (No French name) | 1 × 200 g per person |
| | | Cut from the main rump piece |

The cuts obtained from the fillet include the following:

| | | |
|---|---|---|
| (No English name) | Chateaubriand | 1 × 400 g serves two persons |
| | | Cut from the head of the fillet |

| Fillet steak | Filet be boeuf | 1 × 200 g per person<br>Cut from the head or heart of<br>the fillet |
|---|---|---|
| (No English name) | Tournedos | 1 × 200 g per person<br>Smaller cut than the fillet<br>Often secured with string to<br>retain a round shape<br>Cut from the heart |
| (No English name) | Filet mignon | 3 × 75 g pieces per person<br>Cut from the tail of the fillet<br>Commonly used as part of a<br>mixed grill but may be<br>presented in their own right<br>as a specific dish |

The cuts obtained from the boned-out sirloin (contrefilet be boeuf) include
the following:

| Double sirloin steak | Entrecôte double | 1 × 300 g per person<br>A large steak cut from a boned-<br>out sirloin |
|---|---|---|
| Sirloin steak | Entrecôte | 1 × 200 g per person<br>Cut from a boned-out sirloin |
| Minute steak | Entrecôte minute | 1 × 150 g per person<br>Cut from a boned-out sirloin<br>and batted out until thin |

The cuts of sirloin on the bone (aloyau de boeuf) include the following:

| Porterhouse or<br>T-bone steak | (No French name) | 1 × 650 g per person<br>Cut from a whole sirloin cutting<br>through the bone and<br>including the fillet |
|---|---|---|

Wing rib of beef may also be cut into steaks and grilled but this is not a very
satisfactory way of cooking for this cut.

### Cuts of lamb suitable for grilling

| Fillet | Le filet mignon | 1 × 150 g per person |
|---|---|---|
| Loin chop | Chop | 1 × 150 g per person |
| Double chop<br>or<br>Barnsley chop | Chop d'agneau<br>à l'anglaise | 1 × 250 g per person |
| Chump chop | Chump chop | 1 × 200 g per person |
| Kidney | Le rognon | 100 g per person |

| Best end | Le carré | 2 ribs per person |
|---|---|---|
| | | Serves 2 to 3 persons |
| Rosette | Medaillon | 2 × 75 g per person |
| Noisette | Noisette | 2 × 75 g per person |
| Cutlet | Côtelette | 2 × 75 g per person |
| Double cutlet | Côtelette d'agneau double | 1 × 150 g per person |

## Grilled cutlets
*Côtelettes d'agneau grillées*

1. Season the cutlets with salt and milled pepper.
2. Brush with a little oil.
3. Place on to lightly greased grill tray and grill under a salamander for about 5 minutes on each side.
4. Serve dressed with pommes pailleés (straw potatoes/deep fried), a sprig of watercress and a slice of parsley butter on each cutlet.
5. Top each cutlet with a cutlet frill.

## Lamb kebab
*Brochette d'agneau*

Use a prime lean cut of lamb for this dish, such as best end or loin of lamb.

| | | |
|---|---|---|
| 600 g | Lean lamb, diced into 2 cm pieces | 1½ kg |
| 120 g | Onion, cut into 2 cm pieces | 300 g |
| 120 g | Mixed red, green, yellow peppers | 300 g |
| 50 g | Mushrooms | 150 g |
| 120 ml | Oil | 250 ml |
| 30 ml | Lemon juice or wine | 75 ml |
| | Bay leaves | |
| | Salt and milled pepper | |

1. Lightly season the meat and place into a bowl with the onion, lemon juice, oil and bay leaves. Cover with a cartouche or cling film and leave to stand for at least 2 hours, to marinade before grilling.
2. When ready to use place on to skewers, alternating the ingredients as you progress.
3. Place on to lightly greased grill trays and cook under a salamander for 10–15 minutes, remembering to turn the kebab regularly to allow cooking on all sides.
4. The kebab may also be cooked over a charcoal grill, but must be brushed well with oil to prevent sticking.
5. Serve on a bed of rice pilaff (braised) with a sauce-boat of suitable sauce, such as devilled sauce, barbecue sauce or sweet and sour sauce.

Other meats which may be grilled in kebab form include chicken livers, breast of chicken flesh, lamb and veal kidneys, loin of pork, liver and bacon.
    Kebabs may also be varied by adding other foods such as sausage, tomato, pineapple or peach.

## Mixed grill

| 4 × 100 g | Lamb cutlets | 10 × 100 g |
| 1 dl | Oil | 2 dl |
| 4 | Lambs' kidneys | 10 |
| 4 | Pork chipolatas | 10 |
| 4 | Grilling mushrooms | 10 |
| 4 | Firm tomatoes | 10 |
| 4 | Rashers of bacon | 10 |
| 50 g | Parsley butter | 150 g |
| 50 g | Straw potatoes | 150 g |
| | Watercress to garnish | |

1. Trim and season and brush the cutlets with oil.
2. Remove the skins from the kidneys, cut them open from the back and place them on skewers, season and brush with oil.
3. Place the chipolatas on a grilling tray and coat with oil.
4. Remove the stalks from the mushrooms, wash the mushrooms, add them to the grilling tray, brush with oil and season.
5. Remove the eyes from the tomatoes, cut a shallow cross on the top, add to the grilling tray, oil and season.
6. Place the bacon rashers on the grilling tray.
7. Grill all the ingredients either on a charcoal grill or under the salamander. Note that the kidneys should be slightly underdone. Remove items from the grill tray as they are cooked and place them neatly on to a pre-heated service dish. Place a cutlet frill on each of the cutlet bones and a slice of parsley butter in the centre of each kidney. Garnish the service dish with the straw potatoes and watercress.

### Grilled chicken dishes

Chickens suitable for grilling include the following:

| *Name* | *Age* | *Weight* |
|---|---|---|
| Poussin | 4 to 6 weeks old | 300 g to 500 g |
| Poulet de grain | 3 to 4 months old, fattened bird | small 750 g to 1 kg |
| Poulet reine | Full-grown tender bird | medium 1 kg to 2 kg |

To prepare a whole chicken for grilling:

1. Remove the wishbone.
2. Cut off the claws at the first joint.
3. Put the bird on to its back.
4. Insert a large knife through the neck-end and cut off the vent.
5. Cut through the backbone.
6. Open out
7. Remove the back bone and ribs.

## Grilled chicken with devilled sauce                    *Poulet grillé diable*

| | | |
|---|---|---|
| 250 ml | Devilled sauce | 600 ml |
| 100 g | Straw potatoes | 250 g |
| 100 g | Clarified butter | 250 g |
| 100 g | Fresh white breadcrumbs | 250 g |
| 10 g | Diluted English mustard | 25 g |
| | Watercress | |

1. Brush the chicken liberally with oil and season.
2. Place on to lightly greased grill tray.
3. Grill until half cooked, approximately 10 minutes.
4. Remove from the grill and brush the chicken with mustard and clarified butter and sprinkle with the fresh white breadcrumbs.
5. Finish grilling under the salamander until a deep golden brown colour.
6. Check that the chicken is cooked by looking for signs of blood; if not quite cooked allow to finish cooking in a cooler zone of the salamander.
7. Serve with a sauce-boat of devilled sauce and garnish with straw potatoes and watercress.

## Spiced chicken kebabs
## (Chicken tikka)

| | | |
|---|---|---|
| 1½ dl | Plain yoghurt | 4 dl |
| 4 | Crushed cloves of garlic | 10 |
| 4 cm strip | Peeled and finely chopped root ginger | 10 cm strip |
| 30 g | Brunoise of onion | 75 g |
| 5 g | Chilli powder | 15 g |
| 1 tablespoon | Ground coriander | 2½ tablespoons |
| 1 teaspoon | Salt | 2½ teaspoons |
| 1½ kg | Skinned and boned chicken | 4 kg |

*Garnish*

| | | |
|---|---|---|
| 1 | Large onion sliced into thin rings | 2 |
| 100 g | Thinly sliced tomatoes | 300 g |
| 2 tablespoons | Finely chopped coriander leaves | 5 tablespoons |

1. Mix the yoghurt, ginger, garlic, onion and chilli powder.
2. Add the coriander and salt to taste.
3. Cut the chicken into 3 cm cubes and mix with the marinade.
4. Cover with cling film and stand for 6 hours or overnight.
5. Thread the marinaded chicken on to skewers and grill under a hot salamander on both sides until cooked, 8–10 minutes.
6. Remove from the skewers and serve on a hot service dish. Garnish with onion rings and tomatoes, and sprinkle with the coriander leaves.

**Note:** Chicken breasts or suprêmes may be used in place of the chicken pieces, in which case omit the skewering stage.

## Grilled chicken

*Poulet grillé Crapaudine*

For individual portions use poussins 400 g to 500 g.
For 4 portions use 1 kg to 1½ kg chicken.
For 10 portions you will need 2½ kg to 3½ kg.

1. Cut the chicken horizontally from below the point of the breast over the top of the legs to the wing joints without removing the breasts.
2. Fold the breasts back.
3. Snap and reverse the backbone into the opposite direction so that the point of the breast now extends forward to resemble the nose and face of a toad.
4. Flatten the chicken slightly and remove all the small bones such as the rib cage.
5. Skewer the wings and legs into position.
6. Season with salt and milled pepper.
7. Brush with oil.
8. Grill either on a charcoal grill or more commonly on a lightly greased grill tray under the salamander for between 15 and 20 minutes on each side.
9. Check that the chicken is cooked before serving.
10. Garnish each chicken with two slices of hard-boiled egg for the eyes of the toad with a pupil made from truffle or gherkin.
11. Serve with watercress and a sauce-boat of sauce diable.

*Other grilled meats*

## Gammon steaks

*Jambon grillé*

Allow 1 × 200 g steak per person.
Do not season gammon steak as it has already been seasoned during the curing process. Any further seasoning is likely to make the gammon too salty. Grill as for any of the grilled meats, either under a salamander or on a charcoal grill or even between radiant heat.

*Garnishes*
Gammon may be garnished in many ways; the most popular are as follows:

| | |
|---|---|
| Shallow fried egg | placed on top of the grilled gammon. |
| Glazed pineapple rings | placed on top of the grilled gammon. |
| Glazed peaches | dressed around or on top of the grilled gammon. |
| Vert-pré garnish | dressed around the side of the gammon. |

## Grilled hamburgers

Minced beef, veal and pork are all suitable for this recipe.

| | | |
|---|---|---|
| 360 g | **Raw minced meat** | 900 g |
| 90 g | **Fresh white breadcrumbs soaked in milk and then squeezed of excess moisture** | 225 g |
| 90 g | **Brunoise of onion sweated off in butter without colour** | 225 g |
| 45 g | **Beaten whole egg** | 100 g |
| | **Seasoning** | |
| 1 tablespoon | **Chopped parsley** | 3 tablespoons |

1. Re-mince the meat with the breadcrumbs.
2. Add the brunoise of onion, parsley and seasoning.
3. Mix well together and bind with the egg.
4. Place in the fridge for 1 hour to allow to set.
5. Divide into four or ten portions and shape into medallions.
6. Allow to rest for half an hour before use.
7. Grill as for other meats, and serve in a toasted bun.

### Grilled offal

The following offal is suitable for grilling:

| | |
|---|---|
| *Liver* | *Foie* |
| Lamb's liver | Foie d'agneau |
| Pig's liver | Foie de porc |
| Calf's liver | Foie de veau |

Allow 100 g of raw liver per person.

1. To prepare for grilling, first skin liver and then slice thinly.
2. Pass through seasoned flour just before grilling.
3. Serve with a suitable sauce such as madeira.

*Kidneys*                                                                 *Rognons*

*Lamb's kidneys*                                              *Rognons d'agneau*
2 to 4 kidneys per person.
To prepare for grilling first skin and then slit open, remove the core and thread on to a skewer.
*Pig's kidneys*                                                *Rognons de porc*
1 to 2 kidneys per person.
To prepare for grilling follow the same procedure as for lamb's kidneys.
*Calf's kidneys*                                              *Rognons de veau*
2 to 4 kidneys per person.
To prepare for grilling first skin the kidney and then slice, finally thread on to a skewer.

## Sweetbreads *Ris grillé*

1. To prepare for grilling, first blanch the sweetbreads and braise (*see* braising), allow to cool and press.
2. Cut the sweetbreads in half crosswise, pass through salted butter and gently grill for about 5 minutes on each side.
3. It is also possible to grill sweetbreads when you have passed them through butter and fresh white breadcrumbs as for St Germain. Garnish with béarnaise sauce, purée of peas, buttered carrots and noisette potatoes.

## Barbecued pork spare ribs

Allow 200 to 250 g per person.

*Sauce*

| | | |
|---|---|---|
| 100 g | Brunoise of onion | 250 g |
| 1 | Clove crushed garlic | 3 |
| 60 ml | Olive oil | 150 ml |
| 60 ml | Vinegar | 150 ml |
| 150 g | Tomato purée | 375 g |
| 60 ml | Honey | 150 ml |
| 250 ml | Brown stock | 600 ml |
| 1 teaspoon | Mustard powder | 4 |
| 1 pinch | Thyme | 4 |
| | Salt | |

1. Sweat the onion and garlic in the olive oil; do not colour the onions.
2. Mix in the vinegar followed by the rest of the ingredients.
3. Allow the sauce to simmer for 15 minutes.

| | | |
|---|---|---|
| 2 kg | Pork spare ribs | 5 kg |
| 60 ml | Olive oil | 150 ml |

1. Brush the ribs with olive oil and seal on a charcoal grill on all sides.
2. Brush regularly with the sauce while cooking.
3. When sealed move to a cooler zone of the charcoal grill to finish cooking.
4. Cook for 15–20 minutes.

**Note:** The thyme can be replaced with caraway seeds. Belly pork can be used in place of ribs; this will reduce the cooking time slightly.

## Grilled bacon and sausages

| | | |
|---|---|---|
| 400 g | Sausages | 1 kg |
| 200 g | Sliced bacon | 500 g |

These foods are best placed on lightly greased grill trays and cooked under a salamander, turned during cooking to allow even colouring and cooking. Larger sausages may also be cooked on a charcoal grill.

Grilled bacon and sausages are most commonly found on breakfast menus, luncheon and high tea menus. They are also used extensively as garnishes.

# Grilled vegetables   *Légumes grillés*

Only a limited number of vegetables are suitable for grilling. It is more common to find vegetables finished by this method, by being glazed or gratinated under the salamander to give colour to a dish for service.

The most common grilled vegetables are tomatoes and mushrooms.

### Grilled tomatoes   *Tomates grillées*

Usually served as a garnish when only one would be served. If being served as a vegetable then two to a portion is required.

1. To prepare remove the eyes from the tomatoes and lightly score the opposite end with a shallow criss-cross shape.
2. Place on a lightly greased grill tray with cross-cut uppermost. Brush with oil and season.
3. Cook for 3–5 minutes under a salamander.
4. To serve peel back the four corners of cut skin to form a star, brush with clarified butter and garnish with a sprig of chopped parsley.

### Grilled mushrooms   *Champignons grillés*

| 200 g | Mushrooms | 500 g |
|---|---|---|

1. To prepare, remove the stalks and if necessary peel the cap.
2. Place on a lightly greased grill tray and follow the method as for grilled tomatoes. Cooking time 5–7 minutes.

### New potatoes   *Pommes nouvelles grillées*

New potatoes are excellent grilled. First you need to scrub them, leaving the skins on. Place them into a pan of boiling salted water and simmer until almost cooked. Refresh and then coat with oil, sprinkle with crystals of sea salt and finish cooking on a charcoal grill.

# Grilled fruits   *Fruits grillés*

Fruits which are suitable for grilling, especially over charcoal grills, include pineapple slices brushed very lightly with oil and cooked to a golden brown, and bananas which are cooked in their skins. When the skin is almot black, the banana is cooked. To serve remove the skin by splitting the banana lengthways. Serve both of these dishes with a suitable sauce, such as apricot or cream chantilly.

# Grilled savouries

These savouries are commonly found on snack menus as well as on buffets and as savouries at receptions.

### Angels on horseback                                    *Anges à cheval*

| | | |
|---|---|---|
| 8 | **Fresh oysters** | 20 |
| 4 | **Rashers streaky bacon** | 10 |
| | **Cayenne pepper** | |
| 10 g | **Butter** | 25 g |
| 2 | **Slices of toast** | 5 |

1. Remove the rind from the bacon and oysters from their shells.
2. Wrap each oyster in half a rasher of bacon.
3. Thread on to a skewer and set on to a baking tray.
4. Grill gently, turning to ensure even cooking, until cooked.
5. Sprinkle with a little cayenne pepper.
6. Butter each slice of toast and trim the crusts.
7. Divide each slice into 4 rectangles.
8. Set one bacon and oyster roll on each rectangle and serve on a hot flat with a dish paper and picked parsley.

### Devils on horseback                                    *Diables à cheval*

| | | |
|---|---|---|
| 8 | **Soaked prunes** | 20 |
| 50 g | **Chutney** | 125 g |
| 4 | **Rashers streaky bacon** | 10 |
| 10 g | **Butter** | 25 g |
| 2 | **Slices of toast** | 5 |
| | **Cayenne pepper** | |

1. Remove the rind from the bacon and cut each rasher in half.
2. Remove the stones from the prunes and stuff each prune with a little chutney.
3. Wrap each prune in a piece of bacon.
4. Thread on to a skewer and place on a grill tray and grill gently until cooked; turn during cooking to ensure even cooking.
5. Butter each slice of toast and trim off the crusts.
6. Divide each slice into 4 rectangles, sit a bacon and prune roll on each rectangle and sprinkle with cayenne pepper.
7. Serve on a hot flat with a dish paper and picked parsley.

## Soft roes on toast

| 8 | Soft roes | 20 |
| 10 g | Butter | 25 g |
| 2 | Slices of toast | 5 |
| | Cayenne pepper | |
| | Seasoned flour | |

1. Pass the soft roes through a little seasoned flour.
2. Shake to remove excess flour.
3. Brush with a little oil and butter and grill gently for 3–5 minutes on each side.
4. Butter the toast and remove the crusts.
5. Divide each slice into 4 rectangles and dress with the roe.
6. Sprinkle with a little cayenne pepper and serve on a hot flat with a dish paper and picked parsley.

## Chicken liver and bacon on toast                    *Canapé Diane*

| 8 | Chicken livers | 20 |
| 4 | Rashers of streaky bacon | 10 |
| 10 g | Butter | 25 g |
| 2 | Slices of toast | 5 |
| | Cayenne pepper | |

1. Trim the rind off the bacon and trim the chicken livers.
2. Cut the rashers in half and wrap around the chicken livers.
3. Thread on to a skewer and grill lightly on both sides for 4–6 minutes.
4. Sprinkle with cayenne pepper and keep warm.
5. Butter the toast and trim the crusts.
6. Divide each slice into 4 rectangles and sit a liver and bacon roll on each slice.
7. Serve on a hot flat with a dish paper and picked parsley.

# Chapter 12
# Shallow Frying     *Sauter*

## The competency defined

Shallow frying is the cooking of foods in small quantities of hot fat or oils (including clarified butter), and is performed in a shallow pan, such as a sauté pan (sauteuse), a plat à sauter or a frying-pan. Modern equipment will also include a griddle plate, especially within a fast food area (a 'call-order' unit). There is also 'stir frying' as employed in much of Chinese cookery.

The French term for this method of cookery is 'sauter'. The literal meaning of this word is 'to jump', i.e. the foods are tossed whilst cooking. However, there is another French cookery term which can be confusing to the learner, and this is the word 'meunière', used to describe shallow-fried fish, such as Trout meunière or Dover sole fillets meunière.

Not all foods which are shallow fried, such as eggs, are tossed in the pan, as this action would result in damage to the food.

The term sauter is usually only used in connection with the cooking of meat of first-class quality; poultry items such as chicken cut for sauté or suprêmes; vegetables and potatoes, such as pommes sautées and pommes lyonnaise; fish such as goujons de sole Murat; and fruits such as pineapple slices. These are just some of the examples of items which lend themselves to shallow frying.

## Purpose of shallow frying

The purpose of shallow frying is to:

1. Make food digestible and safe to eat.
2. Give variety to the menu.
3. Give good colour by browning in the pan or griddle.
4. Give a definite flavour.

## Methods of shallow frying

There are basically four methods of shallow frying, as follows:

## 1. Shallow fry

Using the minimum amount of fat or oil in frying-pan or sauté pan. When foods have a presentation side (the best side upwards), this should always be fried first, i.e. presentation side downwards in the pan. The reasons for this are that, firstly, it will allow for a better standard of presentation because the cooking medium will be clean and free from frying debris at the initial stage, and secondly, the item will only need turning once. This will reduce the risk of possible damage to the food from over-handling.

This method is used for smaller tender cuts of meat such as veal escalopes, noisettes of lamb, calf sweetbreads and liver. Fish such as trout and herrings may be cooked by shallow frying, together with certain vegetables, eggs, crêpes and numerous made-up dishes such as Hamburg or Vienna steaks.

However, it is important to understand that, since shallow frying is a fast method of cookery by direct heat, only the best quality foods and the most tender are suitable for cooking in this way.

## 2. Sautér

This is the term which can be used when cooking the tender cuts of poultry and meat in a sauté or frying-pan.

It should be noted that meats which are sautéed are removed from the pan after cooking and kept warm, while the fat is poured away leaving only the sediment. The pan is then swilled out (deglazed) with wine or stock. This process forms an important part of the finished accompanying sauce. Only when the meat is cooked and the sauce has been finished should the two be amalgamated. To cook the meat in the sauce is actually classed as stewing.

The term sauté is also used to describe the cooking of potato dishes, onions or kidneys which are shallow fried. These foods are sliced or cut into small pieces; the potatoes may be shaped into balls with a parisienne scoop for specific dishes, such as pommes parisienne or pommes noisette. Such foods are tossed during cooking until golden brown and cooked through.

## 3. Griddle

This is cooking on a solid metal plate. Foods suitable for cooking on a griddle plate include sliced onions, eggs (usually placed inside a metal ring), hamburgers, bacon, sausages and black pudding. The griddle must be pre-heated and lightly brushed with oil before use. Meat products should be turned frequently during the cooking process. Various hot-plate goods such as pancakes and crumpets are cooked by the griddle method, but should only be turned once.

## 4. Stir fry

This is very fast frying, introduced and made popular in the United

Kingdom in the latter part of the 1970s by the increased number of Chinese restaurants. The cooking is performed in a wok with minimum amounts of oil. Foods which are suitable include strips of the most tender cuts of beef, chicken and vegetables. The technique is to cut everything into fine strips or thin pieces with the object of cooking them for only a few minutes until crisp.

# Organisation and preparation for shallow frying

In the traditional partie system the following members of the kitchen brigade would be involved in organisation and preparation for shallow frying.

| | |
|---|---|
| *Chef saucier*: | Poultry, game, meat, offal (entrées). |
| *Chef poissonnier*: | Fish dishes. |
| *Chef entremettier*: | Vegetable and potato dishes. |
| *Breakfast cook*: | Shallow-fried breakfast dishes. |

For fast and efficient service, a large amount of mise-en-place is usually prepared in advance, particularly sauces and garnishes.

# Advantages of shallow frying

This is a very fast method of cookery for preparing best quality cuts of meat and poultry. As the foods are in direct contact with the heat, the foods cook quickly. It is therefore eminently suitable for an à la carte restaurant service.

# Degrees of cooking

All foods cooked by shallow frying, and specifically meats and poultry, should be cooked through but not over-cooked. The latter will result in the loss of natural moisture (the juices) and make the item tough instead of tender and moist.

# Effects of shallow frying on foods

The effect of the high temperature used for shallow frying produces an instantaneous coagulation of the surface protein and so prevents the escape of most of the food's natural juices. In addition, a small amount of the fat or oil used in shallow frying is absorbed by the food, causing a change in the food's nutritional balance.

# General rules for efficient shallow frying

1. Items of meat, poultry and fish to be cooked by this method must be tender and of the best quality.
2. The foods used should be seasoned before cooking.
3. Always cook the presentation side first.
4. Foods should always be started in hot pans or on pre-heated griddles to prevent the absorption of fat or oil, and the loss of natural juices. However, it is important to remember that different fats have different smoke points, with the smoke point of butter (approximately 140°C; 280°C) being lower than that of oil (see page 363).
5. Pans should be cleaned after each use to get rid of burnt particles.
6. Always 'season' new pans before use, such as cast-iron frying-pans (but not tinned copperware such as a plat à sauter or copper poêle).
7. It is essential to work in a well-ordered and systematic way when performing large amounts of shallow frying.
8. Never allow foods which have been coated with flour prior to cooking to stand for very long, as the flour absorbs the juices from the food and when cooked will form a crust.
9. Always select the correct oil or fat for the item under preparation.

# General safety rules

1. Always select the correct size (and type) of pan for the food being cooked. If the pan is too small the food may break up (fish for example), and it will not colour evenly. If the pan is too large, areas of the pan's surface not being utilised may burn and affect the flavour of the food.
2. Move the hot pans carefully so as not to spill any fat or oil on to the stove.
3. Always use a thick, clean dry cloth (kitchen rubber) when handling hot pans.
4. To avoid being splashed when placing foods into hot pans, always lay the food item into the pan gently, and always away from you—not towards the body.
5. Always wear long sleeves and keep them rolled down to protect your arms from being splashed by hot fat or oil.

# Techniques associated with shallow frying

*Proving or 'seasoning'*: The preparation of frying-pans (not copperware) for use when they are new. Before using, the pans are lightly oiled and heated on the stove top or in the oven for 15–20 minutes, wiped clean and finally coated with a little oil.

*Browning*: Refers to the colouring of foods during cooking. It is achieved by selecting the correct pan and the correct oil or fat, and finally by controlling the temperature during the cooking process.

*Turning*: Refers to the careful turning of food with the aid of a palette knife usually, on to the reverse side; this is done when the presentation side has been cooked to a nice golden brown.

*Tossing*: Refers to the turning of foods by wrist and hand, by flicking the pan so that the food is tossed in such a way that it jumps or turns over. A good example of this particular skill may be demonstrated in the preparation of pommes sautées (sautéed potatoes).

*Holding for service*: Is the keeping of food hot until required for service. With most shallow-fried items it is not an easy task, as they tend to lose much of the initial crispness if they are not served promptly.

# Equipment used for shallow frying

Equipment suitable for the various forms of shallow frying include: bratt pans and griddles, used mainly for large-scale cooking; frying-pans of various sizes (usually made of cast iron); omelette pans; oval frying-pans for fish; plats à sauter and general purpose pans; and woks, used in the preparation of oriental dishes.

# Self-assessment questions for shallow frying

1. What is the French term for shallow frying as a method of cookery?
2. How many methods are there of shallow frying?
3. What do we mean when we refer to the presentation side of a food item?
4. What quality of meats lend themselves to shallow frying as a method of food preparation? Can you give two examples?
5. Why is this particular method of cookery appropriate to an à la carte menu?
6. Can you give four general rules which will help in ensuring efficiency when shallow frying food items?
7. What is the correct method to adopt when placing items into hot pans (for shallow frying)?
8. Why is it important to serve shallow-fried items as quickly as possible?
9. What do we mean by the phrase *proving* or *seasoning* a new frying-pan?
10. Can you name at least four items of equipment suitable for the process of shallow frying?

When you have completed these questions check your answers with your fellow students and chef or lecturer.

# Hot butter sauces

## Introduction to hot butter sauces

These sauces are based on melted butter and are served with grilled or fried poultry, fish, meat, offal and vegetables in place of the traditional thickened sauces found in the boiling chapter.

| **Melted butter** | | *Beurre fondu* |
|---|---|---|
| 100 g | Butter | 250 g |
| ½ | Lemon, juice of | 1 |

1. Gently melt the butter, do not stir, allow the oil and water content to separate (the water and mineral element is known as whey).
2. Pour off the oil into a clean pan.
3. Add the lemon juice. Mix well each time before use.

| **Nut brown butter** | | *Beurre noisette* |
|---|---|---|
| 100 g | Butter | 250 g |
| ¼ | Lemon, juice of | 1 |

1. Gently melt the butter as for beurre fondu.
2. Add the butter oil to a hot frying-pan and cook to a golden brown.
3. Take the pan off the heat, pour in the lemon juice.
4. Stir each time before use.

# Shallow-fried egg dishes

## Introduction to shallow-fried eggs

Eggs may be cooked gently in shallow oil, bacon fat or lard until the whites are firm and the yolk is hot but still soft. They are served at breakfast on the English breakfast menu and are also served as part of the garnish for escalope de veau Holstein and with Vienna steaks. If the fat is too hot the egg white may be cooked and burnt at the edges before the yolk is hot.

| **Shallow-fried eggs** | *Oeufs frits* |
|---|---|

1. Gently heat clean oil, bacon fat or lard in a shallow pan.
2. When the fat or oil is heated, break in the eggs one at a time, frying gently until the whites are firm and the yolk is hot but still soft.
3. While cooking is in progress baste the yolk regularly with fat/oil in the pan.

4. When the egg is cooked remove from the pan using an egg slice, allow the egg to drain well and serve.

**Note:** Should a turned egg be required, this is the turning over of the egg when cooking is almost completed until the egg is well cooked and the yolk is firm.

## Scrambled eggs                                                *Oeufs brouillés*

These are eggs which have been beaten, seasoned and cooked over a gentle heat in a pan with the addition of milk and butter. The mixture should be cooked until firm but fluffy and moist. If the eggs are over-cooked, water and mineral salts will separate from the eggs, leaving them tough and rubbery.

Scrambled eggs may be served at breakfast, lunch and on the high tea menu.

Cooking time is dependent upon the volume being produced, but for 4–10 portions allow 5–12 minutes.

| | | |
|---|---|---|
| 8 | **Eggs** | 20 |
| ½ dl | **Milk** | 1 dl |
| 50 g | **Butter** | 100 g |
| | **Salt and white pepper** | |

For a richer tasting product substitute cream for milk.

1. Crack the eggs into a basin and season with the salt and white pepper; whisk vigorously, but do not make the mixture frothy.
2. Select a sauteuse of suitable size for the volume being produced and gently melt the butter.
3. While the butter is melting, mix the milk into the mixture; note that if you are using cream this goes in after cooking is completed.
4. When the pan is heated pour in the mixture and stir with a wooden spatula or spoon until the eggs have coagulated lightly.
5. Serve as soon as the eggs are cooked. Generally scrambled eggs are served on a slice of hot buttered toast with the crusts removed.

**Notes:**
1. Never make scrambled eggs in an aluminium pan as this will cause them to discolour during cooking, especially if a metal spoon or whisk is used in the pan during the cooking process.
2. If making really large quantities of scrambled eggs, use a pan sat in water (bain-marie). Because the cooking time is longer the risk of scorching is reduced as the eggs are not in direct contact with the heat.
3. When making small quantities, excellent scrambled eggs can be produced in the microwave. Again the cooking time is dependent upon the volume being produced and also the wattage output of your

microwave. For the method see the notes on microwave cookery.

**Scrambled eggs with smoked salmon**     *Oeufs brouillés aux*
*saumon fumé*

1. Allow two small thin slices of smoked salmon per portion.
2. Cook the scrambled eggs and a round slice of hot buttered toast.
3. Arrange the smoked salmon neatly at the side of the eggs, garnished with picked parsley.

# Omelettes

Omelettes are a mixture of eggs and milk with seasoning and additional garnish as required by specific recipes. They can be served as starters, entrées (before main course) or even as a main course.

1. Usually 2 to 3 eggs are used for each omelette, depending upon the size of eggs and which meal the omelette is for.
2. Omelettes may be served flat, folded or rolled cigar shape.
3. Garnishes are added to omelettes in one of three ways depending upon how it is served:

Flat      — The garnish is mixed in before cooking.
Rolled    — The omelette is split down the centre and the hot garnish
            is placed into the split.
Folded    — The garnish is placed in the middle of the omelette just before
            folding, or mixed into the egg before cooking.

4. Omelette pans should have good deep sides which are curved and have a good thick base. They must be kept only for making omelettes and when cleaned should only be wiped with a soft wet cloth in hot soapy water and then rinsed and dried. Never use any form of abrasive on the pan as this will scratch the surface and cause the omelette to stick.
5. New omelette pans need to be 'proved', which is a procedure to seal the surface of the pan and so help to stop the omelette from sticking. To prove an omelette pan, fill the pan approximately two-thirds full with salt and leave on a stove top or in a moderate oven for a good 3 hours. Remove the salt and wipe out the pan with an oily cloth. Re-heat on the stove top until the oil in the pan starts to smoke. Wipe out again with the oily cloth and store away until required for use.

*Degrees of cooking for omelettes*

When an omelette is ready to be served it should be moist and soft in texture. The centre of the omelette should be moist when eaten; this is known as 'baveuse'. The surface of the omelette should be firm and lightly coloured. To make sure that the customer gets the best quality omelette you must cook your omelette to order.

*Preparation of omelettes*                                                                          *Mis-en-place*

Before starting to make omelettes, make sure that you have the following materials: eggs, milk, butter, seasoning, mixing bowls, forks, proved omelette pans, service dishes, plates or flats, garnish, such as parsley.

## Basic omelette recipe

For one person allow 2–3 eggs, 15 g butter, tablespoon of milk.

1. Place your omelette pan on the stove to heat through.
2. Crack the eggs into a small bowl and mix with a fork or whisk.
3. Mix in the milk and seasoning.
4. Place the butter in the pan and allow to get as hot as possible without burning the butter.
5. Pour in the egg mixture and stir vigorously with the base of the fork, scraping around the sides to prevent sticking, and ensuring an even distribution of egg mixture. This action helps to make a light, fluffy omelette.
6. When the omelette has started to set and has coloured slightly on what is the surface, make sure the omelette is loose and then tilt the pan and tap the base on the edge of the stove to move the omelette into a position that will allow you to finish the omelette as required; turned out flat, rolled or folded. If turned out flat, remember to serve the coloured side uppermost.

**Note**: All ingredients given for the following omelette recipes are for 4 and 10 portions.

## Spanish omelette                                                     *Omelette espagnole*

| | | |
|---|---|---|
| 8 | Eggs | 20 |
| 100 g | Julienne of red peppers | 250 g |
| 8 | Anchovy fillets | 20 |
| 60 g | Butter | 150 g |
| 100 g | Tomato concassé | 250 g |
| 8 | Black stoned olives | 8 |
| 100 g | Sweated sliced almonds | 250 g |
| 4 tablespoons | Milk | 10 tablespoons |
| | Finely chopped parsley | |
| | Seasoning | |

1. The garnish is mixed with the eggs before cooking.
2. Serve flat with coloured side uppermost.

## Bacon and cheese omelette

*Omelette lorraine*

| | | |
|---|---|---|
| 8 | Eggs | 20 |
| 4 tablespoons | Milk | 10 tablespoons |
| | Seasoning | |
| 60 g | Butter | 150 g |
| 50 g | Brunoise of grilled bacon | 125 g |
| 50 g | Grated Gruyère cheese | 125 g |
| | Finely chopped chives | |

1. Heat the bacon in the omelette pan.
2. Add the egg mixture with the chives.
3. When the omelette is almost ready for folding, add the grated Gruyère and allow the cheese to commence melting.
4. Fold and serve.

## Omelette Arnold Bennett

| | | |
|---|---|---|
| 8 | Eggs | 20 |
| 4 tablespoons | Milk | 10 tablespoons |
| | Seasoning | |
| 60 g | Butter | 150 g |
| 2½ dl | Cheese sauce | 6 dl |
| 100 g | Cooked and flaked smoked haddock mixed with a small amount of double cream | |
| 50 g | Grated cheese | 125 g |

1. Prepare the omelette as for basic recipe.
2. Roll the omelette when ready to serve.
3. Split the omelette and fill the split with hot smoked haddock mixture.
4. Sprinkle with grated cheese and gratinate under a salamander.
5. Transfer to a service dish and surround with a cordon of cheese sauce.
6. Finish with finely chopped parsley.

## Soufflé omelette

*Omelette soufflée*

| | | |
|---|---|---|
| 8 | Eggs | 20 |
| 60 g | Butter | 150 g |
| 60 g | Castor sugar | 150 g |
| | Pinch of salt | |

1. Separate the egg yolks and whites.
2. Beat the yolk in one bowl.
3. Beat the whites in another bowl and fold in the sugar and salt.
4. Fold the whites into the yolks.
5. Pour the mixture into the hot omelette pan.
6. To cook, place in a hot oven or in the bottom of a salamander.
7. Fold in half to serve.

| **Jam omelette** | | *Omelette à la confiture* |
|---|---|---|
| 8 | Eggs | 20 |
| 120 g | Strawberry or raspberry jam | 300 g |
| 60 g | Butter | 150 g |
| 4 tablespoons | Milk | 10 tablespoons |
| 120 g | Castor sugar | 300 g |

1. Prepare omelette as for basic recipe; do not season.
2. When ready to serve, fill the centre with hot jam.
3. Fold in half and sprinkle with castor sugar.
4. Using a red branding iron, make a simple cross pattern on top of the omelette.
5. Transfer to a service dish and serve straight away.

# Pancake preparation

(**Note:** For pancake batter, see page 37)
If possible, use a special cast-iron crêpe pan which has been well seasoned. Do not wash the pan after using, but wipe round with some absorbent kitchen paper. Make the pancakes as follows:

1. Heat the pan, and add a small amount of clarified butter—just enough to cover the base of the pan. Pour off any surplus.
2. Add sufficient batter to cover the base of the pan thinly.
3. Tilt the pan to allow the batter to flow easily.
4. As soon as the edges of the pancake take on a little colour, turn it with a palette knife, or toss it over, and cook the underside.
5. Slide out on to a sugar-dusted greaseproof paper, and stack one on top of the other.
6. Use as required.

**Note:** Naturally, savoury pancakes will not have any sugar dusting!

**Lemon pancakes** *Crêpes au citron*

1. Make pancakes and dust with sugar.
2. Fold three-corner shape.
3. Serve on a hot dish garnished with a prepared lemon wedge.

**Orange pancakes** *Crêpes à l'orange*

As above but using orange wedges.

**Jam pancakes** *Crêpes au confiture*

1. Spread each pancake with hot jam and roll up.

2. Trim the ends and dust with castor sugar.
3. They can also be folded three-corner ways.

# Shallow-fried fish dishes

### Introduction to shallow-fried fish dishes

This method of cookery is suitable for small whole fish, such as trout, mackerel and sardines; for fillets of fish, like plaice and sole; for other cuts of fish, such as cod, halibut, turbot and for shellfish like scampi and prawns.

The term meunière on the menu denotes a shallow-fried fish dish served with nut brown butter, lemon slice and parsley.

**Basic preparation for shallow frying fish**

For specific weights of fish see individual recipes.
Allow 25 g of butter per person for beurre noisette.

1. For small whole fish (except sardines, which should be left whole), cut and trim the fins, remove the gills and blood running down the spine. Rinse well under cold running water. Remove any scales by scraping gently from the tail to the head using the back of a small knife. Rinse and dry before cooking.
2. For cuts of fish, trim all cuts as required for service before cooking, removing all possible bones. The remaining bones should be removed before serving.

**Basic meunière recipe**

1. Pass the prepared fish through seasoned flour and shake to remove all excess flour.
2. Heat a frying or sauté pan and add a little oil or butter or a mixture of the two.
3. Add the fish to the pan and fry on the presentation side first.
4. When a light golden brown in colour, use a palette knife to turn over the fish and cook on the other side to a light golden brown.
5. When cooked, remove the fish from the pan and place on to a hot service dish.
6. Peel a whole lemon, removing all skin and pith, slice the lemon into discs and allow one disc per portion of fish.
7. Place a disc of lemon on the fish and squeeze a little juice on to the fish.
8. Melt 25 g of butter in a small clean frying-pan, heat until a light brown colour and finish with lemon juice (*see* beurre noisette).
9. Nap the beurre noisette over the full length of the fish.
10. Sprinkle liberally with finely chopped parsley and serve.

## Shallow-fried fish with almonds     *Poisson amandine*

1. Follow the method for basic meunière recipe.
2. Add 15 g of flaked almonds to the beurre noisette just as it starts to go brown.

Menu example: Truite meunière amandines.

## Fish belle-meunière     *Poisson belle-meunière*

1. As for the basic meunière method with the addition of the following garnish per person.

| | | |
|---|---|---|
| 1 | Large mushroom, grilled | |
| ¼ | Segment of peeled tomato without pips | |
| 1 | Soft herring roe, passed through seasoned flour and shallow fried | |

2. Arrange the garnish down one side of the fish on the hot service flat.

Menu example: filet de plie belle-meunière.

## Stuffed squid     *Calamari ripieni*

| | | |
|---|---|---|
| 8 | Squid | 20 |
| 20 g | Fresh white breadcrumbs | 60 g |
| 10 g | Chopped parsley | 25 g |
| 20 g | Grated parmesan | 50 g |
| 2 | Crushed garlic cloves | 5 |
| 1 | Beaten egg | 3 |
| ½ dl | Olive oil | 1 dl |
| | Cayenne pepper to taste | |
| | Salt and pepper to taste | |
| 4 | Whole cloves of garlic | 10 |
| 250 g | Tomato concassé | 600 g |
| 6 g | Dried rosemary | 20 g |
| ½ dl | Dry white wine | 1½ dl |

1. Clean out the squid and chop the tentacles and place into a bowl.
2. Add the breadcrumbs, parsley, cheese, egg, cayenne, a little olive oil and half the crushed garlic.
3. Season and mix well; spoon mixture into the squid and truss the end of the squid to prevent the stuffing falling out.
4. Heat the remaining olive oil in a large sauté pan, add the whole garlic cloves, sauté for 5 minutes.
5. Remove the garlic and add the squid, sauté until light brown on all sides.
6. Stir in the tomato concassé and remaining crushed garlic.
7. Add the remaining ingredients, reduce the heat to a simmer and cook for 25–30 minutes.
8. Place the squid into a hot service dish and remove the string.
9. Slice and arrange neatly, nap with the sauce and serve.

## Scampi in tomato and onion sauce

*Scampi provençale*

| | | |
|---|---|---|
| 500 g | Shelled scampi | 1250 g |
| 1 | Crushed clove of garlic | 2½ |
| 250 g | Tomato concassé | 600 g |
| 1 dl | Tomato sauce | 2½ dl |
| | Chopped parsley | |
| ½ dl | Dry white wine | 1¼ dl |
| ½ dl | Olive oil | 1 dl |
| | Salt and milled pepper | |
| | Seasoned flour | |
| 200 g | Rice pilaff | 500 g |

1. Put the scampi through the seasoned flour and shake off any excess.
2. Select a sauteuse of suitable size and add two-thirds of the oil.
3. Heat until the oil reaches smoking-point, then add the scampi and shallow fry to a light golden brown. Stir and toss throughout cooking to prevent sticking.
4. Drain the scampi.
5. Add the last third of the oil to the sauteuse, add the garlic and sweat for 2–3 minutes.
6. Drain off the excess oil and add the tomato concassé.
7. Simmer for 6–8 minutes.
8. Pour in the dry white wine and simmer until reduced by half.
9. Add the tomato sauce and simmer, season and add the parsley.
10. Add the scampi to the pan and simmer for 4–5 minutes.
11. Serve in a hot entrée dish accompanied with rice pilaff moulded in dariole moulds.

## Frogs legs

*Cuissses de grenouilles*
*Cuisses de nymphes*

Allow 4 legs per person for a starter, 8 for a main course. Quantities given below are for starters, and should be doubled for a main course.

## Frogs legs with herbs

*Cuisses de grenouilles aux fines herbes*

| | | |
|---|---|---|
| 50 g | Brunoise of shallots | 125 g |
| 1 teaspoon | Finely chopped parsley | 1 tablespoon |
| ½ | Fresh lemon, juice of | 1 |
| 1 dl | Beurre noisette | 2 dl |
| | Salt and milled pepper | |
| 50 g | Butter | 100 g |

1. Season the frogs legs.
2. Select a sauteuse of suitable size and add the butter.
3. Heat the pan and add the brunoise of shallots, sweat without colour.
4. Add the frogs legs and sweat for 6–10 minutes, until tender.
5. Add the lemon juice and place on to a hot service dish.
6. Nap with beurre noisette and serve.

350

# Shallow-fried meat dishes    *Viande sauté*

### Introduction to shallow-fried meat dishes

Only best quality meat is suitable for shallow frying as it is a quick method of cookery and so does not allow time for the breakdown of tough connective tissue in meat. The following recipes are popular examples of dishes and meats suitable for shallow frying.

### Shallow-fried steaks

**Sirloin steaks with red wine sauce**     *Entrecôte bordelaise*

| | | |
|---|---|---|
| 4 × 200 g | Sirloin steaks | 10 × 200 g |
| 50 g | Butter | 125 g |
| 1 dl | Red wine | 2½ dl |
| 2½ dl | Bordelaise sauce | 6 dl |
| 100 g | Bone marrow | 250 g |
| | Chopped parsley | |

1. Select a sauté pan of suitable size and heat the butter.
2. Trim the steaks of any excess fat, season both sides and seal quickly on both sides in the sauté pan.
3. Cook the steaks to the required degree and dress on hot service flats.
4. Drain off the fat from the pan and swill out (déglace) with the red wine, simmering until reduced by half.
5. Pour in the bordelaise sauce, bring to the boil and adjust the seasoning.
6. Slice the bone marrow into ½ cm slices and poach in a small amount of stock for 1–2 minutes.
7. Set 2 pieces of marrow on each steak.
8. Nap the steaks with the sauce, sprinkle liberally with chopped parsley and serve.

**Sirloin steaks with chasseur sauce**     *Entrecôte chasseur*

| | | |
|---|---|---|
| 4 × 200 g | Sirloin steaks | 10 × 200 g |
| 50 g | Butter or margarine | 125 g |
| 1 dl | Dry white wine | 2 dl |
| 2½ dl | Chasseur sauce | 6 dl |
| | Finely chopped parsley | |

1. Trim the steaks of any excess fat.
2. Select a sauté pan of suitable size and heat the butter or margarine.
3. Season the steaks and seal quickly on both sides.
4. Cook to a golden brown colour on the surface and to the required degree inside.
5. Remove the steak from the pan when ready and place on one side to drain.

351

6. Swill out (déglace) the sauté pan with dry white wine and simmer until reduced by half its volume.
7. Add the chasseur sauce, bring to the boil and simmer for 3–4 minutes.
8. Adjust the seasoning.
9. Arrange the steaks neatly on a hot service flat and nap with the chasseur sauce.
10. Sprinkle liberally with finely chopped parsley and serve.

**Note:** Shallow-fried steaks may also be garnished as for mixed grill or grilled steaks.

## Beef stroganoff  *Sauté de boeuf stroganoff*

| | | |
|---|---|---|
| 400 g | Tail of beef fillet | 1 kg |
| 50 g | Butter | 100 g |
| 30 g | Brunoise of shallots | 75 g |
| 1½ dl | Double cream | 3½ dl |
| ¼ | Fresh lemon, juice of | ¾ |

1. Prepare the beef by cutting into 1 cm long strips.
2. Select a suitable sized sauteuse and heat the butter.
3. Add the beef, season and cook over a fierce heat for a few seconds, allow to brown lightly but not cook through.
4. Drain the beef in a colander over a bowl.
5. Pour the butter back into the sauteuse, add the shallots and sweat gently until tender.
6. Drain off the butter and pour in the cream.
7. Simmer until the cream has reduced by a third.
8. Add the beef and lemon juice, do not allow the cream to re-boil.
9. Adjust the seasoning as required and serve in a hot service dish.

**Note:** This dish is usually served with plain boiled rice, allowing 30 g (uncooked weight) of long grain rice per portion.

## Lamb dishes

## Breaded cutlets reform  *Cotelette d'agneau réforme*

| | | |
|---|---|---|
| 8 | Lamb cutlets | 20 |
| | Plain flour | |
| | Eggwash | |
| | Breadcrumbs | |
| 30 g | Brunoise of cooked ham | 75 g |
| | Finely chopped parsley | |
| 1 dl | Oil | 3 dl |
| 2½ dl | Reform sauce | 6 dl |
| 60 g | Nut brown butter | 150 g |
| | Watercress | |

1. Mix the finely chopped parsley and brunoise of cooked ham with the breadcrumbs.
2. Proceed to prepare the cutlets by battening out lightly and trimming to remove excess fat.
3. Pass through the seasoned flour, eggwash and breadcrumbs.
4. Re-shape and mark criss-cross patterned using the edge of a palette knife.
5. Select a sauté or frying-pan of suitable size and heat the oil.
6. Shallow fry the cutlets in the oil until golden brown on both sides, 8-10 minutes.
7. Serve on a hot service flat, napped with the nut brown butter.
8. Nap the cutlets with reform sauce and garnish with watercress.
9. Serve accompanied with a sauce-boat of reform sauce.

### Lamb cutlets maintenon                    *Cotelettes d'agneau maintenon*

| | | |
|---|---|---|
| 8 | **Lamb cutlets** | 20 |
| 40 g | **Butter** | 100 g |
| 1½ dl | **Thick sauce soubise** | 3 dl |
| 50 g | **Sieved breadcrumbs** | 125 g |
| 40 g | **Clarified butter** | 100 g |
| 60 g | **Beurre noisette** | 150 g |
| 2½ dl | **Sauce perigueux** | 6 dl |
| | **Picked parsley** | |

1. Select a sauté pan of suitable size and melt the butter.
2. Season the cutlets and seal on one side only.
3. Drain and place on to a lightly buttered tray with the sealed side uppermost.
4. Place a small amount of the thick soubise on to the sealed surface and dome slightly using a palette knife.
5. Sprinkle with the breadcrumbs and melted butter.
6. Place the trays into a pre-heated oven at 190–200°C for 8 minutes to finish cooking.
7. Arrange the cutlets neatly on hot service dishes.
8. Nap the cutlets with the beurre noisette and serve garnished with picked parsley and accompanied with a sauce-boat of sauce perigueux.

### Plain fried cutlets                       *Cotelette d'agneau sauté*

| | | |
|---|---|---|
| 8 | **Lamb cutlets** | 20 |
| 25 g | **Dripping** | 60 g |

1. Select a sauté or frying-pan of suitable size and melt the dripping.
2. Season the lamb and gently fry on both sides to a golden brown.
3. Dress on a hot service dish and garnish with either of the following garnishes.

## Clamart garnish

*Cotelette d'agneaù clamart*

| | | |
|---|---|---|
| 4 | Artichoke bottoms | 10 |
| 50 g | Cooked peas | 100 g |
| 8 | Cocotte potatoes | 20 |

Fill the artichoke bottoms with the cooked peas and arrange cocotte potatoes in small bundles. Arrange the garnish neatly around the service flat.

## Dubarry garnish

*Cotelette d'agneau Dubarry*

| | | |
|---|---|---|
| 8 | Château potatoes | 20 |
| 4 | Cauliflower balls, glazed | 10 |
| 2½ dl | Mornay sauce | 6 dl |

Coat the balls of cauliflower with the mornay sauce and neatly arrange the cauliflower and château potatoes around the hot service flat.

**Note:** Shallow-fried lamb cutlets may also be garnished as for mixed grill, with tomatoes, pommes paillées, watercress and mushrooms.

## Sauté of kidneys turbigo

*Rognons sautés turbigo*

| | | |
|---|---|---|
| 8 | Lamb's kidneys | 20 |
| 8 | Chipolatas | 20 |
| 8 | Button mushrooms | 20 |
| 50 g | Butter | 125 g |
| ½ dl | Dry white wine | 1 dl |
| 2 dl | Demi-glace | 5 dl |
| 4 | Heart-shaped croûtons | 10 |
| | Finely chopped parsley | |

1. Lightly grill or shallow fry the chipolatas in a little butter.
2. Shallow fry the button mushrooms with a little butter and keep warm.
3. Skin the kidneys, cut in half and remove the core.
4. Season the kidneys and sauté, leaving them slightly underdone, and drain in a colander.
5. Drain excess fat from the frying-pan, swill out with the white wine and simmer until it reduces by half its volume.
6. Add the demi-glace and simmer until the sauce has reduced to the required consistency.
7. Strain the sauce through a fine chinois on to the kidneys, chipolatas and mushrooms; simmer but do not allow to boil.
8. Serve in a hot dish with heart-shaped croûtons and sprinkle liberally with finely chopped parsley.

## Pork dishes

### Pork chop Flemish style      *Cotelette de porc flamande*

| | | |
|---|---|---|
| 4 × 200 g | Pork chops | 10 × 200 g |
| 4 | Apple rings | 10 |
| 4 | Soaked and stoned prunes | 10 |
| 60 g | Clarified butter | 150 g |
| | Salt and milled pepper | |
| ½ dl | Oil | 1 dl |
| | Beurre noisette | |

1. Trim the pork chops, removing the rind and excess fat and pass through seasoned flour.
2. Heat the oil and butter in a suitable sauté pan, sauté the pork chops, allow to colour to a light golden brown.
3. Sit the apple rings and prunes on top of the chops, brush with a little oil and butter and finish by sitting in an earthenware service dish and placing in a hot oven until the apple is cooked. Serve garnished with a little watercress.

**Note**: Shallow-fried pork chops may also be served with a mixed grill garnish.

### Escalope of pork Holstein      *Escalope de porc Holstein*

| | | |
|---|---|---|
| 4 | Pork escalopes | 10 |
| 4 | Eggs | 10 |
| | Pané à l'anglaise | |
| 4 | Anchovy fillets | 10 |
| 120 g | Beurre noisette | 300 g |
| 10 g | Capers | 25 g |
| | Finely chopped parsley | |
| 1 dl | Oil | 2 dl |

1. Pané (flour, eggwash and breadcrumbs) the pork escalope.
2. Heat the oil in a suitable size sauté pan and shallow fry the escalopes to a light golden brown.
3. Drain and place on a hot service flat.
4. Nap with beurre noisette.
5. Shallow fry the egg and sit on the escalope.
6. Garnish with a cross of anchovy fillets and sprinkle with heated capers.
7. Sprinkle with finely chopped parsley and serve.

## Chicken dishes

### Preparation of chicken cut for sauté

Remove the legs by cutting the skin where the leg joins the body. Cut to the ball and socket joint, force the leg out, cut the joint, and gently pull off the leg. The legs are then divided into two pieces: the drumstick (pilon) and the thigh (gras de cuisse). On the gras de cuisse, the knuckle is trimmed from each end of the bone. Remove the knuckle end of the pilon and reshape the meat over the area where the bone has been removed. Remove the two small wings, then separate the breast from the carcass and cut across into two. Finally, the two winglets (ailerons) are trimmed at each end to facilitate removal of the bones when cooked.

## Sauté of chicken                                    Poulet sauté

| | | |
|---|---|---|
| 1 | Chicken, about 1½ kg (cut for sauté) | 3 |
| | Seasoning (salt and pepper) | |
| 60 g | Clarified butter | 180 g |
| 285 ml | Jus lié or demi-glace | 850 ml |

1. Choose a shallow heavy pan (sauté pan) which is large enough to hold the chicken pieces on the bottom.
2. Add the butter to the pan and place on a fairly hot stove.
3. Season the pieces of chicken and colour lightly, turning over from time to time.
4. Cover with a lid and place in a hot oven until tender.
5. The white meat will be cooked first; this should be removed after a few minutes and kept warm. The darker meat will take a little longer.
6. When all the pieces are cooked and removed from the pan, drain off the fat.
7. Add the jus lié or demi-glace and simmer for about 5 minutes.
8. Arrange the chicken portions in a suitable shallow dish.
9. Check the seasoning and skim the sauce before passing through a fine strainer.
10. Carefully pour the sauce over the chicken pieces and sprinkle with chopped parsley.

**Note:** In the following recipes, where a final cooking is called for, it should consist merely of five minutes gentle simmering, to acquire the flavour of the garnish and sauce.

## Chicken chasseur                               *Poulet sauté chasseur*

| | | |
|---|---|---|
| 4 | Portions of sautéed chicken | 10 |
| 4 dl | Demi-glace | 1 litre |
| 1 dl | Dry white wine | 2½ dl |
| 100 g | Sliced button mushrooms | 250 g |
| 100 g | Concassé of tomato | 250 g |
| 60 g | Brunoise of shallots | 150 g |
| | Finely chopped parsley | |
| | Finely chopped tarragon | |
| | Salt and milled pepper | |

1. Proceed as for basic recipe to stage 6.
2. Add the brunoise of shallots and mushrooms, sweat without colour.
3. Add the wine and reduce by two-thirds.
4. Add the demi-glace, tarragon, parsley and tomato concassé.
5. Simmer for 10–15 minutes and then pour over the chicken.
6. Serve sprinkled with finely chopped parsley.

### Chicken Maryland                                   *Suprême de volaille*

| | | |
|---|---|---|
| 4 | Chicken suprêmes | 10 |
| 4 | Sweetcorn cakes | 10 |
| 4 | Halves of panéd banana | 10 |
| 4 | Bacon rolls | 10 |
| 4 | Tomatoes | 10 |
| ½ bunch | Watercress | 1 bunch |
| 3 dl | Horseradish sauce (hot or cold) | 5 dl |
| | Flour, eggwash and breadcrumbs | |
| 1 dl | Beurre noisette | 2½ dl |
| 1 dl | Oil or butter | 2½ dl |

1. Pané the suprêmes (flour, eggwash and breadcrumbs).
2. Heat the oil or butter in a sauté pan and shallow fry the suprêmes to a light golden brown colour on both sides.
3. Shallow fry the sweetcorn cakes, deep fry the banana, grill the bacon and tomato.
4. Nap the suprêmes with beurre noisette and arrange the suprêmes neatly on a hot service flat.
5. Arrange the garnish neatly around the suprêmes and serve the sauce in a sauce-boat.

# Shallow-fried vegetable dishes           *Légumes sautés*

## Introduction to shallow-fried vegetable dishes

Few vegetables lend themselves to shallow frying as a method of cooking, and most vegetables which are shallow fried only use shallow frying as a method of re-heating or finishing the dish. The following examples are common dishes found on restaurant menus.

### Macaire potatoes                                   *Pommes Macaire*

| | | |
|---|---|---|
| 500 g | Baked jacket potatoes | 1¼ kg |
| 25 g | Butter | 60 g |
| | Salt | |
| | Milled pepper | |
| | Plain flour | |
| 50 g | Oil or dripping | 125 g |
| | Picked parsley | |

1. Scoop out the flesh from the potatoes and place into a basin.
2. Season and add the butter, mixing in lightly with a fork.
3. Divide the mixture into pieces, allowing 2 pieces for a portion.
4. Using a little flour and a palette knife, mould the potato pieces into small round cakes.
5. Flour lightly.
6. Heat a little oil or dripping in a frying-pan or sauté pan and shallow fry on both sides in very hot fat.
7. Serve on a hot dish, garnished with picked parsley.

### Potatoes Byron                                    *Pommes Byron*

| 50 g | Grated Gruyère cheese | 125 g |
|------|-----------------------|-------|
| 1 dl | Single cream | 2½ dl |
|      | Baked jacket potatoes | |

1. Prepare and cook the potatoes as for Macaire.
2. Using the back of a small spoon make a shallow depression in each potato.
3. Place a little grated cheese in the centre of each potato and pour a little cream over each little pieces of cheese.
4. Brown lightly under the salamander and serve on a hot service dish.

### Sauté potatoes                                    *Pommes sautées*

| 400 g | Steamed jacket potatoes | 1 kg |
|-------|-------------------------|------|
| 80 g | Oil or dripping | 200 g |
| 25 g | Butter | 60 g |
|      | Finely chopped parsley | |

1. Peel and slice the cooked potatoes, into 3–4 mm thick slices.
2. Heat the oil or dripping in a frying-pan or sauté pan with the butter.
3. Season the potato slices and shallow fry in the hot pan until a golden brown colour, tossing occasionally to ensure even colouring of the potatoes.
4. Drain on kitchen paper and serve in a hot service dish sprinkled liberally with finely chopped parsley.

### Sauté potatoes with onions                        *Pommes lyonnaise*

| 300 g | Steamed jacket potatoes | 750 g |
|-------|-------------------------|-------|
| 100 g | Sliced onions | 250 g |
| 80 g | Oil or dripping | 200 g |
| 25 g | Butter | 60 g |
|      | Finely chopped parsley | |

1. Proceed as for sauté potatoes.
2. Shallow fry the sliced onions to a golden brown in a separate pan.
3. When the potatoes and the onions are cooked to a golden brown, gently

toss together, season and serve in a hot service dish sprinkled liberally with finely chopped parsley.

## Shallow-fried vegetables

Pre-cooked and refreshed vegetables are often re-heated (re-chauffed) by shallow frying in clarified butter. Classic examples of this include vegetables such as mangetout, haricots verts, spinach, baby sweetcorn, broccoli heads and sprouts. They are commonly garnished with toasted flaked almonds or julienne (thin slice) of potato. Increasingly popular is a selection of shallow-fried raw vegetables adopted from Chinese cookery known as stir fry. An example would be as follows.

## Stir fry vegetables

| | | |
|---|---|---|
| 100 g | **Fresh beansprouts** | 250 g |
| 100 g | **Broccoli florets** | 250 g |
| 100 g | **Macédoine of carrot** | 250 g |
| 100 g | **Cauliflower florets** | 250 g |
| 100 g | **Bâtons of celery** | 250 g |
| 100 g | **Sliced white button mushrooms** | 250 g |
| 50 g | **Strips of green pimento** | 125 g |
| 50 g | **Strips of red pimento** | 125 g |
| 50 g | **Diced French beans** | 125 g |
| 1 dl | **Olive or sunflower oil** | 2 dl |
| | **Fresh milled pepper** | |
| 5 g | **Ground ginger** | 10 g |
| | **Soy sauce** | |

1. Wash all the prepared vegetables and drain well.
2. Heat the oil in a wok or frying-pan and pour in the prepared vegetables. Stir thoroughly for a full 3 minutes.
3. Add the ginger and cook for a further minute, stirring all the time.
4. Season and add soy sauce to taste.
5. Serve in a hot dish straight away.

## Shallow-fried sweetcorn cakes
*Galettes de maïs sautées*

| | | |
|---|---|---|
| 200 g | **Boiled sweetcorn niblets** | 500 g |
| 2 | **Beaten eggs** | 4–5 |
| 26 g | **Plain flour** | 65 g |
| 1 dl | **Oil** | 2½ dl |

1. Mix the egg, flour and corn to a firm mixture.
2. Season lightly.
3. Heat the oil in a shallow frying-pan and drop small amounts of the mixture into the pan.
4. Lightly press to form a cake and shallow fry to a light brown on both sides.
5. Serve as required as a vegetable or as part of a garnish, such as with chicken Maryland.

# Shallow-fried savouries

As with all savouries, they are used in many ways. The examples given here are commonly used as snacks in their own right or on buffet and high tea menus.

| **Ham and cheese savoury** | | *Croque monsieur* |
|---|---|---|
| 4 | Slices of ham | 10 |
| 8 | Slices of Gruyère cheese | 20 |
| 8 | Slices of hot toast | 20 |
| 50 g | Clarified butter | 100 g |

1. Sandwich one slice of ham between two slices of Gruyère cheese.
2. Place this filling between two slices of hot toast.
3. Select a large round cutter, to fit the slice of toast, and cut out into discs.
4. Heat a sauté pan and add the clarified butter.
5. Gently fry the croque monsieur on both sides to melt the cheese.
6. Serve on a hot flat with a dish paper and picked parsley or straight on to a hot plate with picked parsley.

### Scotch woodcock

| 4 | Eggs | 10 |
|---|---|---|
| 8 | Anchovy fillets | 20 |
| 16 | Capers | 40 |
| 40 g | Butter | 100 g |
| 4 | Slices of toast | 10 |
| | Salt and pepper | |

1. Cut the toast into 4 discs and butter them.
2. Beat the eggs in a basin and season.
3. Melt the remaining butter in a sauteuse and pour in the beaten eggs.
4. Stir over a gentle heat until scrambled.
5. Dome the lightly scrambled eggs on a disc of toast and garnish with a cross of anchovy fillets and 4 capers on each slice.
6. Serve on a hot plate with a garnish of picked parsley.

# Chapter 13
# Deep Fat Frying                    *Frire*

## The competency defined

Deep fat frying is the cooking of foods by total submersion in pre-heated fat or oil.

## Purpose of deep fat frying

The purpose of deep fat frying is to give the food both colour and flavour, and to make it crisp and palatable, whilst providing variety for the diet.

## Methods of deep fat frying

### 1. Blanching

This is partial cooking of foods, and is usually applied to potatoes in the form of chips.

The reason for blanching is to allow the pre-cooking of potatoes in advance—they are softened without being browned. As a mise-en-place item, they can be finished to order (very quickly by frying to a crisp golden brown).

The blanching process is performed at a temperature of approximately 149°C (300°C).

### 2. Deep frying

Deep fat frying is performed at a temperature of about 175°–190°C (350°–375°F). With the exception of potatoes, all foods require a protective coating before they can be deep fried. The reasons for this are as follows:

(a) To protect the surface of foods from the intense heat of the fat or oil.
(b) To prevent the escape of liquids and nutrients from the foods.
(c) To adjust the speed of the penetration of heat from the fat or oil.

The following coatings can be used:

(a) Milk and flour: the starch cells in the flour burst, and the gluten sets when cooked.

(b) Flour, egg and breadcrumbs (pané à l'anglaise): the egg sets on the application of heat, and absorbs and holds the breadcrumbs. The result of correct frying is a nice crisp coating.

(c) Batter: similar to that of flour and milk.

(d) Pastry: such as rissoles (a savoury minced meat enveloped in puff pastry)—the filling is contained within the pastry covering whilst the puff paste expands and is cooked to a nice crisp golden brown.

All foods which are being cooked for service by the deep fat frying method are placed into pre-heated fat or oil and fried until a deep golden brown colour and crisp in surface texture. The item(s) should be well drained and served on a dish paper. Any accompanying sauce should be served separately in a sauce-boat. To achieve a satisfactory standard, deep-fried foods must be cooked to order and served immediately. Otherwise, items will quickly lose their desired crispness and be limp when consumed.

# Organisation and preparation for deep fat frying

In the traditional partie system the following personnel would be involved in the process of deep fat frying:

| | |
|---|---|
| *Chef rôtisseur*: | Deep fried fish, vegetables and potatoes, and also most savouries. |
| *Chef pâtissier*: | Pastry items, e.g. beignets (fritters) and yeast goods (doughnuts). |

For fast and efficient service, food to be deep fried would be prepared prior to the commencement of service on a mise-en-place basis. As stated, potatoes for chips would be blanched. Foods such as whole sole or fillets and croquette potatoes would be coated with their protective coating, such as flour, egg and fresh breadcrumbs (pané à l'anglaise).

## Advantages of deep fat frying

The four main advantages of deep fat frying are as follows:

1. Foods suitable for deep fat frying are cooked quickly and are easily handled at the time of service.
2. The wide variety of protective coatings available means that a good selection of foods can be deep fried.

3. Blanching (of potatoes) allows the item to be held in a partially prepared state prior to service, with a subsequent reduction in the time taken to finish and present the dish for service.
4. Foods which have been coated are sealed very quickly, thus protecting the food from absorbing excess fat or oil, or from losing natural moisture.

# Degrees of cooking

For successful deep fat frying, it is essential to maintain the right temperature.

Continuous cooking of foods, especially at service time, causes a drop in the temperature of the fat or oil. Therefore, time must be allowed for the fat to reach the required degree of heat before placing the next batch of food into the deep fat fryer. If the fat or oil is not up to the correct temperature, the food will absorb excess frying medium (oil or fat), and there is a strong possibility of the item(s) breaking up and so discolouring the frying medium.

When cooking larger pieces of food, the heat should be slightly lower to give the food time to cook thoroughly.

Cooking times vary according to the size and density of the foods being cooked.

### Guide to frying temperatures

| | | |
|---|---|---|
| Chips (blanched) | 149°C | (300°F) |
| Chips (fry off) | 188°C | (370°F) |
| Fish (crumbed or battered) | 175°C | (345°F) |
| Chicken pieces | 175°C | (345°F) |
| Doughnuts | 188°C | (370°F) |
| Fritters | 180°C | (350°F) |
| Choux paste (beignets soufflés) | 170°C | (338°F) |

### Table of fats and oils

| | Smoke point | Flash point |
|---|---|---|
| Beef dripping | 163°C (325°F) | 302°C (575°F) |
| Lard | 221°C (430°F) | 324°C (615°F) |
| Palm | 218°C (424°F) | 321°C (610°F) |
| Vegetable | 218°C (424°F) | 321°C (610°F) |
| *Liquid oils:* | | |
| Groundnut | 238°C (460°F) | 325°C (617°F) |
| Rapeseed | 218°C (424°F) | 320°C (610°F) |
| Corn | 218°C (424°F) | 320°C (610°F) |
| Cottonseed | 238°C (460°F) | 325°C (617°F) |
| Soyabean | 230°C (446°F) | 320°C (608°F) |

# Effects of deep fat frying on foods

When food is deep fried the surface of the food is first sealed by the coagulation of the protein with a small amount of fat absorption.

This leaves the interior of the food in a raw state at first, unless it is already cooked and only needs to be re-heated (réchauffer).

Foods which are not protected by an outer coating will absorb more fat, so affecting the texture of the food and the nutritional value.

Once the high temperature has sealed the surface of the food being deep fried, the liquid inside the food becomes steam as it is heated and this acts upon the solids in the food as a cooking agent.

Foods which have been coated only with flour should never be allowed to stand for any length of time prior to service, as the flour will absorb water from the exterior of the item, resulting in an inferior product. If the flour should become moist it must be washed off and the food dried, and then re-coated with flour immediately before cooking.

# General rules for efficient deep fat frying

1. Clean fat or oil must be used and always strained after use.
2. All items of food should be coated with a protective coating of flour, egg and breadcrumbs or frying batter. The exception is potatoes which do not require a protective coating.
3. Potatoes for deep fat frying should always be dried thoroughly on a clean kitchen cloth before plunging into fat or oil.
4. Fill the fryer to about the half-way mark, and never more than two-thirds deep.
5. Never overfill the fryer with food at any one time. It will result in undue loss of frying temperature.
6. The fat or oil must always be hot enough to seal the exterior of food being fried. The few exceptions are such items as pommes dauphine which require a temperature of about 177°C (338°F). The latter temperature allows for expansion of the food whilst cooking. Choux paste fritters (beignets soufflés) are another example.
7. An orderly system of preparation is essential for a high standard of cooking and service to be achieved.
8. The standard range of deep frying temperatures are between 177°C and 193°C (350°–380°F). For the best results these temperatures are crucial.
9. Always allow time for the fat or oil to recover heat between cooking batches of food.
10. Always remember to turn down the heat on the fryer when not in immediate use, such as during quiet periods of service.
11. Always cover the fryer when not in use to prevent oxidisation.
12. Never try to hold deep-fried foods for too long at point of service; they

will lose their crispness and develop a moist, soggy (and unappetising) texture.

13. Deep-fried foods which are coated in batter should be placed directly into the fryer—without a basket since the batter will stick to the frying basket frame, and make it difficult to remove the item(s) without spoiling the appearance of the food. Always use a spider to remove batter-coated foods.

# General safety rules for deep fat frying

1. Never overfill the fryer with oil or fat.
2. Never overload the fryer with too much food at any one time.
3. Always ensure that foods to be deep fried are free from excess moisture.
4. When placing items of food into a deep fat fryer without the aid of a basket, always place the food in away from you—and gently.
5. Always have a spider to hand in case food needs to be removed quickly.
6. Ensure that a suitable fire extinguisher and fire blanket are close to hand in case of emergency, and that you know how to use them.
7. Always move free-standing fryers with extreme caution, so as not to spill oil or fat on the stove or floor.
8. Always wear long sleeves and keep them rolled down whilst deep frying.
9. During cooking, steam arises from the fryer; avoid placing hands and arms over the heat during cooking.

## Techniques associated with deep fat frying

*Coating:* To protect foods from absorbing too much fat and also to aid moisture retention.

*Blanching:* Refers to the partial cooking of potatoes without colouring.

*Draining:* Refers to the draining of excess fat or oil from food after blanching or frying. This can best be achieved by either draining the food well in the basket by gently shaking, or by placing the food on to absorbent kitchen paper. Deep-fried foods are always served on a dish paper, a practice which will also help absorb any excess frying medium.

*Holding for service:* This is not an easy task when applied to deep-fried foods. Any holding time must be kept to a minimum to avoid foods going soft and soggy in texture.

## Equipment used for deep fat frying

Deep-frying basket     Panier à friture
Spider                 Araignée or écumoire

Two-handled rack                         Grille pour friture
Free-standing frying kettle              Basine à friture
Draining trays for blanched and fried foods
Dry cloths for lifting hot equipment and kitchen rubbers for wiping hands.

All equipment used for deep fat frying should be washed after use in hot soapy water (a good detergent) and rinsed in clean hot water, then dried thoroughly.

### Deep fat fryers

There are many types of fat fryers available to the catering operator. These include models for stove top use, with straight sides and flat bottoms which vary in size and capacity. They can also be round or oval, and usually include a draining rack.

There are also free-standing models with one or more pans which can be heated by gas or electricity. Such fryers are generally designed with features to reduce the accumulation of impurities during a busy deep-frying period. This is done by having a cool zone under the heat source, which traps loose food particles which might otherwise break down the frying medium.

In any case, it is most important to strain the fat or oil at least once each day and, at the same time, clean out the fryer with a good detergent. The final operation is to cleanse the fryer with hot water and dry thoroughly with a clean cloth.

It is generally accepted that the modern fryer will also be fitted with a thermostat device to prevent overheating of the fat or oil. The most recent development has been the introduction of the computerised fryer. The normal manual operations usually associated with deep frying have now been programmed to control the frying cycle to achieve the correct degree of cooking. Such is the degree of sophistication that the actual frying basket will lift automatically to remove the items once the cooking cycle has been completed.

The quality of 'french fries' so produced is superb, with every batch of equal standard. The computer is programmed to deal with a wide range of deep-fried foods, and if necessary, the manufacturer can offer specially designed programmes to suit individual requirements. They are available for either gas or electric operation, and can be installed as a single unit or as multi-product units in modular form. Naturally, they still retain the built-in filter and cool zone and, like the free-standing models described above, both features help to extend the life of the fat or oil whilst at the same time keeping the frying sweet in terms of taste quality.

There are also continuous fryers fitted with automatic timers and temperature control, and pressure fryers which fry foods under pressure— all introduced to cut down on labour costs and production time.

# Self-assessment questions for deep fat frying

1. How would you describe the deep frying process?
2. Can you name the four protective coatings used in deep frying?
3. In a large kitchen brigade, the chef rôtisseur (roast cook) is generally responsible for deep-fried items. Can you name three examples?
4. The practice of blanching deep-fried potatoes (pommes frites) is commonplace. What is its purpose?
5. Why is it preferable to deep fry certain items, such as fish, to order?
6. What is the purpose of a 'cool zone' which is a feature of the modern deep fat fryer?
7. Can you itemise at least three general safety rules appropriate to a deep frying operation?
8. What is the standard range of deep frying temperature?
9. One of the protective coatings when deep frying is known as pané à l'anglaise; what are the ingredients used in the process?
10. It is advisable to deep fry choux pastry fritters (beignets soufflés) at a slightly lower temperature than most other items. Why is this?

When you have completed these questions check your answers with your fellow students and chef or lecturer.

# Deep-fried fish dishes                  *Poisson frire*

### Introduction to deep-fried fish dishes

Fish may be deep fried in fillets and small fish may be deep-fried whole, e.g. whiting or Dover sole.

Most fish are suitable for deep fat frying; however, all must be given a protective coating of batter or breadcrumbs, to protect the fish from frying and burning in the hot fat or oil.

Traditionally, fried fish has always been popular in the British diet, more than on the continent. The following recipes are popular examples of deep-fried fish dishes.

**Whole fish include:**

| | | |
|---|---|---|
| Dover sole | Pané à l'anglaise | 1 per portion |
| Whiting | Pané à l'anglaise | 1 × 200 g per portion |
| Whitebait | Pané à l'anglaise | 100 g per portion |

**Cuts of fish include:**

| | | |
|---|---|---|
| Cod fillets | Batter | 200 g per portion |

367

| Hake | Batter | 200 g per portion |
| Lemon sole | Pané à l'anglaise/batter | 2 fillets per portion |
| Plaice | Pané à l'anglaise/batter | 2 fillets per portion |
| Sole | Pané à l'anglaise/batter | 2 fillets per portion |

**Shellfish include:**

| Oysters | Batter/pané à l'anglaise | 4 per portion |
| Scallops | Batter/pané à l'anglaise | 100 g per portion |
| Scampi | Batter/pané à l'anglaise | 100 g per portion |

**Thin strips of plaice** *Goujons de plie*

Filets of plaice cut into thin strips, pané à l'anglaise, deep fried and served on a hot service flat with a dish paper, garnished with picked parsley and a wedge of lemon per person.
Sole can be cooked in the same way.
Serve with tartare sauce.
Allow 2 fillets per portion.

**Fried fillets of plaice English style** *Filet de plie frit à l'anglaise*

Allow 2 fillets per portion.

1.  Trim the fillets, and remove the skin.
2.  Score the backs of the fillets, that is, the sides which had the skin on. This procedure is known as 'ciseler' and is done to cut the tendons and so stop the fillets curling up when cooked.
3.  Either pané à l'anglaise or pass through flour and batter.
4.  Deep fry to a deep golden brown at 350°C; serve on a dish paper on a hot service flat.
5.  Garnish with picked parsley and accompany with a sauce-boat of tartare or remoulade sauce.

**Fried fillet of plaice French style** *Filet de plie à la française*

Allow 2 fillets per portion.

1.  Proceed as for plaice English style; however, only pass the fish through seasoned milk and flour.
2.  Cook and serve as for plaice English style.

**Deep-fried fish with tomato sauce** *Poisson frit à l'Orly*

Suitable for fillets or cuts of white fish, such as plaice, sole, haddock, cod and whiting.

| 4 | Portions of fish fillets | 10 |
|---|---|---|
| ½ | Fresh lemon, juice of | 1 |
| 1 teaspooon | Finely chopped parsley | 1 tablespoon |
| ½ dl | Vegetable oil | 1 dl |
| | Seasoned flour | |
| 4 dl | Yeast batter | 8 dl |
| 4 dl | Tomato sauce | 8 dl |
| | Picked parsley | |

1. Place the prepared fillets of fish in a shallow tray and add the lemon juice, finely chopped parsley and oil.
2. Season with salt and pepper and cover with a sheet of greaseproof paper.
3. Leave to marinade in the fridge for 20–30 minutes.
4. Pass the marinaded fillets through seasoned flour and gently shake to remove excess flour.
5. Pass through the yeast batter and fry in a pre-heated deep fat fryer at 175°C, to a deep golden brown colour, turning during cooking to ensure an even colour.
6. Drain on kitchen paper and serve on a hot flat with a dish paper and garnish with a piece of deep-fried parsley.
7. Accompany with a sauce-boat of tomato sauce.

## Whitebait
*Blanchailles*

Allow 100 g of whitebait per person.

1. Carefully wash the whitebait and drain well, picking out any imperfect fish.
2. Pass the whitebait through well-seasoned milk and then through seasoned flour.
3. Shake off any surplus flour and place the whitebait into a frying basket.
4. Deep fry in very hot fat and cook until golden brown.
5. Drain well, season with salt and cayenne pepper.
6. Serve on a hot flat lined with a dish paper and garnished with picked or deep-fried parsley and lemon quarters.

Whitebait is most commonly served as a starter or fish course, rarely and usually only at a customer's request is it served as a main course.

# Deep-fried chicken dishes
*Volaille frire*

## Introduction to deep-fried chicken dishes

As with deep-fried fish, chicken also needs a protective coat, usually breadcrumbs, before deep frying to protect the flesh from drying and burning. The following two recipes are classic dishes commonly served in most establishments.

**Chicken Kiev**                    *Suprême de volaille Kiev*

| | | |
|---|---|---|
| 4 | Chicken suprêmes | 10 |
| 100 g | Garlic butter | 250 g |
| | Picked parsley | |
| | Pané à l'anglaise | |

1. Trim the bone of the suprêmes.
2. Cut a small cavity on the inside of the suprêmes and stuff with the garlic butter.
3. Season and pass through flour, eggwash and breadcrumbs (pané à l'anglaise).
4. Place into baskets and deep fry at 350°C to a deep golden brown colour.
5. Drain well on kitchen paper and serve on a hot service flat, lined with dish paper and garnished with picked parsley.

**Chicken cordon bleu**                *Suprême de volaille cordon bleu*

| | | |
|---|---|---|
| 4 | Chicken suprêmes | 10 |
| 4 | Slices Gruyère cheese | 10 |
| 4 | Slices of ham | 10 |
| | Picked parsley | |
| | Pané à l'anglaise | |

1. Trim the bone of the suprêmes.
2. Split open the inside surface of each suprême to make a cavity or pouch.
3. Wrap the ham around the cheese and slot the parcel into the cavity or pouch.
4. Pass through seasoned flour, eggwash, and breadcrumbs (pané à l'anglaise).
5. Place into a basket and deep fry to a crisp golden brown.
6. Drain on kitchen paper.
7. Serve on a hot service flat with dish paper and garnished with picked parsley.

# Deep-fried vegetable dishes

*Introduction to deep-fried vegetable dishes*

Potatoes are readily deep-fried and do not require a protective coating. Other vegetables, however, do need a protective coat. The following recipes are a selection of the most popular deep-fried vegetable dishes.

**Mignonette potatoes**                *Pommes mignonette*

| | | |
|---|---|---|
| 400 | Peeled potatoes | 1 kg |

1. Square off the peeled potatoes and rinse in cold running water.
2. Cut the potatoes into 2 cm × 2 cm × 2 cm slices.

3.  Cut the slices into 2 cm × ½ cm × ½ cm.
4.  Cook and serve as for pommes frites.

## Fried potatoes                                    *Pommes frites*

| 400 g | Peeled potatoes | 1 kg |
|-------|-----------------|------|

1.  Square off the peeled potatoes and rinse under cold running water.
2.  Cut into slices 4 cm × 1 cm.
3.  Cut the slices into 4 cm × 1 cm × 1 cm strips.
4.  Rinse in cold running water and dry in a clean cloth.
5.  Blanch in a deep fat fryer at 165°C; that is, cook the potato without allowing it to colour.
6.  Drain on to kitchen paper until required for service.
7.  To finish for service, cook in pre-heated deep fat at 185°C to a light crisp golden brown.
8.  Drain on kitchen paper and serve on a hot flat with a dish paper, seasoned with a little salt.

Note: Frites and Mignonettes may also be blanched prior to service if required.

## Game chips                                        *Pommes chips*

| 400 g | Peeled potatoes | 1 kg |
|-------|-----------------|------|

1.  Top and tail the potatoes and trim into even-sized cylindrical shapes.
2.  Seat a mandolin and cut the potato to form very thin discs.
3.  Wash in cold running water to remove the starch and drain and dry well.
4.  Cook the discs by placing into pre-heated deep fat at 185°C in a basket and cook to a golden brown; shake gently during cooking to achieve even colouring.
5.  When cooked, drain on kitchen paper and season lightly with salt.

Note: Game chips are used as a garnish to roast game and poultry.

## Lattice or wafer potatoes                         *Pommes gaufrettes*

Proceed as for game chips, but cutting the potatoes on the corrugated blade of the mandolin. Allow half a turn to the potato after each slice—this gives the potato a lattice pattern.

## Straw potatoes                                    *Pommes paillées*

| 400 g | Peeled potatoes | 1 kg |
|-------|-----------------|------|
1.  Square off the peeled potatoes and re-wash in cold running water.

2. Cut the potatoes into fine julienne.
3. Wash in cold running water and dry in a clean cloth.
4. Place in pre-heated deep fat at 185°C and cook to a light crisp golden brown.
5. Remove the straw potatoes using a spider and drain on to kitchen paper.
6. Season with a little salt and use as a garnish to grilled foods.

## Pont Neuf potatoes                                   *Pommes Pont Neuf*

| 400 g | Peeled potatoes | 1 kg |
|---|---|---|

1. Use large, evenly sized potatoes and trim them square.
2. Cut into slices 2 cm × 4 cm.
3. Cut each slice into strips 2 cm × 2 cm × 4 cm.
4. Rinse under cold running water and dry in a clean cloth.
5. Blanch in deep fat at 165°C.
6. Drain on to kitchen paper until required.
7. To finish for service, place into deep fat at 185°C and cook to a light crisp golden brown.
8. Drain on to kitchen paper and season with a little salt.
9. Serve on a hot flat with a dish paper.

## Bataille potatoes                                   *Pommes bataille*

| 400 g | Peeled potatoes | 1 kg |
|---|---|---|

1. Use large, evenly sized potatoes and trim them square.
2. Rinse in cold running water and dry in a clean cloth.
3. Cut the potato in 1 cm slices.
4. Cut the slices into 1 cm strips.
5. Cut the strips into 1 cm square cubes.
6. Cook and serve as for Pont Neuf potatoes.

## Croquette potatoes                                  *Pommes croquettes*

Deep fried potato dishes using duchesse potato mixture as their base must be protected with an exterior coat of breadcrumbs to prevent absorption of fat or oil which will cause the potato to break up.

| 400 g | Duchesse potato mixture | 1 kg |
|---|---|---|
|  | Pané à l'anglaise |  |
|  | Picked parsley |  |
|  | Plain flour |  |

1. Divide the mixture into the required number of pieces, allowing 2 pieces per person.
2. Using a little flour and a palette knife, mould the pieces into cylinders 2 cm × 4 cm.

3. Pass the cylinders through the flour, eggwash and breadcrumbs (pané à l'anglaise) and remould to give a neater shape.
4. Place into frying baskets and deep fry in hot fat 180–185°C to a deep golden brown colour.
5. Drain on kitchen paper and serve on a hot flat with a dish paper and garnished with picked parsley.

## Almond potatoes                                  *Pommes amandines*

| | | |
|---|---|---|
| **400 g** | **Duchesse potato mixture** | **1 kg** |
| | **Nibbed almonds** | |
| | **Flour** | |
| | **Picked parsley** | |
| | **Eggwash** | |

Proceed exactly as for croquette potatoes, coating the potato mixture with flour, eggwash and nibbed almonds in place of the breadcrumbs.

## Other vegetables

Depending on which vegetable is to be deep fried, a variety of coatings may be used to protect it.

## Aubergine fritters                        *Aubergine frit à la française*

| | | |
|---|---|---|
| **300 g** | **Aubergines** | **700 g** |
| | **Seasoned flour** | |
| | **Milk** | |
| | **Picked parsley** | |

1. Top and tail the aubergines; peel off the skin using a small sharp knife.
2. Cut into slices ½ cm thick.
3. Pass through the milk and seasoned flour.
4. Deep fry at 190°C to a deep golden brown.
5. Drain well on kitchen paper.
6. Serve on a hot service dish lined with a dish paper.
7. Sprinkle lightly with salt and garnish with picked parsley.

**Note:** Aubergine fritters may also be cooked and served coated in a yeast batter.

## Deep-fried onion rings                    *Oignons frits à la française*

| | | |
|---|---|---|
| **300 g** | **Onions** | **700 g** |

1. Peel the onions and slice into thin rings.
2. Separate the rings and remove any small rings.
3. Pass through milk and seasoned flour.
4. Cook and serve as for aubergine fritters.

**Note:** Onion rings may also be cooked and served coated in a yeast batter.

## Deep-fried baby marrow

*Courgettes frites à la française*

| 300 g | Courgettes | 700 g |

1. Trim the ends and cut into ½ cm thick slices.
2. Proceed to cook and present in the same way as for aubergine fritters.

**Note:** Courgettes, also known as zucchini and baby marrow, may also be cooked and served coated in a yeast batter.

## Deep-fried mushrooms

*Champignons frits*

| 300 g | Button mushrooms | 700 g |
| | Pané à l'anglaise | |
| | *or* | |
| | Yeast batter | |
| | Picked parsley | |

1. Wash the button mushrooms and remove the stalks. If necessary also peel the button mushrooms. (Keep the stalks and peeling for stock or sauce making.)
2. Pass the mushrooms through flour, eggwash and breadcrumbs (pané à l'anglaise) or through flour and batter.
3. Deep fry to a deep golden brown at 190°C.
4. Drain well on kitchen paper.
5. Serve on a hot service dish lined with a dish paper and garnished with picked parsley.

**Note:** Deep-fried mushrooms are often served as a starter, accompanied with a suitable mayonnaise-based cold sauce, such as tartare.

Deep-fried mushrooms served as starters may also be stuffed before coating. Stuffings commonly used include pâté, Stilton cheese or duxelle. To stuff mushrooms, dome the stuffing into the cavity created by removing the stalk. Coat with breadcrumbs before cooking and serve with a suitable sauce.

## Deep-fried cheese

*Fromage frit*

Use a soft cheese such as Camembert or Brie.

| 8 | Wedges of cheese | 20 |
| 1 | Beaten egg | 3 |
| 60 g | Fresh white breadcrumbs | 150 g |

1. Pass the cheese through the beaten egg and then through the breadcrumbs.
2. Deep fry at 190°C to a golden brown colour.
3. Drain well on kitchen paper.
4. Serve on a hot service flat with a dish paper.

5. Garnish with picked parsley and accompany with a suitable cold sauce, e.g. mayonnaise.

# Deep-fried réchauffé dishes *Réchauffé frire*

### Introduction to deep-fried réchauffé dishes

Réchauffé dishes are dishes made out of cooked foods which are then reheated and served, usually with a sauce. They are often found on restaurant or snack bar menus. The following recipes are popular examples of réchauffed dishes.

The recipes are based on the same basic recipe, using different cooked meats and sauces.

All the dishes produced should be presented for service on hot service flats lined with a dish paper. The accompanying sauce should be served in a sauce-boat.

**Basic recipe for cooked forcemeat**

| | | |
|---|---|---|
| 260 g | Cooked meat | 650 g |
| 1 dl | Thick béchamel | 2½ dl |
| 2 | Egg yolks | 5 |
| | Finely chopped parsley | |
| | Pinch of nutmeg to taste | |
| | Salt and pepper | |
| | Flour, eggwash and breadcrumbs | |

1. Dice or mince the cooked meat, season and bind with the thick béchamel.
2. Bring the mixture to the boil; make sure that the mixture is stiff enough to hold its shape for moulding.
3. Remove the mixture from the heat and mix in the nutmeg, parsley and egg yolks; adjust the seasoning.
4. Pour the mixture into a buttered tray, lined with greaseproof paper.
5. Chill until set and then divide into the required number of portions, moulding into the required shapes.
6. Pané à l'anglaise (flour, eggwash and breadcrumbs).
7. Re-shape and deep fry at 175–180°C until a deep golden brown colour.
8. Serve on a hot service flat, lined with a dish paper and garnished with fresh or deep-fried picked parsley and a sauce-boat of the required sauce.

**Rissoles** *Croquettes*

These are small puff pastry cases filled with savoury minced meat and deep fried, commonly found on buffet tables or as a starter.

| 100 g | Minced meat | 250 g |
|---|---|---|
| | (lamb, beef, ham or chicken) | |
| 1 | Beaten egg | 2 |
| 30 g | Sweated brunoise of onion | 70 g |
| | Finely chopped parsley | |
| 200 g | Puff pastry trimmings | |

1. Mix the meat, egg and chopped parsley in a bowl.
2. Season and divide into portions.
3. Roll out the pastry thinly and cut into 10 cm square or round discs.
4. Moisten the edges, place a small amount of filling in the centre and fold over in half.
5. Seal the edges and deep fry at 175°C to a deep golden brown.
6. Drain on kitchen paper and serve on a hot service dish with a dish paper.
7. Garnish with fresh or deep-fried picked parsley, serve with a sauce-boat of piquante sauce or other suitable sauce.

### Lentil and nut rissoles

| 4 dl | Water | 1 litre |
|---|---|---|
| 160 g | Red split lentils | 400 g |
| 60 g | Brunoise of onion | 150 g |
| 100 g | Finely chopped assorted nuts | 250 g |
| | (almonds, brazils, walnuts, peanuts) | |
| 100 g | Curd cheese | 250 g |
| 70 g | Fine breadcrumbs | 175 g |
| | Finely chopped parsley | |
| 3 dl | Tomato sauce | 7½ dl |
| | *or* | |
| | Mornay sauce | |
| | Plain flour and eggwash | |

1. Place the lentils in a pan with brunoise of onion and add the water.
2. Bring quickly to the boil, skim to remove any surface scum.
3. Reduce the heat to simmer and cook for 45 minutes or until the lentils are tender and the water has been absorbed.
4. Chill the lentils; when cold mix in the curd cheese, breadcrumbs and parsley and season to taste.
5. Form into croquette shapes and pass through the seasoned flour, eggwash and finely chopped nuts.
6. Deep fry at 175–180°C to a light golden brown colour.
7. Drain well on kitchen paper and serve on a hot flat with a dish paper and picked parsley.
8. Accompany with a sauce-boat of tomato or mornay sauce.

## Fish cakes                    *Medaillons de poisson frits*

| 200 g | Flaked cooked white fish | 500 g |
| 160 g | Dry purée of potato | 400 g |
| 1–2 | Beaten eggs | 2–4 |
| ¼ dl | Anchovy essence | ½ dl |
| | Finely chopped parsley | |
| | Salt and pepper | |
| | Flour, eggwash and breadcrumbs | |
| 3 dl | Tomato or parsley or anchovy sauce | 7½ dl |

1. Mix the fish, potato, parsley and anchovy essence together and bind with beaten egg.
2. Divide into the required number of portions.
3. Mould into round cakes (medaillons) and pané à l'anglaise (flour, eggwash and breadcrumbs).
4. Re-mould to neaten the shape.
5. Deep fry in pre-heated fat at 189°C to a deep golden brown.
6. Drain well on kitchen paper and served dressed on dish papers on hot service flats.
7. Garnish with fresh or deep-fried picked parsley. Accompany with a suitable sauce, such as tomato, anchovy or parsley.

## Scotch eggs

| 4 | Hard-boiled eggs | 10 |
| 400 g | Sausagemeat | 1 kg |
| | Seasoned flour | |
| | Eggwash | |
| | Fine breadcrumbs | |

1. Shell the eggs and divide the sausagemeat into equal quantities.
2. Wrap the eggs in the sausagemeat and seal without cracks.
3. Pané à l'anglaise and deep fry to a dark golden brown colour.
4. Serve on a dish paper, placed on a hot service flat.
*or*
Serve cold with salad.

## Durham cutlets

| 200 g | Cooked minced beef | 500 g |
| 100 g | Dry purée of potato | 250 g |
| 60 g | Sweated brunoise of onion | 150 g |
| 2 | Egg yolks | 4 |
| | Finely chopped parsley | |
| | Salt and pepper | |
| | Flour, eggwash and breadcrumbs | |
| 3 dl | Piquante sauce | 7½ dl |

1. Mix the beef, potato, onion, egg yolks and parsley together in a bowl.
2. Season and mould into cutlet shapes.

3. Pané à l'anglaise (flour, eggwash and breadcrumbs) and then re-shape.
4. Insert a piece of blanched macaroni in the end of the cutlet to form a mock rib bone.
5. Deep fry to a golden brown at 175°C; drain well on kitchen paper.
6. Serve on a hot flat on a dish paper garnished with deep-fried or fresh picked parsley; accompany with sauce-boat of piquante sauce.

**Note:** Durham cutlets may also be shallow fried.

# Deep-fried pâtisserie dishes *Pâtisserie frire*

### Introduction to deep-fried pâtisserie dishes

The following recipes are a selection of sweet dishes which are deep fried and served hot or warm. They are served on warm plates with dish papers and are usually accompanied with sauce-boats of apricot sauce.

**Doughnuts, fermented**

1. Scale off plain bun dough at 40 g pieces. Mould round and place on to greased trays. Prove to double the size, remove carefully, and drop into hot fat individually; fat temperature 193°C.
2. Turn over when half cooked and finish the other half.
3. Remove, and drain well on cake wires.
4. Roll in coarse granulated sugar, then fill carefully with red jam and/or whipped cream.
5. If filled with whipped cream, dust heavily with icing sugar.

**Powder doughnuts**

| | |
|---|---|
| 500 g | Cake flour |
| 35 g | Baking powder |
| ¼ teaspoon | Salt (scant measure) |
| ½ teaspoon | Grated nutmeg |
| 175 g | Castor sugar |
| 250 ml | Milk |
| 50 g | Milk powder |
| 60 g | Melted butter |

1. Sieve the flour, baking powder, salt, milk powder and nutmeg.
2. Beat the eggs, add the sugar, stir in the milk and melted butter.
3. Add to the flour mixture and blend well together.
4. Turn out on to a lightly floured surface, and roll out to 1–1½ cm thickness.
5. Cut out shapes with a ring cutter and fry in deep fat to golden brown.
6. Dust with icing sugar or roll in granulated sugar.

The dough may be scaled off at 55 g pieces and moulded finger-shaped. Fry off to golden brown, drain and cool. Fill with whipped cream and dust with icing sugar.

### Apricot fritters

*Beignets d'abricots*

| | | |
|---|---|---|
| 8 | Whole apricots | 20 |
| 25 g | Castor sugar | 50 g |
| ½ dl | Kirsch | 1 dl |
| | Plain flour | |
| 5 dl | Yeast batter | 1 litre |
| | Icing sugar | |
| 3 dl | Apricot sauce | 6 dl |

1. Split the apricots in half and remove the stones.
2. Place in a suitable basin, cover with the sugar and kirsch and stand in the refrigerator for at least 1 hour, turning occasionally.
3. Drain the apricots and dry well (add the liqueur to the apricot sauce).
4. Pass through the flour, shaking off excess flour.
5. Dip into the batter and place them in a deep fat fryer at 180°C, one at a time so they do not stick together.
6. Fry to a deep golden brown colour.
7. Place on a grill tray, dredge with icing sugar and glaze under a hot salamander.
8. Arrange on a flat with a dish paper and serve with a sauce-boat of apricot sauce.

### Pineapple fritters

*Beignets d'ananas*

Proceed exactly as for apricots using 3 slices of pineapple per portion.
A slight variation to this dish is to add freshly milled black pepper to the batter.

### Banana fritters

*Beignets de bananes*

Proceed as for apricot fritters allowing 1 banana cut in half lengthways per person.

### Apple fritters

*Beignets de pommes*

| | | |
|---|---|---|
| 2 | Cooking apples | 5 |
| 25 g | Castor sugar | 50 g |
| 2 g | Ground cinnamon | 5 g |
| ½ dl | Demerara rum | 1 dl |
| ½ | Lemon, juice of | 1 |
| | Plain flour | |
| 5 dl | Yeast batter | 1 litre |
| | Icing sugar | |
| 3 dl | Apricot sauce | 6 dl |

1. Peel, core and slice the apples into ¾ cm rings.
2. Lay in a bowl of suitable size and cover with the sugar, cinnamon, rum and lemon juice.
3. Leave to stand for at least 1 hour, turning regularly.
4. Drain and dry the apple slices.
5. Proceed as for apricot fritters from stage 4.

## Choux paste fritters                     *Beignets soufflés, sauce abricot*

| 4 dl | Choux paste | 1 litre |
|------|-------------|---------|
|      | Icing sugar |         |
| 3 dl | Apricot sauce | 6 dl |

1. Using dessert spoons, mould the choux paste into small oval shapes. Dip the spoons in hot fat to stop the paste sticking to the spoons.
2. Lower the moulded choux paste into deep fat at about 150°C.
3. Fry to a deep golden brown (8–10 minutes). Occasionally turn the fritters gently to ensure even colouring.
4. Remove and drain well on kitchen paper.
5. Dredge with plenty of icing sugar.
6. Serve with a sauce-boat of apricot sauce.

## Cheese fritters

| 4 dl | Choux paste | 1 litre |
|------|-------------|---------|
| 100 g | Grated cheese | 200 g |
|      | Cayenne pepper |      |
|      | Grated parmesan |     |

1. Mix the grated cheese into the choux paste along with the cayenne paper.
2. Mould as for beignets soufflés
3. Cook as for beignets soufflés.
4. Drain as for beignets soufflés.
5. Dredge with parmesan cheese before serving.

# Chapter 14
# Microwave
# Cookery

*Micro*
*Onde*

## The competency defined

This is one of the most modern methods of cookery, involving the cooking and re-heating of foods by electromagnetic waves. The power source is electricity, although no heat is generated in the oven cavity, only in the food itself. Since their inception in the early part of the 1960s, microwave ovens have developed many new features including browning and turntable facilities. The microwaves agitate the water molecules in the food which in turn causes heat by friction. This friction of the water molecules causes foods to cook, or if pre-cooked, to be re-heated very quickly.

## Purpose of microwave cookery

There are several reasons for using this specialised method:

1. From a hygiene point of view, re-heating by microwave is extremely rapid. This discourages the growth of harmful bacteria.
2. Foods being cooked from the raw state will take only a fraction of the time taken by more conventional methods, and if the correct timing and power setting is observed, the results can be impressive.
3. Frozen foods across the entire range can also be defrosted by microwaves both safely and efficiently due to the speed at which the microwaves react.

## Organisation and preparation for micro-wave cookery

Microwave ovens can be used for pre-prepared dishes, sauces, soups, meats, poultry, game, fish and a wide range of sweet items. All areas of the kitchen can produce dishes suitable for cooking by this method. The most up-to-date microwave ovens are fitted with halogen heat lamps to aid 'browning' of certain dishes. There are dual-purpose microwave and convection ovens, some of which also have salamander facilities fitted. Certainly, one may find a microwave oven sited in any area of the modern kitchen from the pastry to the stove section.

However, it is worth noting some points which will assist with the successful completion of microwave cookery.

1. Always make sure that you check recipes for time and power settings. Most important!
2. When purchasing a microwave oven you need to know its power output, whether 400 W, 550 W, 650 W, 700 W, or with larger industrial units, 1500 W plus. An industrial microwave/convection oven can produce a tray of perfect, crisp baked potatoes in 10 minutes. By contrast, a domestic microwave oven would take 10 minutes to cook 2–3 potatoes.
3. Always allow for standing time: this is the time allowed after removal from the microwave, for foods to finish cooking.
4. Not all foods are ideally suited for cooking in a microwave. Some of those which are better suited to more traditional methods include rice, pasta, pastry and eggs (unless scrambled).
5. The internal oven capacity of microwave ovens in general only allows for foods to be cooked in small quanitites. However, depending upon the food under preparation, cooking time is so short that many dishes can be cooked to order.
6. Not all containers are suitable for use with a microwave oven, and certainly not metal. They act as a barrier to the waves and prevent the foods from getting hot. Tinfoil containers are not recommended, nor any item of china ware which has a gold or silver pattern. Special dishes are now available for use in microwave ovens.
7. Other factors to be considered are: the starting temperature; the size of the foodstuff; the quantity of the item being processed; consistency or density of the food; and recommended cooking times.

# Advantages of microwave cookery

Two of the main advantages must be time and fuel costs. Cooking by microwave can save up to 70 per cent cooking time on certain foods, so that vegetables which take from 20 minutes by conventional boiling will be ready in 3 minutes in a microwave. This sort of example is applicable to a very wide selection of items.

Labour is also a major consideration. Foods can be cooked in their serving dishes. For example, vegetables can be prepared raw and cooked in their service dish, to order. This facility eliminates pre-cooking, refreshing and re-heating. Microwaves have also enabled employers to offer a 24-hour round-the-clock meal service, by pre-plating meals and leaving staff with access to self-service microwave ovens.

In addition, microwave meals usually retain their flavour and nutritional value, and provided the foods are not over-cooked, there is minimum shrinkage or loss of moisture.

# General safety rules

The rules for safety in this area are few and basic. Microwaves are safe and easy to use if looked after with care. All commercially available ovens comply with British Standard 5175 which requires that the power density should be less than $4 \, mW/cm^2$ (5 milliwatts per sq. centimetre) at points 5 cm or more from the external surfaces of the appliance.

Always wipe out the interior of the oven after use and make sure that you wipe around the door seal, ensuring that the seal is unbroken. If there is any doubt about the seal, do not use the oven; escaping waves can present a hazard.

All microwave ovens have a built-in safety switch that automatically cuts off the power supply when the door is opened.

Never operate a microwave oven when empty.

# General rules for efficient cooking by microwave

1. Always check that power settings and times are correct, and never allow foods to over-cook.
2. Make sure that you only use plastic, china or glass in the oven. Foil or metal can damage the apparatus.
3. Try to avoid 'doming' or piling up foods unevenly, as this will cause the commodity to cook unevenly.
4. Always allow sufficient room in dishes/utensils for stirring during the cooking process.

# Techniques associated with microwave cookery

1. Wherever possible cover foods to prevent excess loss of moisture, condensation and spluttering inside the oven.
2. Never try to cook eggs in their shells as they will explode.
3. Such items as potatoes and apples (in their skins) should be pricked with a skewer to prevent them splitting whilst cooking.

# Equipment available for microwave cookery

As stated, there are a number of types of machines available, with different power settings and combinations. Most models are equipped either with a turntable facility, or operate on a deltawave principle, where the waves move round rather than the foods.

Always disconnect microwaves from the power supply before cleaning, and use a damp cloth to wipe out the oven, after which wipe dry with a clean, dry cloth. The best utensils for use in microwave ovens are ceramic, glass, plastic or paper.

Microwave thermometers are available for use with meat and poultry; ordinary thermometers should not be used as they contain mercury.

Special stacking rings can be used which allow up to three plated meals to be heated at any one time. However, there must be air space between the plates and you must remember to cover the top plate.

# Design features of the microwave oven

A microwave cooker consists of a supply unit which takes the normal domestic electricity power supply and passes it through a *magnetron* which generates electromagnetic waves of very high frequency (microwaves). These high frequency waves are carried into the cooking cavity or 'oven'.

All components are contained in a cabinet on which the controls are fixed, and the front of the cabinet has a drop-down, hinged or slide-up door. The microwaves 'bounce' off and across the metal sides of the oven cavity in a regular pattern and, to make sure that all the food in the cooking space is heated as evenly as possible, a slow 'fan' or 'stirrer' is fixed to diffuse the energy evenly. Microwaves operating at a very high frequency agitate the molecules in food or liquid which then oscillate at over two thousand million times per second, and in so doing create heat within the food. The greatest penetration of the microwave is 5 cm.

# Microwave oven components

*Door screen*: Perforated metal screen which allows the user to see food whilst it is cooking. The screen is designed so that light can pass through, but not the microwaves.

*Automatic door latch*: When the door is closed, the latch will automatically lock it shut.

*Manual timer*: Some models have one control, like a minute timer. Others have two: one calibrated in seconds up to about 5 minutes and the other calibrated in minutes up to about 30 minutes. Items can then be pre-set to the desired cooking time.

*Spatter shield*: Protects the ceiling of the oven, the stirrer and the *magnetron* (the part which generates electromagnetic waves of very high frequency) from splashes during the cooking process.

*Stirrer*: The six-bladed stirrer operates whenever the oven is in use. It provides distribution of microwave energy throughout the cooking area.

*Oven light*: This turns on when the power switch is activated, and remains on until the power switch is turned off.

*Cooking tray*: This helps the food to receive a more even distribution of microwaves on top, sides and bottom.

*Air filter*: Located at the bottom front of the oven; the filter allows air to be drawn into the oven during cooking, and keeps out dust and lint.

*Cook button*: This turns on the *magnetron* and during the cooking process, if the door is opened for any reason, the cook button must be reactivated to restart the oven.

*Cooking light*: The light will glow red when the *magnetron* is operating.

*Power button*: This turns on the current, the oven light and the magnetron cooking fan.

# Microwave cooking, general notes

The recipes given are for microwave cookers of no less than 650 W power output. If your microwave is of a lower capacity output allow the following extra time:

600 W—add 10 seconds for every minute given in the 4-portion recipe
500 W—add 15 seconds for every minute given in the 4-portion recipe

*Always* allow for standing time and check the food just before cooking time is completed to avoid over-cooking.

In this section we will work on three power settings:

High        100 per cent power output
Medium      60 per cent power output
Defrost     30 per cent power output

Note that high is always 100 per cent output no matter what size wattage the machine is.

Foods which cook well include soups, vegetables, sauces, preserves, hot and cold puddings and suet pastry. This is due to their water content and chemical make-up.

Foods which do not cook well include Yorkshire pudding, soufflés, choux paste, deep-fried foods, casseroles, roast vegetables and pasta. This is because these foods need browning, rising or lack moisture. Modern microwaves now combine grills and convection ovens allowing foods which were previously unsuitable for microwaves to be cooked by combined methods, so speeding up the process of cooking.

### Cooking times

For certain recipes given it will be necessary to allow extra cooking time for 10 portions than the stated times which are for 4 portions.

# Self-assessment questions for microwave cookery

1. How do microwaves affect the cooking of foods?
2. Why are some materials not suitable for cooking in microwave ovens?
3. What other factors should be considered when processing foods by microwave?
4. What are some of the advantages of cooking by microwave?
5. What are the general safety rules when cooking by microwave?
6. Why is is advantageous to cover foods while they are being cooked in a microwave oven?
7. Why should an ordinary thermometer not be used to test meat and poultry items?
8. Explain what standing time is and why it is important.
9. What problems may occur when cooking eggs in a microwave?
10. Explain the principle of how a microwave cooker works.

When you have completed these questions check your answers with your fellow students and chef or lecturer.

# Microwaved soups and sauces

*Introduction to microwaved soups and sauces*

Microwave cookery or cuisine à micro is, of course, well suited to soup and sauce cookery. The following dishes cook quickly and efficiently by microwave. These dishes have been selected for their simplicity for use by people new to microwave cookery. The large-scale recipes should only be used in industrial machines.

**Mushroom soup** *Crème champignon*

| | | |
|---|---|---|
| 25 g | Butter or margarine | 60 g |
| 60 g | Brunoise of onions | 150 g |
| 220 g | Brunoise of mushrooms | 550 g |
| 3 dl | Milk | 7½ dl |
| 6 dl | Hot chicken stock | 15 dl |
| 1 teaspoon | Fresh chopped parsley and basil | 3 teaspoons |
| | Salt and pepper | |
| 25 g | Cornflour | 60 g |

1. Place the butter, onions and mushrooms in a 3 litre or 8 litre bowl.
2. Cover with cling film, leaving exposed at one corner for steam to escape.
3. Cook on high for 7 minutes or until the onions are tender. Stir the ingredients half-way through cooking.
4. Gently stir the liquid into the vegetables and the parsley and basil,

386

season and cook on high for 10 minutes or until the soup has thickened, stirring every 2 minutes.
5. Liquidise the soup and adjust the seasoning.
6. Serve in hot soup bowls.

**Note**: If required, finish the soup with a swirl of single cream or plain yoghurt. Be sure to inform your customers if the soup is finished with yoghurt in place of cream.

## Hollandaise sauce                                    *Sauce hollandaise*

| 50 g | Butter | 125 g |
|------|--------|-------|
| 2 | Eggs | 5 |
|   | Seasoning |   |
| 1 tablespoon | Fresh lemon juice | 2 tablespoons |

1. Place half of the butter in a 1 or 2 litre jug and melt.
2. Beat in the egg yolks and cook uncovered on high for 15 seconds.
3. Beat until the sauce is smooth.
4. Add the remaining butter in small pieces and beat into the mixture, a little at a time.
5. Season.
6. Beat in the lemon juice and use as required, e.g. poached asparagus, eggs, steaks or poached salmon.

## Basic white sauce                                              *Béchamel*

| 50 g | Margarine or flour | 100 g |
|------|--------------------|-------|
| 50 g | Plain flour | 100 g |
| 6 dl | Milk | 12 dl |
|   | Seasoning |   |

1. Melt the butter in a 1 or 2 litre jug.
2. Stir in the flour and cook on high uncovered for 30–45 seconds.
3. Blend in the milk and cook uncovered on high for a further 3–4 minutes or until the sauce thickens, stirring the sauce every minute to avoid lumps.
4. Season and use as required.

This sauce may be extended as for any of the basic white sauce recipe extensions given in the boiling chapter.

## Basic sweet white sauce

| 1 tablespoon | Cornflour | 2 tablespoons |
|--------------|-----------|---------------|
| 3 dl | Milk | 6 dl |
| 2 tablespoons | Castor sugar | 4 tablespoons |
| 2 | Drops vanilla essence | 4 |
| 10 g | Butter | 20 g |

1. Mix the cornflour to a smooth paste with a small amount of the milk, in a 1 or 2 litre jug.
2. Stir in the rest of the milk, sugar and vanilla essence.
3. Cook uncovered for 3 minutes or until the sauce has thickened. Stir every minute to avoid lumps.
4. Stir in the butter and use as required.

*Extensions:*
Coffee sauce—Replace half the milk with strong black coffee.
Chocolate sauce—Add an equal quantity of cocoa powder to the cornflour and proceed as for the basic sauce.
Orange or lemon sauce—Add the grated zest of one orange or lemon to each 3 dl of sauce, add with the milk.

**Notes:**
1. Quantities of sauce over 6 dl are best made by boiling as a conventional method of cookery.
2. Always use containers which are large enough not to allow the sauce to boil over.

# Microwaved meat and fish dishes

*Introduction to microwaved meat and fish dishes*

Great care must be taken when cooking meat and fish dishes not to over-cook the food. Over-cooking will cause loss of flavour, hardening of texture or excess loss of moisture resulting in an indigestible dish.

**Liver pâté**                                                    *Pâté de foie*

| | | |
|---|---|---|
| 4 | Rashers rindless streaky bacon | 10 |
| 40 g | Brunoise of onion | 20 |
| 1 | Crushed clove of garlic | 2 |
| 230 g | Chicken, lamb's or turkey livers | 560 g |
| 1 teaspoon | Finely chopped fresh herbs | 2 teaspoons |
| 100 g | Margarine or butter | 250 g |
| ½ dl | Double cream | 1 dl |
| | Salt and pepper | |
| | Lemon wedges | |
| | Picked parsley | |
| | Slices of toast | |

1. Finely chop the bacon and place into a 2 or 5 litre bowl with the onions and garlic.
2. Cover with cling film, prick the surface to allow steam to escape, cook on high for 5 minutes.
3. Stir in the chopped livers and herbs, re-cover and cook on high for 4

minutes, stirring after 2 minutes.
4. Cut the butter into small pieces and mix in with the livers, re-cover and cook on high for 2 minutes.
5. Leave to stand covered for 3 minutes, mix in the cream.
6. Blend in a food processor and season.
7. Place the pâté into individual ramekins and cap with a little aspic or clarified butter.
8. Leave to set in the refrigerator.
9. Serve garnished with lemon wedges and picked parsley, accompanied with buttered toast.

## Fish kebabs       *Brochette de poisson*

| | | |
|---|---|---|
| 50 g | Tomatoes | 125 g |
| 100 g | Courgettes | 250 g |
| 100 g | Field mushrooms | 250 g |
| ½ | Lemon | 1½ |
| 500 g | Diced monkfish | 1½ kg |
| 25 g | Butter | 75 g |
| 1 teaspoon | Fresh chopped dill | 3 teaspoons |

1. Wash and thickly slice the courgettes, quarter the mushrooms and halve the tomatoes.
2. Slice the lemons
3. Thread the ingredients on to wooden skewers, alternating as you do so, tomato, courgette, fish, lemon, mushroom, repeat until all ingredients are used.
4. Melt the butter with the dill.
5. Brush each kebab liberally with the dill-flavoured butter.
6. Arrange the kebabs on a dish and cook uncoverd for 4–6 minutes on a high setting or until the fish and vegetables are cooked.
7. Serve on a bed of rice and accompany with a sauce-boat of hollandaise sauce.

## Pork escalopes with grapes       *Escalope de porc aux raisins*

| | | |
|---|---|---|
| 8 × 50 g | Pork escalopes | 20 × 50 g |
| 25 g | Margarine or butter | 60 g |
| 25 g | Plain flour | 60 g |
| 1½ dl | Pure unsweetened apple juice | 3¾ dl |
| 1½ dl | Hot chicken stock | 3¾ dl |
| | Salt and pepper | |
| 175 g | Black grapes | 435 g |
| 1 tablespoon | Double cream | 2½ tablespoons |
| | Finely chopped parsley | |

1. Arrange the pork escalopes, overlapping in a shallow dish.
2. Cover with cling film, pricking to allow steam to escape.
3. Cook on high for 6 minutes, turn over after 3 minutes.
4. Place the butter in a 1 or 3 litre jug and cook uncovered on high for 45

seconds or until melted.
5. Stir in the flour and cook uncovered on high for 30 seconds.
6. Mix in the apple juice a little at a time and then mix in the stock.
7. Season and cook uncovered on high for 2½ minutes. Stir every minute.
8. Cut the grapes in half and remove the seeds, stir into the sauce and cook uncovered for 1 minute or until hot. Stir in the cream and season.
9. Arrange the pork escalopes on a hot service dish and nap with the sauce; sprinkle liberally with finely chopped parsley and serve.

| **Chicken with tarragon and garlic** | | *Suprême de volaille à l'estragon au ail* |
|---|---|---|
| 4 × 100 g | **Chicken suprêmes** | 10 × 100g |
| 40 g | **Margarine or butter** | 100 g |
| 2 | **Crushed cloves of garlic** | 5 |
| 2 teaspoons | **Fresh chopped tarragon** | 5 teaspoons |
| 4 | **Rashers of back bacon** | 10 |
| | **Picked parsley** | |

1. Remove the fillets from the suprêmes and trim out the sinew.
2. Lightly batten the suprêmes, make a small pocket in each suprême and tuck in the fillet.
3. Mix the butter, tarragon and garlic together and spread over the chicken.
4. Roll the suprêmes with the butter on the inside.
5. Remove the rind from the bacon and stretch the rasher around the chicken. If necessary secure the chicken with a wooden cocktail stick.
6. Sit the parcels in a circle on an oven-proof dish and cover with cling film; prick to allow steam to escape.
7. Cook on high for 11 minutes, reposition after 5 minutes.
8. Leave to stand while still covered for 2 minutes. Remove the cocktail sticks and serve in a hot service dish. Garnish with picked parsley and brush with a little of the melted garlic and tarragon butter.

# Microwaved eggs and farinaceous dishes

*Introduction to microwaved eggs and farinaceous dishes*

These recipes have been selected because of their frequent use in today's restaurants and eating houses. Pasta and rice can be difficult to cook if instructions are not followed carefully. It should also be noted that the cooking times for pasta and rice are not greatly reduced by using microwave cookery so having no advantage over traditional boiling.

## Lasagne/spaghetti

1. Place the lasagne in boiling water, allowing 1 litre to 175 g of pasta, along with a tablespoon of olive oil and a little salt.
2. Cover with cling film, prick to allow steam to escape.
3. Cook on high for 9 minutes and stir gently every 3 minutes.
4. Allow to stand for 10 minutes, drain, refresh and use as required.

## Macaroni

1. Place the macaroni into boiling water with oil as for spaghetti.
2. Cover with cling film, prick to allow steam to escape.
3. Cook on high for 15 minutes.
4. Allow to stand for 10 minutes, drain, refresh and use as required.

**Notes:**
1. Always use a large container to avoid the water boiling over and to allow the expansion of the pasta. (The same rule applies when cooking rice.)
2. Pasta is best reheated when bound with a sauce.

## Rice

1. Allow 8 dl of water to 250 g of rice; add a little oil and cover with cling film.
2. Cook on high for 13 minutes, stir after 5 minutes.
3. Allow to stand for 10 minutes and then fluff with a fork.
4. Either refresh and use as required or serve straight away.

**Note:** Brown rice should be cooked in the same manner as white rice, but allow slightly longer cooking times.

## Tarragon eggs                                    *Oeufs à l'estragon*

| 4 | Eggs | 10 |
|---|---|---|
| 1 teaspoon | Double cream | 2 teaspoons |
| 1 teaspoon | Fresh tarragon, chopped | 2 teaspoons |
| | Sea salt | |
| | Milled pepper | |
| | Butter | |

1. Lightly butter 4 or 10 cocotte dishes and season them with the salt and pepper.
2. Sprinkle a small amount of tarragon in the base of the dish.
3. Crack the eggs into the dishes and prick the yolks with a cocktail stick (this is to prevent the sealed yolk exploding in the cooking process).
4. Mix the cream with the remaining tarragon and add a little salt and pepper.
5. Pour the cream mixture over the eggs and cook uncovered on high for 1 to 3 minutes depending on the number of eggs being cooked.

391

**Note:** Eggs will cook well in microwaves provided the yolk is always pricked prior to cooking. If the yolk is not pricked the yolk will expand during cooking, building up pressure inside its skin until the pressure forces the skin to explode.

### Macaroni cheese

| | | |
|---|---|---|
| 225 g | Macaroni | 560 g |
| 1 tablespoon | Vegetable oil | 2 tablespoons |
| 1 litre | Water | 2½ litres |
| | Seasoning | |
| 40 g | Butter or margarine | 100 g |
| 40 g | Plain flour | 100 g |
| 5 dl | Milk | 1 litre |
| ½ teaspoon | Mustard | 1 teaspoon |
| 60 g | Grated parmesan | 150 g |
| 60 g | Grated Gruyère | 150 g |
| | *or* Cheddar cheese | |

1. Cook the macaroni as for the instruction given for cooking pasta.
2. Place the butter into a 2 or 4 litre jug and cook uncovered for 45 seconds on high.
3. Stir in the flour and cook uncovered for 30 seconds.
4. Mix in the milk, mustard and seasoning.
5. Cook uncovered for 6 minutes on high, stirring every 2 minutes, or until the sauce is thickened.
6. Mix the parmesan and grated cheese into the sauce, reserving a third of the cheese to top the macaroni.
7. Mix the drained macaroni with the sauce and pour into a deep hot service dish.
8. Top with the remaining grated cheese and finish by browning under a hot grill.

# Microwaved vegetable dishes

### Introduction to microwaved vegetable dishes

Most vegetables are suitable for cooking by microwave, especially those which are high in water content such as carrots, potatoes, broccoli, etc. The following recipes are a cross-section of these vegetables.

### Jacket potatoes                    *Pommes en robe de chambre*

| | | |
|---|---|---|
| 4 | Equal-sized jacket potatoes | 10 |
| ½ dl | Single cream | 1 dl |
| | Seasoning | |
| 20 g | Butter | 50 g |
| | Picked parsley | |

1. Set the potatoes on kitchen paper on a shallow tray and cook on high for 13 minutes; turn over half-way through cooking.
2. Wrap the potato in foil and leave to stand for 5 minutes.
3. Cut the potatoes in half lengthwise and scoop out the flesh, leaving the skins unbroken.
4. Mix the flesh with the cream and season.
5. Pipe the mixture into the jacket potato skins and cook on high for 3 minutes or until hot.
6. Garnish with sprigs of parsley and serve.

## Glazed carrots                                    *Carottes glacées*

| | | |
|---|---|---|
| 40 g | Butter | 100 g |
| 2 teaspooons | Soft brown sugar | 4 teaspoons |
| 400 g | Peeled and sliced carrots | 1 kg |
| | Seasoning | |
| | Finely chopped parsley | |

1. Place the butter and sugar in a bowl of 2 or 5 litres and cook on high for 1 minute.
2. Mix in the carrots, cover with cling film and prick to allow steam to escape.
3. Cook on high for 8 minutes and then leave to stand for 3 minutes while still covered.
4. Season and serve in a hot serving dish garnished with finely chopped parsley.

## Buttered cabbage                                  *Choux au beurre*

| | | |
|---|---|---|
| 400 g | Cabbage | 1 kg |
| 40 g | Butter | 100 g |
| | Salt and pepper | |
| | Finely chopped parsley | |

1. Cut the cabbage into segments and remove the core.
2. Finely shred the cabbage and place into a suitable dish with a small amount of water in the base.
3. Cover with cling film and prick to allow steam to escape.
4. Cook on high for 8 minutes until tender, stirring after 4 minutes.
5. Drain and stir in the butter, season and serve in a hot dish. Sprinkle liberally with finely chopped parsley.

## Broccoli with lemon                               *Brocolis au citron*

| | | |
|---|---|---|
| 700 g | Broccoli | 1750 g |
| 20 g | Butter or margarine | 50 g |
| 40 g | Brunoise of onion | 100 g |
| 1 | Clove crushed garlic | 3 |
| 1 | Lemon, juice of | 2 |
| 1½ dl | Vegetable stock | 4 dl |
| | Seasoning | |

1. Place the onion, garlic and butter into a 3 or 7 litre bowl. Cover with cling film and prick to allow the steam to escape.
2. Cook on high for 5 minutes until the onions are tender.
3. Trim the broccoli and set on top of the onion.
4. Sprinkle the broccoli with the lemon juice and zest.
5. Pour in the stock, re-cover and cook for 7–8 minutes or until the broccoli is tender, stirring half-way through the cooking.
6. Season and serve.

# Microwaved pâtisserie dishes

## Introduction to microwaved pâtisserie dishes

Many sweets, especially cakes and sponges in general, are suitable for cooking by microwave. The following recipes are a cross-section of sweet dishes suitable for cooking by microwave.

**Hot chocolate pudding**                        *Pouding au chocolat*

| | | |
|---|---|---|
| 100 g | **Broken plain chocolate** | 200 g |
| 50 g | **Pieces of butter** | 100 g |
| 3 dl | **Milk** | 6 dl |
| ¼ dl | **Sweet sherry** | ½ dl |
| 50 g | **Soft brown sugar** | 100 g |
| | **Vanilla essence to taste** | |
| 2 | **Eggs, separated** | 4 |
| 150 g | **Fresh white breadcrumbs** | 300 g |
| 1½ dl | **Double cream** | 3 dl |
| 50 g | **Grated chocolate garnish** | 100 g |

1. Melt the broken plain chocolate in a 1 or 2 litre jug. Stir every minute and then place on one side.
2. Bring the milk to almost boiling-point and then beat into the chocolate.
3. Mix in the sherry, vanilla, sugar and egg yolk.
4. Beat in the breadcrumbs.
5. Whisk the egg whites until stiff and fold into the mixture.
6. Pour into a 1 litre or 2 litre dish and cook on high for 4 minutes. Stir every two minutes.
7. Reduce the power to defrost and cook for a further 4 minutes.
8. Pour on the double cream, leave to stand for 4 minutes and serve sprinkled with grated chocolate.

## Christmas pudding

*Pouding de Noël*

| | |
|---|---|
| 75 g | Shredded suet |
| 50 g | Plain flour or wholemeal flour |
| 1 teaspoon | Mixed spice |
| ½ teaspoon | Cinnamon powder |
| ½ teaspoon | Nutmeg, grated |
| | Pinch of salt |
| 50 g | Castor sugar |
| 50 g | Soft brown sugar |
| 45 g | Soft white breadcrumbs |
| 50 g | Chopped glacé cherries |
| 50 g | Chopped mixed peel |
| 110 g | Currants |
| 125 g | Sultanas |
| 50 g | Walnuts, crushed, or nibbed almonds |
| 50 g | Grated apple, peeled |
| 1 | Zest and juice of orange |
| 2 | Beaten eggs |
| ¼ dl | Brandy |

1. Mix all of the dry ingredients together and stir in the zest and juice of the orange.
2. Mix in the eggs and milk.
3. Add the ¼ dl of brandy and mix into the pudding.
4. Pour the mixture into a greased pudding basin and make a small dip in the centre of the pudding.
5. Cover with cling film, not too tightly, to allow for expansion.
6. Cook on defrost for 20 minutes, remove from the microwave and lift a corner of the cling film to allow steam to escape.
7. Stand for 5 minutes.
8. Increase power to high, cook for 4 minutes and allow to stand for a further 5 minutes, allowing the steam to escape.
9. Turn out on to a service plate and serve with brandy sauce or rum sauce.
10. The pudding may also be served dusted with icing sugar.

## Rice pudding

*Pouding au riz*

| | | |
|---|---|---|
| 5 dl | Milk | 1 litre |
| 50 g | Carolina rice | 100 g |
| 25 g | Castor sugar | 50 g |
| 15 g | Butter | 30 g |
| | Grated nutmeg | |

1. Place all the ingredients into a 3 or 7 litre bowl and cook uncovered on high for 8 minutes or until the mixture starts to boil. Stir every 4 minutes.
2. Reduce heat to defrost and cook uncovered for 35 minutes or until the rice is soft and cooked. Stir every 10 minutes.
3. Serve as required.

# Glossary of Technical Terms

| | |
|---|---|
| **Acidulated water** | Water with addition of lemon juice or vinegar. |
| **Aiguillettes** | Any items of fish, poultry or meat cut into fine strips. |
| **Aloyau** | Sirloin of beef. |
| **Aromats** | A blend of herbs and vegetables used to impart flavour. |
| **Arroser** | To sprinkle or baste during cooking. |
| **Au bleu** | Used to describe the method of cooking fish in a court-bouillon. |
| **Au four** | Baked in the oven. |
| **Bain-marie** | A water-bath or large shallow pan used to hold water into which pans and fire-proof dishes are put to heat and cook foods which should not boil. Also used to keep food, such as sauces, hot. |
| **Bake** | Exposure of any item of food to a hot oven. |
| **Ballotine** | Meat, usually chicken or game birds, which is boned and stuffed. |
| **Barder** | To cover game birds and poultry with thin slices of pork back fat or fat bacon. |
| **Bardes de larde** | Thin slices of fat bacon or pork cut to the required size for covering the breasts of game birds prior to roasting. |
| **Barquette** | A boat-shaped mould or pastry tartlet. |
| **Béchamel** | Basic milk-based white sauce, one of the foundation sauces. |
| **Beignets** | Sweet or savoury fritters. |
| **Beurre manié** | Equal parts of butter and flour blended to a paste used for thickening sauces. |
| **Beurre noisette** | Nut brown butter, as poured over fish cooked meunière style. |
| **Blanch** | 1. To partly cook without coloration, as with deep-fried potatoes. <br> 2. To plunge into boiling water, for skinning. <br> 3. To partially cook certain vegetables (make limp), such as leeks and celery, prior to braising. <br> 4. To whiten and remove impurities, in poultry and meat, and reduce acridity by bringing to the boil. <br> 5. To place a food item into boiling water in order to preserve its natural colour. |
| **Boil** | A method whereby the article(s) are immersed in sufficient liquid to cover, after which any scum is removed when boiling-point is reached. Dependent upon the items to be boiled, some are started off in cold liquid, whilst others may be plunged into boiling liquid. |
| **Bombe** | A rich iced confection made in a mould of the same name. |
| **Bonnet** | A metal cover which is put over cakes to preserve the moisture during the baking process. A bonnet insulates the cakes from the direct heat of the oven. |
| **Bouchées** | Small puff-paste cases like a miniature vol-au-vent. |
| **Bouquet garni** | A faggot of herbs, such as thyme, parsley, bayleaf, |

396

| | |
|---|---|
| | usually tied together in a piece of leek or celery. |
| **Braise** | A method of cooking which is suitable for the less tender joints/cuts of meat and poultry. It is a long, slow process which is carried out in a suitable pan with a tight-fitting lid to conserve the natural juices and avoid undue evaporation. |
| **Brider** | To truss with needle and string. |
| **Brochette** | A skewer. |
| **Caffeine** | One of the important elements in tea and coffee. It acts as a mild stimulant. |
| **Cartouche** | A greased round of paper for covering meat dishes during cooking. |
| **Carbohydrate** | A nutrient which helps to provide the body with energy. Carbohydrates are derived from sugar, starch and cellulose. The latter is, however, indigestible and acts as roughage in the diet. |
| **Cellulose** | The fibrous element contained in vegetables, fruit and grains, which acts as dietary roughage. |
| **Chemiser** | To line a mould with aspic jelly or ice cream prior to filling with another flavour or colour. |
| **Chinois** | A conical strainer which can be of varying grades of mesh. |
| **Chill-cookery** | A seven-stage process of food preparation and short-term food preservation based on rapid chilling techniques, and precise temperatures of chilled refrigeration for a period of one to five days. |
| **Ciseler** | To shred into strips with a knife. |
| **Civet** | A brown stew of jugged hare or other game. |
| **Coagulation** | Part or complete solidification of protein matter by heat, as in scrambled eggs. |
| **Concasser** | To chop roughly. |
| **Contiser** | The process of making incisions at regular intervals for the insertion of truffle, garlic or other material. |
| **Court-bouillon** | A stock of water, vinegar or white wine, herbs and seasoning for poaching fish. |
| **Crème pâtissière** | A custard-like filling cream. |
| **Croûtes** | Fried bread used for dishing small roast game birds, and tournedos. |
| **Croûtons** | Bread cut into various shapes and either fried or toasted. |
| **Curd** | The mixture of casein and butter fat which separates from the whey during cheese making. |
| **Curdle** | The process of turning into curd. |
| **Cutlet** | A cut of meat from the best-end of lamb, veal or pork. |
| **Cuisine minceur** | A technique of food preparation designed to eliminate or much reduce the fats and rich carbohydrates inherent in most traditional recipes. It is a much lighter style of cookery. |
| **Cuisson** | The liquor in which something has been cooked; the cooking liquor. |
| **Darne** | A slice of round fish cut through the centre bone to form a steak. |
| **Déglacer** | To swill out a pan that has been used for sealing or frying foods with wine, stock or water in order to use the |

|  |  |
|---|---|
| | sediment for a sauce or gravy. |
| **Dégraisser** | To remove the grease from stews, stocks and sauces. |
| **Despumate** | To boil out sauce, such as espagnole. |
| **Dorer** | To eggwash with beaten egg before cooking, as with pies. |
| **Duxelle** | Chopped shallots and mushrooms cooked in butter. |
| **Ecumer** | To skim. |
| **Emincer** | To cut into thin slices. |
| **Escalope** | Thin slices, such as escalope of veal. |
| **Estouffade** | Brown stock; a brown beef stew. |
| **Etuver** | To cook slowly under cover with minimum of added liquor. |
| **Fat** | One of the six nutrients, derived from animal, vegetable or marine sources. In cookery, its function is to improve the eating qualities and keeping qualities of foodstuffs, especially in pastry work and confectionery. Nutritionally, fat is also a valuable provider of energy. |
| **Fécule** | A starch or thickening agent, such as cornflour or arrowroot. |
| **Feuilletage** | Puff paste. |
| **Fines herbes** | A mixture of herbs such as chervil, tarragon, parsley and chives. |
| **Fleurons** | Small items of puff paste which are crescent shaped. |
| **Fonds de cuisine** | Basic stocks or essences. |
| **Fermentation** | A process of aeration brought about by the action of yeast on sugars which produces a gas called carbon dioxide. It is the latter which causes yeast doughs to expand during the proving period. |
| **Fillet** | A cut of fish without the bone. |
| **Fouet** | A whisk. |
| **Fouetter** | To whisk something. |
| **Fourré** | Anything stuffed. |
| **Frappé** | To serve chilled. |
| **Friandises** | Another name for petits fours. |
| **Friture** | A deep-frying utensil usually made of heavy duty steel. |
| **Fricassée** | A white stew of meat or poultry. |
| **Fumet de poisson** | Fish stock made from white fish bones, together with lemon juice, parsley stalks, onions, bayleaves and peppercorns. |
| **Glaze** | 1. To colour under the salamander. |
| | 2. To cover an item with boiling apricot jam, such as a fruit flan. |
| | 3. To coat a savoury item with aspic jelly. |
| | 4. The constant basting of meats and poultry with their own liquor to achieve a nice glaze. |
| | 5. The cooking of vegetables, like carrots, until all the liquor is absorbed and a shiny coating remains. |
| **Gluten** | Formed from the non-soluble proteins in flour when mixed with water to form a dough. It is an elastic-like substance, the amount of which is determined by the protein content of the flour. |
| **Gratinate** | To sprinkle with breadcrumbs/grated cheese and colour golden brown under the salamander or in the oven. |

| | |
|---|---|
| **Grill** | A method of cooking by radiant heat either from above or from below. Such heat may be gas, electricity, charcoal or coke. |
| **Gros sel** | Freezing salt, coarse salt. |
| **Hacher** | To chop finely. |
| **Hachis** | Mince, such as hachis de boeuf (minced beef). |
| **Hors-d'oeuvre** | The first course or appetiser course usually in the form of a variety of cold, piquant dishes. |
| **Jardinière** | Bâtons of vegetables, cut 2 cm long × ¼ cm wide × ¼ cm deep. |
| **Julienne** | Anything cut into fine strips. |
| **Jus** | Gravy. |
| **Jus lié** | Thickened gravy. |
| **Knock back** | The process of de-gassing a fermented dough after the latter reaches the correct degree of proof. The operation can be performed by hand or mechanically according to the amount of dough being handled. |
| **Kromeski** | A type of meat croquette. |
| **Lard** | Bacon or salt, fat pork. |
| **Larder** | To lard, to thread strips of fat with a larding needle into lean meat. |
| **Lardons** | Strips of fat pork or bacon used for larding. |
| **Liaison** | A thickening or binding agent, usually of egg yolk and cream or butter. Used to thicken and enrich soups and sauces. |
| **Lamination** | A process of layers such as those built up when making puff paste. |
| **Macédoine** | Items, often vegetables and fruit, which are cut into dice approximately 5 mm. |
| **Macerate** | To allow items to steep in a liquid, such as wine or liqueur, in order to absorb flavour. |
| **Marble icing** | Also known as feathering. A decorative effect caused by running one coloured icing into another to create a marble effect. |
| **Masking** | To coat a cake surface with one or more different mediums, such as cream, buttercream, or toasted nuts. It can also apply when masking savoury items with a sauce. |
| **Mignardises** | An alternative name for petits fours. |
| **Meunière** | Meunière-style cooking, meaning 'after the fashion of the miller's wife'. It refers to items which are passed through seasoned flour, and shallow fried in butter then finished with beurre noisette (nut brown butter), lemon juice and chopped parsley. |
| **Mijoter** | To simmer slowly. |
| **Minerals** | One of the six nutrients which control body processes and promote growth and tissue repair. |
| **Mis-en-place** | Things in place; basic preparations ready beforehand. |
| **Mortifier** | To hang game and meat, to become tender and flavoursome. |
| **Morue** | Salt cod. |
| **Mousseline** | Smaller sized mousse-type preparation, usually of an individual sized portion and served hot. |

| | |
|---|---|
| **Mousse** | Sweet or savoury items with a foam-like nature, usually made in moulds sufficient to serve several portions. |
| **Napper** | To coat with sauce. |
| **Navarin** | A type of brown, lamb stew. |
| **Noisette** | A boneless portion, such as cutlet of lamb, trimmed of bone and excess fat. |
| **Noix de veau** | A cushion of veal; cut from the rump. |
| **Nouilles** | Noodles. |
| **Nutrients** | The six components necessary in a healthy diet, i.e. carbohydrates, fat, water, vitamins, minerals and protein. |
| **Offal** | The edible parts obtained from the innards of the animal, such as liver, kidneys, heart and sweetbread. |
| **Oignon clouté** | An onion studded with a clove. |
| **Pané** | To coat with breadcrumbs. |
| **Palette knife** | A flat or crank-bladed knife used for spreading purposes. |
| **Parfait** | A frozen ice-cream confection made in special moulds. |
| **Paillettes** | Cheese straws. |
| **Panada** | A binding agent, usually a thick roux-based white sauce. |
| **Papillotes** | Paper cases, for cooking in paper wrapping. |
| **Paupiettes** | Thin, flattened slices of meat or fish, stuffed and rolled. |
| **Pickling** | A method of food preservation by which items of food are placed in a solution, such as brine, which will prevent the development of harmful micro-organisms. |
| **Piquante** | Sharp or spicy in flavour. |
| **Plier** | To fold over, as with fish fillets. |
| **Poach** | A method of cooking whereby the item(s) are never allowed to boil, but are kept just below boiling temperature. Such foods are generally cooked in a minimum amount of liquid to conserve the flavour. |
| **Poêler** | A method of oven cooking similar to braising or pot roasting. Only first-class food items are suited to this method, such as duckling and chicken. |
| **Pojarski** | Minced veal shaped in cutlet form and re-assembled on the cutlet bone. |
| **Potage** | Simply a class of soup, usually of the thick kind. |
| **Printanier** | A garnish of mixed spring vegetables cut to various shapes and sizes. |
| **Primeurs** | Spring vegetables. |
| **Protein** | One of the main body-building nutrients. Sources include milk, cheese, meat and fish. |
| **Pulses** | Dried pod vegetables. |
| **Purée** | 1. A soup which has been passed through a sieve or blender and which is thickened by means of its main constituent.<br>2. Any food mass which has been passed through a sieve or blender. |
| **Rafraîchir** | To cool under running cold water; also by surrounding with ice. |
| **Ragoût** | A stew. |
| **Réchauffé** | Reheated. |

| | |
|---|---|
| **Rapé** | Grated. |
| **Reduction** | To reduce, as with a sauce or stock. |
| **Rissoler** | To fry to golden brown in shallow fat. |
| **Rondel** | A ring or round slice. |
| **Roux** | A thickening agent made from melted butter or other fat and an approximate amount of flour. The mixture is cooked to a sandy texture. |
| **Roast** | To cook by means of a dry heat with the aid of a little fat, either in an oven, or in front of or over a spit. |
| **Rondeau** | A large shallow pan. |
| **Russe** | A stew pan. |
| **Saignant** | Underdone. |
| **Salmis** | A game stew. |
| **Salpicon** | A mixture of diced vegetables, meats or fruits used as a filling. |
| **Sauté** | The shallow frying of tender cuts of meat, fish and poultry, which are of good quality. They are tossed in shallow fat and allowed to colour evenly all over. Potatoes and some other vegetables are also suitable. |
| **Singe** | To brown or colour in the oven. |
| **Smoked** | With reference to smoked bacon, achieved by smoking cured sides of bacon pig over oak or elm wood dust for two or three days to impart its own special delicious flavour. |
| **Soufflé** | A sweet or savoury item which is very light in texture. May be hot or cold as in hot cheese soufflé or cold lemon soufflé. |
| **Spatule** | A flat spoon. |
| **Starch** | A carbohydrate found in cereal grains, some vegetables and farinaceous items. |
| **Stew** | Applies generally to those foods, usually meats, which are of a more fibrous nature, and which demand long, slow cooking. |
| **Stock** | The basic liquid obtained from the long, slow simmering of meat and poultry bones, together with aromats in order to extract the flavour and essence of the chosen produce. Fish stock is derived from fish bones. |
| **Suprême** | The choice part or cut, e.g. suprême de volaille (the wing and breast). |
| **Sweat** | To cook slowly in fat (under cover) without coloration so that the items are limp and the natural juices are released. |
| **Terrine** | An earthenware cooking vessel with lid. The item gives its name to the pâté cooked in the utensil, such as terrine de gibier. |
| **Tranche** | A slice or cut. |
| **Tronçon** | A slice of fish on the bone. |
| **Turban** | Dish moulded in the shape of a turban, often by means of a savarin mould. |
| **Turbotière** | A turbot kettle. |
| **Velouté** | Literally meaning 'velvet', applied to smooth thick-textured white soup or sauce. |
| **Voiler** | To veil, as with spun sugar. |

| | |
|---|---|
| **Vol-au-vent** | A puff pastry case. |
| **Waterzoi** | A type of fish stew, usually made from fresh water fish. |
| **Zabaglione** | An Italian sweet made from whisked eggs, sugar, wine or liqueur, the whole whisked over hot water to a mousse-like consistency. |
| **Zest** | The outer rind of lemon, orange or other citrus fruit. |

# Addresses of Professional Bodies and Trade Association

**The Hotel and Catering Trades Centre**
3 Denmark Street
London WC2H 8LR Tel: 071 497 2047

Cookery and Food Association
1 Victoria Parade
by 331 Sandycombe Road
Richmond
Surrey TW9 3NB Tel: 081 948 3870

Chefs and Cooks Circle
13 Underne Avenue
Southgate
London N14 7ND

The Hotel and Catering Training Company
International House
High Street
Ealing
London W5 5DB Tel: 081 579 2400

# Recipe Index

# General Index